LANGUAGE IN SOCIETY 11

Pidgin & Creole Linguistics

LANGUAGE IN SOCIETY

1 Language and Social Psychology
Edited by Howard Giles and Robert N. St Clair

2 Language and Social Networks
Lesley Milroy

3 The Ethnography of Communication
Muriel Saville-Troike

4 Discourse Analysis
Michael Stubbs

5 The Sociolinguistics of Society
Introduction to Sociolinguistics, Volume I
Ralph Fasold

6 The Sociolinguistics of Language
Introduction to Sociolinguistics, Volume II
Ralph Fasold

7 The Language of Children and Adolescents
The Acquisition of Communicative Competence
Suzanne Romaine

8 Language, the Sexes and Society
Philip M. Smith

9 The Language of Advertising
Torben Vestergaard and Kim Schrøder

10 Dialects in Contact
Peter Trudgill

11 Pidgin and Creole Linguistics
Peter Mühlhäusler

Pidgin & Creole Linguistics

Peter Mühlhäusler

Basil Blackwell

First published 1986

Basil Blackwell Ltd
108 Cowley Road, Oxford OX4 1JF, UK

Basil Blackwell Inc.
432 Park Avenue South, Suite 1503,
New York, NY 10016, USA

British Library Cataloguing in Publication Data

Mühlhäusler, Peter
Pidgin and creole linguistics—
(Language in society; 11)
1. Creole dialects 2. Pidgin languages.
3. Sociolinguistics
I. Title II. Series
417′2 PM7802
ISBN 0-631-13573-1
ISBN 0-631-13574-X Pbk

Library of Congress Cataloging in Publication Data

Mühlhäusler, Peter.
Pidgin and Creole linguistics.
(Language in society; 11)
Bibliography: p.
Includes index.
1. Pidgin languages. 2. Creole dialects. I. Title.
II. Series: Language in society (Oxford, Oxfordshire); 11.
PM7802.M78 1986 417′.2 85-30683
ISBN 0-631-13573-1
ISBN 0-631-13574-X (pbk.)

Typeset by Katerprint Typesetting Services, Oxford
Printed in Great Britain by T.J. Press Ltd, Padstow, Cornwall

To Jackie, Beverly and Tim

Contents

Editor's Preface ix
Preface xi
Acknowledgements xii
1 Names and Definitions 1
2 The Study of Pidgins and Creoles 22
3 The Socio-historical Context of Pidgin and Creole Development 51
4 Theories of Origin 96
5 Linguistic Development of Pidgins and Creoles 134
6 The Relevance of Pidgin and Creole Studies to Linguistic Theory 251
7 Conclusions and Outlook 276
Notes 285
Bibliography 297
Index 318

Editor's Preface

The investigation of pidgin and creole languages offers one of the most exciting of all those areas of study that can be included under the heading of language and society. These languages provide a very clear example of how essential it is to study language within its social matrix if we are to achieve a clearer understanding not only of the social forces at work in language change and development but also of the mental and linguistic factors that are involved. They also give us an opportunity to relate our linguistic studies to the study of social history and geography in a way that is truly interdisciplinary and that has a breadth and scope denied to many of those who are working within more narrowly confined areas of linguistics.

The present book is written by a scholar who knows more than most about pidgin and creole languages and the processes of pidginization and creolization, and one who has gained this knowledge at first hand through extensive and often very difficult fieldwork, as well as through a deep and wide-ranging study of the work of other creolists. His book provides a comprehensive, insightful and up-to-date discussion of all the central theoretical issues connected with pidgin and creole languages: it investigates the often very difficult and controversial problems of terminology; it discusses the history of pidgin and creole study and plots its course from an undervalued and peripheral activity to one that is today at the heart of a number of important linguistic concerns; it investigates the origins and development of pidgin and creole languages from both a social and linguistic point of view; and it relates the findings of linguists working in this field to general linguistic theory. The book will certainly offer novices an excellent introduction to the topic, but the author's original approach and depth of understanding mean that it will also have a lot to say to scholars already working in the area. It is also possible – and most sociolinguists would certainly hope that this will be the case – that theoretical linguists will find there is something for them here too.

Peter Trudgill

Preface

Writers on pidgins and creoles find it difficult to escape from two limitations imposed on them by the very nature of their work. The first involves what Bickerton (1981: 83) has called the First Law of Creole Studies, which reads: 'Every creolist's analysis can be directly contradicted by that creolist's own texts and citations'. Despite my efforts, this law may well be found to apply at some point in this book. A second limitation is what I would like to call the Second Law of Creole Studies: 'Given the choice between neat and untidy data, creolists feel compelled to deal with the latter'. In addition, and this is what makes them invidious to their publishers, creolists tend to insist that whatever argument they put forward should be illustrated with an extensive list of examples. The book you hold in your hands is no exception. Such was its size when the first draft was completed that it was no longer an economically viable proposition. Of the two remedies suggested to me, either to condense the volume as a whole or to drop a few chapters, I have opted for the second strategy as the less painful one. As a consequence, the chapters on the sociology of language, pidgin and creole literature and education have disappeared. What remains is a detailed description of the processes of pidginization, creolization and pidgin and creole development, and a discussion of the major theoretical issues related to these languages. I have not given up hope of publishing my findings in sociolinguistics and applied linguistics, and I would not wish to argue for a strict separation of theoretical and applied creolistics. However, the greatest need I perceived in pidgin and creole studies is to clarify what constitutes their dynamic character and to isolate the most important forces underlying it.

The cut-off point for writings considered in this book is about October 1984. Since then some quite significant work has appeared, particularly in the area of substratum grammar and language and identity. However, at the time of writing this introduction, I do not feel that my arguments stand in need of major revision. Since creolistics is almost as dynamic and changing as its subject matter, some such revision will no doubt become necessary eventually and I hope that this book will stimulate such changes.

Acknowledgements

This book is the product of many years of involvement with pidgin and creole languages and it is not possible to mention all those who have influenced my thinking during these years. However, I would like to give particular thanks to Stephen Wurm of the Australian National University, who first provided me with the opportunity to carry out fieldwork on pidgins and creoles and who has encouraged my work in this area ever since. I am grateful to those who influenced my linguistics as teachers and colleagues: Rudie Botha at Stellenbosch, Peter Trudgill at Reading, Don Laycock and Tom Dutton at the Australian National University, C.-J.N. Bailey at the Technische Universität Berlin, and Roy Harris, Tony Bladon and Suzanne Romaine at Oxford. I am indebted to those who have over the years regularly supplied me with their data and writings, in particular Derek Bickerton, Annegret Bollée, Michael Clyne, Manfred Görlach, John Holm, Roger Keesing, Jürgen Meisel, John Rickford, Bruce Rigsby, John Sandefur, Gillian Sankoff, Anna Shnukal, Jeff Siegel among many others. I would also like to thank my mother for supplying me with many hard-to-obtain archival materials on pidgins and creoles, and my wife Jackie for a great deal of advice and editorial help with this book.

The author and publishers would like to express thanks for permission to use the following tables and figures: figures 1.1, 4.1, 6.2 are from R. A. Hall jr., 'How Pidgin English has evolved', which first appeared in 1961 in the *New Scientist*, London, the weekly review of science and technology; figure 1.4 is from Ross Clark, 'In search of Beach-la-Mar', *Teo Reo*, 1979; table 2.1 is taken from D. DeCamp, 'Analysis of a post-creole speech continuum', in D. Hymes (ed.), *Pidginization and Creolization of Languages*, Cambridge University Press, 1971.

Above all, I am indebted to my informants in various parts of the Pacific and Australia for their patience and for letting me study their language. It is my hope that this book will be of help to them.

1

Names and Definitions

> To a creolist, almost everyone else's definition of a creole sounds absurd and arbitrary; yet creolists communicate and collaborate with their colleagues just as Slavicists and Amerindianists do.
>
> (DeCamp: 1977:4)

The term 'pidgin'

When telling a new acquaintance that I have spent most of my academic career studying Pidgin English, this statement is met either with an outburst of laughter or else the question 'Where does the word pidgin originate?' I hope that this book will dispel any notion that the study of pidgin and creole languages is a frivolous waste of time, although I may need several chapters to convince the more sceptical of my readers. My reply to the second reaction is much more straightforward.

There have been a number of proposals as to the etymology of the term 'pidgin'. The more widespread of these include:

1 the definition given by the *OED* of a 'Chinese corruption of English "business"';
2 a Chinese corruption of the Portuguese word *ocupação*: 'business';
3 Hebrew *pidjom*: 'exchange, trade, redemption';
4 Yago (a South American Indian language spoken in an area colonized by Britain) *pidian*: 'people';
5 South Seas pronunciation of English 'beach' (*beachee*) from the location where the language was typically used.

I have come to the conclusion that all of these etymologies may be genuine, the reason being that such a conclusion is most in agreement with the nature of pidgin languages. Because they emerge as vehicles of intercommunication between speakers of many different languages, coincidence of form and similarity of meaning across languages will give a word a high survival rate. I have found, for instance, that in the early formative years of Tok Pisin (New Guinea Pidgin English), up to 50 per cent of the lexicon could be traced back to more than one language, including the following examples of lexical encounter between English and Tolai:

Tolai	*English*	*Tok Pisin*
atip 'thatched roof'	on top	antap 'on top, roof'
bala 'belly, bowels'	belly	bel 'belly, seat of emotions'
ikilik 'small'	little bit	liklik 'small, little bit'
mari 'pretty'	Mary, marry	meri 'woman'

More than two sources appear to have been involved in some instances. A particularly intriguing case of lexical conflation is that of *sanga* 'pliers, hand of crayfish, forked post, slingshot', which appears to be related to German *Zange* 'pliers', Malay *tiang* 'forked branch' and Australian English *Shanghai* 'slingshot'. Lexical encounters in other pidgins are probably equally numerous, although they have not always been identified. The earliest reports of this phenomenon are by Schuchardt (1979: 30; originally 1909) for the Lingua Franca, where he observes that 'many [Arabic loans] give the impression that they were introduced due to similarity with corresponding Romance forms'. For Eskimo Trade Jargon, Stefánsson observes in the same year on the entry *miluk*:

> This is in a way, an interesting form. The whites who use it consider it a corruption of the English 'milk', while to the Eskimo it is their own word 'mi'-lūk', which refers to any milk (human, caribou, etc.). (Stefánsson 1909: 227)

Other well-known examples include Jamaican Creole *dati* 'dirty', which can be traced back to English 'dirty', and West African Twi *doti* 'dirty', or the term *kanaka* 'black labourer' in Queensland Kanaka English, which some linguists relate to both Polynesian *kanaka* 'human being' and English 'cane hacker'. Australian Kriol *kan* 'can't' has recently been traced to both English 'can't' and Walmajarri *kaya* a 'negative used to express inability', and many similar cases have become known. Sometimes pidgins also develop compounds of dual origin such as Fanakalo *tshisa-stik* (fuse lighter) from Zulu (Z.) *shisa* (set alight, burn) and E. *stick*; *makaza-mbitshan* (cool) from Z. *amakhaja* (cold) and Afrikaans (A.) *bietjie* (slightly); *tshisa-mbitshan* (warm from Z. *shisa* (burn) and *mbitshan*; *sokismude* (stocking) from E. *socks* and Z. *omude* (long). Such compounds are reminiscent of those produced by some bilingual children.[1]

Lexical encounters and mutual reinforcement may continue throughout the history of a pidgin. I have met many speakers of Tok Pisin who insisted that the name of the language meant 'language of the birds' (from English 'pigeon'), because it was given to human beings by birds, a very common account of the origin of languages throughout Melanesia.

A name, as we shall see shortly, is not in itself a reliable indicator of the existence of a language, language form or any other linguistic entity. Pidgin languages were used long before the label 'pidgin' was invented (in 1850 according to the *OED*). Examples of such early pidgins include Mediterranean Sabir or Lingua Franca, Pidgin Portuguese of West Africa, and an as yet ill-documented plantation pidgin spoken in medieval Cyprus. Indeed, little is known about the many contact pidgins in use in the countries of the Third World before the arrival of the European colonizers. As regards the label 'pidgin', even today it is not used with consistency. In the speech of non-specialists, it overlaps with terms such as 'lingua franca', 'argot', 'sabir', 'patois' or 'koine', and the definitions and delimitations given by professional linguists also differ. This, I feel, should not upset us, for it is the common fate of everyday expressions which assume a more specialist meaning within a field of scientific inquiry. The vagueness of the term 'pidgin' is thus no different from that of other metalinguistic labels, such as 'text', 'sentence', 'construction' or 'topic', as can easily be ascertained by consulting one of the numerous lexicons or encyclopaedias of linguistics. For the time being, however, I suggest we accept the popular view of a pidgin as a structurally reduced trade language. How this popular definition is elaborated in the scholarly discussion of pidgin languages will be the topic of the next section.

Terminological issues: 'pidgin'

Pidgin studies have suffered for a long time from terminological and definitional problems, as has been discussed by Mühlhäusler (1974: 11–25) and Samarin (1975). Since definitions often determine the direction of research, it would seem profitable to look at some of them in more detail. The term 'pidgin' has been defined, among other things, as:

> A variety whose grammar and vocabulary are very much reduced . . . The resultant language must be native to no one. (Bloomfield 1933: 474)

> A language which has arisen as the result of contact between peoples of different languages, usually formed from mixing of the languages. (Unesco 1963: 46)

> The vocabulary is mainly provided by the language spoken by upper stratum [*sic*] of a mixed society, adapted by the lower stratum to the grammar and morphology of their original language. (Adler 1977: 12)

> the grammatical structure has been simplified very much beyond what we find in any of the languages involved in their [pidgins'] making. (Jespersen 1922: 227)

> Two or more people use a language in a variety whose grammar and vocabulary are very much reduced in extent and which is native to neither side. Such a language is a 'pidgin'. (Hall 1966: xii)

> It [i.e. Pidgin English] is a corrupted form of English, mixed with many morsels from other languages and it is adapted to the mentality of the natives; therefore words tend to be simply concatenated and conjunction and declension are avoided. (Baessler 1895: 23–4, translated from German)

Note that there are a number of problems with such definitions. First, those who stress the makeshift character of pidgins – a 'supplementary tongue for special forms of intercourse' (Reinecke 1964: 537) – ignore the fact that pidgins can develop to a considerable degree of stability and complexity.

Second, there is a tendency to confuse simplification (greater grammatical regularity) with impoverishment (lack of referential and non-referential power). There is also considerable uncertainty as to whether simplification is greatest in incipient or extended pidgins. Studies in the area of interlanguage (e.g. Corder 1976; Traugott 1977: 132–62) have drawn attention to the insufficiency of the notion of simplification (or simplicity) in some pidgin and creole studies. The complex problem as to the relationship between simplification in the sense of rule generalization, on the one hand, and naturalness and markedness, on the other, cannot be solved here. However, data from developing pidgins support the view that impoverishment and simplification are inversely related: as the referential and non-referential power of a language increases, so its content must become more structured. A basic jargon used to exchange information in a limited contextual domain does not need structure. In its initial phase it is little more than a list of phrases or lexical irregularities. We thus get the following picture:

incipient pidgin	maximally impoverished	minimally simple
	↓	↓
developed pidgin	fully expanded	maximally simple (regular)

One can therefore no longer uphold Agheyisi's view that:

> It is possible that most of the factors which contribute to the development of the simplified variety known as the pidgin are most active during the pidginization process. This process is said to extend chronologically from the period of initial language contact through the stage when the resulting pidginized speech becomes sufficiently regularized and stabilized. (Agheyisi 1971: 24)

The third problem to note is that pidgins are not mixed languages in the sense most often intended. It appears that the most mixed component of grammar is the lexicon, where syncretisms of various types are common, and not syntax. In addition, mixing at the syntactic and morphological levels is virtually absent in the formative phase of pidgins and becomes more important only after stabilization and considerable expansion have taken place. It is most pronounced in the post-pidgin phase, that is when a pidgin comes into renewed contact with its original lexifier language.

Finally, pidgins are classified and often defined as being based on a principal lexifier language, typically the language spoken by the socially dominant group. Two objections can be levelled against this view (for a more detailed discussion of this issue, see Walsh 1984). As pointed out by Dennis and Scott (1975: 2), 'we will avoid calling the creoles "English-based" or "Portuguese-based" etc., since we can see no grounds for deciding that the lexicon is the base of the language, as opposed to the semantic–syntactic framework of the language.' The second objection is that the mixed or compromise character of pidgin lexicons is typically ignored.

In view of the above considerations, I would like to propose a new definition of pidgin:

> Pidgins are examples of partially targeted or non-targeted second-language learning, developing from simpler to more complex systems as communicative requirements become more demanding. Pidgin languages by definition have no native speakers, they are social rather than individual solutions, and hence are characterized by norms of acceptability.

Implicit in this definition is the assumption that there are qualitatively different stages in the development of a pidgin. These have been given labels by a number of scholars. Here follow my own preferred labels, side by side with others commonly in use:

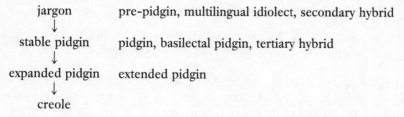

jargon	pre-pidgin, multilingual idiolect, secondary hybrid
↓	
stable pidgin	pidgin, basilectal pidgin, tertiary hybrid
↓	
expanded pidgin	extended pidgin
↓	
creole	

The term 'creole'

The origins of the term 'creole' are not much less complex than those of 'pidgin'. According to Valkhoff (1966: 38–46), it is widely held that the word originated in one of Portugal's colonies in the sixteenth century. Both form and meaning suggest an etymology *criar* 'to nurse, breed, nourish', but there may also have been reinforcement from another, as yet unknown, source language. Originally the meaning of *criolho* was 'slave in European employment, particularly around the house, white man or woman originating from the colonies', but the word has since adopted a number of additional meanings. Its most common meaning in English, according to the *Concise Oxford Dictionary*, is '(descendant of) European or Negro settler in W. Indies, or stemming from these areas' and is used with nouns referring to something like 'exotic' or 'spicy'.

Perhaps the linguistic layman's most common association with the term creole is that of mixture of culture and race, and it is commonly assumed that linguistic mixture goes hand in hand with these.

The terminological debate in creole linguistics

Problems with the linguistic definition of creoles are legion and many of the central issues remain unresolved. The uninitiated reader will probably agree with Givón's (1979: 4) characterization of creole studies as something like a 'mythological safari across the equally mythological African jungle of lore' and will find them 'liberally strewn with boobytraps and quicksands of idiosyncratic linguistic features'. Still, it would seem that the numerous characterizations and definitions of creole can be reduced to three major types:

1 creoles are regarded as mixed languages typically associated with cultural and often racial mixture;
2 creoles are defined as pidgin languages (second languages) that have become the first language of a new generation of speakers;
3 creoles are reflections of a natural bioprogram for human language which is activated in cases of imperfect language transmission (cf. Bickerton 1981).

As in the case of the definition of 'pidgin', both social and linguistic aspects tend to be found in the above categories. Let us now consider each type in some more detail.

In discussing the question whether English is a creole language, Bailey and Maroldt (1977) state: 'by creolization the authors wish to indicate gradient mixture of two or more languages; in a narrow sense, a creole is the result of mixing which is substantial enough to result in a new system, a system that is separate from its antecedent parent system' (1975: 21). A number of researchers, including Bailey and Maroldt, have concluded from their assessment of the role of mixing in the emergence of Middle English from Anglo-Saxon that English is indeed a creole. Very similar arguments have been put forward in the case of Italian as spoken in the USA (Haller 1981: 181–94) and in the case of Afrikaans, a Dutch-derived language spoken in Southern Africa. Valkhoff (1966: 26) increased the controversiality of the debate by declaring that there is 'an ancient relation between miscegenation and creolization', implying that Afrikaans developed in the context of intense racial mixture in the early years of Dutch colonization of the Cape. This view was understandably unpopular with the large group of white pro-apartheid speakers of Afrikaans, who prefer to regard their language as a continuation of white dialects of Dutch (cf. Raidt 1983). In discussing issues such as these, we should heed Schuchardt's cautionary remarks on the relationship between linguistic and racial mixture:

> Linguistic mixture tends to be connected with a more or less pronounced mixture of culture. With the crossing of races, which at least has no influence upon the latter, it coincides only externally; or, to express myself more cautiously, it is not associated in any demonstrable degree with it. (Schuchardt 1889b: 508)

Indeed, inasmuch as pidgins and creoles develop as indicators of social distance between members of two different races (as they have done over and over again), one is tempted to suspect that large-scale racial mixture tends to discourage the development of creoles.

Leaving aside the problem of correlating linguistic with social factors, there is another issue which has not as yet been addressed by the proponents of the equation creolization equals language mixing: that is, the possibility that not every linguistic consequence of linguistic encounters is alike. Indeed, there is mounting evidence that one is dealing with many different types of language mixing, some increasing and some decreasing the naturalness of the affected linguistic systems.[2]

A creole, according to the second definition, is a pidgin that has acquired a community of native speakers. This occurs, for instance, when parents from different linguistic backgrounds communicate among themselves and with their offspring in a makeshift pidgin, which is elaborated and adopted as a means of intercommunication by the next generation. Thus the children in this situation: are exposed to imperfect, reduced language input; elaborate this input using new grammatical devices gleaned from internal resources, that is, by appealing to their innate linguistic knowledge; and eventually speak a language that is both quantitatively and qualitatively different from that spoken by their parents and, in many cases, not intelligible to them.

Creolization in this sense thus appears to be an ideal test case for claims about the nature of the human language acquisition device and universal linguistic knowledge. It can be represented schematically as follows:

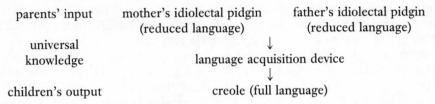

parents' input	mother's idiolectal pidgin (reduced language)	father's idiolectal pidgin (reduced language)
	↓	
universal knowledge	language acquisition device	
	↓	
children's output	creole (full language)	

Although numerous creole languages are in existence today, there are a number of problems when it comes to testing the creolization hypothesis. Observations concerning the differences between the second-language pidgin and the ensuing first-language creole should preferably be made with first-generation speakers, as creoles may change through borrowing and for internal reasons, like any other language, once they have come into being. A comparison of a present-day creole with a pidgin that was spoken centuries ago is unlikely to yield satisfactory evidence. Further, the pidgin input may vary considerably. Thus, creolization can occur: (a) with pidgins that are very rudimentary and unstable, that is, so-called jargons; (b) with elementary stable pidgins; and (c) with stable expanded pidgins. Consequently three main sociolinguistic types of creoles can be distinguished according to their developmental history:

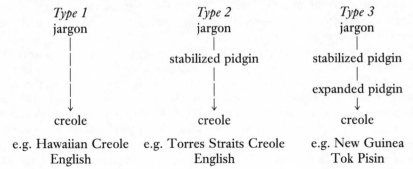

Type 1	*Type 2*	*Type 3*
jargon	jargon	jargon
|	|	|
	stabilized pidgin	stabilized pidgin
|	|	|
		expanded pidgin
↓	↓	↓
creole	creole	creole
e.g. Hawaiian Creole English	e.g. Torres Straits Creole English	e.g. New Guinea Tok Pisin

If any second language becomes the first language of a speech community, its deficiencies need to be repaired. The nature of this repair will depend on the developmental stage at which creolization sets in.

Of the cases of creolization that can be observed in situ today, most belong to type 3 (for example, New Guinea Tok Pisin, New Hebridean Bichelamar, West African Pidgin English) and a smaller number to type 2 (North Australian Kriol, Torres Straits Creole). There are no known instances of type 1, the most interesting type from the point of view of psycholinguistic evidence, with the possible exception of Hawaiian Pidgin English and Unserdeutsch of former German New Guinea. Even this subcategorization of creole types is very abstract and should be supplemented with additional types, such as sheltered/unsheltered creoles as suggested by Bailey (personal communication), a difference depending on the presence or absence of a creole's original lexifier language. The need to differentiate between a number of different types of nativized pidgins and to regard the term creole in the sense of the second definition (p. 6), as a gradient term, springs from the difficulty of distinguishing between first and second languages. In his introduction to the perhaps best known reader on these languages (Hymes 1971), DeCamp (1971a: 16) expresses this by saying that a creole is 'a native language for most of its speakers'. However, both Nigerian Pidgin English and Tok Pisin have viable creole communities, while continuing to serve as second languages for most of their speakers. Thus, Mafeni points out:

> While this [distinction between a pidgin and a creole language] is a useful distinction, it does not always prove possible to make such a neat separation . . . West African Pidgin . . . runs the gamut all the way from true creole – as a mother tongue and home language – to what one might call 'minimal pidgin', the exiguous jargon often used between Europeans and their domestic servants. (Mafeni 1971: 95–6)

It is important to remember at this point that a speaker's dominant language may not be his or her first language in the sense of order of acquisition. Therefore, to avoid confusion, one may adopt the term 'primary language' to designate the language that is best mastered. This is not necessarily the mother tongue. All other languages of a bilingual individual are secondary languages. The functional and structural differences between a primary pidgin and its corresponding creole may thus be minimal.

A further complication encountered in distinguishing between pidgins and creoles and first and second languages is the fact that first-language creoles can become either partially or totally repidginized. An instance of partial repidginization of a creole are plantation creoles, where first-generation creole speakers are supplemented with raw recruits from elsewhere. Thus, in the case of Sranan, the English- and Portuguese-derived creole of Surinam, mortality on the plantations was so high during the first hundred years of its existence that the majority of plantation workers had to be recruited from overseas. Thus, creole speakers of Sranan were outnumbered by second-language speakers of the language for a large part of its existence. Total repidginization is documented in the case of Tok Pisin on Rambutyo Island in the Admiralties. A group of plantation workers from many parts of New Guinea founded a new village on this island, where children began to speak creolized Tok Pisin within a generation. However, because of the very limited usefulness of this language, the second generation of children grew up speaking Rambutyo as their first and Tok Pisin as their second language.

From such observations, it emerges that it is difficult to study pidgins and creoles as two separate phenomena rather than two aspects of the same linguistic process.

Before giving the third definition of 'creole', it may be of interest to explore briefly why such a definition should have emerged. The existence of so many different manifestations of creole appears to have led linguists to search for an 'ideal' creole, a search which would seem comparable to that for the invariant idiolect of latter-day American structuralists or the ideal speaker–hearer of transformational generative grammar. The method adopted is to discard all superficial and incidental properties (whatever these may be) and retain the essential core. Thus the purest types of creole, as defined by Bickerton (1981: 4), are those that meet the following conditions:

1 they arose out of a prior pidgin, which had not existed for more than a generation;
2 they arose in a population where not more than 20 per cent were native speakers of the dominant language and where the remaining 80 per cent was composed of diverse language groups.

Bickerton argues that in this narrowly defined social context only one type of linguistic development is possible: that which is governed by an innate bioprogram. We will explore this hypothesis below.

If I have suggested, in the discussion of the various definitions of the term 'creole', a trend towards narrower and more idealized types of language, this was not meant to exclude the numerous attempts by linguists to identify and classify the non-ideal types. For the purposes of this introductory chapter, only the two principal non-ideal types will be mentioned, the creoloid and the post-creole continuum.

The need for the concept of 'creoloid' arose out of a number of observations, made from the late 1960s onwards, including the following.

1 Whereas true creoles develop where there is a radical break in language transmission, many languages appear to have developed with only a partial break.
2 A number of languages with no known pidgin ancestor nevertheless exhibit many of the alleged typological properties of creole languages.
3 Next to mixing between fully developed linguistic systems one also finds mixing between full systems and developing systems, such as pidgins. The results of this second type of mixture tend to be structurally similar to established creoles.

The term 'creoloid' (semi-creole or quasi-creole) has been applied to a motley collection of languages, including recently emerged ones such as Singlish (a form of English spoken in Singapore, see Platt 1975), Afrikaans (see Markey 1982), Pitcairnese (see Ross 1964) and County Tyrone Irish English (see Todd 1975), as well as old languages such as Marathi, which is said to exhibit signs of intensive contact between Indo-Aryan and Dravidian languages (Southworth 1971), East African Mbugu, which contains Bantu and Hamitic elements

(Goodman 1971), and, in the even more remote past, Egyptian (Zyhlarz 1932–3), Germanic (Feist 1932) or the Melanesian languages (a discussion of the latter is given by Lynch 1981). The usefulness of the term 'creoloid' rapidly declines with increasing time depth, since every language history is characterized by a certain amount of mixing and discontinuity of transmission. It is most useful in those cases where new linguistic systems can be shown to have emerged within a very short timespan, as is the case with Singlish.

The term 'creoloid' reflects gradience of social and linguistic parameters in the formative period of languages; the term 'post-creole continuum', on the other hand, was coined (by DeCamp 1971b) to cater for differential developments in the subsequent history of creoles. A distinction needs to be drawn between creoles like Krio of Sierra Leone, Kriol of Northern Australia and Jamaican Creole, which exist in a community where the related lexifier language is also spoken and is a continuous influence on the creole, and creoles that do not coexist with a standard variety of their lexifier language. Examples of the latter are English-derived Sranan of Surinam, a former Dutch colony, and Negro Dutch (Negerhollands) of the former *Danish* Antilles.

The pressure of standard lexifier languages can result, given the right social circumstances, in the development of a linguistic continuum. Such a continuum is called *a restructuring continuum* and is characterized by the fact that the different varieties located on it are roughly of the same linguistic complexity. It thus contrasts with the *developmental continuum*, where differential complexity is encountered. This contrast can be depicted as follows:

developmental dimension ↓	jargon		
	stable pidgin		
	expanded pidgin	post-pidgin continuum	lexifier language
	creole	post-creole continuum	
restructuring ⟶			

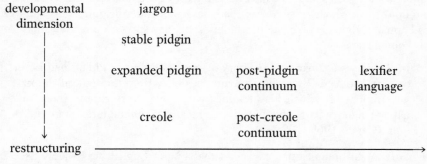

The varieties on the left side of the above graph are called *basilect*, the related standard lexifier language *acrolect*, and the varieties intermediate between the two, *mesolects*. The social context in which mesolectal varieties develop is one of increasing social mobility and bilingualism, commonly found in post-colonial societies.

A final term which has created some confusion is that of 'koine'. In a recent paper, Siegel (1983a), draws attention to the following points.

1 A koine is the result of mixing between language subsystems that are either mutually intelligible or share the same superimposed standard language.

2 Koineization, unlike pidginization, is typically a slow and gradual process.
3 The social correlate of koine development is sustained intensive contacts and gradual assimilation of social groups.

Thus, although some of the linguistic consequences of koineization can be similar to those identified in pidgin development (for example, simplification of inflectional morphology), koines do not involve the drastic reduction characteristic of early pidgin development. Siegel's insistence on a terminological distinction between pidgin and koine seems well motivated in the light of recent findings, which suggest that there are differential linguistic consequences of the encounters between separate systems, on the one hand, and subsystems of the same superordinate system on the other.

It can be seen that the terminological problems addressed in this section are a reflection of the complexity of the subject matter under investigation. The definition of a pidgin or a creole turns out to be comparable to the definition of human language. The uncertainties encountered when defining these languages as types are reflected in our next problem, that of identifying individual pidgins and creoles.

The identification of pidgins and creoles

In the course of my academic life I have carried out fieldwork on a number of pidgins and creoles, one of which was a pidgin whose speakers' existence was in no doubt, but whose existence as a language was under dispute. This language is Papuan Pidgin English, about which Capell, an expert on the linguistic scene in Papua, states:

> In Papua, as against the Territory of New Guinea . . . Pidgin had never been introduced. By early Government policy from the days of the first government of British New Guinea right up to very recent times, one native language had been chosen as a means of general intercommunication. (Capell 1969: 109)

I managed to demonstrate, however, that Pidgin English was widely used in many parts of Papua until fairly recently (Mühlhäusler 1978a), and I had no trouble finding informants who could still speak it.

In another piece of research, I discovered a pidgin whose existence, together with that of its speakers, was not known. Thus, Samoan Plantation Pidgin, the language spoken by workers imported from former German New Guinea, was forgotten for two reasons: because the New Guineans were officially classified as Solomon Islanders by the New Zealand Administration of Samoa; and both speakers and non-speakers believed the language to be English and not a pidgin. By discovering that these English-speaking Solomon Islanders were in fact speakers of an early fossilized form of Tok Pisin, I was able to fill in many gaps in the social and linguistic history of Tok Pisin.

Next comes the case of a language whose existence was known and which had been reasonably well documented, but whose speakers' existence was until very recently not known, Queensland Kanaka English. Officially, all Melanesian sugar-plantation workers had been repatriated from Queensland by 1906, but unofficially many had stayed on, and they and their descendants continued to use this pidgin (cf. Dutton and Mühlhäusler 1984). Again, it was perfectly easy to locate these speakers and to elicit their language.

Finally, I have also worked on a number of pidgins where both the existence of the language and its speakers was beyond doubt, the most straightforward case being Tok Pisin of Papua New Guinea.

What emerges from this is that because people at the bottom of the social ladder are frequently pushed aside or ignored, little tends to be known about them or their language, and it is commonly believed that they speak the standard language in a country. Moreover, many of the lower-class pidgin and creole speakers are not aware that their language is a separate one. Thus, in the case of Papuan Pidgin English, my informants claimed to be speaking English, not Pidgin. The term 'pidgin' has only recently become known to Pacific islanders and asking older inhabitants whether they speak pidgin is unlikely to make sense to them. In a similar fashion, I obtained samples of New Guinea Pidgin German by merely asking my informants to speak German, and I have no doubts that many other nameless pidgins and creoles could be elicited in this fashion.

Even where speakers may be aware that they speak a separate linguistic system and have their own name for it, they may not wish to admit to this fact, particularly not to fieldworkers from outside. Thus, when Tom Dutton and I started recording Queensland Kanaka English, we visited a house where, on entering, we heard the couple speak in this variety. However, when explaining the purpose of our visit, they vigorously denied having any knowledge of the language and kept using standard language, until the atmosphere was sufficiently relaxed and until we demonstrated our own knowledge of Pidgin English. The explanation for this behaviour is that speakers of Queensland Kanaka English follow the widely used convention of non-white speakers of Australian Pidgin or Creole English that these languages are not to be used in the presence of whites.

In addition to such practical problems in identifying pidgin and creole languages, there are also a number of theoretical ones. The question as to what constitutes *a language*, as against a dialect, argot or patois, has received considerable attention in the past, and detailed studies of the theoretical issues are found in Harris (1980) and Romaine (1982b). It is almost a truism to believe that problems which have become blurred in fully developed 'old' languages are identified much more neatly in the younger pidgins and creoles, and the question of language identification is no exception. Thus, it appears that, in the past, many writers have failed to acknowledge any problem in defining a pidgin or creole, and have merely followed the well-known formula[3] of naming pidgins after their location (1) and their principal 'lexifier language' (2), as in:

1	*Pidgin*	*2*
Chinese	Pidgin	English
Nigerian	Pidgin	English
West African	Pidgin	Portuguese
New Caledonian	Pidgin	French

This practice has been of considerable use in the initial phase of identifying and locating pidgin languages. However, it has a number of serious drawbacks, including the following.

First, speakers of these languages are becoming increasingly aware of the negative connotations of the term 'pidgin' and have therefore introduced new names. These are either user-based, such as Tok Pisin (New Guinea Pidgin), or broken (for Torres Straits Pidgin English), or else invented by linguists, as with Neo-Melanesian, Neo-Solomonic (Robert Hall's creations) and Cameroonian instead of Cameroons Pidgin English (see Todd 1979).

More seriously, pidgins can 'fly': that is, a pidgin found in one location today may have been transported there only recently. Thus, Fernando Póo Pidgin English was spoken by mainland West Africans originating from Nigeria and the Cameroons; New Guinea Pidgin English (Tok Pisin) was imported from Western Samoa (see Mühlhäusler 1978b); many of the Queensland Aboriginal Pidgin varieties probably started in New South Wales (see Dutton 1983a); Fijian Pidgin English (Siegel 1984) appears to be simply Kanaka English transported from Queensland; and, as has been demonstrated in a recent book by Baker and Corne (1982), the label Indian Ocean Creole French is a misnomer, as the social and linguistic histories of Mauritian and Réunion Creole French are quite separate. In the light of their high geographic mobility, it appears inadvisable to associate pidgins and creoles too closely with a single well-defined location.

It is further known that in the course of their history pidgins can change their lexical affiliation, a process referred to as relexification. Thus, present-day Hiri Motu may be partially relexified Papuan Pidgin English (cf. Dutton and Mühlhäusler 1979) and New Caledonian Pidgin French may have resulted from relexification of an earlier Pidgin English (but see Hollyman 1976). It should be obvious that ongoing relexification poses special problems of language identity over time.

It is true that the problems raised above have been realized, at least implicitly, by a number of observers, and we thus find a few notational devices which alleviate them. An example is the use of non-localized (or only very generally localized) labels, such as Beach-la-Mar (the lingua franca spoken 'between the meridians 140° and 180° and between the Equator and the Tropic of Capricorn', according to Reinecke 1937: 727), or West African Pidgin English. Another relaxation is the interpretation of 'Chinese' in Chinese Pidgin English as indicating 'speakers of Chinese origin' rather than 'spoken along the China coast'.

Nevertheless, problems remain and continue to slow down the discussion of the complex linguistic and sociolinguistic dimensions of pidgin and creole languages. I will now show, with examples from the Pacific, that having a name for an entity is not a sufficient condition for the reality, meaningfulness or usefulness of what is supposed to be referred to. Put differently, many of the available names are rough and ready classification devices, but misleading as descriptions or explanations.

An illustration: counting pidgins and creoles in the Pacific

Even a superficial look at the vast literature on Pidgin and Creole English in the Pacific[4] will soon reveal a general lack of agreement both as to whether Pidgin English is spoken in a certain area or not and whether such a pidgin is the same as or different from other known pidgins. Since, in the past, studies of pidgins were at best the by-product of other linguistic studies and at worst anecdotal travellers' tales, disagreement as to the existence of a pidgin in a certain area is understandable.

Most earlier sources (for example, Churchill 1911; Friederici 1911) speak of only one South Seas Pidgin English, referred to by such names as Sandalwood English, Trepang English or Beach-la-Mar. This view is continued in Reinecke (1937: 751), and it is only in more recent work that different languages are distinguished. For instance, figure 1.1, the family tree given by Hall (1961),

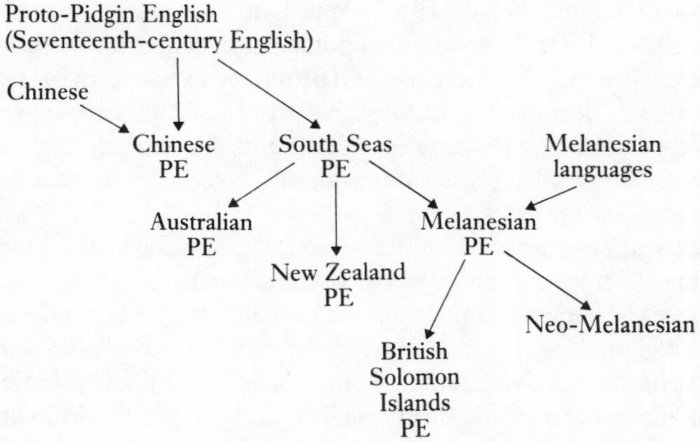

Figure 1.1 Hall's family tree (from Hall 1961)

recognizes several varieties. Melanesian Pidgin English in this tree roughly corresponds to the former Beach-la-Mar. The reason for the separate development of British Solomon Island Pidgin is given as follows: 'BSI Pidgin is, in its grammatical structure, very close to Neo-Melanesian . . . In vocabulary, however, BSI Pidgin is distinctly archaic and closer to English than is Neo-Melanesian.' (Hall 1955a: 68–9). Hall's arguments were not universally accepted and other classifications are given by subsequent authors. Thus, Voegelin and Voegelin (1964: 57) state: 'Neo-Melanesian, or Pidgin English, is spoken in the Australian Territory of New Guinea (including the Bismarck Archipelago), in the Solomon Islands and adjacent islands.' The only other variety mentioned by them is nineteenth-century Beach-la-Mar.

Two more comprehensive accounts appeared in 1971. The first, that of Wurm, lists a reasonably large number of pidgins, which could be arranged in the type of family tree shown in figure 1.2. A number of comments need to be

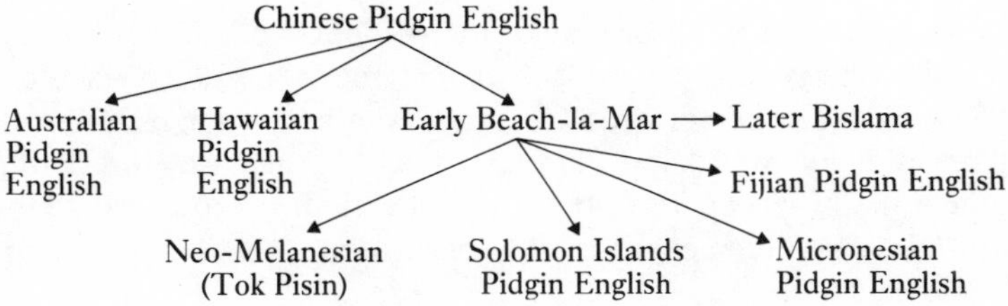

Figure 1.2 Wurm's family tree (from Wurm 1971)

made on Wurm's classification. Its principal virtue lies in the fact that it is based on first-hand observation and that it contains a number of valuable details, such as that Beach-la-Mar is still known in Fiji (Wurm 1971: 1008), a fact borne out in a recent paper by Siegel (1984). Wurm is also correct in stressing that Australian Pidgin English varieties cannot be regarded as direct descendants of Beach-la-Mar (p. 1013). There are two problems in his account, however: the first is that he underrates the differences between nineteenth-century Beach-la-Mar and present-day Bislama (p. 1008); and the second, that he may have given Chinese Pidgin English too important a role in the formation of Pacific Pidgin English varieties.

Hancock's often-quoted classifications (1971, 1977a) suffer from different shortcomings. Thus, one could construct the family tree shown in figure 1.3 from Hancock's remarks. This tree not only assigns a very different place to Australian Pidgin English; it also suggests that 'a Neo-Melanesian-like substratum seems to be discernible' (Hancock 1971: 509) in Hawaiian Pidgin English, a fact which is difficult to establish and even more difficult to accommodate in a family tree. More serious is the confusion between Tok Pisin (Neo-Melanesian) and Papuan Pidgin English. It is repeated on the accompanying

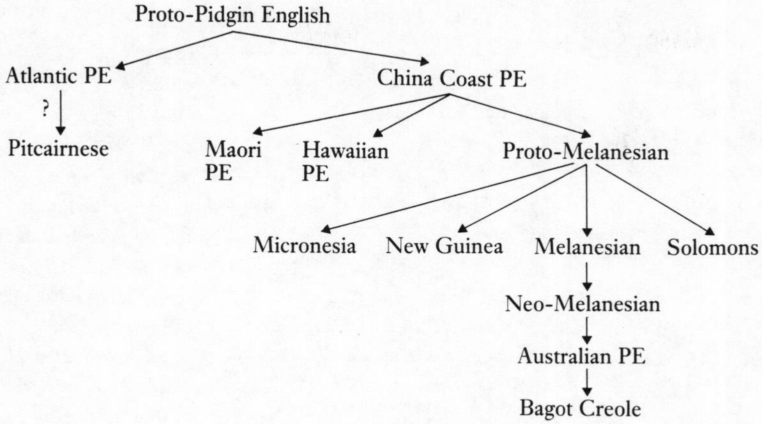

Figure 1.3 A family tree constructed from Hancock's classification (from Hancock 1971)

map, where the locations for 'New Guinea or Papuan Pidgin English' (74) and 'Melanesian Pidgin English' (75) are given as the New Guinea mainland (New Guinea or Papuan variety) and the Bismarck Archipelago (Neo-Melanesian = Tok Pisin) respectively.

That Australian Pidgin English is not a direct development from Neo-Melanesian, as claimed by Hancock, should be evident from the fact that the former antedates the latter. The problems of the 1971 classification are not resolved in Hancock's later proposals (1977a). The decision to group all geographic and temporal varieties of Melanesian Pidgin English together (1977a: 378, entry 115) seems particularly difficult to justify.

In contrast, a number of very closely related Australian varieties of Pidgin English receive separate entries; the distinction between entry 107 (creolized English on the Bagot Aboriginal Reserve near Darwin, Australian Northern Territory) and entry 108 (Northern Territory Pidgin) is particularly puzzling. In actual fact, it would be more appropriate to regard these two varieties as different developmental stages of the same language, Northern Australian Kriol. Equally puzzling is Hancock's decision to provide two separate entries for the historically and structurally closely linked Norfolk Island and Pitcairn Island Creoles.

The main excuse for the shortcomings of the classifications discussed so far is the absence of reliable data on many varieties and the lack of any consistent criteria for separating or grouping different pidgins. These problems are partly overcome in two more recent accounts of Pidgin English in the Pacific. Both Clark (1979) and Wurm et al. (1981) take into account fieldwork and archival work carried out on a number of lesser-known Pacific pidgins and creoles,

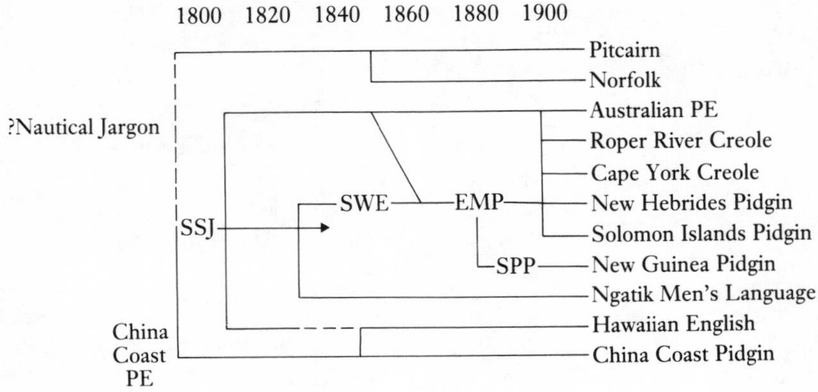

SSJ South Seas Jargon (Polynesia and Micronesia)
SWE Sandalwood English (New Caledonia, Loyalty Islands, New Hebrides)
EMP Early Melanesian Pidgin (New Hebrides, Solomon Islands, Queensland, Fiji)
SPP Samoan Plantation Pidgin

For the sake of simplicity, the positions of vernacular languages have not been shown.

Figure 1.4 Historical relations indicated by comparative and documentary evidence

including Samoan Plantation Pidgin, New Caledonian Pidgin, Queensland Kanaka English, Ngatik Men's language and Papuan Pidgin English. The principal virtue of Clark is his awareness of changes over time in the relationships between different pidgins (and derived creoles). His family tree (1979: 48) clearly shows that what was one language at one point may be two or more at a later period (see figure 1.4).

It would seem that Clark's account demonstrates the limits of what a family-tree model may reveal about the relationships between the various Pacific pidgins. Although it results from a careful assessment of many sources and observation of comparative methodology, it still suffers from a number of shortcomings, including the following.

1. A continuous development is assumed, where in reality there may have been many historical breaks, caused by non-optimal patterns of transmission.
2. Geographical location is relied upon even in those cases where there have been considerable population movements between pidgin-speaking areas.
3. As in all family trees, the role of convergence and mergers of pidgins is ignored.
4. Shared substratal influence is not depicted.

These points will be raised again later in this book. A last attempt at 'counting' and mapping Pidgin English in the Pacific is made in a map (designed by Wurm et al.) in the recent *Language Atlas of the Pacific* (1981). The authors of this map have paid considerable attention to overcoming the limitations of a purely geographically based classification. In particular, they have distinguished typographically between flourishing, dying and dead varieties; and mapped areas of (putative) origin as well as areas where the languages were later spoken.

The most important aspect of their classification is the distinction between the *linguistically ill-defined* Pacific Pidgin English, whose spread and appearance in many different parts of the Pacific (Loyalties, Tahiti, Samoa, etc.) is documented, and *linguistically distinct* varieties such as Tok Pisin, Papuan Pidgin English, Bislama and Solomon Pidgin English. Although such a distinction would seem to be a sound basis for counting and classifying pidgin in the Pacific, a number of problems remain unsolved, the first of which is the fact, mentioned in the text, that 'a number of regional dialect forms persisted in the New Hebrides' until fairly recently. This may be indicative either of the lack of stabilization of the language or the fact that indigenes from different parts of the archipelago traditionally went to work on different plantations. A second problem is that it is not clear whether Micronesian Pidgin is a separate unitary phenomenon. Apart from its origin in general Pacific Pidgin, it was also influenced by Melanesian Pidgin, which was imported by labourers from German New Guinea, and the employment of Micronesians in the Samoan plantations in the 1860s and early 1870s. None the less, the compilers of the map have made significant progress in sorting out the complex picture of Australian pidgin languages, by stressing the basic unity of the northern Australian creole varieties, the complexities of the preceding pidgin situation, and the presence of a number of imported pidgins.

To conclude, when one looks back on the many attempts to classify and list English-based pidgins and creoles in the Pacific, a rather desolate picture emerges. The contradictory and haphazard nature of all but the most recent accounts renders them almost useless as a basis for historical or comparative work. Furthermore, an extremely complex network of relationships is hidden by misleadingly simplistic descriptive accounts.

The message contained in the discussion of Pacific pidgins and creoles should be well heeded by those who wish to use these languages as examples or test cases in theoretical linguistics. In particular, one should avoid deducing general principles of historical development from a comparison of earlier and later stages of different languages, and also one should refrain from postulating universals on the basis of pidgins which are in fact historically linked. Both sins have been committed in the past and will continue to be committed as long as solid knowledge of the socio-historical context in which these languages developed is lacking.

Increased sensitivity to the matters just raised is certainly very much in evidence in recent pidginist–creolist writings and at conferences. As the number of linguists working in this area increases, new pidgins and creoles are discovered and described, and general statements about these languages are revised in accordance. It might be interesting to list briefly just a few languages that have been added to the list of pidgins and creoles over the last twenty years:

Pidgins	*Creoles*
Tarzanca (Foreigner Talk Turkish, Tourist Turkish)	Ngatik Men's language (Micronesia – English based)
Pidgin Koriki (Papua)	Unserdeutsch (Creole German of New Guinea)
Pidgin Afrikaans (South Africa)	Palanquero (Columbian Creole Spanish)
Samoan Plantation Pidgin English	Berbice Creole Dutch (Guayana)
Chinese Pidgin German (Kiautschou)	Karipuna (French based in French Guayana)
Singapore Bahasa Rojak	

Often, new discoveries are first announced in the *Carrier Pidgin*, the newssheet for workers in this area. Whether or not such new discoveries constitute separate languages and traditions is not always clear at first, nor do we have information, in many cases, as to the extent of their stabilization and institutionalization. However, initial data collection remains an important part of pidgin/creole studies and in many cases time is running out. I personally wish I had the time and opportunity to follow up the as yet undescribed languages mentioned to me in informal conversations: the Pidgin Spanish–English of Melilla (Spanish North Africa), the simplified Manam (New Guinea) used by nut collectors from this island, and the French–English Pidgin allegedly spoken in some Canadian coal-mines. The social and geographical marginality of such languages does not mean that they could not be of considerable importance to our theoretical developments.

Conclusions

The field of pidgin and creole linguistics in more than one way illustrates the predicament of anyone engaged in pre-theoretical inquiry. This predicament is compounded by the fact that, for many, pidgin and creole studies are supposed to deliver insights into the nature of abstract autonomous language systems, while at the same time such languages can be studied only in their socio-historical context. In fact, pidgins and creoles are the paradigm illustration of the adage that all linguistic systems leak.

As regards the two principal questions addressed in this chapter, the definition of pidgins and creoles, and their identification as separate languages, no unequivocal answers can be given, as is only to be expected at this phase of inquiry. It is hoped, however, that the discussion has been helpful to the development of a future explicit theory of these languages. Fortunately, one can learn much about a phenomenon without having agreed on definitions, as is suggested by the quotation at the beginning of this chapter. An awareness of the uncertainties and disagreements is certainly of greater benefit to the field than consensus about something which turns out to be a myth.

2

The Study of Pidgins and Creoles

> The creole dialects which have grown out of different European languages grafted on African stock, though inferior in general interest to even the rudest languages of native growth, are in some respect well worth attention.
>
> (Van Name 1869: 123)

Introduction

When the history of linguistics in the twentieth century comes to be written, a separate chapter should be devoted to the question 'What did linguists regard as legitimate topics of investigation?' For a long time only a few languages were thought worthy of attention; the remainder were given labels such as 'ungrammatical' or 'deviant'.

Grammarians in earlier centuries regarded the classical languages Hebrew, Latin and Greek as the only ones deserving of grammatical study, and it was commonly accepted that all other languages fell short of this ideal. Languages with no inflection, such as English, were said to be 'grammarless'. This view is found in Sir William Temple's *An Essay upon the Ancient and Modern Learning*, first published in 1690:

> The three modern tongues most esteemed are Italian, Spanish, and French, all imperfect dialects of the noble Roman; first mingled and corrupted with the harsh words and terminations of those many different and barbarous nations, by whose invasions and excursions the Roman empire was long infested; they were afterwards made up into these several languages, by long and popular use, out of those ruins and corruptions of Latin.

The rise of European nationalism brought a major reorientation, in that languages such as German, French and English were now regarded as systems on a par with the classical languages. At the same time, the belief that primitive peoples from other parts of the world communicated by means of barbarous tongues remained firmly established. In fact, it was hoped by eighteenth-century linguists that the study of languages spoken by 'culturally primitive' and illiterate people could throw light upon the origin of human language.

It is not very long ago that the Reverend Farrar could publish a long list of language freaks including the following (1899: 36–7):

> What shall we say, for instance . . . Of the Yamparico, 'who speaks a sort of gibberish like the growling of a dog', and who 'lives on roots, crickets, and several bug-like insects of different species'? Of the aborigines of Victoria, among whom new-born babes are killed and eaten by their parents and brothers, and who have no numerals beyond three? Of the Puris of Brazil, who have to eke out their scanty language by a large use of signs, and who have no words for even such simple conceptions as 'to-morrow', and 'yesterday'? Of the naked, houseless, mischievous, vindictive Andamaner, with a skull hung ornamentally round his neck? Of the Fuegians, 'whose language is an inarticulate clucking,' and who kill and eat their old women before their dogs, because as a Fuegian boy naively and candidly expressed it, 'Doggies catch otters, old women no'? Of the Banaks, who wear lumps of meat, artistically suspended in the cartilage of the nose? Of the negroes of New Guinea, who were seen springing from branch to branch of the trees like monkeys, gesticulating, screaming, and laughing?

When observers began to look at the so-called 'primitive' languages, however, they often met with intricacies of grammatical organization that were unfamiliar to them. Thus, the notion that there were developed and under-developed languages began to make way, in the late nineteenth century, to the now widely accepted view that all human languages are of comparable grammatical complexity and that the many surface dissimilarities are all manifestations of a deeper universal 'human language capacity'.

The question as to what constitutes equality when comparing languages has not as yet been settled, and claims in this area tend to be made on emotional rather than empirical grounds. The earlier view of a close link between grammar and culture has now given way to one in which all languages are regarded as 'natural'. It would seem that both views are mistaken, however: the former in believing that 'primitive man' reveals himself as ignorant and 'natural' in matters of language, the latter in ignoring that what seems 'natural' to the uninitiated observer turns out to be to a large extent man-made and cultural. This criticism implies that there may be differences in the extent to which human languages can be said to be 'natural', and it is suggested that pidgins and creoles play a key role in this debate. This question, together with that of evaluating linguistic systems, will be taken up again later in this book.

It is interesting that the very data relevant to the question of equality were for so long ignored, and that the status of true languages has continued to be denied to a number of linguistic phenomena, namely child language, pidgins (and creoles), and second-language learners' approximative systems. What is common to these languages is that they are linguistic systems in development.

The view that such developmental systems were deviant in some way was dominant prior to 1970, and linguists lacked the conceptual paradigm to describe the dynamics of language development in time and space. Thus, the utterances made by a child were regarded as faulty imitations of the parents' mode, and Pidgin English was labelled 'bad' or 'broken' English. Recent child language studies, however, show that, far from being faulty imitations, the utterances made by a child reflect a separate language system.

In spite of some pioneering attempts by scholars such as Schuchardt and Hall in the field of pidgin and creole studies, the view that these are parasitic rather than independent language systems is still widely found. However, a close study of pidgins reveals that they are systems in their own right. Like child language, pidgins are highly dynamic, becoming more complex as the communicative demands of their users increase. As with child language, a pidgin illustrates the capacity of human beings to create efficient communication systems, the principal difference between the two being that children are communicating in an established language community, whereas pidgins develop to serve new language communities.

Since pidgins illustrate how adults learn and create new languages, their study has become a major research area in second-language teaching and learning. It is now becoming clear that the errors committed by, say, a second-language learner of English are to a large extent systematic and can be described in terms of natural developmental processes. In contrast to the development of pidgins, which takes place without formal tuition or pressure to conform to a pre-existing standard, a formal second-language-learning context introduces elements that may run counter to the natural learning order. A close study of pidgins as examples of naturally learnt languages may well result in more efficient second-language teaching.

Today, there are few areas of human communication that are not regarded as a legitimate field of investigation. What is more, developmental systems such as child language and pidgins are increasingly regarded as central to the study of human language and language-learning capacity.

The reasons why pidgins and creoles have been regarded in the past as marginal are not just socio-cultural, however; their neglect also sprang from the lack of both adequate recording facilities and the availability of descriptive models capable of dealing with variability, rapid change and context-dependency. The motifs underlying the few studies of these languages that were undertaken in spite of the unattractiveness of the topic will be explored shortly.

Grammar as a gentleman's pastime

Many of the early accounts of pidgins and creoles come from the pen of gentleman travellers and administrators whose attention they had attracted because they appeared to them as caricatures of the civilized European tongues. Thus, in the preface to one of the first accounts of Jamaican Creole English (Russel 1868), we read: 'This little work has never intended originally to meet the eye of the Public; the writer merely prepared it as a source of social amusement to such of his friends as are of a literary turn.' A similar sentiment is expressed by William Churchill, sometime consul-general of the United States in Samoa and Tonga, (1911: 31) in his remarks on Beach-la-Mar, the cover term referring to the various English-based pidgins and creoles of the Western Pacific: 'Beach-la-mar is an amusing speech; in this brief treatise we have studied it with gaiety of enjoyment which it would be a shame to have repressed.'

We can thus see the establishment of a tradition which survives in present-day journalism, where expert and non-expert alike could agree, and where dilettantes could achieve easy recognition and acknowledgement of their own superiority. Pidgins and creoles, at the lowest levels, have become an after-dinner joke or, to borrow an expression widely used in expatriate circles, a 'tropicism', a typical example being this extract from *The Rabaul Times*:

> *Those Esses and Tees*
>
> We all know how the New Britain native – around Rabaul more especially – mixes up his esses and tees. He calls a cup of tea 'cup sea' and the Post Office 'Hout Pote'.
>
> Had a puzzling illustration of this t'other evening. Driving along from Kokopo in one of Tex Roberts' cars the lad suddenly brought the six cylindered juggernaut to a standstill.
>
> 'Why the thusness?' I enquired, somewhat bewildered, in my pidgin-ese.
>
> 'Me like pus him sail lice,' came the response, as he switched on the red light at the rear. – Joy Rider (21 July 1933)

It is only a small step from such light-hearted abuse to outright racist nastiness. Thus, a comment on West African Pidgin English (by M. Buchner, in the *Deutsche Kolonialzeitung* of 1885: 220) begins with the statement: 'One likes the negro because of his droleness; at the same time one hates him because of his infamity' (my translation). Pidgin English is seen by Buchner as the result of such ambivalent attitudes, the funny side being illustrated by the names given by Europeans to their servants, including Bloody Fool, Dirty Fellow, Peasoup, Brandy, Empty Bottle, Mustard and the like. Such linguistic observations are often handed down from one generation of amateur linguists to the next.

A case in point are the numerous reports on the name for 'piano' in Pacific Pidgin English. In 1902, Baron von Hesse-Wartegg (1902: 53) reports the form '*big fellow box spose whiteman fight him he cry too much*'; and Daiber writes in the same year (1902: 255): 'It was a Papuan who, horrified, told of *big fellow box white fellow master fight him plenty too much, he cry* (of the big box which the white man beats so much that it screams)'. Later, one finds '*big fellow bokkes, suppose missis he fight him, he cry too much*' (Friederici 1911: 100), *big fellow box, stop house, suppose you fight him, him cry* (reported for SPP by Neffgen in the *Samoan Times* of 27 March 1915); Shelton-Smith (1929) mentions the more likely version of *fight im bokis moosik* for 'to play the piano'; more recently, Mihalic (1969: 39) mentions the form *him big fella box, suppose you fight him, he cry* without claiming the authenticity of this version; and lastly (but perhaps not finally), Balint in his 1969 dictionary lists the entry *bikpela bokis bilong krai taim yu paitim na kikim em*. It may be noted that none of the sources quoted has the same 'name' for a piano.

Very little has changed over the years; perhaps the most important shift is that new technologies are reflected in equally dubious circumlocutions, such as *mixmaster bilong Jesus Christ* for 'helicopter'. Whereas such expressions serve to illustrate the perceived 'brighter side' of the colonized races, the absence of grammatical distinctions present in related European lexifier languages is frequently appealed to illustrate their mental inferiority, unreliability or brutishness. Only a few of the many examples can be mentioned here. Thus, Adam (1883, quoted from Hesseling 1905: 52) opines that 'creoles are adaptions of French or English to the phonetic and grammatical mentality . . . of a linguistically inferior race' (author's translation).

Linguistic examples often accompany such statements. Very prominent are comments on the absence of the copula, which is also included in this statement by Churchill (1911: 23): 'In our system of formal grammar the only thing which at all approximates this idea is the verbal noun. The savage of our study, like many another primitive thinker, has no conception of being in the absolute; his speech has no true verb "to be".'

Overt racism is found in the following lexicon entries in a booklet on Fanakalo (Pidgin Bantu of Southern Africa):

> AS adv. . . . sa. Unbelievable but true. Proves that the native mind works in the opposite direction to ours . . .
> BEAT, vb. . . . chaiya. 'I'll beat you.' 'Mena chaiya wena.' If you are going to get any effect do it first and talk later.
> GO, vb. int. . . . hamba (hortative-footsack).
> LIE, vb. . . . It is extraordinary that there are so few words to describe this national pastime of the native Africans . . . (Aitken-Cade 1951, quoted from Cole 1953: 553)

Contempt for pidgins and creoles and their speakers sometimes goes hand in hand with a different emotion, that of pride that the pidgin or creole concerned was derived from the writer's own superior native tongue. Thus, while complaining that the 'natives' have rendered the European language a 'debased mongrel jargon', 'a crude macaronic lingo', 'a perversion' or one of the many similar expressions found in the relevant literature, even in its debased form the European language remains superior to what the 'primitive natives' had before. Thus Grimshaw writes on the adoption of Papuan Pidgin English by the inhabitants of Rossel Island:

> To be addressed in reasonably good English of the 'pidgin' variety, by hideous savages who made murder a profession, and had never come into actual contact with civilisation, is an experience perplexing enough to make the observer wonder if he is awake. Yet this is what happens on Rossel Island. English is the 'lingua franca' of the place, filling up the gaps – and there are many – in the hideous snapping, barking dialect that passes for speech along the coast, and making communication possible among the tribes of the interior, who vary so much in language that many of them cannot understand one another. How did this come about? I fancy, through the unsatisfactory nature of the Rossel dialects. Any that we heard were scarcely like human speech in sound, and were evidently very poor and restricted in expression. Noises like sneezes, snarls, and the preliminary stages of choking – impossible to reproduce on paper – represented the names of villages, people, and things. (Grimshaw 1912: 191–2)

The folkviews expressed by the gentlemanly and not so gentlemanly writers of the passages quoted here have influenced professional linguists, educators and administrators for a long time and often still do.

Studies in defence of pidgins and creoles

The distorted characterizations and attacks on pidgins and creoles just outlined were effective for a number of reasons, not least because the speakers of these languages could not defend themselves, being illiterates at the bottom of the colonial hierarchy. Their voice could be heard only through the mediation of a small number of understanding outsiders and, in a very few cases, members of their own community who had risen to a position of respect within their society. One of the earliest defenders of a creole, Surinam Negro English, was the philologist and superintendent of the editorial department of the British and Foreign Bible Society, William Greenfield. The full background to his *A defence of the Surinam Negro–English version of the New Testament* . . . (1830) is given by Reinecke (1980). Greenfield's defence followed an attack in the *Edinburgh Christian Instructor* on the Negro English (Sranan) translation of the New

Testament by the Morovian Brothers in 1829. The translators were taken to task for being 'at pains to embody their barbarous, mixed, imperfect phrase in the pages of schoolbooks, and to perpetuate all its disadvantages and evil consequences by shutting them up to it as the vehicle of God's word'. The attacker concludes that with a little birch and patience broken English could be replaced by good English in Surinam.

Greenfield's defence includes many points that have come to make up the standard repertoire of those protecting a pidgin or creole from its detractors. For instance:

1 Creoles and related lexifier languages are mutually unintelligible.
2 The creole is a mixed language, (that is, a separate system) comparable to Middle English which had developed out of Anglo-Saxon and French and which, in earlier times, had similarly been accused of being 'a barbarous jargon, neither good French nor good Saxon'.
3 Etymological spelling can give a totally distorted view of a pidgin and creole.
4 Creoles may be more simple in the sense of more regular than their source languages, but not necessarily less developed in expressive power. They are as systematic as any other language.
5 Creoles are not infrequently suppressive, but represent a medium through which people can express their own feelings and bring about their own liberation.

Greenfield was far ahead of his time, however, and his spirited defence of Sranan did little to convince those in charge of mission language policies. Similar cycles of attack and defence were to be repeated with languages such as Afrikaans (see Valkhoff 1966), Haitian Creole French (Fleischmann 1978) and Tok Pisin (Mühlhäusler 1979). Many of Greenfield's arguments are also found in the later history of Sranan, for instance in the defence of the language by the missionary Wullschlaegel in his 1858 dictionary.

The fact that the poverty of expression in creoles is mainly in the minds of those with insufficient knowledge of the language is also a main theme in Thomas's 1869 defence of Trinidad Creole French. Born the son of freed slaves, John Jacob Thomas became a highly respected teacher and a vocal defender of the rights of the members of his race. His realization that misunderstandings of the language were at the root of many social problems resulted in his publication of his *Creole Grammar.* Closer to our own time, Robert A. Hall began to defend a number of pidgins and creoles in Oceania and the Caribbean, his best-known defence being *Hands off Pidgin English* (1955b), a staunch piece of writing. The book was written in direct reaction to a United Nations pronouncement in 1953 deploring the use of Tok Pisin in the Australian-administered Trust Territory of New Guinea.

Hall's involvement in the politics of pidgins and creoles has had considerable impact on this field of study. It can be seen to be causally related to two recent developments: first, the widespread support of professional linguists for many pidgin and creole languages and the rights of their speakers, often in the face of continued public animosity; and second, the fact that most of the defence of these languages remains in the hands of expatriate experts, although a small number of pidgin and creole speakers from the countries concerned have now also taken up these issues. This situation can lead to conflict, as it has indeed done in a number of instances. Interesting comments are given by Eades (1982: 62 ff).

Early missionary and pedagogical grammars

We have already noted conflicting views of mission bodies on pidgin and creole languages. On the one hand, missionaries aimed at quick and efficient communication with the peoples they were trying to convert, but, on the other, there appears to have been a widespread feeling that the word of God should not be debased by being written or preached in an 'inferior' language. It is in this situation of conflict between everyday preoccupation and long-term goals that most of mission grammar writing and lexicography for pidgins and creoles was done. The best results were obtained in those areas where the pidgin or creole and its related lexifier language did not coexist, or where missionaries were not native speakers of the lexifier language. How different missions dealt with their communicative problems will now be illustrated with a few case studies.

Virgin Islands Creole Dutch (Negerengels)

The islands of St Thomas, St John and St Croix were settled in the early eighteenth century by Dutch planters and their slaves. Soon after they were taken over by the Danes, who eventually sold them to the United States in 1915. A Dutch-based creole appears to have sprung up within a very short time, and this language was used by both Danish and German missionaries operating on these islands. J. M. Magens in 1770 produced *Grammatica over det Creolske sprog*, based on a Latin model. It is the first systematic account of any creole. This was followed by a burst of publishing activity, and another grammar for the use of German missionaries appeared around 1802. As the language has very severely declined since (there were six known speakers in 1969), it would probably have remained unrecorded without such missionary activities.

Annobón Creole Portuguese

The island of Annobón in the Gulf of West Africa was settled by Portuguese planters and their slaves at the beginning of the sixteenth century. It was ceded to Spain in 1777, but proper Spanish control does not predate 1850. The first priest was also installed at about that time, and a mission station was opened in 1882 to serve the 1,800 inhabitants of the island. Two of the first Spanish missionaries, M. Barrena and I. Vila, wrote grammars of Annobonese, both modelled on traditional classical grammars. A catechism and other religious writings followed, although both missionaries made it perfectly clear that this was an interim measure only and that a mastery of Standard Spanish by the entire population was the ultimate aim.

Chinook Jargon

This language, based on Chinook spoken at the mouth of the Columbia River, was an important trade language in pre-European times,[1] but spread and developed considerably with the advent of European fur traders and settlers. Most of the important grammar and dictionary writing for this language is due to the efforts of the Catholic and, to a lesser extent, assorted Protestant missions, in particular Le Jeune's practical vocabulary (1886).

A large body of religious writings is also due to missionary influence. As observed by Reinecke (1937: 640): 'In so far as the Jargon has a literary form it is due to the missionaries, chiefly Roman Catholics.' Such early graphization and standardization incidentally pose a considerable problem for those who would like to regard Chinook Jargon as a paradigm case of a non-European-derived pidgin. What initially seemed a natural language again turns out to be one that is heavily influenced by culture, not least European culture.

Sango

Sango is the pidgin version of a small vernacular (about 5,000 speakers) in the Central African Republic. Since its modest beginnings as a riverine lingua franca in the 1890s, it has experienced considerable linguistic and social expansion in the wake of European penetration of the area (see Samarin 1982). It is today the most important language of this African nation. A number of smallish vocabularies were in currency at the turn of the century, but genuine descriptive work does not predate 1953, when Samarin's pedagogical grammar, published by the Mission Evangelique de Oubangui-Chari, appeared.

Papuan Pidgin English

We have so far considered cases where missionaries, for reasons best known to themselves, have been the initiators and promoters of pidgins and creoles and their study. However, one should not forget that missionaries have also been instrumental in suppressing these languages and preventing their study. On the debit side of mission activities, we find languages such as Papuan Pidgin English, Mauritius French Creole and Town Bemba.

In spite of the fact that Papuan Pidgin English was at one time probably the most widely understood language of Papua, its existence was played down and denied by both government and missionaries. Arguably the missionaries who controlled most teaching as well as other important areas of communication, are to be held responsible for the decline of this language. Newton appears to reflect the prevalent attitudes of the missionaries towards Papuan Pidgin English when he deplores its use in religious services in Samarai prison:

> It would approach blasphemy were one to put in print the form in which truths of religion appear in 'Pidgin' English, as for instance the way in which the Almighty is spoken of, or the relation of our Blessed Lord to the Eternal Father, even though the close connection of the sublime and the ridiculous has elements of humour . . . For my own part, when I have taken the gaol service I could never bring myself to use 'Pidgin' English, and not simply because I am not familiar with it. (Newton 1914: 26–7)

No dictionaries or grammars were ever compiled, and none of the scriptures ever translated into this language. Instead, the missionaries developed a number of indigenous languages as mission lingue franche for restricted areas and, for the remainder, lent their support to Hiri Motu, the Motu-based pidgin (see Dutton forthcoming). The legacy of such policies is a Papua New Guinean nation that is split into two: Pidgin English-speaking (Tok Pisin) former German New Guinea and Hiri Motu-speaking former British/Australian Papua. The political and financial disadvantages of this are very considerable.

Mauritius French Creole

The case of Mauritius again illustrates the more general principle that speakers of a superimposed European language frequently find it difficult to accept a lexically related pidgin or creole. Thus, on Mauritius extensive passages of the bible were translated into Creole by Protestant missionaries of English extraction, while the French-speaking Catholic missionaries discouraged this language. A good illustration is the title of a paper written by Father Louis Ducrocq in 1902: 'L'idiome enfantin d'une race enfantine' (The childish language of a childish race).

Town Bemba

Town Bemba, a partially pidginized and creolized language spoken in the Zambian copperbelt, appears to have been discouraged by European missionaries until the very recent past. Heine reports:

> Amongst the Europeans, 'Town BEMBA' up to today has not much been in vogue. In comparison with BEMBA of the rural districts it is designated as 'slang', 'broken BEMBA', 'English with BEMBA grammar', or 'mixed gibberish'. This also applies to the missionaries, who had declared against the use of 'Town BEMBA', but had on the other hand significantly promoted the tribal language of BEMBA as language of education in the schools. (Richardson 1961: 27, quoted in Heine 1970: 59)

The reason for these mission attitudes may be related to the widespread mission aversion to urban modes of life and speech.[2]

Further examples of missionary activities leading to the decline of lingue franche are cases where an existing language was associated with Islam, as Bazaar Malay in German New Guinea (cf. Seiler 1982) and Swahili in some parts of East Africa. In sum, missionary work on pidgins and creoles, in spite of all its shortcomings, constitutes one of the major sources of information on earlier stages of pidgins and creoles. Missionaries were involved insiders in language and communication matters, and were often forced to develop communicative solutions on the basis of limited information and resources. Although most missionary writings are of a descriptive type, some comparative and theoretical material is available. A recent contribution illustrating this point is Markey (1983: 110–13).

Pidgins and creoles in philology

Linguistics in the nineteenth century was dominated by the comparative and historical paradigm. Among the opinions widely held by the scholarly establishment of the day were the following:

1 that it was possible to reconstruct family trees for languages and to trace back contemporary languages to an original ancestral language;
2 the idea of linguistic evolution: highly inflected languages were often regarded as developmentally more advanced;
3 that languages change from within, following natural laws: both language mixing and man-made changes were regarded as marginal, and sound changes, in particular, were regarded as mechanical exceptionless processes;
4 scientific treatment is seen as historical.

It is easy to see why pidgins and creoles were not popular within this paradigm. In particular:

1 they apparently resulted from convergent (mixture) rather than divergent processes;

2 they had few inflectional properties;
3 regular sound changes and correspondences were difficult to establish: even more frequently than in the case of the older languages studied by the philologist, exceptionless sound laws turn out to be a myth;
4 as pidgins and creoles were short lived, their study must have appeared unlikely to throw any light on the question of an ancestral human language.

It is for reasons such as these that the father of pidgin and creole studies, Hugo Schuchardt (1842–1927), was regarded as a rebel against the established neo-grammarian doctrine. Although Schuchardt set out to disprove the notion of regularity of sound change with pidgin and creole data, he soon became interested in other aspects of these languages, particularly the interaction between typologically and historically different grammars, and in his late writings the operation of language-independent universal forces in their formation. This latter interest links him to some of his lesser-known predecessors, such as the Portuguese scholar Coelho. Schuchardt remains a source of inspiration for present-day scholars for a number of reasons, notably his highly detailed descriptions of many of the world's lesser-known pidgins and creoles, in particular those related to Portuguese, and because he advanced ideas far ahead of his times, such as the post-creole continuum, species-specific language, and the relationship of Black American English to its creole predecessors.

Schuchardt's considerable creativity and originality of thought are balanced, unfortunately, by a number of shortcomings. He appears to have been unable to construct a coherent model out of his numerous observations, and he often mixes irrelevant details with pertinent theoretical remarks. This, together with his lack of skills in academic politics, accounts for the fact that his writings have remained relatively unknown until recently. The appearance of two edited translations of major writings on pidgins and creoles by Markey in Schuchardt 1979 and in Gilbert 1980 hopefully signals a new era of appreciation (see also Gilbert 1983).

In addition to his topic being regarded as marginal by his colleagues, the Dutch scholar Hesseling (1859–1941) faced the problem of writing in a minority language. Like Schuchardt, he had gone through the mill of Indo-European studies and subsequently held the chair of Byzantine and Modern Greek at Leiden University. His principal interest, koiné Greek, appears to have led him to the study of contemporary languages of a similar nature, in particular semi-creolized (creoloid) Afrikaans and Negro Dutch of the Danish Antilles (Negerhollands). In later life he also looked at creoles based on languages other than Dutch and worked on generalities in the construction of these languages. Unlike Schuchardt, whose major concern was that of substratum grammar, Hesseling regarded language-independent modes of second-language acquisition as the most powerful agents of pidgin and creole formation. Like Schuchardt, Hesseling was regarded as a minor figure, even in his home country. A revaluation of his work has now begun to appear, however, beginning with Valkoff's writings on Afrikaans (1966, 1972) and a recent translation of some of Hesseling's creolist writings (Markey et al. 1979).

Pidgin and creole studies continued to be discussed within the framework of comparative and historical linguistics until very recently. On the whole, existing methodology was adopted, and their overall impact on philological studies has been almost negligible. We can only single out a few later studies in our brief survey.

Around 1925, a number of scholars suggested pidginization and/or creolization as a major factor in the development of language families. Examples are Sydney Ray's *A Comparative Study of Melanesian Island Languages* (1926), where the so-called Pidginization Hypothesis of Melanesian languages was proposed. According to this theory, Melanesian languages were regarded as a mixture between Papuan and Indonesian languages:

> The IN [Indonesian] in MN [Melanesian] is a foreign element, introduced by colonists from the west. These settled on some of the smaller islands which became centres of trade and influence in the sea round about, the pidgin-IN of the settlement eventually modifying and introducing a certain amount of likeness into the originally different dialects . . . The IN words found in Melanesia have the characteristics of a pidgin-tongue. (Ray 1926: 597)

It is not clear whether the present-day Melanesian languages should be seen as continuations of contact pidgins or whether they are more in the nature of mixtures of two full systems. Neither Ray nor any of his successors (discussed in Lynch 1981) have a sufficiently powerful model of mixing and pidginization to come up with genuine explanations. Similar problems are also found with Feist's (1932) suggestion that the origin of the Germanic family of languages involved pidginization, and a later study by Politzer (1949) making similar claims for the Romance languages. Finally, one should mention recent work on the emergence of Middle English (Bailey and Maroldt 1977) and Domingue (1977). Again, as was the case with explanations of the origin of Melanesian languages, the distinction between creolization, pidginization and mixing tends to be insufficiently precise, and questions as to whether Middle English can be regarded as a continuation of a medieval French–Anglo-Saxon contact jargon (Albert 1922) cannot be meaningfully asked.

The role of pidgin and creole research as a corrective against overly dogmatic models of linguistic relationship and change thus remained minimal. In contrast, the influence of established comparative historical methodology on the study of these languages has been considerable. In spite of the unsuitability of this model, it has been applied over and over again to pidgin and creole data. We can discern two motifs in such studies: the older one of relating pidgins and creoles to their European 'parent' languages; the more recent one of determining inter-relationships among pidgins and creoles. A staunch defender of the validity of this genetic model is R.A. Hall Jr, and it may be this linguistic conservatism which, more than anything else, made pidgin and creole linguistics acceptable in North America and elsewhere. Hall regards both Schuchardt's claims that the existence of mixed languages invalidates the genetic model and Meillet's counterclaims that creoles are direct descendants of languages such as French (for example, Meillet 1921: 85) as pseudo arguments, based on too stringent criteria for linguistic continuity.[3] Instead, he proposes (Hall 1958: 369) that by genetic relationship we simply mean: 'when we find systematic correspondences in all aspects of language structure . . . between two languages . . . we conclude that one must be a later stage of the other, or else that they must have come from a common source'.

Although such a view enabled Hall to reconcile historical comparative linguistics with American structuralism, it had two damaging consequences: first, it removed sociolinguistic considerations from the analysis of pidgins and creoles; and second, it gave respectability to static comparison, a method hardly suited to highly variable and rapidly changing linguistic entities. It is by dint of such simplifications and assumptions that Hall managed to establish the fundamental structural identity of pidgins and creoles and their related European lexifier languages.

Partly in reaction to Hall's claims, Douglas Taylor, one of the most active creolists of the 1950s, pointed to a number of unacceptable consequences of the traditional model of genetic relationships. In particular, he raised the question of apparently changing genetic relationships that appear to alter over the history of a creole; he illustrated his arguments with languages such as Papiamento, spoken on the Dutch Antilles, which allegedly changed from a Portuguese-based to a Spanish-based creole, and Sranan of Surinam, which changed from a Portuguese creole to an English one. Taylor's argument was subsequently developed and named *relexification theory* by scholars such as Thompson (1961), and it was studied in great detail for the Surinamese creoles Sranan, Saramaccan and Djuka by Voorhoeve (1973). These studies indicated not only that shifts in genetic relationships can occur in creoles, but also that, in most parts of grammar, there are considerable differences between European languages and their creole daughters, casting doubts upon claims as to a genetic link.

A second application of comparative and historical linguistics to the study of pidgins and creoles is the reconstruction of their genetic relationships, sometimes with the additional aim of isolating ancestral proto-pidgins. A first major attempt was made by Goodman in 1964 who, after a detailed study of about forty lexical and grammatical features, concluded that there must be a common origin to all French creoles and that the most likely place of origin appears to be West Africa. A similar conclusion for the English-based creoles of the New

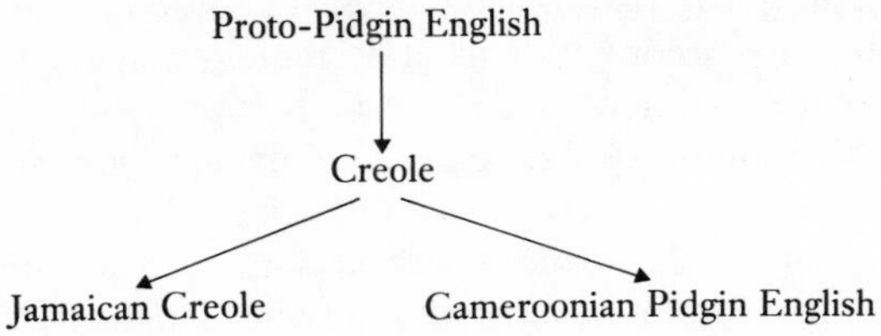

Figure 2.1 Gilman's family tree (from Gilman 1978)

World is arrived at by Hancock (1969), where a single proto-Pidgin English with some local variants is identified as occurring on the West African coast in the sixteenth century. In a more recent paper (1983), Hancock supplements structural and lexical evidence with socio-cultural information, paying attention to factors such as migrations, labour recruitment, shift of political boundaries and nature of contacts. That such information is an essential rather than a dispensable constituent of historical work on pidgins and creoles has yet to become widely accepted. Thus, in spite of the excellent models provided by Clark (1979) and Hancock, so-called 'extralinguistic' factors continue to be ignored in many comparative studies. An example of how this practice affects results is a study by Gilman (1978). The author suggests that Jamaican Creole English and Cameroonian Pidgin English both derive from the same language, Proto Pidgin English, and he implies a family tree of the type shown in figure 2.1. However, the available historical evidence suggests that Cameroonian Pidgin English as spoken today is not a continuation of earlier West African coastal Pidgin English, but a more recent import from Sierra Leone Krio (see Todd 1979), and that Krio, in turn, may be either a direct descendant of or heavily influenced by Jamaican Creole and possibly other West Indian Creole Englishes. The resulting family relationships would consequently be considerably less tree-like and would more closely resemble figure 2.2.

Thus linguistic comparisons should be made between an earlier creole and a

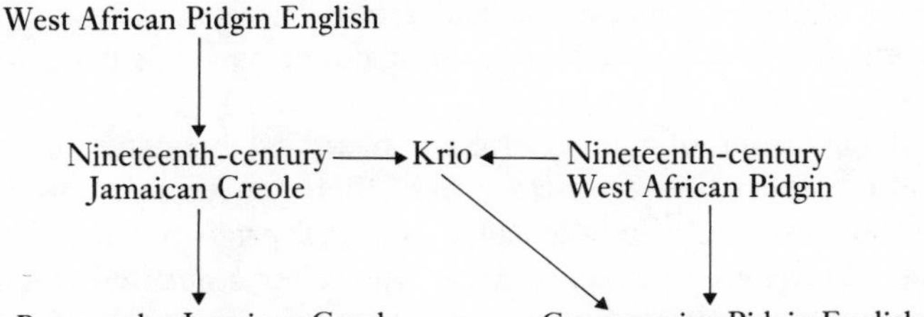

Figure 2.2 Relationship between Krio, Cameroon Pidgin English and Jamaican Creole

later pidgin, and not between contemporary systems. A comparison between present-day Jamaican Creole and Cameroon Pidgin English would certainly not seem to be a sound procedure for establishing a proto-language.

Anthropological linguistics and sociolinguistics

In a recent review of the field of pidgin and creole studies, Bickerton (1976: 169–93) expresses astonishment at the fact that it has consistently been classified as part of sociolinguistics. I have personally experienced the same reaction from many of my linguistic colleagues (that is, a readiness to label me a sociolinguist simply because most of my work is concerned with pidgins and creoles). On closer inspection, one finds that genuine sociolinguistic work on these languages is a relatively recent phenomenon. Symptomatic of this is the absence, within classical anthropological linguistics in the United States (i.e. Boas and Sapir), of any attempt to analyse the linguistic and social dimensions of the many American Indian–European contact languages found in North America, a point discussed in greater detail by Silverstein (1972b).

It is further symptomatic that Reinecke's monumental doctoral thesis of 1937, 'Marginal Languages', has remained unpublished and virtually unknown to anthropologists and sociologists, in spite of the fact that it summarizes and critically discusses virtually the entire body of sociological and anthropological writings on pidgins and creoles before 1935. A similar fate overtook the often misquoted article by Schultze (1933), which was the first attempt to provide a systematic classification of pidgins and creoles according to sociological criteria.

If an integrated view of pidgins and creoles has been lacking within anthropological linguistics and sociology until very recently, studies of individual languages, with or without critical remarks on their ethnography of speaking, have been made by numerous anthropologists. Indeed, our knowledge of the early stages of many pidgins and creoles would be very deficient without such studies. Let me illustrate this point with the example of Papuan Pidgin English. The most extensive reports on this language are remarks by Ray in 1907, following the Cambridge Anthropological Expedition to Torres Straits. In 1918, the Scandinavian anthropologist Landtman published 'The Pidgin English of British New Guinea', accompanying a volume containing a vast collection of traditional stories in this language (1917). A similarly valuable collection of texts covering the Torres Straits as well as the Papuan coast is given by the Swiss anthropologist Laade (1968).

In short, the recent upsurge in pidgin and creole studies again is due, to a very significant extent, to the interest paid to these languages by anthropologists and anthropological linguists such as Hymes, Silverstein, Sankoff, Rigsby and Keesing, and by sociolinguists such as Labov, Bailey and Trudgill.

Structuralist studies

The period of structuralism in linguistics extends from the early 1920s to the 1960s. It is impossible to do justice to the many developments of structuralism, but it seems worth while to single out a few areas which affected pidgin and creole studies. These include:

1 the emphasis on description;
2 the association with behaviourist learning theories;
3 the tendency to regard languages as self-contained systems.

The belief that linguists should describe and not prescribe, combined with the strong insistence on the inherent equality of all human languages, undoubtedly created an atmosphere wherein it was possible to produce scholarly descriptions of these once-despised languages. The most productive figure in this enterprise is Robert A. Hall Jr, who attempted comprehensive descriptions of Tok Pisin (1943), Chinese Pidgin English (1944), Sranan (1948), Haitian Creole (1953) as well as grammatical sketches of a number of other pidgins and creoles. Also of interest are the descriptive writings of those working on non-European-based languages, such as Samarin's work on Sango (1953) and Wurm and Harris's early writings (1963) on Hiri Motu (then called Police Motu). Common to most of the descriptive work of this kind is the relatively uncritical adherence to established structuralist methods. The legacy of this is a large body of data arranged in a very similar manner and thus well suited to comparative work (if indeed structuralism did allow the comparison of elements across systems).

Perhaps the greatest impact of structuralism on pidgin and creole linguistics was the promotion of a particular model of language acquisition, based on behaviourist learning theories. Since languages were thought to be learned by imitation, pidgins were said to reflect the foreigner-talk register used by speakers of the superordinate language when addressing uneducated foreigners. In addition to imitation, interference (or substratum influence) was considered a second force in the development of pidgins. According to Bloomfield:

> Speakers of a lower language may make so little progress in learning the dominant speech, that the masters, in communicating with them resort to 'baby-talk'. This 'baby-talk' is the master's imitation of the subjects' speech. There is reason to believe that it is by no means an exact imitation, and that some of its features are based not upon the subjects' mistakes but upon grammatical relations that exist within the upper language itself. The subject, in turn, deprived of the correct model, can do no better now than to acquire the simplified 'baby-talk' version of the upper language. (1933: 472)

Such a model could provide plausible explanations for the origin of pidgins, albeit not for their subsequent development, but it was certainly not an adequate model for creolization, since the qualitative differences between the second-language pidgin and the following generation's first-language creole exclude imitation as the primary explanation. The only explanation consonant with behaviourism is the appeal to substratum influence, which is developed parallel to interference in the learning models appealed to at the time. In fact, Hall states:

> creolization is simply one manifestation of a broader process which, for want of a better term, we can call 'nativization'. A language is nativized when it is taken over by a group of speakers who have previously used some other languages, so that the new language becomes the native language of the group. (1966: xiii)

It is interesting to observe how the role of children and their rule-changing creativity is played down in this explanation.

The view of pidgins and creoles as self-contained systems can be seen, like the two views just discussed, as an attempt to ignore possible 'leaks' in grammars, in particular the element of time. Hall has justified this as a useful abstraction (1975: 138): 'a purely descriptive analysis . . . is . . . dependent simply on a convenient fiction of the complete removal of the time element from a description'. Also ignored are those areas of grammar that are notoriously gradient: that is, phonetics and semantics, and the social forces shaping the creation of variation. Instead, we are given abstract common core or overall pattern accounts. Their neatness and symmetry are achieved at high cost, however. With pidgins and creoles exhibiting greater variability and a faster rate of change than most older established languages, idealized descriptions are even more remote from the goal of observational adequacy. They also reinforce the social myth that pidgin and creole users live in static societies and are dependent for the improvement of their lot upon the crumbs that fall from their colonizers' tables.

Transformational generative grammar

In his *Selective Chronology of Creole Studies* (1981), Reinecke observes that transformational generative grammar (TGG), first widely publicized in 1957, has been 'immensely influential in the field of creole studies as in all linguistic theory'. What Reinecke did not say is that it has been an almost constant love–hate relationship between the two, resulting in eventual divorce.

In many ways TGG theory and practice remained at the very centre of structuralism. This can be seen in the following features, which are of particular importance for our present discussion.

1 Transformationalist practice is minilectal, that is, it is concerned with single idiolects or varieties at a single point in time.
2 Strict separation is made between structure and use.
3 Linguistic systems are kept separate, with a consequent aversion to fusion and mergers.
4 Synchronic and diachronic grammar are separate.

Such considerations apart, TGG has succeeded in motivating a sizeable number of scholars to do work on previously investigated aspects of pidgins and creoles. Thus, on the positive side, the availability of a more refined model of description led to considerable progress in the understanding of the syntax of pidgin and creole languages. Whereas in the early days of TGG writers attempted global descriptions of individual languages (the paradigm case being Bailey's (1966) grammar of Jamaican Creole), later writers increasingly restricted themselves to smaller subgrammars and carried out in-depth studies of constructions such as verb chaining, complementation or relative-clause formation.

A second area of research which was greatly promoted by TGG was the quest for linguistic universals and/or universals of language.[4] It is no coincidence that a number of scholars (Agheyisi 1971; Givón 1979; Kay and Sankoff 1974; Mühlhäusler 1974) should come up independently with the suggestion that pidgins are probably the universal base from which other languages can be derived by means of language-specific transformations. Whatever the limitations of this view, it certainly directed researchers to an inquiry into the common features of pidgins, and thus indirectly promoted the study of non-European-based pidgins and creoles.

A third innovation of TGG of interest to pidgin/creole scholars was its mentalism. Language learning was not seen as imitation, but as a productive process reflecting innate mental structures. As the operation of the language acquisition device (LAD) was said to be encountered mainly before puberty, and as it was generally held that grammars of adult speakers change, if at all, by minor alteration, TGG was, strictly speaking, not suited to explaining the formation of pidgins by adults, but only creole formation. In spite of this, the mentalist learning model was applied to pidgins; moreover, some traditional explanations that smacked of behaviourism, such as baby talk or substratum influence (mixing), were discarded. It is only very recently that a growing number of scholars have come to acknowledge that pidgin formation involves a number of strategies, including universals, substratum influence and imitation, and that these factors often conspire to give a result which can be traced to any single factor.[5] It is also now more widely accepted, mainly as a result of numerous studies in the area of second-language acquisition (interlanguage), that adults retain the capacity to restructure and drastically change linguistic systems (cf. Corder and Roulet 1976).

In addition to these shortcomings, one can identify two areas of TGG which have become particularly bothersome to pidgin and creole linguists, and which have led many of them to propose alternative models. These are:

1 methodological problems with the use of intuitions;
2 conceptual problems involving the notions of linguistic competence and ideal speaker–hearer.

The use of intuitions in pidgin and creole linguistics, rather than a corpus of observed data as the basis of analysis, causes problems beyond the more general ones outlined by Labov (1972). This is particularly true of pidgins that are second languages acquired and spoken by adults with wide-ranging differences in proficiency. As pointed out independently in a number of publications (Ardener 1971; Mühlhäusler 1974; Silverstein 1972a), it is simply impossible to obtain reliable answers about acceptability, let alone grammaticality, from pidgin speakers. When I first set out to undertake linguistic fieldwork on Tok Pisin of Papua New Guinea, I had carefully prepared a questionnaire designed to test speakers' intuitions about a number of constructions. These questionnaires ended up as a fire over which a billy of tea was made. I had come to realize that asking questions about decontextualized isolated sentences was no more regarded as a meaningful activity by my informants than asking random speakers in a Western speech community what colour skunks prefer. The main difference is that Western people feel obliged to answer even such questions,[6] whereas most Papua New Guineans do not, unless they belong to a culture where question-answering is socially mandatory, in which case they tend to provide those answers they expect the researcher to want to hear. In addition, it should be noted that many of the metalinguistic labels linguists would wish to employ in such questions (for example, sentence, word) have no counterpart in the languages under investigation. Heavy reliance on a corpus is thus unavoidable, and great care must be taken to obtain a representative sample of the language.

The question of representative data is also of importance in establishing how far pidgins and creoles can be related to a Chomskyan notion of grammatical competence (that is, the system of rules that an ideal speaker–hearer has internalized and that determines the relationship between the sound and meaning of sentences). The problems are greatest with two developmental stages: namely, incipient pidgins and decreolizing creoles.

Both Bickerton (1977) and Silverstein (1972a) hold that there is no such thing as grammatical competence in an incipient pidgin or jargon. Rather, speakers use a number of strategies, most prominently that of calquing the grammars of their own first languages with the addition of shallow adjustment rules, which creates superficially similar surface structures. Deeper levels of grammars of different speakers would not be affected. An illustration is given in the following surface structure of Tok Pisin:

man ya i haisim ap plak
this man hoists up the flag

This may be analysed as either:

noun—determiner—predicate marker—verb—particle—noun

or:

noun—determiner—predicate marker—verb—verb—noun

The verb-particle analysis is preferred by European speakers (and European analysts such as Hall 1943), whereas the verb-chain interpretation is common among Papua New Guineans.

The problem of grammatical competence in creoles (Le Page 1973) and post-creole situations again involves inter-speaker differences. Let me illustrate the latter situation with an example given by Bickerton (1977: 31), who asked twenty undergraduate students of the University of Guayana to translate the English sentence 'I was sitting' into their native Guayanese Creole English. He recorded the following thirteen answers:

1 a woz sitin.
2 ai de sidong.
3 mi bin sidong.
4 a de sitin.
5 a bin sitin.
6 a did sidong.
7 ai biin sitin.
8 mi bina sidong.
9 ai bin sitin dong.
10 a bina sidong.
11 a woz sitin dong.
12 a did sitin.
13 mi bina sit.

To describe the kind of variations encountered along the post-creole continuum as optional or free variation leads to two major problems:

1 that of selecting the obligatory forms/rules of which the remaining forms are said to be expansions or derivations;
2 the fact that the selection of 'optional' rules in many instances is not free, but severely restrained by superimposed implicational rule patterns.

Thus a transformational grammar without optional rules will underdescribe the language, whereas one with such optional rules will generate numerous forms which are in clear violation of the rules of the creole concerned. It is thus understandable that most serious scholars specializing in pidgin/creole studies have found the TGG paradigm inadequate or, at best, have adopted it as an interim makeshift solution. As pointed out by Muysken in the introduction to a volume entitled *Generative Studies on Creole Languages* (1981), 'most generativists . . . have shied away from Pidgin and Creole languages because of the variability hinted at or described in the literature'. Indeed, of those who have reviewed this volume, two (Markey 1981 and Romaine 1984) have pointed out that the title was a contradiction in terms and that some of its papers were anti-TGG in content and aim.

It could be argued that generativists have probably lost more by ignoring pidgin and creole evidence than pidgin and creole scholars have lost by ignoring ongoing theoretical work in TGG. The reason for this suspicion is that pidgins and creoles would seem to provide the best test cases for the central question asked within the generative paradigm: how can one account for the acquisition of human language?

Post-generative models

In his introduction to Bailey's *Jamaican Creole Syntax* (1966), Le Page commented:

> The descriptive analysis of an idiolect at any given moment may reveal a great many overlapping systems, some of which are coming to the end of a period of change, others just beginning. The descriptive analyst freezes for a moment what is in fact a highly dynamic system, and describes it in static terms. The quantum mechanics era in linguistics has not yet arrived, but I believe that the study of Creole languages will help it forward, since it appears generally true that the kinetic energy within creole systems is greater than that within older systems. (Le Page 1966: xi–xii)

It is not by chance that this quantum linguistics should emerge first within the description of highly fluid pidgins and creoles. The first writer to point out ordered patterning in an apparently messy instance of a post-creole language was DeCamp (1971b). He observed that basilectal, mesolectal and acrolectal features or rules cannot be combined in any order, but that the possible combinations are highly constrained. These constraints are such that the presence of the most acrolectal feature implies the presence of all other acrolectal features, but not vice versa. DeCamp illustrated this with data from Jamaican Creole English (see table 2.1).

Table 2.1 Some variant features of Jamaican Creole English

Acrolectal features		*Basilectal features*	
+A	child	−A	pikni
+B	cat	−B	nyam
+C	/Θ − − t/	−C	/t/
+D	/ð − − d/	−D	/d/
+E	granny	−E	nana
+F	didn't	−F	no ben

He then established that only seven of the numerous mathematically possible combinations could actually be observed or elicited. These are shown in table 2.2.

Table 2.2 Observed feature distribution

Speakers						
1	+A	+B	+C	−D	+E	+F
2	−A	+B	−C	−D	+E	+F
3	−A	+B	−C	−D	−E	−F
4	−A	−B	−C	−D	−E	−F
5	+A	+B	+C	+D	+E	+F
6	+A	+B	−C	−D	+E	+F
7	−A	+B	−C	−D	+E	−F

These seven permitted combinations can then be arranged in such a way that each speaker differs from the next one by just one feature,[7] to yield the arrangement shown in table 2.3.

Table 2.3 Rearranged data

Speaker						
5	+A	+B	+C	+D	+E	+F
1	+A	+B	+C	−D	+E	+F
6	+A	+B	−C	−D	+E	+F
etc.						

Such an arrangement can tell us that feature D is the most acrolectal one, in that its presence in a given speech event implies the simultaneous presence of all other acrolectal features. It excludes combinations such as *no ben* for 'didn't' and [ð] in the same speech event.

In its most abstract form, the panlectal grid will look as shown in table 2.4.

Table 2.4 The Panlectal grid

Speaker/lect	*B*	*E*	*F*	*Feature* *A*	C	*D→more acrolectal*
5	+	+	+	+	+	+
1	+	+	+	+	+	–
6	+	+	+	+	–	–
2	+	+	+	–	–	–
7	+	+	–	–	–	–
3	+	–	–	–	–	–
4	–	–	–	–	–	–

This rearrangement clearly demonstrates what implicational patterns can occur. A plus implies pluses only to its left, and a minus implies minuses only to its right. The presence of a plus makes no predictions of what is found to its right; the implications are unidirectional. Instead of associating each horizontal line of pluses and minuses with a single speaker, we can make the more realistic assumption that all speakers are polylectal and hence proficient over a greater or lesser span of a polylectal grid. Although the implicational patterns are constant for all speakers of a post-creole-speaking community in this model, individual competences can differ, as can the perceptive and productive competence of single individuals.

The model suggested by DeCamp was subsequently developed by Bailey, Bickerton and others and has become widely used not only by pidginists and creolists, but also by sociolinguists and theoretical linguists. As the model will be referred to in several places in this volume, it would seem advisable to consider briefly some of its advantages and drawbacks here.

On the positive side, we find that it is capable of displaying, in an orderly fashion, highly variable data; that it can map differences between perception and production which tend to be particularly strong in the rapidly changing pidgins and creoles; and that breaks in implicational patterns can be used as indicators of breaks in continuity of transmission.

A number of limitations must be noted, however. First, the model is a way of displaying rather than explaining data. Second, although it is highly useful for displaying variation in a small area of grammar (local variation), it is extremely cumbersome for mapping all dependencies such as might hold in a language. This leads to the following more serious deficiencies. In the absence of any procedures for identifying dependencies for the entire grammar and lexicon, the distinction between linguistically motivated implications, historically motivated implications and accidents of the descriptivists' selection cannot be made. Implicational scales of the type $A \subset B \subset C$ map, first and foremost, the addition of linguistic features/rules over time,[8] C being added after B, which in turn is added to the grammar after A. In an ideal world, the same implications would hold for all speakers of a speech 'community'. In actual fact, because of discontinuities of transmission, prestige borrowing, hypercorrection and the non-homogenity of so-called speech communities, an implicational grid is an idealization, though admittedly considerably less so than a static monostylistic model such as TGG.

Later writers have seen the limitations of the original model and have suggested various ways of overcoming these. Perhaps the most important innovation is the appeal to linguistic naturalness. What it means is that the least cost for language development is where language changes from[9] $\overset{>}{m}$ to $\overset{<}{m}$ (or less natural to more natural), and that compelling external factors are held responsible for all other changes.

The emergence of pidgin and creole studies as a separate field of inquiry

Having commented on the status of pidgin/creole studies *vis-à-vis* the main directions within modern linguistics,[10] I will now examine their emergence as a separate subdiscipline of linguistics.

The first international conference on creole studies, attracting a total of thirteen participants, was held in Jamaica in 1959. Many of the questions which were subsequently to dominate the field, such as monogenesis, the use of TGG and the status of abstract descriptions, were postulated at this gathering. DeCamp (1971a: 14) contends that: 'the birth of the field of pidgin–creole studies may be dated from that April afternoon in Jamaica, when Jack Berry suddenly remarked "All of us are talking about the same thing"'. At the conclusion of the 1959 conference a considerable amount of agreement had been reached both as to the questions to be asked within a separate subdiscipline of pidgin and creole studies, and as to the methodology to be used, in particular field recordings. Last, but not least, there was also consensus as to the social role of creole studies – that is, that of promoting an understanding of these languages and their speakers, in particular in defending them against the claims of cultural imperialists and colonialist/racist policies.

The second international conference was again held in Jamaica, in 1968, attracting more than 50 specialists. It demonstrated the significant quantitative and qualitative growth of the new field. Of particular importance was the re-establishment of strong links with anthropology and sociology, and the beginnings of alternatives to TGG.

By 1975, the venue of the third international conference on pidgins and creoles had been shifted to Hawaii, a shift signalling the growing awareness of the role of the Pacific in the formation and development of these languages. It was, incidentally, the first such conference attended by the writer, leaving lasting impressions of conversations with John Reinecke, David DeCamp and many of his future colleagues. We can observe, with this conference, the beginning of specialization within pidgin and creole studies. The expressed aim of the conference organizers was to solicit papers from the following three areas: universals in pidgins and creoles; challenges to linguistic theory; uniqueness and specificity in individual pidgins and creoles. The largest number of contributions fell into the second category, illustrating the fact that pidgin and creole research had begun to shake off the limitations of pre-existing models of description and explanation. Instead, the focus was on the explanation of linguistic variability. In linking synchronic variability to diachronic development, for a number of participants the traditional division into synchronic and diachronic linguistics became blurred. The most influential development in the first category was Bickerton's remarks on linguistic universals and his arguments, against Sankoff, Givón and myself, that natural (i.e. corresponding with the basic neurological equipment of the species) universals do not occur in pidgins, but only in first-generation creole speakers. This argument is still being debated, as will be made clear later in this book.

Further specialization of the field is suggested by the title of the 1979 conference, 'Theoretical Orientations in Creole Studies', held at St Thomas in the Caribbean. In his incisive introductory remarks to the proceedings of this conference, Alleyne (1980) gave a highly self-critical appraisal of the field and its practitioners, pointing, in particular, to the continued dominance of an outmoded and inappropriate (Euro-centric) conceptual bias. At the same time, he drew attention to two particularly strong points of the field: the wide range of questions to be discussed makes it come closest to an integrated theory of language; and a high level of social consciousness is paired with active academic interest. Another important development at this conference was the link-up between second-language acquisition studies and pidgin/creole studies.

A final international conference to be considered here is the one held at York in 1983 under the title 'Urban Pidgins and Creoles'. This choice of topic suggests a move away from the conservative basilectal varieties to the rapidly restructuring ones of acculturating urban communities. It also provided an avenue for the study of the rapid stylistic diversification of urban pidgins and creoles, enabling them to fulfil the ever-changing stylistic needs of unstable urban communities.

It is evident from these conferences that a rather brief period of unity is being followed by a new diversity. This is apparent in the growing gap between theoretical and applied studies, as well as in the often heated debates between those who subscribe to genetically transmitted creole structures and those who see them as a result of social interaction. Furthermore, the tendency towards regionalization has remained and even increased, with conferences dealing with a geographically limited area or a special group of languages such as Tok Pisin (1969, 1973), Papiamento (1981) or Romance languages in contact with other languages (1976).

It is hard to see how things could be otherwise in the light of the flood of new information relating to the field. Whereas barely a decade ago I could manage to read virtually all publications in the field, I now find it increasingly difficult to keep up with recent developments. I hope that future international conferences will retain a wide scope, in order to give scholars the opportunity to familiarize themselves with the research activities outside their immediate regional and theoretical area of interest.

Outlook

In the business of making predictions, the likelihood that one will be proven wrong is an unavoidable hazard, and my having been involved in pidgin and creole linguistics for some time is of little advantage. However, it certainly has helped me to determine those developments which, from my own point of view, would seem to be beneficial to the field. In assessing his own predictions, made on the occasion of the second international conference on pidgins and creoles in 1968, Dell Hymes remarked:

> In 1968 . . . it seemed inevitable that attention to pidginization and creolization would unite the linguistic and social in a specially revealing way. How we underestimated the resourcefulness and creativity of linguists and psychologists. After a decade, the inescapable embedding of pidgin and creole languages in social history remains a theme to be argued for, a topic to be rediscovered. (Hymes 1980: 389)

Before presenting my own views, I would like briefly to consider two other earlier predictions regarding the pidgin/creole field, namely those of Figueroa (1971: 503–6) and Bickerton (1974), as they appear to represent two opposite poles.

Figueroa's principal concern is for the political, social and educational applications of the field: that is, how being a pidgin or creole speaker affects one's life. He also makes an implicit plea against too much reliance on expatriate white analyses. At the time of his writing, the extent to which cultural factors can influence the analyses of and views on a pidgin or creole was ill understood. That they are indeed of very considerable importance has been demonstrated in a recent article of mine on indigenous and expatriate approaches to Tok Pisin (Mühlhäusler 1984b). However, such factors will remain of marginal interest as long as the wider question of how culture-bound metalinguistic systems affect linguistic argumentation and analysis remains unexplored (cf. Lyons 1981). Figueroa hopes that sympathetic research will demonstrate the equality of creoles *vis-à-vis* their source languages. However, linguists appear unprepared to address seriously the qualitative differences, and a study of this kind could well produce results which Figueroa might find unacceptable. In pidgin and creole studies, as in other fields of inquiry, premature and socially undesirable findings tend to meet with little enthusiasm, and, in the present social and intellectual climate, some questions regarded as important by the writer of this article are perhaps best left alone.

Bickerton (1974), unlike Figueroa, considers the most urgent priority in creole studies to be the provision of answers to a number of questions in the area of theoretical and historical linguistics asked by Schuchardt, in particular:

1 How do languages get mixed?
2 What is the nature of linguistic continua?

He has since added to these questions (in particular, in Bickerton 1981), again relating to questions of general linguistic interest:

3 What is the relationship between first-language acquisition, phylogenetic development of human language and creole development (in first-generation speakers)?

Because of the importance attached to Bickerton's *Roots of Language* (1981), where this last question is discussed, the issues raised therein are likely to dominate the field for some time to come. One hopes that the long-overdue question of the relationship between child language acquisition and pidgin and creole formation will receive more attention as a result. There can be little doubt, however, that the renewal of the conspiracy between psycholinguists, neurolinguists and creolists will further postpone Hymes's expected *rapprochement* between the social and linguistic.

Bickerton's proposals are also likely to promote the study of links between the sign languages of deaf people and pidgins and creoles (cf. Edwards and Ladd 1983), as it is expected that the same natural patterns of encoding will emerge in all communication systems that have been developed without sufficient input. Although such a development would advance the frontiers of knowledge in the area of linguistic naturalness, there is a danger that the cultural forces instrumental in shaping pidgins and creoles will be neglected. Moreover, many aspects of pidgins and creoles only appear to be natural; in reality, they are cultural products, the results of conceptual frameworks that are so familiar to us as to pass unnoticed. I thus sympathize with Hymes's fears that an integrative view of pidgin and creole communication will yet again be postponed, and that questions which I would regard as important will be regarded as marginal, including the following.

1 Does ontogenetic, phylogenetic and creole development take place in a smooth continuous fashion[11] or in (to quote Figueroa 1971: 503) 'sudden Lamarckian jumps'?
2 What is the extent of social influence on structural development, and how far are we dealing, when discussing pidgin and creole structures, with

man-made cultural products? What is the relationship between such cultural and biological/genetic factors?

3 What can abstract deductive models of creole development tell us about the actual historical process? Should we study the emergence of grammar in preference to the emergence of social communicative abilities?
4 How do we best link up phylogenetic and pidgin/creole development? There is still a tendency to accept Chomsky's statement (1968) that: 'It is quite senseless to raise the problem of explaining the evolution of human language from more primitive systems of communication that appear at lower levels of intellectual capacity.' Undue concentration on the denotative–predicative aspects of language and arbitrary signs appear to have led to the above statement. However, in explaining the development of connotative/emotive dimensions of creoles and their indexical and iconic aspects, a link with ethology could well turn out to be necessary. To analyse, for instance, patterns of verbal aggression without reference to wider aspects of the development of human aggression would seem to be a rather limiting enterprise.

My view of future priorities for creole studies, then, is that they should remain broadly based and that, next to questions of linguistic theory, links should be retained with ethology, sociology, anthropology and communication sciences.

To gain a better understanding of these languages as cultural products would seem to be of particular importance. There are at least two reasons for this wish. First, if pidgins and creoles should turn out to be maximally natural and culture-neutral, they may represent the level of structure at which human beings could most easily be manipulated.[12] If, on the other hand, pidgins and creoles are significantly shaped by human actions, one should take a closer look at the agencies that have shaped them. Thus, a language influenced by colonial attitudes, missionary policies and other authoritarian bodies may not be an ideal instrument for political liberation. There is no reason to expect that creole and pidgin language development will not lag behind social and political changes. In sum, then, I would like to advocate that grammatical studies of these languages be supplemented with studies of their rhetorical dimensions, and that, in particular, the communicative factors which gave birth to them be studied more seriously.

3

The Socio-historical Context of Pidgin and Creole Development

> The inescapable embedding of pidgin and creole languages in social history remains a theme to be argued for, a topic to be rediscovered.
>
> (Hymes 1980: 389–90)

Introduction

In this chapter I shall investigate the external[1] factors constitutive of and contributing to the development of pidgin and creole languages. Languages, be they first or second ones, do not arise in a social vacuum. Wolf children and children who grow up in conditions of severe social deprivation, such as Genie (see Curtiss 1977), do not develop language. There are two conditions which have to be met before languages can come into being: first, a need for verbal communication, i.e. communicative pressure; and second, access to a model. These two factors will determine the relative complexity of the evolving language as well as its genetic and typological affiliation.

Non-verbal communication and pidgin development

In view of the frequency of silent bartering, it is somewhat surprising how little attention has been paid to it in the literature on pidgins and creoles. A major pilot paper is Dutton's as yet unpublished 'On the Frontiers of Contact: Non-verbal Communication and Peaceful European Expansion in the South-West Pacific' (1982). In the absence of any detailed records, and with reliance on sporadic indirect evidence, it is difficult to assess the stability and success of such early non-verbal attempts to communicate across linguistic boundaries. It seems certain, however, that the number of culture-free signs which were available to the interacting parties was extremely limited (cf. Morris et al. 1979). Possible candidates for 'natural' signs include gestures for cutting, killing, eating and location. It also seems certain that communication was impaired by frequent misunderstandings, even in the small domain of topics needed.

Let me illustrate this with examples relating to the recruiting of indigenous labourers in the Pacific for the plantations of Queensland, New Caledonia, Fiji and Samoa. Holthouse describes a typical early encounter:

> Lacking interpreters for the countless native languages of Melanesia, the recruiters resorted to pantomime, often of the sketchiest kind. To indicate to the kanakas that they were being engaged to work for three years, the expression 'three yam' was used – supposed to be the time taken to grow three crops of yams. Reduced to pantomime it often came down to showing the native a yam and holding up three fingers. (Holthouse 1969: 22)

Even at such a basic level, cultural factors can severely impair communication. The most interesting example is that for many Melanesians the show of three fingers means the number two, as they work with a subtractive rather than an additive system. Further, the limitations of the yam symbol to represent the timespan of a year are pointed out, with no mincing of words, in the report of a Royal Commission into Labour recruiting for Queensland:

> The edible tuberous root which we call 'yam' has a different name in nearly every island, and *quá* root does not suggest a period of time. No dependence can accordingly be placed on the use of the word 'yam', or its equivalent as an edible root, or of the words employed for season or feast, as conveying to the minds of natives from numerous and widely separate islands a fixed term which they would at once understand as a period of service. The employment of the word 'yam' at the port of arrival, in explaining a three years' engagement, was, therefore, altogether illusory. (Royal Commission into Labour 1885: xxi)

In the south-west Pacific, silent bartering apparently never developed, as it did in other parts of the world, into a fully developed sign system.[2] Instead, under the growing pressure for verbal communication, it was added to and eventually replaced by a verbal code, Jargon English. At first, this involved the use of single words and holophrases. Later, grammar covering longer utterances was added.

The complementary nature of non-verbal and verbal means of communication in incipient pidgins has often been remarked upon. An example is Hale's observations on Chinook Jargon:

> Finally, in the Jargon, as in the spoken Chinese, a good deal is expressed by the tone of voice, the look and the gesture of the speaker. The Indians in general – contrary to what seems to be a common opinion – are very sparing of their gesticulations. No languages, probably, require less assistance from this source than theirs. Every circumstance and qualification of their thought are expressed in their speech with a minuteness

> which, to those accustomed to the languages of Europe, appears exaggerated and idle – as much as the forms of the German and Latin may seem to the Chinese. We frequently had occasion to observe the sudden change produced when a party of natives, who had been conversing in their own tongue, were joined by a foreigner, with whom it was necessary to speak in the Jargon. The countenances which had before been grave, stolid and inexpressive, were instantly lighted up with animation; the low, monotonous tone became lively and modulated; every feature was active; the head, arms, and the whole body were in motion, and every look and gesture became instinct with meaning. One who knows merely the subject of the discourse might often have comprehended, from this source alone, the general purport of the conversation. (Hale 1890: 18–19)

More recently, similar observations have been made for Japanese Pidgin English after the Second World War:

> Although it is very difficult to analyze these non-verbal systems componentially, individuals from different cultural backgrounds seem to develop instinct for them early and quickly, and a few of the terms of these systems should be mentioned here. The meaning of the smile, for example, in English and Japanese symbolizes several of the same things. Both peoples tend to use the smile in moments of social uncertainty and as a means of suggesting vague good will. Although the Japanese see the smile also as a mask of much greater kinds of distress, the smile easily becomes a working diamorph (?) of non-verbal pidgin. Similarly, the giggle is used by both peoples in moments of embarrassment, astonishment, and indecision. In the realm of gestures, both peoples touch each other to indicate reassurance and friendliness, and the slap on the shoulder is almost immediately understood on both sides. (This slapping borders on another and broader inter-cultural similarity, that of a love for joking and mild horseplay.) This process is, more broadly, probably one of the discovery of a set of gestural diamorphs followed by a sorting out of one or the other in social context. (Goodman 1967: 48)

However, other studies on Japanese–English communication have demonstrated (e.g. Neustupný 1983) that many of the non-verbal patterns of communication that emerge cannot be explained in terms of the rules of either culture in contact. Rather, both parties appear to undergo a considerable degree of behavioural regression.

Sometimes, the very early heavily contextualized stages of a pidgin can still be recovered by looking at socially or geographically marginal varieties of otherwise more developed pidgins. Thus a pronounced reliance on extralinguistic signals can be observed in Bush Pidgin (the bush varieties of Tok Pisin, see

Mühlhäusler 1979), and Todd (1982: 286) has found, in contemporary West Africa, 'a very basic sort of English (often associated with market mammies) consisting of little more than lexical strings augmented by gesture: buy okra, okra fine, bring money, what of banana?'

Pidgin/creole research has, in the past, paid relatively little attention to such phenomena, assuming that the development of a linguistic means of intercommunication can be studied in isolation from its gestural predecessors. This, I feel, is a great shortcoming, as there appears to be an interesting relationship between the complexity of a sign language and that of the simultaneously employed verbal means of communication. With video-recording techniques becoming widely available, there is no reason why detailed research in this area should not be undertaken.

Verbal means of communication: general remarks

Although there are many studies on the verbal aspects of pidgins, relatively few of them pertain to the very early unstable stages of development. The reasons for this are not hard to find: neither the people involved in initial jargon contacts nor the situations in which communication took place lent themselves to systematic observation or recording. Moreover, in the absence of modern recording technology, a considerable amount of filtering out and distortion must have occurred. A major victim of this were instances of unsuccessful or partially successful communication: development all too often is seen as a sequence of successful stages, rather than a process involving regression, discontinuity and failure.

In the absence of reliable information on situational and other external factors, it is difficult to be confident about their role in pidgin and creole formation. However, it would seem that at least some claims can be made with relative confidence. Before putting them forward, however, I would like to remind the reader of an important distinction, that between formation and development.

I would suggest that the main difference between these two processes can be characterized as follows:

> The formative period of pidgins and creoles embraces their development up to the point where a socially accepted grammar emerges, that is, a grammar which is transmitted without significant restructuring, to a subsequent group of speakers. As a rule, formation occurs within a single generation of speakers. By development I mean the subsequent history of the language over a number of generations.

By this definition, the formative period for Tok Pisin or Pidgin English of New

Guinea falls between 1865 and 1890, whereas its subsequent development, after initial stabilization, begins around 1890. For a pidgin, the formative phase ends with stabilization. For a creole, it ends once the first generation of speakers have attained adulthood.

Although such a distinction helps us to distinguish language-formation processes without a model from others where a model has been transmitted by a previous generation, it is not without its problems, the main one being discontinuities arising out of subsequent breaks in transmission. Thus a creole may be acquired as a second language by a group of non-native adult speakers and thus become repidginized: instances of this are the fate of West Indian Creole Englishes in West Africa and the prolonged repidginization of Sranan in Surinam. Similarly, an already stable pidgin may become rejargonized, that is, subject to individual language learning strategies, if it is acquired by no socially viable group of speakers. An interesting example is provided by Tok Pisin which, fifty years after its initial stabilization in the coastal areas of Papua New Guinea, was adopted and destabilized by New Guinea Highlanders (see Salisbury 1967).

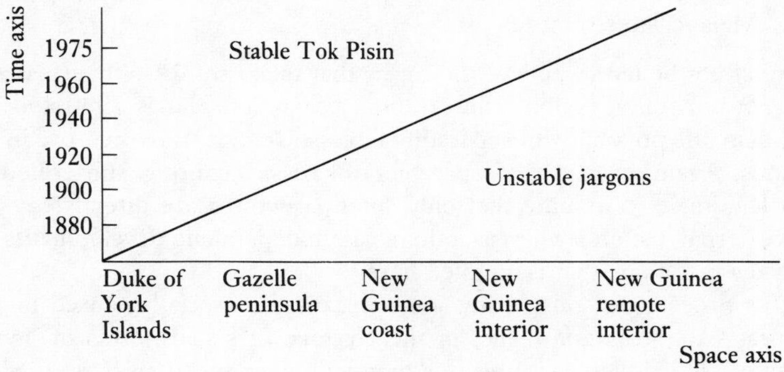

Figure 3.1 Relationship between geographic remoteness and stabilization in Tok Pisin

Consequently, in order to understand what happens at a particular stage in the formation and development of a pidgin or creole, we can appeal to the uniformitarian principle,[3] that is, observe the phenomena of the past synchronically by moving along the geographical and stylistic[4] dimensions of the language. I have done this for Tok Pisin when reconstructing the early unstable varieties of the language. The relationship between geographic remoteness and stabilization in this language can be depicted as shown in figure 3.1. Although this is an idealization, there can be no doubt that significant insights into language history can be gained from the uniformitarian method.

Social forces as constitutive factors in pidgin formation

As already mentioned in the previous chapter, a major source of disagreement in pidgin and creole studies has been the role of external or social factors in pidgin/creole formation and structural development. The two opposing views are that:

1 a distinction between social (external) and structural (internal[5]) factors must be made: internal development proceeds of its own accord, with external factors determining the speed of this development;
2 external factors crucially shape and determine grammatical and lexical structuring. As suggested by Turner (1966: 208):

> The structure of Neo-Melanesian [Tok Pisin] derives from the social situation in which the intermediary language was used. Some grammatically important morphemes and some more general details of syntactic structure may derive from one or another of the 'terminal' languages, but it is doubtful whether the importance of these is equal to the importance of the social setting in determining Neo-Melanesian structure.

One must not be led to believe, however, that these are the only explanations. An as yet not fully developed integrationist view (cf. Harris 1980 and 1981) would deny the possibility of separating linguistic codes from their use in social situations. Again, even if the separability of these factors is subscribed to, it seems legitimate to assume that only some structures are directly caused by social/external factors, whereas others are independent developments. The latter view is the one that is adopted here.

Let us proceed to considering some instances of socially caused linguistic structures. At the jargon stage, in the absence of social norms of linguistic interaction, individuals are free to adopt a number of different strategies for cross-linguistic communication (see Meisel 1983). This choice appears to be very much determined by personality factors, educational background and cultural-group membership. Thus speakers concerned with grammatical correctness are more likely to make use of the grammatical structures of their first language, that is, their strategy is transfer or use of substratum. Other speakers who simply want to get a message across tend to regress to earlier stages in their own language development or universals of grammar. A speaker's previous exposure to other pidgins and creoles is also likely to be reflected in his or her grammar. In the early developmental stages of many pidgins, one party in the linguistic exchange was a member of the geographically highly mobile group of sailors, traders and plantation overseers.[6] In some extreme cases, this may have led to relexification (that is, the replacement of the lexicon of an existing pidgin or creole with that from another source language). The role of geographical diffusion certainly cannot be easily overrated with pidgins and creoles.

Equally important is the role of certain culture-derived stereotypes, typically associated with foreigner talk registers, in early jargon formation. Reduplication and repetition, the use of special word order, and grammatical elements and special lexical items are documented for speakers of such widely different lexifier languages as German, English and Motu. The acceptance of foreigner talk input depends both on the already mentioned individual learning strategies, and the next factor, the nature of the social relationships between the groups in contact. Such relationships are mirrored not only in the relative percentage of lexical items in the resulting contact language, but also in its composition and parts of grammar. Thus the asymmetrical social relationship in many culture-contact situations tends to be mirrored in pronoun and address systems. Members of the socially subordinate group are addressed with T (from French *tu*) rather than V pronouns (from French *vous*), as in Vietnamese Pidgin French:

toi donner moi cadeaux = you give me a present

or New Guinea Pidgin German:

Du geben mir Geschenk = give me a present

against the special forms of address signalling deference used when indigenes address their colonizers, as in:

Monsieur donner moi cadeau = Sir give me present
Herr geben mir Geschenk = Sir give me present.

Similar discriminatory vocabulary is also found in non-address forms in many pidgins and creoles that developed in a stratified colonial society. Thus, Tok Pisin distinguishes[7] between *boi* 'male indigene' and *masta* 'male European adult' as well as between *meri* 'indigenous woman' and *misis* 'expatriate woman'. Similar distinctions were also made in Hiri Motu, where the items *taubada* 'male European' and *sinabada* 'female European' had special status in both reference and address. Such asymmetrical pairs tend to be less pronounced in the later developmental stages of pidgins and creoles, that is, when horizontal rather than vertical communication becomes the dominant mode.

Another example of external factors promoting structural developments is that of accessibility to the target/lexifier language. The stability of a pidgin is greatly promoted by the absence of a model, as there is then little scope for system-destructing hypercorrection. A good illustration is afforded by contrasting the two pidgin Englishes found in the New Guinea area. Whereas in British/Australian Papua, Papuan Pidgin English remained at a very low level of stabilization throughout its existence (cf. Mühlhäusler 1978a), in German-controlled New Guinea a stable Pidgin English (Tok Pisin) emerged within a few years. In fact, the German administration indirectly contributed to the stabilization of Tok Pisin in two ways: by removing English as a lexifier language; and by creating social conditions in which communication between members of many different linguistic backgrounds became established, giving rise to what Whinnom (1971) refers to as a 'tertiary hybrid'. Whereas the constitutive role of external factors in the formation of pidgins is relatively clear, for creoles it is much less so. One reason for this is that adults are much more capable of choice and active manipulation of language than young children.

The extent of external influence in the formation of creoles appears to be linked primarily to one factor: the linguistic input that children are exposed to. A subsidiary factor is the size and composition of the community in which creoles emerge. To take this second point first, it appears that for a creole to develop at all there must be a viable community in which it can be used. By this I mean there must be a large enough number of children whose only means of communication is the creole. Thus, in the case of a nuclear family where two parents communicate in pidgin, no creolization is likely to occur; instead children will speak one or both of their parents' languages and/or end up being linguistically deprived,[8] as in the instance of mixed-race children in former German New Guinea:

> The mission could not remain indifferent to the sad plight of these children. It began to collect them and when their numbers continued to grow it founded its own institution in 1897 where they were to be educated by the sisters. Now that was a really difficult enterprise. The whites are generally ignorant of the natives' language and in conversation with them make use of pidgin English, the workers' language, which is a mixture of corrupted English and native dialects. The halfcastes mostly speak only this pidgin English with a few bits of native language heard from their mother, which of course differs according to the home. On their arrival at the mission station they are therefore hardly able to make themselves understood. (Janssen 1932: 150)

As soon as a larger community of children is established, however, a qualitative change sets in. Thus the very same children that spoke little broken German or Tok Pisin (in the above quotation) developed a sophisticated creole, Unserdeutsch, within a single generation. This language is structurally very different from its potential models of Tok Pisin, Pidgin German and Standard German (cf. Mühlhäusler 1984b). That the structural viability of a creole is dependent on its social viability is also seen elsewhere. Thus Samoan Plantation Pidgin English (see Mühlhäusler 1978b) was the first language of many children on the German plantations of Samoa, but proved of little use to their later life because the plantation society remained dominated by linguistically less progressive adults; and the language was spoken only within a small ghetto and not outside these plantations. Consequently these creole speakers adopted the more useful Samoan language as their exclusive means of communication.[9] When it was brought to Papua New Guinea by returning labourers, however, the language (now Tok Pisin) was in a much better situation. Viable creole communities developed here around two types of settlements: the non-traditional rural settlements, such as the government oil palm project at Hoskins, which attracted families from many parts of the country; and the large urban centres with frequent intermarriage between speakers from different linguistic backgrounds and no dominant local language.

Detailed studies of a number of creole communities in New Guinea have been made by Sankoff (e.g. 1975a, 1975b) and Mühlhäusler (1979a), confirming the fragility of creole innovations under adverse social conditions. Thus those grammatical innovations that deviate most from established second-language norms tend to be given up by creole speakers once they begin to communicate as adults. In other instances, a creole is replaced by a more useful local lingua franca, and in yet other cases heavy reliance is placed on English for structural and lexical innovations.

A number of conclusions can be drawn from such case studies. First, the development of viable creoles (with socially sanctioned grammars) depends on their functional usefulness and social viability. Children's innovations have little chance of survival in an adverse social environment. Further, creolization is not the only solution for children whose parents provide them with insufficient linguistic input. The solutions eventually adopted may include bilingualism, language shift, and dual-lingualism.[10]

The second way in which external factors can influence creoles is in the nature and availability of linguistic input from the lexifier language. Many writers draw the simple distinction between access to lexical structures and access to grammatical ones. Whereas lexical borrowing is regarded as a relatively unconstrained process, borrowing of grammar is regarded as exceptional by many. It must be borne in mind, however, that the boundary between lexicon and grammar is language-specific rather than universally motivated, since what is done by means of grammar in one language may be lexicalized in the next. Consequently even lexical borrowing can predetermine much of a creole grammar in the formative years and change the course of subsequent development. An interesting case is the borrowing of lexicalized causatives such as 'kill', which can block the development of grammaticalized morphological or periphrastic causatives.

Access to lexical and structural resources of the lexifier language (and substratum languages) can be related to a number of other external factors, including the numerical relationship between speakers of each language, whether or not the socializers (caretakers, not necessarily parents) of creolizing children had access to the lexifier language, whether there was any formal teaching, and prevailing linguistic attitudes. Linguists investigating creoles must constantly keep in mind that access does not necessarily mean acceptance of the model. Pidgin and creole speakers are not passive recipients of the crumbs that fall from the linguistic tables of speakers of 'more civilized' tongues, but active makers[11] and users of languages. Differences from the 'model' may well reflect the wish to be linguistically different, that is, it could refer to the indexical rather than the referential/grammatical functions of these languages.

The differential effects of the relative absence of a target lexifier language are illustrated by the cases of Réunion and Mauritius (Ile de France) Creole French, a detailed description of which is given by Baker and Corne (1982). Réunion was first settled in 1663 mainly by *petits blancs* (lower-class French settlers), Malagassies and Indo-Portuguese women, with the French outnumbering all other races during the formative years of Réunion creole (that is, until about 1720). As observed by Corne:

> At the end of the first period RC has emerged in a situation of linguistic diversity wherein French, in various guises, was the dominant factor. As a consequence, RC has remained structurally close to French such that it might even be called a creoloid. (1982: 107)

The situation on Mauritius was quite different: speakers of other languages outnumbered those of French from the start and, during a long period of British colonial control, standard French was virtually withdrawn as a target language. In fact, as in some other plantation communities, the creole could develop in virtual independence from its related lexifier language for most of its history. A similar comparison can be made between the creoloid Afrikaans and Virgin Islands Dutch Creole, as has been shown by Valkhoff (1966).

Nature and nurture

The concept of 'naturalness' is widely found in linguistic writings, although it is often used in an ill-defined way. In a loose sense, the label 'natural language' is used to contrast vernaculars such as English, Hindi or Quechua with artificially created languages such as Volapük, Esperanto or computer languages. The naturalness of the former systems is related to the fact that their rules and conventions are mainly unconscious and, it is argued, are not directly amenable to human interference. This argument seems unconvincing, however, in the light of recent work on the socio-historical context of language development, which highlights the importance of conscious interference with language development. To take the example of English, the use of *you* as both singular and plural pronoun (rather than a *thou–you* or *you–ye* distinction), or the rule which selects *he* as the pronoun in utterances such as 'mind the child – he may be deaf' can be traced back to historical events (cf. Silverstein n.d.). Again, the morphological complexity of many languages of Melanesia appears to be man-made (cf. Wurm 1983). Cultural games such as backslang, rhyming slang and pig-Latin have left traces in the grammar of many languages. It would thus seem more realistic to admit that most of the so-called 'natural languages' are in fact a mixture of nature and culture.[12]

The question whether pidgins and creoles are natural languages in this first sense has been debated, and it is not by chance that they have often been grouped together with artificial languages in linguistic bibliographies. Reasons for believing them not to be natural languages include the fact that some non-expert observers believe that pidgins are invented languages. Reed (1943: 271) reports the view that Tok Pisin 'was invented and introduced by the Germans in order that they might speak before the natives in their own tongue without being understood'.[13] Also, a number of professional linguists regard pidgins as reduced parasitic systems, rather than 'full' languages (that is, systems that can be explained only by reference to a full 'natural' language). The first view has no empirical support, and the second can be dismissed on the grounds that pidgins exhibit constructions and developmental tendencies which cannot be related to their lexifier language and/or their substratum languages. It could further be argued that 'structural complexity' or 'fullness' of a language is a rather shaky concept, as there is little empirical support for the widely held assumption that all natively spoken languages are of equal complexity.

The reader of this book will by now have got used to the idea that for most views on pidgins and creoles there is also any opposite view. Thus it is not surprising that, applying roughly the same meaning of naturalness, pidgin languages have been characterized as maximally natural. In support of this view, the following arguments have been adduced. First, since pidgins are used as a means of communication between members of different cultures, they have to be culture-neutral. Second, pidgins are very young languages, that is, they have not been exposed to cultural forces for long enough to have absorbed cultural rules. In spite of the initial plausibility of such arguments, one must not overstate the case: the imperviousness of pidgins to cultural forces appears to be restricted to the very early period of formation and development; at later levels they are influenced by a man-made social context.[14]

As regards creoles, these have been denied the status of natural languages on very much the same grounds given for pidgins, that is, their being parasitic degenerate systems. However, this view is not heard in linguistic circles, as it is generally admitted that without a knowledge of the history of a language one cannot determine whether one is dealing with a creole. They are thus assigned the status of 'full' natural languages.[15]

The term 'naturalness' is also used in a second, more technical sense, and again pidgins and creoles are included in the ongoing discussions. Indicators of naturalness are both system-internal and system-external. Language-internal natural rules are characterized as being more resistant to change; more frequent (token frequency); more frequent cross-linguistically; more likely to be the basis of neutralization; and more likely to be the model in analogical change than an abnatural category. Language-external parameters of naturalness are acquired earlier; less subject to speech errors; lost later in language death; or lost later in aphasia. A more detailed discussion is given by Edmondson (1984).

Ever since the technical notion of naturalness was introduced into linguistics, observers have been quick to point out the prolificity of natural rules and categories in pidgins and creoles. Thus one of the principal syntactic characteristics of pidgins, their derivational shallowness, was seen to reflect the more general principle that natural rules do not produce intermediate forms that are not also acceptable surface structures. In 1972, I examined the following categories: predilection for a syllable structure CVCV; the absence of highly marked sounds, such as rounded front vowels, clicks, the replacement of voiced sibilants by voiceless ones, etc.; the loss of tonal distinctions; the loss of the passive; the infinitive present form for verbs; a preference for continuous constituents; the use of masculine for all genders, when languages with a gender system become simplified; the use of singular in all cases; and relational words. For each of these categories, it was found that pidgins prefer the more natural (less marked) alternative. More about the theoretical implications of this finding will be said below.

The view that pidgins are maximally natural languages was attacked by Bickerton (e.g. 1975d), who points to language mixing, structural inconsistencies and similar abnatural phenomena in his data relating to early nineteenth-century Hawaiian Pidgin English. He further points out that subsequent creolized varieties of this language are better candidates for natural linguistic systems.

This apparent conflict can be resolved by considering developmental and gradient aspects of pidgins and the notion of naturalness. Naturalness must be regarded as a scale ranging from more to less natural phenomena, the latter being referred to as abnatural.[16] Further, naturalness must be related to the individual as well as the social character of pidgins and creoles. Individual pidgin developers have at their disposal a number of strategies, only one of which is that of selecting the most natural solution. A mixture of different strategies can thus be expected in early jargons such as Hawaiian Pidgin, referred to by Bickerton. Once a pidgin stabilizes as a result of the encounter of numerous unstable jargons, natural solutions definitely have an edge over others, because they tend to optimalize production and/or perception. Again, if a pidgin expands as the language of an otherwise multilingual community, the cost of adding natural rules is less than adding others, so that – all things being equal – expanding pidgins will prefer natural solutions.

It can be argued that naturalness goes hand in hand with unconscious language developments, such as those found in children acquiring a first language or adults under great pressure for communication.[17] As soon as the language begins to be used for social purposes such as group identification, stylistic aims and so forth, less natural solutions are inevitably added. In the case of pidgins and creoles, there is one prime source of abnatural constructions and rules: linguistic borrowing from the superimposed related language. In many instances, such borrowing serves the primary function of enhancing a speaker's prestige. Human beings seem to be prepared to accept a considerable cost in linguistic simplicity and communicative efficiency in order that their language should promote their social standing. In sum, maximally natural solutions tend to be sensitive to external social pressure, and consequently are differentially realized at different points in the developmental and restructuring pidgin–creole continua. This can be portrayed as in table 3.1.

Table 3.1 Nature and nurture in the development of pidgins and creoles

Stage	*Natural solution preferred*	*Socially sanctioned grammars*	*Access to superstrata*
Jargon	+ –	–	limited
Stabilization	+	+	minimal
Expansion	+	+	minimal
Creolization	+	+	minimal
Post-pidgin	–	+ –	considerable
Post-creole	–	+ –	considerable

These findings can be summarized as follows:

1 Natural categories emerge most readily in socially sanctioned grammars.[18]
2 Natural solutions are favoured by the absence of a particular target language.
3 Natural solutions are found with both children and adults.
4 The cost of linguistic and social prominence is reduced inter-intelligibility and greater cognitive load.

Finally, languages seem gradually to move away from their natural basis and become cultural artefacts. This is happening, or has already happened, with many of the older pidgins and creoles. Consequently, to rely on naturalness criteria to set these languages apart typologically may turn out to be unsatisfactory in the absence of a good knowledge of their socio-cultural context.

Variability of contextual factors

It has been emphasized repeatedly in this book that, in order to understand pidgins and creoles, one also has to understand variability and change. In this section, the main stress will fall on variability of the social factors promoting or causing the linguistic diversification of these languages. The dimensions along which such variation is commonly located[19] are social, geographical and stylistic. In discussing them, I will be concerned with linguistic markers and indicators, rather than individual free variation and fluctuations such as are found with jargon speakers. This would serve to demonstrate that even pidgins are rarely the monostylistic languages they are sometimes said to be, but rather that they share the important design feature of human language of serving in a number of indexical functions above and beyond their referential one.

Sociolectal variation

For most of the history of the better-known pidgins and creoles, sociolectal variation has been a relatively unimportant factor. Typically, a distinction could be drawn between the language of the colonized (a basilectal pidgin or creole) and the language of the colonizers (the acrolect or its foreigner talk register), although some other dimensions of variation could occasionally be found. Thus, in many pidgin and creole-speaking areas, the domestic servants' language was considerably more acrolectal than that of the plantation workers and villagers. Again, among the colonizers there tends to be a small group of people who need to communicate in the basilect, including missionaries, administrative officers and plantation owners. The effects of a rigid colonial system are nicely illustrated in the following quotation relating to Tok Pisin in the 1920s:

> 'Pidgin' is such a language that there are only two white masters of it in the Mandated Territory of New Guinea. That is, there are only two who speak it so fluently that if they were out of sight they would be mistaken for kanakas. The ordinary resident of the islands is far from being an expert. (Shelton-Smith 1929: 1)

Almost half a century later, the situation had not changed very dramatically. Bell (1971: 38) expresses the opinion that 'A rough and hopeful guess is that one in fifty can understand Pidgin as spoken by the indigenes to each other.'

Once the original asymmetrical power relations begin to disappear and once social mobility sets in, new language forms, intermediate between the basilect and the acrolect, can develop[20] and often signal newly emerging social groups. The development of such a mesolectal continuum can be illustrated by Nigerian Pidgin English, Bickerton reports:

> In Nigeria, in the early years of the present century, there was a small handful of educated Nigerians who spoke English, a fair number of uneducated Nigerians, particularly along the coast, who spoke Nigerian Pidgin, and nothing in between. The situation there was much more similar to that of Papua New Guinea than was the Guyanese one, since in

> Nigeria, as distinct from Guyana, the vast bulk of the population retained its vernacular languages; moreover, the situation persisted until the end of colonial rule came in sight.
>
> Over the last twenty years, however, there have been very considerable changes. Both English and pidgin have spread widely, the former through education, the latter both through the growing geographic mobility of the working class, as here, and through the utility of a contact language in a country divided between many language communities. The result, once again, was the birth of a wide spectrum of varieties intermediate between Nigerian Pidgin and English. (Bickerton 1975a: 25–6)

Initially, speakers of the more targeted (anglicized) varieties may not be aware of the differences between their speech and that of basilectal speakers. However, after a while such awareness begins to emerge, as reflected in metalinguistic labels such as Tok Pisin *Tok Bilong Bus* 'Bush Pidgin', *Tok (Pisin) Bilong Asples* 'Village (rural) Pidgin' and *Tok Skul* 'School Pidgin' or *Tok (Pisin) bilong Taun* 'Urban Pidgin'.

The nature of linguistic variation is often taken as an indicator of types of social change. Thus, in those cases where there remains a clear division between the majority of the population and a small urban post-colonial elite (as, for instance, in the cases of Haiti and Guinea Bissau), the coexistent systems show few signs of merging or being linked by a linguistic continuum. However, to what extent a linguistic continuum can be taken as a direct reflection of certain social conditions remains to be seen. Observers of languages such as Hawaiian English or Haitian French Creole differ in their assessment of the linguistic situation.[21]

Next to the correlation between social class and linguistic structures, one also finds special forms of language associated with other types of social groups. Thus, as pidgins and creoles are often standardized by expatriate missionaries and used for evangelizing purposes, special church varieties are common: for example, different varieties of Virgin Islands Negerhollands used to be associated with different mission groups, and in the case of Sranan a special archaic church register has been reported (Voorhoeve 1971). Linguistic differences are often the result of accidental factors, but in at least some instances missionaries have exploited existing differences for their own purposes. Thus language standardization of Tok Pisin in the 1920s was implemented in a number of different ways by different missions, making it difficult, for instance, for a Catholic to follow a Methodist service or vice versa. Table 3.2 shows the differences that could be observed in the area of doctrinal terminology. An even more drastic step is the alleged policy of the Seventh Day Missionaries in New Hanover to make use of Solomon Islands Pidgin instead of Tok Pisin, thus setting believers and non-believers linguistically apart. Deliberate acts of language creation in Tok Pisin are also reported of the numerous cargo

Table 3.2 Some doctrinal terms of Tok Pisin

Gloss	*Terms used by different missions*		
'acolyte'	ministran (G)	altaboi (CP)	kundar (L)
'incense'	wairau (G)	insens (E)	smel smok (CP) smok smel (PH)
'church'	kirke (G)	sios (E)	haus lotu (PH)
'cross'	diwai kros (PH)	kruse (LA)	bolo (L)
'to believe'	bilip (E)	nurnur (L)	to i tru (PH)
'heart'	bel (Ex)	hat (E)	liva (Ex)
'procession'	prosesio (LA)	varvaliu (L)	
'rosary'	roseri (E)	kurkurua (L)	corona (LA)
'holy'	holi (E)	santu (LA)	takondo (L)
'to pray'	pre (E)	beten (G)	raring (L)
'sin'	sin (E)	pekato (LA)	
'hell'	hel (E)	imperno (LA)	bikpaia (CP)
'to forgive'	pogivim (E)	larim (Ex)	lusim (Ex)
'virgin'	vetsin (E)	virgo (LA)	meri i stap tambu (PH)
'ascension'	goap bilong Jesus (PH)	asensio (LA)	

E = English; G = German; L = local languages; CP = compounding; Ex = extension of meaning; LA = Latin; PH = phrase formation.

movements[22] found in Papua New Guinea. Backslang, changes in meaning, and new coinings in secret Tok Pisin serve to exclude certain groups, particularly Europeans, missionaries and mission helpers, women, children and strangers, from gaining knowledge of a particular cargo cult. The use of secret meanings for a number of doctrinal terms, for instance, has often prevented European missionaries from noticing significant differences between their own interpretation of utterances and that intended by members of the community in which they were working. Thus, in the 1920s, shortly after the introduction of Tok Pisin as a mission language, the situation in the Madang area was such that 'relations between natives and missionaries, although on the whole extremely amicable, were nevertheless based on complete mutual misunderstanding' (Lawrence 1964: 85).

A second reason for the use of secret vocabulary in the cargo movements was the belief that words were vested with power of the kind needed to obtain the desired cargo. Brash writes:

> It is significant that some recent cult leaders have used Pidgin, and that they and their followers have imbued certain Pidgin words with supernatural power from other sources. For example, Yali's cult in the Madang District was conducted primarily in Pidgin, and used expressions like *lo*

bos (law boss) for assistant leaders of the cult, and *rum tambu* (forbidden room) for Yali's holy room. Yali would often speak in symbolic language – *tok bokis* (story with a spiritual meaning like a parable) or *tok antap* (public statement with spiritual meaning and force). (Brash 1975: 326)

A particularly fertile environment for the development of new subvarieties of pidgins and creoles are towns. The impact of urban modes of living on these languages was the topic of the York Conference on Pidgins and Creoles in 1983, and I would like to single out two cases discussed on this occasion: Afrikaans of Sophiatown and Rastafarian varieties of West Indian Creole English.

Sophiatown Afrikaans, Taal or Tsotsi Taal (described by Janson 1983) is interesting in that it shows that urbanization can have the opposite effect from that commonly postulated for a post-creole situation. In the absence of any incentives to merge with white Afrikaans speakers, Sophiatown Afrikaans developed away from the acrolectal norms as the language of an anti-group living in a black ghetto. The enforced move of many traditional black urban dwellers into the new township of Soweto has recently brought about yet another move away from Afrikaans in the direction of local Bantu languages. In spite of close historical links between standard Afrikaans and Sophiatown Afrikaans, mutual intelligibility is low. As pointed out by Janson (1983: 8): 'My main informant G remarked that Taal was popular precisely because it was not understandable to white Afrikaaners.'

Rastafarian varieties of West Indian Creole English (for example, Pollard 1983) are associated with a religious movement found mainly in the urban areas of the West Indies and also in many British towns.[23] They illustrate the role of active human interference in language development. As was the case with some of the cargo varieties of Tok Pisin above, one aspect of Rastafarian language change is the replacement of seemingly misencoded lexical items by others which, from the viewpoint of their ideology, appear to be in a more iconic relationship with what they stand for. Thus, because of the positive values attached to seeing, 'cigarettes' are referred to as *blind-garettes*. Since to 'oppress' means 'to keep someone down', *downpress* is used, and for similar reasons 'informer' becomes *outformer*.

Geographical variation

Perhaps the most important recent finding in dialectology is that correlations between linguistic systems or subsystems and geographic entities can rarely be satisfactorily established. The fundamental rationale of dialectology, that geographic isolation leads to the development of new subvarieties, is difficult to apply to pidgins and creoles, as one of the principal functions of the former has been that of promoting cross-linguistic and inter-regional communication. As regards the latter, incipient creole communities are often too small to be liable to splitting-up processes. There are, however, a number of cases where regional differences have been observed in pidgins and creoles.[24] They tend to be associated with certain external factors.

As a first factor, different colonial powers may come to control a previously united communication area. Thus, Pidgin English-speaking German Kamerun was divided between France and Britain after the First World War, with consequent differences in lexical borrowing and structural stability.[25] Another example is Indian Portuguese Creole, where one can observe differences between varieties spoken in territories such as Goa, Diu and Damão that remained Portuguese until the very recent past and varieties spoken in other territories which were taken over by colonial powers such as England (Calcutta), France (Pondichéry) or Denmark (Tranquebar).

A second factor is the differences in the social and functional uses of the language. Thus the dividing line between a pidgin and a creole form of the same language may well be a geographic one, as in the case of Northern Australian Kriol (see Sandefur 1984). An interesting case is that of Swahili, which gets significantly reduced in form and function as one travels from the East African coast inland to places such as Katanga. Moreover, in areas where this language is spoken side by side with vernacular Swahili, as in Mombasa, Pidgin Swahili tends to become depidginized. Similar observations have also been made for Hiri Motu, which exists in two main, geographically defined varieties: one is spoken in the vicinity of Motu-speaking Port Moresby, which is heavily influenced by Motu foreigner talk and simplified learners' Motu; the other is a much more structurally independent pidgin Hiri Motu, spoken in the more outlying areas to the east and west (see Taylor 1978).

A third factor is the different foci of innovation, mainly larger urban centres. Thus, with Tok Pisin, the principal regional varieties are those influenced by the former capital Rabaul and the coastal town Madang. These two centres are also the centre of Catholic and Lutheran mission activities respectively, and mission language-planning efforts are partly responsible for observed regional differences. A comparable situation obtains with Northern Australian Kriol, where different varieties, according to Sandefur (1984), are associated with urban centres such as Bamyili, Fitzroy Crossing and Halls Creek. However, because of the complex history of pidgin and creole development in all these cases, convergent developments (merging of different pidgin and creole traditions) as well as divergent processes (splitting up of a single tradition) have probably been involved.

Finally, pidgins or creoles can be transported to new areas miles away from their original focus of development. Thus, Samoan Plantation Pidgin English was taken back to Papua New Guinea by returning plantation workers. For many years (1880–1914) there were continuous population movements between these two areas, but after 1914 the contacts ceded. Other similar cases involve Black American English transported to the Bahamas and guest-worker Pidgin German transported to Australia (Clyne 1975).

We still have insufficient knowledge of the regional and geographical factors in pidgins and creoles. Most available studies have concentrated on synchronic analysis, but this appears to be the least profitable way of approaching the phenomenon. What is needed is the study of the regional distribution and diffusion of pidgin and creoles using sophisticated geographic models such as the ones suggested by Trudgill (1983).

Stylistic variation

There are many uses of the term 'style'. For the purposes of this chapter, I shall accept something close to Labov's (1972) meaning, that is, I shall examine the influence of varying degrees of formality and monitoring of speech, rather than the development of poetic traditions. It should also be noted that under this approach style is determined by factors present in the immediate situation of an utterance, but not by factors internal to a speaker such as his or her sex or age.

The isolation of a unidimensional notion of style is not without its problems, and its precarious theoretical status has been pointed out by a number of observers (e.g. Traugott and Romaine 1982). However, because it facilitates the comparison of existing source materials, it would seem best to discuss contextual style separately for pidgins and creoles. Pidgins have often been labelled monostylistic, as can be seen from the following observation by Samarin:

> a speaker of a pidgin, as a *normal* human being in a normal society, can be expected to have more than one code-variety for different uses. The pidgin, on the other hand, is not normal, and when a person is speaking a pidgin he is limited to the use of a code with but one level or style or key or register, to cite some terms used for this aspect of the organization of language. (Samarin 1971: 122)

However, whereas this may be true for the very first stages in their development, it is well documented that stylistic diversification can set in well before creolization. Unfortunately, very few studies of this phenomenon exist and what will be said about Tok Pisin may not apply to other pidgins. The two principal sources for diversification in a pidgin (and probably all other languages as well) are backsliding (that is, recourse to developmentally earlier stages) and borrowing from other systems. In addition, one finds internally motivated development of new stylistic variants, mainly as a result of the introduction of new media such as broadcasting or printing.

In a rapidly developing system such as Tok Pisin (there have been at least three systems over the last hundred years of development which are almost mutually unintelligible, referred to as *Nambawan Tok Pisin*, *Nambatu Tok Pisin* and *Nambatri Tok Pisin* in the metalanguage of some speakers), there is ample scope for backsliding. Developmentally earlier, less grammaticalized stages are used not only in more informal unmonitored speech, but also to achieve certain deliberate effects. Thus, among Tolai speakers of Tok Pisin, the distinction between [s] and [t] is given up on occasions in unmonitored speech, but it is also used in monitored speech to portray a hillbilly mentality.

Because Tok Pisin remains a second language for the majority of its speakers, backsliding is common in situations of stress, with advancing age and when discussing complex topics. For the same reason, the stylistic range of younger speakers tends to be greater than that of their fathers. A well-known example of development in Tok Pisin is the gradual reduction of the original 'future marker'[26] *baimbai* (from English by and by) to the shorter forms *bambai*, *babai*, *bai*, *ba* and *b'* (cf. Sankoff and Laberge 1973). Whereas very old speakers only have *baimbai* at their disposal, younger speakers are proficient along a shorter or longer span of the continuum between *baimbai* and *b'*. Similar choice is found with other prominent grammatical markers such as the adjective ending *pela*, which can be shortened *pla*, and the preposition *bilong*, which is also realized as *bolong*, *blong* and *blo* or even *blə*.

Although such changes promote optimalization of production, especially in allegro speech, there is a considerable price to pay, namely that of decodability. Therefore such stylistic variants can only emerge once the majority of pidgin speakers are reasonably proficient. As soon as a pidgin is used to communicate with less sophisticated speakers, the phonological condensation will be abandoned again.

The effects of borrowing are in many ways opposite to those of backsliding, that is, the result is often less natural and hence more difficult to articulate. Thus, whereas rural Tok Pisin has *sekan* 'shake hands, make peace' with variants such as *seken*, *skan* and *sken*, in anglicized urban varieties renewed contact with English has led to the restoration of the final cluster to yield *sekand* or even *shekand*. Such pronunciations are common in carefully monitored styles.

So far the examples chosen have related to phonological properties. Stylistic variation is equally manifest at other levels of grammar. Thus, to return to *baimbai*, developmentally later varieties tend to have this 'future marker' closer to the verb and, for some speakers, the shorted *ba* has become a verbal prefix. In sliding back and forth along the developmental continuum, speakers can fluctuate between synthetic and analytic constructions to express the same grammatical meaning.

The same is true for word formation. Many speakers have at their disposal three different methods of causative encoding: lexicalization, circumlocution and morphological affixation. Thus, in the same speech event one may find *kilim* 'to hit or kill', and *mekim i dai* 'to make die, kill', or *mekim i bagarap* 'to destroy' and *bagarapim* 'to destroy'. These and many other examples point to the conclusion that earlier stages of language development are not simply replaced, but remain accessible to speakers and are used for stylistic purposes.[27]

An excellent theoretical discussion of the forces that promote stylistic flexibility in creoles is given by Labov (1971a). His paper examines why creoles develop a highly redundant tense system, instead of perpetuating the redundancy-free encoding of some of their pidgin predecessors. More precisely, he studies the transition of tense/time encoding by means of optional adverbs as against encoding by affixation. He concludes that creoles develop affixes for stylistic reasons:

> in tracing the development of tense so far, it appears that the *essence is a stylistic one.* There is no basis for arguing that tense markers express the concepts of temporal relations more clearly than adverbs of time. What then is the advantage that they offer to native speakers, the advantage which native speakers seem to demand? *The most important property which tense markers possess, which adverbs of time do not, is their stylistic flexibility.* They can be expanded or contracted to fit in with the prosodic requirements of allegro or lento style. (Labov 1971a: 61)

He could have added a second consideration, had natural morphology been developed at the time. According to the proponents of this theory (e.g. Mayerthaler 1978), there is a tendency towards greater naturalness in morphological development, which manifests itself in constructional iconicity: those aspects of the message that are central should be perceptually more prominent than marginal ones. Thus, the lexical meaning of a word should be encoded by means of a fully stressed word, whereas its grammatical 'accidents' are best encoded by means of unstressed affixes.

As in the case of pidgins, creole speakers also have to pay the price of increased complexity in decoding for their stylistic flexibility. Thus, instead of the relative derivational shallowness of early pidgins, there can be a considerable distance between more surficial and deeper structures in creoles. An example of this depth is the variable pronunciation of Hawaiian Creole auxiliary *wen*. Whereas rules of morphophonemic condensation are virtually absent with older pidgin speakers, creole-speaking members of the young generation produce numerous variants of this form, including the reduced forms *wen*, *wn*, *en*, *n*, *we* and *w*. Labov (1971a) illustrates some of these in the following sample sentences:

45 a So they wen walk [dew·ɔk.] pas' the bridge.
   b We wen looking [w:nlukinn] for the guy

46 I wen go [° go] kick one of 'em

47 So I went look [al: k] by the door

He points out that the reductions are due to the operation of a number of phonological rules, whose application appears to depend on stylistic factors.

Again, in addition to such phonological condensation, which can be thought of as reflecting internal development, speakers of Hawaiian Creole English also have the option of borrowing from the superimposed English language and producing the form *went*. This last example illustrates the fact that creoles exhibit a stylistic distinction to which their speakers refer by expressions such as heavy (basilectal) and light (acrolectal like). Typically, the light creole is influenced by and mixed with the related superimposed language, but by no means identical with it. Sandefur's data on heavy and light Northern Australian Kriol suggest that this distinction is not just a matter of different varieties linked by ordered phonological or other rules, but a much more complex phenomenon involving lexicalization and lexical diffusion. Thus *dog*, which can mean 'dog' and 'talk' in heavy Kriol, becomes *dog* 'dog' and *tok* 'talk' in the light variety, suggesting that the English model rather than a phonological rule is responsible (cf. Sandefur 1984: 132).

These last examples illustrate the complex interplay between the many factors underlying variation in pidgins and creoles. At the same time they also suggest why they should be more variable than most other languages. Their condensed developmental history and the ready access to a model from which lexicon and structures can be borrowed provide an enormous pool of stylistic and other sources of variability. As they develop from mere media for the exchange of information to carriers of indexical and personal dimensions of meaning, more and more of these potential variants are exploited.

Social typology of pidgins and creoles

After our discussion of the major social forces shaping the formation and development of pidgins and creoles, one may wish to ask whether such factors and their combinations define subclasses of these languages. A number of attempts have indeed been made, the best known being that of Schultze (1933), who distinguishes four main types (table 3.3). This classification is of little help for our purposes, as the languages of the first and third category, strictly speaking, fall outside the scope of this book. A critical discussion of Schultze's classificatory attempt is found in Reinecke (1937: 34 ff), as is Reinecke's own classification (table 3.4).

Since Reinecke's proposals were first put forward, various comments about criteria to be used in classification have been made, but no attempt, to my knowledge at least, has ever been undertaken to pull all these criteria together into a comprehensive sociology of pidgins and creoles. In the following pages, I shall discuss a number of parameters useful in this area. I have to insist, however, that the resulting classification is quite preliminary, and that no claims about any direct correlations between a linguistic and a social typology are implied.

Table 3.3 Schultze's classification

Type	*Example*
Colonial jargon	Afrikaans, Pennsylvania Dutch
Trade jargon	Chook Jargon, Lingua Geral Brasilica[a]
Languages of the study table	Esperanto
Slaves' and servant's languages	Pidgin English

[a] This label relates to a number of former and present-day contact varities of Brazilian Portuguese spoken in the country as well as spoken by migrant groups. A full analysis of the various types of language involved here is still outstanding. However, it seems clear that one is not dealing with a unitary linguistic or social phenomenon.

Source: Schultze 1933.

Table 3.4 Reinecke's classification

Type	*Example*
Immigrant's mixed dialects	Imperfect acquisition of a new language by immigrants
Trade pidgins	Chinese Pidgin English
Plantation creole dialects	Jamaican Creole

Source: Reinecke 1937: 34 ff.

Indigenous versus European pidgins and creoles

A prominent distinction made by many creolists is that between indigenous and European-derived (or based) pidgins and creoles. This distinction, it should be noted, is usually made on linguistic grounds and is often inapplicable to a sociology of language.

The principal problem with a linguistic distinction is that pidgins or creoles based on indigenous languages often developed in response to European colonial expansion. Thus Pidgin Fijian (e.g. Siegel 1982) and Fijian Pidgin Hindi (Siegel 1975) both emerged in the context of the sugar plantation system brought to Fiji by British colonizers; Hiri Motu or Police Motu, unlike a number of other pidgins used by the Motuans,[28] developed in the police force, prisons and government patrols introduced by the British and Australian administrations; and many African lingue franche such as Lingala and Bantu A–70 can again be regarded as the results of colonial social structures.

In contrast, a number of pidgins and creoles associated with European languages arose with only minimal contact with European colonizers. Thus the spread of Tok Pisin into the interior of New Guinea often preceded the advent of expatriate missionaries and administrators, and the social conventions governing the use of this language tend to reflect local New Guinean patterns. The same appears to be true of some Australian pidgins derived from English. The creoles used in some early maroon communities again are spoken by peoples who, with the exception of a period of forced displacement, had little access to the social and linguistic models of their colonizers.

The principal criteria for determining whether a language is indeed indigenous should therefore be as follows:

1 Has the language resulted from European colonial expansion?
2 Has the language been used, to a significant degree, in communication between indigenes and Europeans?
3 Is the language indigenous to an area or has it been transported?

Even this classification leaves certain problems unresolved. It is not obvious, for instance, why European colonial expansion should be singled out as a special case. The Malay expansion across Indonesia to New Guinea, for instance, has had similar results to Portuguese or English expansion in the area. Again, one may ask why the little-known trade languages used between Arab traders and their partners in India and China should be labelled indigenous. In some cases there may even have been a gradual transition, involving relexification over a considerable period of time, from a pre-existing indigenous pidgin to a subsequent European-based one. A possible example is Pidgin Macassarese, which was spoken in the North of Australia before it was replaced with an English-derived pidgin.[29]

The problem of finding good objective criteria for distinguishing between indigenous and European pidgins and creoles is aggravated by subjective factors. Speakers of pidgins and creoles may differ considerably in their view as to whether their language is a European or an indigenous phenomenon. Thus recent surveys of attitudes towards Kriol discussed by Sandefur (1984) suggest that the majority of its second-language speakers and first-generation creole speakers regard it as a European phenomenon. Second-generation creole speakers, on the other hand, overwhelmingly consider it an Aboriginal language and do not use it in the presence of whites. I have experienced something similar with Tok Pisin. Older speakers report that the language was brought to them by the whites and often do not even distinguish it from proper English, whereas the younger generation often maintain that it was handed down to them by their ancestors, by God, or by speaking animals.

In conclusion, a European linguistic classification of pidgins and creoles is hardly adequate. We need to consider two factors. First, pidgins and creoles can change both their structural/linguistic and pragmatic/linguistic affiliation over time. Second, European influence is of importance in the formative years of many pidgins and creoles, but is often absent later; in such cases we should refer to later stages as nativized pidgins or creoles.

Classification according to domain

It has often been suggested that the linguistic and social character of pidgins is linked to their narrow domain of communication, thus distinguishing them from full languages. It is also suggested that qualitative differences[30] between pidgins may reflect the type of domain they are employed in, the following types being frequently singled out as prominent: trade; military purposes; migrant labour; tourism; domestic purposes; and so on. Most of the older pidgins belong to the trade category, although more recently overseas military involvement and tourism have become increasingly common. Thus American involvement in Asia has given rise to varieties such as Japanese Pidgin English (e.g. Goodman 1967), Thai Pidgin English (Gebhard 1979) and Vietnamese Pidgin English. The impact of mass tourism on pidgin development has not been studied in most areas.[31] However, an account on a Turkish-derived pidgin by Hinnenkamp (1982) suggests that many insights can be gained from such systems.

Perhaps the best-studied pidgins are those involving migrant labour. Many regard the plantation system with its large displacement of populations as *the* most important context for the development of pidgins and creoles. Whether recruitment of forced labour for plantations results in a pidgin or a creole depends on a number of factors. First and foremost, one should distinguish between those plantation areas where labour was employed permanently and those where employment was for limited periods, as in the Pacific – the usual duration for employment in Queensland, Samoa, New Caledonia and Fiji was three to five years, with an annual turnover of about one-third of the labourers. This system meant that a number of functionally restricted stable pidgins were handed down from one group of second-language speakers to the next in a narrowly defined social context.

A similar situation, until recently, was found with the numerous workers from Eastern and Southern Europe who came to work in the industrial centres of Germany, the Netherlands or Scandinavia. Again, the so-called guest-worker pidgins were employed in a relatively narrow social context and were passed on from one generation of second-language speakers to the next.[32] In the recent past, it has become apparent that many of the guest workers have become permanent migrants. Some of the linguistic consequences of this change in social environment have been that children do not develop a creole or speak their parents' vernacular, but become integrated linguistically into the host community. The same thing happened with the small number of plantation workers who remained after termination of their labour contract: thus, in present-day Queensland, we find a community of about 10,000 Melanesians who have become speakers of Australian English.

Temporary employment abroad often promotes the spread of pidgins. Thus the spread of Pacific Pidgin Englishes to the Solomons, Papua New Guinea and Vanuatu is largely the result of tens of thousands of ex-workers taking their newly acquired linguistic skills home. It is interesting to note that such was the usefulness of Pidgin English in their home areas that it soon expanded socially and linguistically beyond its plantation past.

Where we are dealing with permanent population displacements, the role of the plantations is even more important, as observed by Sankoff:

> The plantation system is crucial because it was unique in creating a catastrophic break in linguistic tradition that is unparalleled. It is difficult to conceive of another situation where people arrived with such a variety of native languages; where they were so cut off from their native language groups; where the size of no one language group was sufficient to insure its survival; where no second language was shared by enough people to serve as a useful vehicle of intercommunication; and where the legitimate language was inaccessible to almost everyone. (Sankoff 1979: 24)

One should not forget, however, that in spite of the many discontinuities caused by plantation slavery, some continuities of linguistic and cultural transmission remained. Thus the import of new slaves may occur over a prolonged period of time, particularly where local mortality on the plantations was high, as, for instance, in Surinam. Thus the relative importance of natural human reproduction and replenishment of human resources from the outside would seem to be useful parameters in a social classification of creoles. Continuity was also provided by the relative homogeneity of origin in some plantations and the consequent survival of many linguistic and cultural habits. Contrary to the often expressed belief that plantation societies were a totally new start, links with the homeland were maintained over a long period. It is dangerous to generalize here and it seems advisable to carry out a detailed study of the local conditions to avoid unwarranted conclusions.

The geographical mobility of slaves was, for obvious reasons, considerably less than that of indentured workers, and the spread of plantation creoles was less than that of plantation pidgins for many years. It was only with the manumission of slaves and their resettlement in places like Liberia or Sierra Leone that the creoles of the New World were returned to the Old World. One may wish to conclude that the label 'plantation creole' does not characterize a uniform phenomenon sociologically.

Pidgins and creoles that developed out of trade contacts are documented for many different areas, and it is certain that they refute Sankoff's claim that 'we know of no cases where a "pidgin" has developed in conditions other than those of modern European colonial expansion' (1979: 24). Counterexamples are very often not well documented, mainly because those speaking such trade pidgins were hardly in the business of recording them and in most cases were probably illiterate. Among such lost languages one can mention Pidgin Macassarese in Northern Australia, Arabic Chinese Pidgin of Canton,[33] Pidgin Siassi of New Guinea, and American Indian trade languages spoken in pre-Columbian days (see Silverstein 1972b).

Among the pre-colonial trade pidgins that have become better known, I would like to single out Mobilian (Haas 1975) and the two trade pidgins employed by the Motuans of Papua (Dutton 1983b). Early reports on Mobilian (so called because of its currency at Mobile, the trade centre of the Gulf region of the Mississippi) suggest that this language was spoken in addition to their native language by most of the Indians from the east side of the Mississippi, that is, it was widely used as a trade language by numerous tribes before Europeans arrived. Linguistically, the language was derived from Choctaw. Its structures exhibit most of the simplifications one has come to expect with European-derived pidgins, such as the drastic simplification of its morphology. Its lexical composition appears to have differed from area to area, probably in reflection of the relative power of the partners in trade. A fairly mixed lexicon, something which is often associated with trade between equals, is found in the variety among the Alabama (Haas 1975: 259):

	Alabama	*Choctaw*	*Mobilian*
fish:	*tato*	nani	*šlašu*
squirrel:	ipto	*fani*	*fani*
horse:	ělěoba	*(is)suba*	*suba*
dog:	ifa	*ofi*	*ofi*
eat:	ipa	*apa*	*apa*
fire:	tikba	*lowak*	*lowak*
water:	*oki*	oka	*oki*
rain:	*oyba*	omba	*hoyba*

Traces of this language still survive and it is hoped that a detailed analysis of it will be made before it disappears.

In contrast to the wide geographic spread of Mobilian, the two trade languages used by the Motuans on one of their annual trading expeditions to the Gulf of Papua were highly restricted: an Eleman Hiri Trade Language was used with the Eleman people west of Cape Possession (Papua), and a Koriki Hiri Trade Language was spoken with the Koriki, who lived further west in the delta area of the Puari River. The existence of two trade languages rather than one, which could have been transported as trade spread further west, suggests the precarious position of the Motu traders *vis-à-vis* their hosts: in order to be accepted, they had to accept the languages of their host communities as their linguistic models[34] and, moreover, they also had to observe the strict social conditions attached to their use, such as not addressing women.

The desire of the Motuans' trade partners to maintain non-intimacy is reflected in the highly restricted vocabulary of both trade pidgins, containing perhaps not more than 300 words relating to the immediate context of the exchange of goods. Their grammatical structures, as far as they are known, again exhibit many of the simplifications of morphology, the absence of derivational depth and an avoidance of embedding. However, there are some important differences between the two varieties, indicating that different strategies of pidgin formation and development must have been operative. As the trade relations typically involved speakers of only two different languages, we are dealing with secondary hybrids (in the sense of Whinnom 1971) and thus can expect a higher degree of mixing than in multilingual environments.

Other trade languages that have become better known include Russonorsk (e.g. Neumann 1965), the Chinese–Russian trade jargon (Neumann 1966) and Chinook Jargon in its various forms (Thomason 1981). Somewhat surprisingly, these languages have been studied more or less in isolation from one another. I feel that comparative work on the social and linguistic nature of trade jargons and pidgins would be an enterprise well worth undertaking.

The duration and nature of trade in the above cases differed considerably and in most contexts the preconditions for the development of a creole out of a trade pidgin were not met: that is, there was insufficient permanency, no intermarriage and clearly defined social roles. In some instances, however, notably with some Portuguese-based creoles, a trade language was probably the origin of a creole.

One example which has recently been studied in more detail (Kihm 1983a) is Bissau Criolho,[35] a language brought to former Portuguese Guinea by so-called lançados, that is, adventurers and other marginal characters from the Cape Verde Islands, who settled in order to trade slaves with other overseas territories. The version of Portuguese they brought with them (probably a pidgin) became a stable creole in the small mixed-race community that subsequently sprang up around Cacheu and other fortified places. The development of Portuguese-based pidgins into fully fledged creoles depended crucially on the relative absence of Portuguese as a target language. Whereas creolization was interfered with in those areas that remained under Portuguese control for a long time after the establishment of an initial trading post (as also in Portuguese Goa, Diu Damão, Macau and Timor), it could develop unconstrained in some other places such as Ceylon (see Schuchardt 1889b), Malacca (see Baxter 1985), or the Moluccas. Macanese, the Portuguese creole that had developed in Macau, has become virtually absorbed by Portuguese in this possession, but has remained a separate language in nearby Hong Kong (Thompson 1967). A particularly interesting fate is that of the trade Portuguese of Ternate in the Moluccas in the seventeenth century. It is suggested (e.g. by Molony 1973) that after the language became a creole in this small trading post, it was brought to the Philippines towards the end of the seventeenth century by about 200 migrants, all of whom were Christians, led by their priest who did not want them to be open to attacks by Muslims and heathens after the termination of European control of Ternate. Subsequently this language and its offspring partly relexified under Spanish influence.

All the trade pidgins and creoles known to me underwent creolization following the prolonged stabilization and expansion of a pidgin. Thus, whatever their sociological interest, these languages will have little appeal to linguists looking for bioprogram universals. They should, however, afford interesting insights into the impact of social conditions on the lexicon.

Military pidgins, unlike trade pidgins, tend to reflect unequal power relations. The best-known cases relate to the recent past, in particular American involvement in South-East Asia, although it is likely that many existed long before.

Military influence manifests itself in two ways: first, in the formation of new pidgins and, second, in the spread and structural expansion of existing pidgins. Military and paramilitary forces were instrumental, for instance, in spreading Police Motu (later Hiri Motu) throughout Papua, particularly during the Second World War, and the extensive use of Tok Pisin during the military propaganda campaigns of the Japanese and American/Australian forces in New Guinea and other parts of Melanesia provided a tremendous boost to the pidgins of this area.

A case where military operations triggered off the large-scale creolization of a pidgin is that of Northern Australia. During the Second World War, in reaction to the threat of a Japanese invasion, large numbers of Australian troops were moved to the Northern Territory and parts of northern Queensland. To facilitate the control and use for military purposes of the local Aboriginal population, Aborigines of different regional and tribal affiliations were brought together in large camps. This had a twofold effect. On the one hand, it weakened the social position of the indigenous vernaculars; on the other, it provided a tremendous boost to Aboriginal Pidgin English (cf. Sandefur 1984).

It is also interesting, in this connection, to observe that the first structural descriptions and language teaching programmes of the various Melanesian Pidgin Englishes were commissioned by military agencies during the Second World War. Such indirect military involvement may have similarly influenced the development of quite a few other pidgins and creoles.

Pidgins that are restricted to the domestic domain are rare, but the domestic context is an important force in their formation and development. A pidgin that has remained restricted is Indian Butler English, first discussed by Schuchardt (1891). He predicted its early demise, but, in spite of the passing of British colonial control in India, it continues alive and well (cf. Hosali 1983). In other areas, the gradual disappearance of the domestic servant system has dealt a severe blow to the numerous kitchen pidgins that were in use in colonial times; many of these were very much ad-hoc inventions, such as the Pidgin German of the missionary kitchens of Alexishafen in New Guinea, but others were more institutionalized. Often, because of the reluctance of white colonizers to acquire an indigenous vernacular, pidgin or creole proper, kitchen jargons survive in a fossilized condition at a much lower developmental stage than the varieties spoken outside. Thus, although on the plantations and goldmines of Papua a relatively sophisticated pidgin had developed, and although most government agencies had begun to use pidginized Motu (Police Motu, later Hiri Motu), unstable[36] English-derived kitchen jargons survived in colonial households. The following is an example spoken by Eka Kave of Sinaka Settlement, outside Port Moresby. Eka had been a domestic servant for many years, and was an old man when the recording was made in 1976:

> Ai go haus, mekim kaikai nau, mekim twelv klok, orait, kuk, mekim kopti, ai putim tebol, ai got hia fok, spun, naif, mi putim de. Ai go, ai putim sia. Masta i sidaun, hevim kaikai, hevim kaikai, gut, em i go haus, kam bek, o wokabaut, i orait. We i go? Ai go we? Ai go de, siksmail o [unclear] i tufar, o Waigani a hamas nem? Ai kam bek hom, mekim haus, slip haus, taim finis, mi go kaikai, kopti, orait, mi slip haus inse ivening, inse haus. Orait, sik, inse haus, no wok, no wok ai mekim, ai sik inse haus.

An interesting kitchen jargon still in use is pidginized Afrikaans spoken by domestic Bantu servants in white households in South Africa. Although such varieties are often marginal, some at least perform important roles. In many colonial societies, it was customary for white children to be brought up by a black nanny. Thus the minimal differences between black and white Southern States American English, the many Black constructions in white Bahamian English (Shilling 1980), and the development of a creoloid Afrikaans were probably caused by this factor. Domestic personnel had greater access to standard forms of the superimposed language and thus transmitted these to black outsiders. This, however, was not universally so. In most colonial societies, there was an ongoing debate as to the desirability of servants who were sufficiently fluent in their masters' language to overhear conversations at table. Thus the domestic pidgin or creole favoured was often lexically unrelated to the whites' language. Much early debate as to whether German or Pidgin German should replace Tok Pisin as the lingua franca of German New Guinea centred around such an argument. Friederici (1911: 97) discusses this point and remarks on 'the inconvenience of not having a language at the disposal of the master race once German had become generally known, a language in which one could not be understood or overheard by unauthorized natives'.

Similar attitudes probably prevented the development of other pidgins. Thus the Dutch policy in the Dutch East Indies (present-day Indonesia) until the middle of the last century was to prevent indigenes from learning any form of Dutch, by which time a pidginized form of Malay, the precursor of present-day

Bahasa Indonesia, had become the language of dealings between colonizers and colonized.

We have now examined some of the domains of human intercommunication that particularly favour the development of jargons and pidgins. What is common to them is the original geographic, social and linguistic distance of the parties involved. In most cases, there remains a desire to maintain the social distance, and it is this desire that keeps jargons and pidgins alive. We have also seen how a jargon or pidgin depends on its social usefulness, or its viability. Survival chances are enhanced considerably if it is used in a number of domains or if it becomes creolized, the most favourable conditions for the latter being created by slavery and the plantation system. As we have seen, however, other social uses of a jargon or pidgin can also lead to the development of a creole.

Classification according to function

By function, one understands the communicative purpose to which language is put in a particular utterance. In the same way as there is no utterance without style, there is no utterance without function, although in both instances attempts have been made to portray decontextualized statements as the reference point for both style and function. These problems cannot all be discussed here. Remarks pertaining to the discussion of linguistic functions can be found in Bell (1976), Halliday (1974), Robinson (1974) and Silverstein (1977).

For the purposes of our present discussion, two assumptions will be made:

1 that pidgins and creoles should be regarded as developing entities at the structural and functional levels;
2 that there is no reason for the assumption that the cognitive (representations, communicative, referential) function is primary in human communication.[37]

We will further assume, while being aware of the fundamental difficulties, that one can isolate a finite number of linguistic functions and we shall draw these functions from the lists compiled by Halliday (1974) and Jakobson (1960). The most important ones for our purposes are:

Functions	*Role in communication*
Propositional (referential)	The message itself, the information exchanged, information whose truth value can be established
Directive	Getting things achieved, manipulation of others
Integrative	Creation of social bonds, use of language as an index of group membership
Expressive	Expression of own personal feelings towards the message or interlocutors

Phatic	Keeping open channels of communication, counteracting socially undesirable silence, creation of rituals
Metalinguistic	Use of language to discuss language
Poetic	Use of language to focus on the message for its own sake, to play with verbal material
Heuristic	Use of language for obtaining information

Remember again that this is a pre-theoretical classification and that different observers have used different labels and/or different characterizations of individual functions.

Pidgins have long been described as functionally reduced, that is, they are not used in all the above functions. As pointed out, for instance, by Smith (1972: 50), the primary function of a pidgin is the propositional (referential) one. In this article, Smith arrives at this and related important insights. Unfortunately his views are based on a rather undifferentiated three-function model and are still within the static paradigm (that is, he ignores the possibility that even a pidgin with no native speakers can undergo functional expansion). It seems that at least some functions are added relatively early in the pidgin–creole life-cycle. Using the above functions, and applying them to a number of pidgins, I have tentatively arrived at the following hierarchy of development:

propositional
heuristic
directive
integrative
expressive
phatic
metalinguistic
poetic

We can project these onto the developmental stages of pidgins discussed earlier in this book. Thus early jargons serve the purpose of exchanging simple information in a restricted domain, simple statements and questions (propositional and heuristic functions) being sufficient. At this stage, equal power relations prevail. Even in situations of contact between colonizers and colonized, the numerical proportions are such that power cannot be exercised by the former. Instead, and this purpose is served well by a jargon, individual attempts at cross-communication emphasize non-intimacy and non-involvement.

This situation changes once expatriate domination becomes consolidated. At this point, white foreigner talk becomes the dominant model, although pressure for more efficient communication may also result in some stabilization of rules not found in the white input. The principal direction of communication is now vertical, between master and servant, and the directive function of the language is emphasized. Many pidgins have remained associated with giving orders in a colonial context; this has promoted a negative attitude towards them by language planners and educators in newly independent countries.

However, pidgins can develop considerably beyond this mainly directive function, as pointed out by Wurm:

> The fact that the use of Pidgin as opposed to English may at times in the past have been indicative of social distinctions is not something that can sensibly be held against any language: very much the same situation prevailed with regard to English versus French in Norman days . . . (Wurm 1969: 39)

However, in accordance with the retentionist view of pidgin development adopted in this book, one suspects that traces of earlier functions continue to survive at later stages, and that the earlier a function emerges, the more dominant it is later. Sankoff has made some pertinent observations about Tok Pisin in rural areas and its continued association with power and non-solidarity:

> Though . . . Tok Pisin is now a common denominator, even a language of equality among urban New Guineans from diverse linguistic groups, it has retained its associations with and connotations of power and authority at the village level, learned by each new generation in the context of giving orders and shouting at people, as well as playful imitation of such contexts. (Sankoff 1976: 302)

As Sankoff further demonstrates, it is used predominantly where forced regimentation plays a role (such as village meetings where people line up to receive orders about the work for the day) and by persons in a position of authority (such as village leaders, the big men, etc.). It may be an awareness of this which accounts for the widely found rule in expanded pidgins and even creoles that the language is not to be used in the company of or towards whites and also for the related objection of many pidgin and creole speakers at being addressed in these languages by an expatriate. One certainly cannot ignore the indexical value of language choice in pidgin and creole-using societies.

The change from vertical to horizontal (between indigenes of comparable power in the communication process) communication is the principal reason for stabilization of a pidgin. In the absence of prestige norms, language universals rather than language or speaker-specific solutions emerge in lexicon and grammar. Language-internal word formation begins to replace borrowing from prestige languages, and natural structures supplement or replace those borrowed from the previously dominant language. The function most closely associated with this process is the integrative one. Speakers now identify with a new type of society, which is neither traditional nor that of the colonizer, with its own social and linguistic norms. The plantation is a typical context for this development, and some pidgins of this type include Pidgin French of the New Caledonian Plantations, Pidgin Fijian and the Pidgin English spoken on some West African islands such as Fernando Póo.[38]

A vivid picture of the functional limitations of such a stabilized pidgin is given by Bateson describing early Tok Pisin:

> The language and its tones of voice and the things that are said in it are a rudimentary third culture, neither native nor white, and within the conventions of this third culture the white man and the native can meet happily, though the culture is germane to neither of them . . . But neither the white man's philosophy of life, nor that of the native, crops up in the neutral and special fields of Pidgin English conversation. It is not that democracy and private enterprise could not be described in Pidgin, it is just that, in fact they are not. (Bateson 1944: 139)

Continued use of a stable pidgin by speakers from many different language backgrounds, particularly when transported from the plantation to a larger multilingual society such as that of Papua New Guinea or Vanuatu, led to further functional and structural expansion. On the one hand, the permanency of contacts required the encoding of personal feelings; on the other, social norms of politeness such as small talk were needed. The addition of the expressive function typically goes hand in hand with a widening of domain. In many instances, the use of a pidgin for religious purposes triggered this new functional use. Phatic communion (a term introduced by Malinowski 1923) is associated with new domains (meetings, social gatherings, etc.) as well as new media. In using a pidgin for telephone conversations, for instance, certain devices referring to this channel of communication and its functioning are required.

It has to be kept in mind, at all times, that pidgins are second languages and that any new functions have to be seen in relation to the functional use of a speaker's first language. The use of a jargon – that is, a language for propositional and heuristic functions only – typically has little effect on a speaker's vernacular. It is simply added to it. The same is true with beginning stabilizing pidgins and many older stable pidgins: they are additional to traditional vernaculars, which continue to remain intact and to be used in all functions relevant to the traditional society in which they are spoken.

With the ongoing functional and structural expansion of a pidgin, however, its relationship with the speaker's first language tends to become changed. Instead of being added to, traditional languages tend to be replaced in an increasing number of domains and functions. This is particularly striking with the expressive function in the domains of religion and abuse. Thus the religious experiences transmitted by expatriate mission bodies to the indigenous population tend to be incompatible with traditional modes of religious expression and pidgins, or mission lingue franche are preferred.[39] Prayer, services and discussion of religious matters thus are associated with speakers' second languages. The same is true of insults, expletives and other forms of strong language. For Tok Pisin among the Kwoma, Reed observed:

> We found that youngsters not only counted and sang in pidgin but also used it in the new game of football – especially in angry altercations. Their own language was not lacking in terms of abuse, but those in pidgin were preferred. (Reed 1943: 286)

Conventions for talking about talking differ from society to society. For some languages, such as central African Gbeya (Samarin 1969), only two metalinguistic labels – translated as 'good' and 'bad' – are reported. In other cases, such as central American Tzeltal (Stross 1974), a profusion of labels is in use. It thus seems that metalinguistic conventions are very much culture-specific and culture-dependent and to be expected late, if at all, in the development of a pidgin. With the exception of scattered remarks on metalinguistic systems in various pidgins and creoles (e.g. Sandefur 1984 on Kriol), no comparative or developmental studies are at hand and the following brief case study of Tok Pisin may turn out to be quite atypical. In a pilot paper on this question, I distinguished a number of stages:

1 awareness of Tok Pisin as a language separate from English;
2 awareness of distinct varieties within Tok Pisin:
  a indigenous versus non-indigenous varieties;
  b socially determined varieties;
  c diachronic varieties (developmental stages);
  d stylistic varieties;
3 awareness of grammatical units such as sense group, word classes and word-formation processes.

Labels referring to these categories emerged over a period of more than one hundred years. It took roughly fifty years for the difference between English and Tok Pisin to be expressed, another twenty-five years before socially determined varieties were labelled, and it is only recently that one can talk about diachronic and stylistic varieties and grammar. This, incidentally, causes a major problem for the fieldworker, since the absence of metalinguistic labels signals not only pidgin speakers' difficulties in talking about their language, but also their lack of interest in this matter. Most pidgins are not languages that reflect on themselves.

This lack of self-reflection also means that the poetic function of the language is late to emerge. The poetic use of language means that attention is drawn to the language itself as used in a message. Examples include word plays, puns, rhymes, artistic metaphors and other tropes. Such stylistic devices were conspicuous by their absence in Tok Pisin. As observed by Mead (1931: 333): 'To the unaccustomed ear, pidgin has a terrific monotony because of the

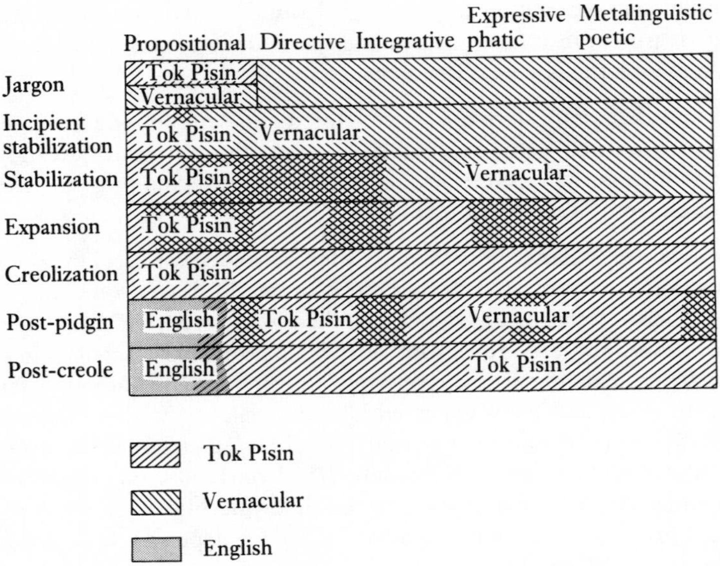

Figure 3.2 Functional expansion of Tok Pisin

constant repetition of three words, belong, along and fellow.' The use of Tok Pisin in the poetic function has emerged only recently and is restricted to younger urban speakers.[40] Examples of contexts in which the poetic function is dominant and the linguistic devices used for poetic purposes are discussed by Wurm and Mühlhäusler (1983). Again, the poetic use of Tok Pisin typically implies the reduction of a speaker's use of his or her first language in this function.

Summing up the functional expansion of Tok Pisin, it seems obvious that this can happen with second-language speakers and that, as it were, the process of creolization of a language can occur over a prolonged period of time with widespread bilingualism. The functional range that individual speakers occupy can be distributed over a number of languages, and one typically finds a change from initial compound to later coordinate bilingualism, followed again by compound bilingualism with the growing importance of English. Schematically, a highly idealized picture could be drawn up as shown in figure 3.2. The development outlined here is from a monostylistic, monofunctional language to a polyfunctional one. It is likely that other expanding pidgins, as well as second languages learned in a more formal context, may follow a similar development. This functional expansion of a pidgin differs dramatically from the functional development found with first-language acquisition. For instance, Halliday's investigations (1974) of the development of language function in first-language acquisition suggest the following hierarchy:

Halliday (1974)	*Other common terms*
instrumental	
regulative	(directive, social control)
interactional	(phatic)
personal	(expressive)
heuristic	
metalinguistic	
imaginative	(poetic)
representational	(referential, propositional)

The endpoint of first-language acquisition, if the hierarchies developed by Halliday and myself are correct, is thus the point of departure for pidgin development. Whereas a first language develops in the social security of parent–child interaction and eventually enables the child to correlate to the world outside, pidgin speakers are faced first with a hostile and dangerous outside world and only gradually do they develop the structural and functional means to make this world a home. One is tempted to do two things:

1 to correlate the functional expansion of a pidgin to its structural growth;
2 to explain the differences in the development of first languages and pidgins as being derived from differences in functional development.

Table 3.5 Correlation of the functional expansion of a pidgin to its structural growth

Functions	*Structures*
Cognitive	Simple sentence structures, but no grammar beyond the sentence, list-like lexicon
Directive and integrative	Development of systematic aspects in the lexicon, e.g., address-system forms that marks politeness, emergence of socially determined lexicon and grammar, some syntactic variants for requests
Expressive	Additions to lexical inventory, beginnings of word formation, emergence of devices for focalization, grammar beyond sentence
Phatic	Increase in stylistic variation at the lexical and syntactic levels
Metalinguistic	Emergence of lexical items for speaking about language, hypercorrection
Poetic	Socially determined variation of earlier stages of a developmental continuum can become stylistic devices, productive word-formation providing lexical synonyms, stylistic syntactic transformations, development of conventions for metaphorical expansion

At this point, however, correlations can be only very rough guidelines indeed, principally because we simply lack comparative data and, secondly, because single structures can be used in a number of different functions and vice versa. It is in this light that one has to see table 3.5. Our discussion of functional development has been restricted to pidgins. As regards creoles, it is usually assumed that they exhibit the same functional potential as any other language, although the continued presence of lexifier languages and associated diglossia may invalidate such a claim for certain groups of speakers.

No studies of the sequence in which such functions emerge in a first-generation creole, or indeed in child language in older creoles, have yet been made, although they would form highly desirable complements to Bickerton's claims about bioprogram grammar (1981, 1984). If language ontogeny recapitulates language phylogeny, as he claims, then a study of the likely early non-cognitive dimensions of creole development may be of considerable importance.

Other bases for the classification of pidgins and creoles

The number of parameters proposed in the social classification of pidgins and creoles is large and it does not seem profitable to consider them all here. However, to conclude this chapter a few will be discussed, mainly because they have been influential in the development of the field, in spite of their limited usefulness in empirical testing and theory formation.

First, a few words have to be said about an oft-quoted suggestion by Stewart (1962) designed to set pidgin and creoles apart from other languages by appeal to social factors alone. Stewart suggests the following criteria:

	Pidgin	*Creole*
Standardization	–	–
Historicity	–	–
Vitality	–	+
Autonomy	–	–

On closer inspection, such criteria turn out to be of very limited diagnostic value. Thus standardization (particularly planned standardization) has been observed in many pidgins and creoles; in some cases, such as in Tok Pisin or the Surinam creole of Sranan, more than 50 per cent of their total lifespan is characterized by direct human interference with their development. Other pidgins and creoles have become the object of standardization more recently, including Haitian (cf. Hall 1972), Bahasa Indonesa, Bislama, Northern Australian Kriol, Seychellois French Creole and Papiamento. Proposals for language standardization exist for other pidgins and creoles, including indigenous ones such as Naga Pidgin described by Sreedhar (1977). A recent summary of standardization in pidgins and creoles is given by Samarin (1980) and a rejoinder by Wurm (1980).

As regards historicity, Stewart would seem to place too much emphasis on absolute time. Because of this rapid development, one might argue that changes that take a thousand years in old languages may only take one hundred years in a pidgin and creole. Note that historicity in relative time is manifested in the present-day variability of these languages, allowing the analyst to recover a considerable portion of their development by means of internal reconstruction. Historicity is also found when one considers them as products of human social history: their development in times of rapid social change again means that many past social forces are reflected in present-day structures. Pidgins and creoles are not spoken by people without a history, unless one argues that only uniformitarian changes are genuine history.

The criterion of vitality is used to set apart pidgins from creoles. This idea is related to Hall's concept of a life-cycle, which implies that:

> normal languages do not have life cycles. A language is not an organism, but a set of habits, handed down from one generation of speakers to another . . . To this general principle, however, there is one exception. Pidginized languages normally come into existence for a specific reason, last just as long as the situation which called them into being, and then go quickly out of use. (Hall 1962: 152–3)

This view, again, is quite problematic. As recent studies on language death have shown (for example, studies in Dressler 1977b), all languages depend for their continued existence on certain numbers of speakers and certain social purposes. The grammar of a dying language, as Trudgill has pointed out (1977), can in many ways be regarded as the mirror image of the grammatical enrichment processes occurring in creolization or pidgin development in expanded pidgins. Again, first languages need not be primary languages, and, to make things even more confused, pidgin and creole forms, vital and dying forms of one and the same language, are often found within a single speech community.

Finally, the criterion of autonomy seems to imply the need for an external language for purposes of structural and lexical development. We already know that access to a lexifier language varies considerably at different points in pidgin and creole development. Most recent studies of structural development suggest that much of the enrichment is not due to borrowing. Instead, through restructuring and possible borrowing from universals of grammar, pidgins and creoles can develop powerful mechanisms of growth and perhaps they borrow no more than other languages. One consideration which seems relevant here is Whinnom's (1971) barriers to mixing. As a general rule, the more tightly structured a system, the more likely it is that borrowing will lead to dramatic restructuring or destruction of the system. Pidgins (particularly expanded ones) and first-generation creoles have highly systematic grammars and hence a drastically reduced syncretic capacity. Borrowing occurs only when there are no drastic linguistic consequences, and when the social gain is greater than the communicative cost incurred. The fact that many post-pidgins and post-creoles are found must not be taken as an indicator of lexical and structural dependency.

Although Stewart's criteria thus seem incapable of differentiating between pidgins, creoles and other languages, they are of some use in subclassifying the first two. Thus a distinction could be drawn between planned and unplanned, vital (stable or expanding) and non-vital (unstable and contracting), and autonomous versus non-autonomous pidgins and creoles. Linguists have tended to prefer the vital, autonomous and unplanned kind for purposes of structural analysis, but there is no reason why the other varieties should not also be given serious attention.

A last dimension I want to mention is that of oral versus literate modes of speaking. Such a distinction has been known for a long time, some interesting early sources being Churchill's (1911) study of Beach-la-Mar and Bloomfield (1933). However, detailed investigations are rare and were probably discouraged by some of the assumptions prevailing in structuralist and transformationalist grammar, including the following:

1 that of the primacy of speech, a view under which written and indeed literate language are often regarded as derivatives;
2 the preoccupation with 'natural' language and the belief that the most informal style is the one most deserving analysis.[41]

The distinction between oral and literate mode is not simply one between spoken and written forms. In fact, many of the early attempts to reduce pidgins to writing are very much extensions of the oral mode. The difference is characterized by Romaine and Traugott 1983 as follows:

> Oral modes of expression, whether spoken or written, focus on contextualized participant interaction, especially shared speaker–hearer interaction, and present material (i.e. topic) in rhapsodic or chunking fashion with action starting *in medias res* (cf. Homeric epics, Modern Greek narratives), whereas literate modes focus on decontextualized, non-participant, presentation of material organized according to logical sequence in preference to shared knowledge (this is a matter of ordering effects). (Romaine and Traugott 1983: 10 000)

The evidence I have surveyed suggests that in their formative years all pidgins and creoles are very much oral languages and many of them will remain so until very late in their development. In the case of pidgins, the reasons are obvious. Until well into their expansion phase the structural devices needed for subordination and logical discourse patterning are absent.[42] Even their presence or potential presence in expanded varieties and creoles does not mean that a literate mode will develop or become dominant. No exhaustive study of the factors contributing to its development has been made, but, in the case of pidgins and creoles, the following are of importance:

1 There has to be a social function for such a use of language, for example, public speaking and verbal skills may be seen as the symbol of leadership, as is the case in many Melanesian societies. The ability to address an audience in a Melanesian Pidgin English as well as in one or more native vernaculars was regarded as a highly desirable skill for big men (see Salisbury 1972).
2 A literary mode is promoted by non-egalitarian and socially mobile societies, in particular post-colonial ones.
3 The presence of language-standardization agencies, such as missions and language academies, which engage in grammar and dictionary making.
4 The use of the language in a number of media, for example, newspapers, radio and television.
5 The absence of restrictions on public use of the language, and, in particular, the absence of a diglossic situation where the related lexifier language continues to serve as that of public discourse.
6 The speech community must be of sufficient size to ensure that its members have differential access to information and thus need to use the language in a cognitive function on many occasions. Open communication networks rather than closed ones (see Milroy 1980) again appear to favour a literate mode.

For most pidgins and a large number of creoles such favourable conditions do not appear to exist. In the case of creoles, this indeed raises the question of qualitative differences between languages. Thus, if the literate mode should turn out always to emerge after the oral mode, one may be justified in assigning the status of more elaborate languages to the former. Note that nothing has been said about their speakers at present; in many instances where creoles have remained oral languages these speakers are bi- or multilingual.

We have now surveyed a large number of factors to be used in the social classification of pidgins and creoles, and we have seen how these factors contribute to the considerable social typological differences found within these languages. In as much as these factors influence their formation and development, we can expect an equally large field of linguistic types. With regard to pidgins and creoles, we are indeed faced with a situation characterized by Bollée as follows:

> The more the investigation of pidgins and creoles advances, the more difficult it appears to become to find generally valid characterizations for the languages traditionally described by these labels. (Bollée 1977: 48, my translation)

There are a number of possible responses to this realization.

1 As we have already indicated, one can justify the unity of pidgins and creoles in developmental (diachronic) terms: individual languages may be more or less advanced in terms of a universally valid developmental continuum. This view presupposes the possibility of separating linguistic from non-linguistic factors, as well as the primacy of the former.
2 One can observe a number of cases and arrive at certain inductive generalizations, the method implicit in much early research.
3 One can attempt to isolate the ideal social environment for pidgin and/or creole development and study. I shall refer to this latter approach as the 'desert-island' approach.

The desert-island approach

Sociologists and linguists have often speculated upon the social and linguistic consequences of the development of new societies and languages when shipwrecked individuals are thrown together on a desert island. One of the principal insights derived from such speculations is that only the essential and not the accidental aspects of society and/or language would emerge in the first generation. In view of the multitude of social factors and linguistic consequences noted in pidgin and creole development, it would seem reasonable to concentrate on at least some cases where the number of variables is drastically reduced.

The search for such cases can take two forms: first, the scrutiny of actual desert-island speech communities; and second, the setting up of an artificial experiment on such a desert island. These two possibilities will now be discussed.

Although most pidgins and creoles developed in a context with access to established languages, at least in theory,[43] some were indeed established on a desert island. These include:

1 Pitcairnese on Pitcairn Island;
2 Tristan da Cunha English;
3 Portuguese Creole of Annobón;
4 Portuguese Creole of the Cape Verde Islands;
5 French creoles of the Indian Ocean;
6 Creole English of Providence Island in the Caribbean.

On closer inspection, however, it appears that even these languages may not be ideal test cases. Thus, in the cases of Annobón and the Cape Verdes, a fairly developed form of Portuguese Pidgin was brought along by the first settlers, together with some Standard Portuguese. Similar objections can be raised against Creole English of Providence, and possibly against the French Creoles of the Indian Ocean. (For a detailed account of the latter, see Baker and Corne 1982.) The relevance of the Tristan da Cunha data (Zettersten 1969) is diminished greatly by the fact that speakers of Standard English have been dominant throughout its history; thus this leaves, as the only genuinely interesting case, that of Pitcairn Island.

Pitcairn Island was settled by the mutineers of the *Bounty*, led by Fletcher Christian in 1790. Christian brought with him eight English-speaking sailors, their Tahitian and Tubuaian spouses, and nine others from Tahiti or Tubuai. Most of the male inhabitants succeeded in killing one another off, mainly over women, in the next few years, and by 1808 one first-generation male, John Adam had survived.

The language which developed in the first twenty years of total isolation was thus determined mainly by the linguistic input of mothers (possibly pidginized varieties of Tahitian and Tubuaian, as well as some English), male caretakers (English and some broken Tahitian), and the linguistic inventions of the children themselves. At this time hardly any Pidgin English had become established in the Pacific; as a consequence, virtually none of the diagnostic pidgin features for this area (see Clark 1979) have found their way into the language.

The absence of a prior pidgin model, the almost total isolation in the formative years, and the mixed composition of the island's population thus seem to make Pitcairnese an ideal test case. Its relevance for the so-called bioprogram theory of creole development is discussed by Le Page (1983b).

The scarcity of such 'pure' cases of pidgin and creole development and the difficulties in perceiving the parameters operative in the 'impure' cases have led Bickerton and Givón to proposing a controlled experiment. A more detailed description of this experiment is found in Bickerton (1979: 17–22). It involves the following procedures:

1 Take sixteen subjects from four different language backgrounds to an uninhabited Pacific island. Their languages should be historically unrelated and typologically maximally divergent.
2 Ensure that you recruit couples with children, so that both adult and child linguistic adaption can be studied.
3 Provide all the necessary social and medical facilities.
4 Give them a highly restricted (about 200 words) lexicon containing the names of the most useful objects and activities in this social context.

Bickerton and Givón expected that within a year a simple pidgin would have evolved, and that later a creole would develop among the children. As the project was rejected by the bodies they applied to for funding, we can only speculate as to its outcome.

The two weakest points of the experiment appear to be the possibility that individual culture-dependent second-language-learning strategies might have prevailed, if the personality of a leader had been strong enough; and even more problematic is the decision to make English vocabulary available. The boundary between lexicon and syntax is very much a culture and language-specific matter, and the provision of certain lexical resources is likely to prevent the emergence of certain circumlocutory and other syntactic devices. Again, a totally culture-neutral natural communication system is probably unrealizable, although experiments of the kind devised by Bickerton and Givón are certainly useful in that they help us control some of the numerous variables in pidgin and creole formation and development.

Summary

The principal aim of this chapter has been to demonstrate that pidgins and creoles can be understood only if they are seen as social solutions to the discontinuities in social and linguistic traditions and to the communicative pressures developing in cross-linguistic intercourse. Although the social forces differ from language to language, making it very difficult to establish a coherent social definition of either pidgins or creoles, a number of prominent factors are found again and again. My own assessment is that discontinuity of transmission is probably the most powerful factor. This discontinuity manifests itself in the imperfect transmission and reinvention of pidgin languages, and in the break between one generation's pidgin and the next generation's creole in many creole situations.[44]

A second finding is that those who invent pidgins and creoles are not necessarily powerless victims or clean slates ready to be imprinted with the categories of universal grammar. Instead, one should seek for a view in which deliberate human actions determine the degree to which cultureless natural linguistic categories are used in the formation of such new linguistic systems.

It has been accepted for methodological reasons that a distinction can be made between linguistic and extralinguistic (social) factors in the development of pidgins and creoles. It is further acknowledged that the linguistic development can be characterized as possessing its own internal dynamics, governed by considerations such as naturalness. The language that is determined entirely by a natural developmental programme is the one that is least costly in terms of perception and production.[45] In the first instance, its very uniformity makes it useless as a signifying device for different social identities. Thus speakers will invent deviations from natural grammar in order to increase its indexicality. Second, it is not certain, at this point, how powerful natural grammar is. It may well fall short of the communicative requirement encountered even in limited pidgin contexts. Consequently, language in a number of domains and functions will require human inventions. Third, certain units and constructions may be endowed with special prestige, regardless of their status on a naturalness hierarchy. Prestige forms can develop from within or be introduced from other systems. It is because of such considerations that social factors are seen as both triggering and constitutive of certain (by no means all) aspects of pidgin and creole development.

A number of case studies have been presented here and more are needed for a fuller understanding of the complex inter-relationship between linguistic and social factors. As Sankoff states 'to understand what happened in any particular case, we must become better historians' (1979: 25).

4

Theories of Origin

> The real creole is always in the process of receding over the horizon . . . and creole grammars tend to be normalized descriptions of an earlier phase of the language that no one is quite sure was ever spoken by anyone.
>
> (Labov 1971a: 40)

Introduction

In this and the following chapter, I will address the linguistic and structural characteristics of pidgins and creoles. This will be done in two parts: first, by concentrating on the question of their origin and formation; and second, by examining the nature of their development. One can phrase the first question, one which has dominated the pidgin/creole field for many years, as follows: 'Why do pidgins and creoles exhibit structural affinities among themselves which are often closer than their affinities with perceived lexifier languages?' Underlying this question is the assumption that there are certain typological similarities.[1] Opinions as to how these similarities came about differ greatly and tend to be, as already discussed in chapter 2, related to current views of language and language relationship. Since the various theories of origin have been discussed in detail elsewhere (for example, in Bollée 1977; Todd 1974), my discussion of them will be rather short. However, as frequent reference is made to them, the reader should be reminded of what is at issue here.

With regard to the origin of pidgins, the following theories have been proposed:

1 language-specific theories:
   a nautical language theory;
   b foreigner talk/baby talk theory;
2 general theories:
   c relexification theory;
   d universalist theories.

In addition, we find theories that stress observed differences between pidgins. They include:

e common-core theories;
f substratum theories.

In the past, a distinction between pidgin and creole formation often was not made, and virtually all of the above explanations have also been applied to creoles. The only theory that specifically solely addresses the formation of creoles is Bickerton's recent bioprogram theory (1981).

I shall start by discussing each of these theories in isolation, although it seems unlikely that any single cause will be sufficient to explain the complex processes which call these languages into being.

Nautical jargon theories

The importance of nautical speech in the formation of pidgins and creoles was realized early and can be traced back to the popular view expressed, for instance, by F. Robertson:

> The recipe for the language is interesting: Take one sea full of British sailormen, hardy, daring, very British and profane, and leave it in a cool place for two days; extract their speech; then bring to boil and extract what speech remains. Add a coconut shell each of Chinese, Malay, German and Kanaka and bring to boil a hundred or so times, then season with a little war or two; add a few drops of Mission sauce and sprinkle with blackbirder pepper and recruiter salt. Strain through Kanaka lips and serve with beer on boat days, or with undiluted Australian any other time. (Robertson 1971: 13–14)

This folkview is usually restricted to individual source languages and, accordingly, I shall look at two such languages – English and French – separately. The first comprehensive account of South Seas Beach-la-Mar (Melanesian Pidgin English of the nineteenth century) is given by Churchill (1911), who emphasizes the contributions of sailors. The alleged lack of grammar in Beach-la-Mar is traced back to the speech habits of this class of people:

> I have already commented upon the fact that the white man, who is without particular intention or principle of philology dominating the production of the mongrel speech for his own greater convenience, is a man of little or no education. The categories of grammar are far above his experience; the few rules and the many exceptions which form the science of our speech have never been feruled into his intelligence – perhaps it was in avoidance of them that he ran away off to sea and became a part of a life of dingy adventure. (Churchill 1911: 13)

Unfortunately, little actual information as to the peculiar dialect of these sailors is given by Churchill and direct evidence is restricted to anecdotal material such as that given by Schellong:

> The tribe that happens to have the numerical superiority in the encounter of people from several island groups is likely to gain linguistic superiority as well. Captains and mates are amused by this confusion of languages. They hear this or that strange word and occasionally employ it instead of the English equivalent. Thus, on our cutter *quillequille* is always used for 'quick', *kaikai* instead of 'eat', *bulmakau* instead of 'meat' and so forth. (Schellong 1934: 97–8, author's translation)

The nautical jargon theory was developed subsequently by Reinecke, who points out that:

> One of the most favourable situations for the formation of such dialects is found aboard merchant vessels which ply the seven seas and ship large numbers of foreign sailors – and indeed the seaman is a figure of the greatest importance in the creation of the more permanent makeshift tongues. (Reinecke 1937: 434)

The role of nautical English also features prominently in the work of Hall. He claims that by applying the comparative method to pidgin English data, one will find that:

> If we have to assign a specific locality to our proto-pidgin-English, it will have to be somewhere in the lower reaches of the Thames, on either bank of the river, in the docks and settlements in such parts of London as Bermondsey, Rotherhithe, Wapping, Shadwell and Limehouse, and in other English seaports such as Plymouth. (Hall 1966: 120)

Although much of these earlier statements were based on informed guesswork, Hancock (1976: 23–36) actually undertook extensive comparative work between the Atlantic creoles and what is known of nautical English of the seventeenth century. There remain problems with such an approach, however. First, nautical English is not a stable monolithic language, but a highly variable and developing one. Second, there is very considerable overlap between nautical English and other forms of non-Standard English. Finally, even if nautical English was the model, it was not imitated in full, but acquired by the non-British interlocutors of these sailors in a more or less modified form. The precise learning contexts, the time of exposure and other social variables remain unknown.

Parallel to a nautical origin of Pidgin English are attempts to relate pidgin and creole French to maritime varieties of French. On the linguistic side, Jules Faine (1939) and Alexander Hull (1968) have attempted 'to reconstruct a hypothetical maritime French . . . a form of language which might have been used on French ships engaged in the slave trade and in commerce with American ports' (Hull 1968: 255). In his discussion of this theory, Baker sums up:

> The former existence of a patois such as Faine envisaged appears to be less than an established fact, but it would be unreasonable not to allow both that sailing, as an occupation, must have required its own rather specialized terminology, and that the conditions of living in the restricted environment of a ship must have been particularly favorable to dialect leveling. If something not totally different from Faine's 'composite patois' had indeed existed, it would have been readily available to the extent that there would have been speakers of this on board every French ship which visited the various French trading posts and colonies overseas. But wherever settlers from different parts of France were brought together, one would expect a certain amount of dialect leveling to result . . . common elements in geographically distant French Creoles are not necessarily attributable to a specifically *nautical* 'composite patois'. (Baker 1982: 243)

More important, Baker supplements his arguments with a highly detailed study of the verbal contacts that could have occurred both on board recruiting vessels sailing to Mauritius and in ports. His social data indicate that 'numerically speaking, sailors are clearly a statistically significant factor'. He continues to point out, however, that 'there is nothing to indicate that just one "nautical patois" existed, or that the collective expertise of sailors in communicating with non-Francophones would have equipped them all with a single uniform pidgin'.

The criticisms made against a uniform English and French nautical jargon also appear to hold for other creoles and creoloids which have, at one time or other, been regarded as continuations of sailor's speech, including Afrikaans (e.g. Hesseling 1979: 8). A tentative conclusion to this is that although sailors were instrumental in diffusing language material over vast distances,[2] their role in shaping the lexicon and grammars of the languages thus diffused remains to be proven.

Baby talk and foreigner talk theories

There is some terminological confusion with 'baby talk' and 'foreigner talk', as, in everyday speech, they tend to be associated with both the language used by babies and/or foreigners and the language used by adult native speakers when addressing these groups. This latter meaning, however, is the only one used in modern linguistics. In older writings on the origins of pidgins and creoles, this confusion is often found. Thus Leland (1876) writes of Chinese Pidgin English: 'What remains can present no difficulty to anyone who can understand negro minstrelsy or baby talk.'

Support for a foreigner talk origin is found in some of Schuchardt's writings, in particular in his article of 1909 on the lingua franca. Thus, in Markey's translation, we read:

> All atrocities performed on language derive from its inherent possessors in the same manner as child language depends on the speech of the wet nurse. Or to use another image: it is not the foreigners who break away single stones from a splendid, well-appointed edifice in order to construct meager huts, but the owners themselves who put them to such ends. (Schuchardt 1979: 28)

However, in his later article on Saramaccan (first published in 1914), Schuchardt offers a more cautious assessment:

> The White was teacher to the Black; the latter repeated the former. And the White always used the most emphatic expressions, exaggerations as they occasionally occurred to him too, in communication with his compatriots. He did not say: 'you are very dirty,' but 'you are too dirty,' and thus it may be explained that 'very' in Pacific Beach-la-mar is *too much* and *tumussi* in Sranan Black English (SBE). It is difficult for us to appraise such relationships correctly. We involuntarily regard our language as the model, and we have no feeling for the fusions and obfuscations, the inconsistencies and eccentricities, by which they excel all other languages; we perceive the splinter in the stranger's eye, but not the beam in our own. (Schuchardt 1979: 74)

This last quotation affirms the learner's productive role in pidgin formation as well as the possibility of inconsistencies in the input. Such caution was not always exercised within structuralist linguistics, particularly in the writings of Bloomfield, who, in 1933, wrote the following famous passage:

> Speakers of a lower language may make so little progress in learning the dominant speech, that the masters, in communicating with them resort to 'baby-talk'. This 'baby-talk' is the master's imitation of the subjects' incorrect speech. There is reason to believe that it is by no means an exact imitation, and that some of its features are based not upon the subjects' mistakes but upon grammatical relations that exist within the upper language itself. The subject, in turn, deprived of the correct model, can do no better now than to acquire the simplified 'baby-talk' version of the upper language. (Bloomfield 1933: 472)

At the time, his behaviourist views compelled him to assume a virtual equivalence between the baby or foreigner talk input and the learner's pidgin. Bloomfield's views were taken over by a number of influential scholars, such as

Hockett, although virtually no empirical support for the claims implicit in the above quotation were ever sought.

Such support has appeared more recently in three forms:

1 experiments involving the elicitation of foreigner and baby talk in formal settings;
2 observation of contextualized behaviour;
3 archival research.

Considerable input has also been made by studies in the area of second-language acquisition. It has become common practice to see both learning and the provision of a model for the learner as active processes, and to combine both behaviourist and mentalist views of pidgin formation, as in Clyne (1978) or Ferguson and DeBose (1977).

Experimental elicitation of foreigner talk was pioneered by Ferguson (1975) for English, and has since been carried out for some other languages such as Dutch (Werkgroep 1978) and German (Hinnenkamp 1982), though not, to my knowledge, for any non-Indo-European language. The results of such tests are that a number of morphological, syntactic and phonological simplifications promoting greater naturalness are found for all languages tested; and that such foreigner talk simplifications are variable rather than categorical.

The input given to foreigners in many cases is quite inconsistent. Let me illustrate these points using results obtained applying Ferguson's test to Australian adults with no previous experience of a pidgin or creole: individual speakers differ markedly in the application of the various simplificatory devices, as can be seen from the following versions of the sentence *I haven't seen the man you're talking about*:

1 I no see this man.
2 Me no see man you talk about.
3 No see man. (head shaking)
4 Me (point) no see (eyes) man you (point) talk about. (wild gestures)
5 No seeum man you say.
6 Man you talk about, I not see.
7 No seen man you talk.
8 You talk man. I not seen.
9 Me no look him man you say.

The following strategies deserve particular mention:

1 The avoidance of embedded constructions is in evidence in most responses. It either takes the form of loss (as in 1, 3) or replacement by parataxis (as in 8).
2 The expressed feeling that the linguistic message needs to be reinforced by gestures.

3 The avoidance of do- support in negative clauses. *No* is used as a negator in most responses. This is probably the result of a strong tendency towards one form–one meaning in simplified registers.
4 The avoidance of tensed verb forms.

Apart from these tendencies, which seem to reflect natural categories, there are a number of other changes of a clearly cultural type. They include:

5 The addition of *-um* or *him* to verb forms.
6 Lexical replacement: *talk* 'to say' or *see* 'to look'.
7 The selection of the *me* rather than *I* form of the pronoun as the basic pronominal form.

A number of other processes appear to be difficult to fit into the natural-cultural dimensions and may be random. Most notable here are changes in word order. The tentative conclusion from these and similar experimental data is that baby talk or foreigner talk is governed by cultural conventions as well as natural tendencies towards input simplification. Consequently it does not provide an optimal model for second-language learners, although it does offer one which is considerably easier to acquire than the full standard target language.

A second source of foreigner talk data is actual observations. Because of the lack of recording techniques, and indeed interest in this matter, in the past, one has to rely on secondary evidence such as literary varieties of foreigner speech,[3] for traces of foreigner talk dating back more than ten years. I have recently investigated German foreigner talk (Mühlhäusler 1984b) and traced back its history to the early nineteenth century, although its use in literature obviously does not reflect actual usage. The earliest passage is found in the speech of a German servant who poses as a Russian traveller in Kotzebue's play *Pagenstreiche* (around 1810):

> Das sein der reichste Mann in ganz Russland. Er haben Gueter von Wolga bis Irtich.
> Braut kann warten. Der Fuerst schicken kostbare Diamanten. So is. Peterburch sein Hauptstadt in Ukrain.
>
> He is the richest man in the whole of Russia. He owns land from the Wolga to the Irtich river.
> The Bride can wait. The duke send precious diamonds. That's so. Petersburg is the capital of the Ukraine.
> (my translation)

The writer of this passage employs a number of strategies that are also documented in later foreigner talk and pidgin varieties of German, including:

1 use of the infinitive instead of inflected verb forms;
2 variable absence of the definite article;
3 omission of surface dummy *es* 'it'.

An interesting feature of this, and indeed many later texts, is the presence of the copula (here in its uninflected form); according to Ferguson (1971), the absence of the copula is one of the most widespread properties of foreigner talk varieties. Note that its presence in the input does not mean that it will be acquired by a learner. However, it again indicated that foreigner talk is in part a cultural form of language.

Perhaps no better illustration of this claim can be given than the reduced forms of German employed by Karl May. The importance of this writer of adventure stories in shaping a German tradition of foreigner talk was first mentioned by Clyne (1975: 3), who quotes a number of Pidgin German passages from *Winnetou*, the most widely read of Karl May's works. Clyne observes that although the syntax exhibits a number of pidgin characteristics such as the use of the infinitive instead of inflected verb forms, there is no loss of copula and the lexicon has not undergone a similar simplification.

It is interesting to note that Karl May portrayed different degrees of simplification with different characters in his stories. Thus, whereas an Italian artist in *Der Peitschenmueller* (originally published in 1886) approximates the syntax and lexicon of Standard German in many of his utterances, the Basuto in *Das Kafferngrab* (originally published in 1879) uses a considerably more pidginized form of German. Let me illustrate this with some text material from *Der Peitschenmueller*:

Ein Koenig? Welch Entzuecken! Was fuer ein Koenig wird er sein? . . . Unmoeglich! Koenig Luigi kommen nie in Bad, sondern sein sehr einsam, sehr . . . Nicht? Oh, ich glauben daran, sehr, sehr. Ich wissen genau, dass wahr sein. Sie sein da oben begraben und spiel in der Nacht Violin in Grab. Nein, es sein Wahrheit.

A King. What delight. What King will it be? . . . Impossible! King Ludwig never visits the spa, but he is very lonely, very . . . No? I believe in it very very much. I know for sure that it is true. She is buried up there and plays violin in her grave at night. No, it is the truth.

Foreigner talk features reflecting genuine use of more natural grammar include:

1 variable omission of verb inflections;
2 omission of surface dummy *es*;
3 variable absence of subject pronouns.

On the other hand, one encounters fairly complex features such as the passive construction and (variably) inverted word order in the appropriate grammatical context. Note also the presence of coordination and subordination. Some German lexemes are replaced and/or are followed by Italian ones. However, one misses the stereotyped Pidgin German lexemes such as *capito* 'savvy?' and *avanti* 'quick, come on'.

Compare this text with the following passages from *Das Kafferngrab*:

Mynheer rett Quimbo. Mynheer helf arm Quimbo. Quimbo will nicht gut schmeck Strauss, oh, oh, Mynheer, aber Mynheer nicht treff Quimbo, denn Quimbo bin sonst tot.	Mynheer save Quimbo. Mynheer help poor Quimbo. Quimbo no want good taste ostrich, oh, oh, Mynheer, but Mynheer not hit Quimbo, for Quimbo otherwise be dead.
Quimbo lass liegen Sau? Oh, oh, Mynheer Quimbo ess viel schoen Sau.	Quimbo let lie pig? Oh, oh Mynheer Quimbo eat much beautiful pig.
Quimbo kenn Tschemba; Quimbo hab red schon gross viel mit Tschemba.	Quimbo know Tschemba; Quimbo have talk already big much with Tschemba.

I have only selected a very small portion of the many relevant passages in this story. However, it should be clear that we are dealing with a much more drastically reduced form of German than in the previous sample. This is obvious from the following features:

1 Consistent use of verb stem (rather than infinitive), instead of inflected verb forms, the only exceptions being the inflected copula. This usage may have been modelled on the Cape Dutch spoken when this story was written. However, the Italian in the previous story uses either inflected forms or infinitives.
2 Absence of articles and other determiners. This is unlike Cape Dutch (Afrikaans) and in contrast with the variable presence of articles in the previous text.
3 Uninflected attributive adjectives, similar to Cape Dutch. The Italian speaker uses mainly inflected adjectives, though often with an inappropriate ending.
4 The use of *viel* 'much' instead of *sehr* 'very', unlike Cape Dutch. The Italian speaker uses *sehr.*
5 The use of proper nouns instead of pronouns gives this passage a particularly childish quality. Again, the Italian in the previous text uses the appropriate pronouns.
6 There are few examples of passives and they differ from that used by the Italian through the use of a verb stem instead of a past participle, as in *Quimbo darf nicht werd fress von Loewe* 'Quimbo must not be eaten by a lion'.
7 Logical order is frequently expressed by sequential order, as in *Pferd lauf viel schnell Quimbo verlier Arm* 'if the horse runs very fast, Quimbo will lose his arm'.

The differential use of such features by literary Italians and Bantu relates to an important rule for the use of foreigner talk: most of its cultural features (such as lexical replacement) and some of its natural features are employed more readily when the addressee is perceived to belong to an inferior culture; dressed accordingly; and when there is power differential.

I have stressed repeatedly that a distinction has to be drawn between culture-specific and universal or natural conventions for foreigner talk. A comparison of the various foreigner talk conventions found with Indo-European languages and those of a number of non-Indo-European languages would make a fascinating study indeed. An excellent basis for an initial comparison would be simplified Motu (of Papua New Guinea). The first missionaries who settled around Port Moresby in the latter half of the nineteenth century were addressed by the Motuans in a highly simplified foreigner talk version of their language,[4] although for a long time they were under the impression that they had been taught genuine Motu. They even began to translate the scriptures into this foreigner talk, until the difference was pointed out to them by their own children, who had grown up in a Motu-speaking environment (cf. Taylor 1978).

Another task for the future is the analysis of variability in the literary foreigner talk registers of individual common lexifier languages such as English and French. Some real-life situations have been studied in recent years, notably for Melanesian varieties of Pidgin English, Pidgin German and Pidgin Turkish.

Some of the main findings derived from a study of English Foreigner Talk and its role in the formation and development of Tok Pisin (see Mühlhäusler 1981a) are as follows. First, the use of foreigner talk can carry on a long time after its functional usefulness has disappeared. In the case of Tok Pisin, a special foreigner talk register of English – referred to as Tok Masta by the indigenes – continued to be used, in spite of the fact that it was badly understood and that indigenous Tok Pisin had developed along totally different lines. A conclusion is that the importance of foreigner talk is restricted to the very early stages of pidgin formation, but of little relevance for later development.[5] Second, in later stages of Tok Pisin's life, Tok Masta assumes the role of an index of social superiority. The desire not to mix with perceived inferiors finds its linguistic expression in the growing gap between Tok Masta and the indigenous varieties of Tok Pisin. Third, only indigenes in close contact with Europeans or those with a knowledge of English know foreigner talk. Finally, both structurally and lexically, Tok Masta is highly variable and not a systematic simplification of English. Apart from fairly stable lexical conventions, no normative tendencies have been observed.

A more positive assessment of the social role of foreigner talk is found in studies by Hinnenkamp (1982, 1983) on German and Turkish varieties. As regards Pidgin German and German foreigner talk, Hinnenkamp's research, which is based largely on anonymously taped conversations between native speakers of German and Turkish, suggests that there is a very large amount of inconsistency in German foreigner talk input.[6] He also reports that the use of foreigner talk is not necessarily regarded as bad: a number of informants perceive its role in simplifying communication between speakers of different languages; and that simplification has to be regarded as a continuum. These findings agree with earlier ones, such as those of Bodemann and Ostow (1975) or Amsler (1952).

Hinnenkamp goes on to explore affinities with Tarzanca, the foreigner talk variety of Turkish. His data comprise exchanges between Turkish villagers and German tourists in a tourist resort. The types of deviations from the standard language closely parallel those in German foreigner talk and include (1983: 4):

1 loss of pre- and post-positions;
2 loss of nominal inflection and agreement;
3 deletion of the copula;
4 generalization of the infinitive;
5 change in word order;
6 loss of overt question marking;
7 external placement of propositional qualifiers;
8 juxtaposition of subordinating clauses;
9 lexical and grammatical multifunctionality;
10 periphrasis.

Hinnenkamp notes that, although the particular linguistic processes found in German and Turkish foreigner talk are language-dependent, their outcome is pretty well the same. This view is also supported by initial observations on simplified Motu (Dutton forthcoming).

The importance of the last source of our knowledge of foreigner talk, archival research, is underlined by Naro's valuable research into Pidgin Portuguese. His conclusion, reached on the basis of a close scrutiny of historical chronicles, missionaries' accounts and other documents, is that (1978: 341): 'Portuguese pidgin . . . had its origin in EUROPE, not in Africa, beginning with the officially instituted training of translators. Its basic structural peculiarities resulted primarily from conscious modifications of their speech by the Portuguese.'

We have now surveyed some studies of foreigner talk. Although the data basis available at present is small and the criterion of observational adequacy has hardly been met (this last point is particularly true for actually employed or primary foreigner talk), a number of conclusions still appear to be warranted. First, foreigner talk tends to be a mixture of cultural conventions and genuine natural intuitions on language simplification. It probably involves a good deal of speakers' regression to developmentally earlier stages of their own language. Second, because of its mixed nature and considerable inconsistency in its use, foreigner talk is not the ideal simple model some structuralist linguists imagined it to be. Finally, the importance of foreigner talk in pidgin formation appears to be restricted to relatively early stages of development.

It is difficult to assess the relative importance of foreigner talk in the formation of different pidgins, but considerable differences can be expected. Foreigner talk is an input in the formative years of pidgins and thus should be considered. However, it would be wrong to conclude that imitation and rote learning has been established as a major factor in this process.

Relexification theory

In its strongest form, relexification theory claims that most European-based pidgins and creoles are related via a special process involving the maintenance of grammar and the replacement of lexical units. The grammar is said to be that of sixteenth-century Pidgin Portuguese or possibly medieval Mediterranean Sabir. The possibility of relexification, or, as Hall (1975: 183) puts it, 'the substitution of vocabulary items for others, with the maintenance of a stable syntactic base', was first suggested by Thompson (1961). He surmises that the West African slaver's jargon (Pidgin Portuguese) (p. 113) 'may have been the pattern for all the West Indian Creoles just as, in the Eastern and Pacific worlds Portuguese creole dialects, well known to Europeans of many nationalities may have provided the model for the two great branches of Pidgin English, China coast pidgin and Neo-Melanesian'.

Other writers go even further back in history and regard the Mediterranean Lingua Franca as the ancestral language underlying most pidgins and creoles; yet others make much weaker claims as to the continuity of the transmission of pidgin or creole grammar. Thus Laycock (1970a: ix) merely considers the possibility that relexification of pidgin Portuguese may have played some part in the development of Melanesian Pidgin English.

It is interesting that with most writers who support relexification:

1 the possibility of non-European predecessor languages to European-based pidgins and creoles is never raised;
2 no proper distinction is drawn between its role in the formation of pidgins and creoles and in their subsequent history;
3 the question of discontinuity in development is not considered.

As regards the first point, it is not impossible that some pidgins and creoles with strong lexical affinities with English may in fact have been modelled on pre-existing indigenous lingue franche. Thus Kriol of North Australia could be a relexified version of a Pidgin Macassarese, which was widely used in trade with outsiders and as an intertribal lingua franca until the beginning of this century (see Urry and Walsh 1981), and many of the Portuguese creoles in Asia may have been continuations of earlier Arabic-based trade languages. As regards the second point, it should be noted that relexification is a timeless concept and ignores the fact that pidgins are developing entities. It is not made clear at what point relexification occurred.

Since the very early stages of a pidgin stable grammar, relexification is not plausible for those pidgins with unstable jargon predecessors. As regards the relexification of stable pidgins, there are two possible scenarios, depending on whether a given instance of relexification constitutes an abrupt break in linguistic tradition or not. For this, the analyst requires information as to the absolute length of time needed for relexification, communicative problems, and changes in the composition of the pidgin-using community.

The difference between the two types of relexification can be illustrated by the following examples from Tok Pisin:

	Gradual change (a)		*Abrupt change (b)*	
Stage 1	beten	'to pray'	'binen'	'bee'
Stage 2	beten o prea	'to pray'		
Stage 3	prea	'to pray'	'bi'	'bee'

In case (a), continuity is maintained by the joint use of both lexical items in a synonym pair. In case (b), the word for 'bee' was introduced twice at different stages in the development of Tok Pisin by different speakers. The external explanation for this difference is that the discussion of non-traditional religion has been one of the central functions of Tok Pisin for most of its existence. On the other hand, there is no such tradition for bee-keeping. A comparison of arbitrary stages of the language, as practised in diachronic structuralist analyses, would not capture this difference, although no descriptive problems would arise within a developmental framework such as that proposed by Bailey (1980).

Gradual relexification is associated with a prolonged period of bilingualism and the simultaneous presence of more than one prestige lexifier language. Thus, in the case of German New Guinea, although the relative status of English and German changed over time, both languages were partially accessible for lexical borrowing for a considerable part of its development. At the height of German colonial control, a number of New Guineans who already spoke English-based Tok Pisin introduced more and more lexical items of German origin, creating mixed German–English and predominantly German forms of pidgin. The close parallelism between Tok Pisin and the Pidgin German of Fritz from Ali Island can be seen in the following text:

P.G. (Pidgin German): Ja frueher wir bleiben. Und dann Siapan kommen.
T.P. (Tok Pisin): Yes bipo mipela stap. Na bihain Siapan kam.
Eng. (English): Yes, at first we remained. Then the Japanese came.

P.G.: Wir muss gehen unsere Boot. Wir bleiben und bikples, a, festland gehen.

T.P.: Mipela mas go bot bilong mipela. Mipela stap na go bikples.
Eng.: We must go to our boat. We stayed for while and then we went to the mainland.

A similar process could be observed in a second German colony, Kiautschou in north-east China. Again, both English and German were important languages, and Pidgin English was common among those Chinese involved in trade with Europeans. The growing importance of German appears to have led to a gradual change-over to a Pidgin German via intermediate mixed varieties. One example of such an intermediate pidgin in the process of changing lexical affiliation is discussed by von Hesse-Wartegg in his comments on the proprietor of the Hotel Kaiser:

> The proprietor with his friendly smile had already learned German. 'Ik sabe Deutsch,' he addressed me while making deep bows. 'Gobenol at gebene pamischu open Otel, Kommen Sie, luksi, no hebe pisi man, no habe dima, bei an bei.' Since this Spanish–English–German–Chinese dialect differs from native to native, I want to add the German translation: 'Ich kann Deutsch, der Gouverneur hat mir Erlaubnis gegeben, ein Hotel zu eroeffnen, kommen Sie, besehen Sie es; ich habe noch keinen Gast, weil ich keine Zimmer habe, aber nach und nach.' The words *pamischu*, *luksi*, *pisi*, and *bei an bei* are not German, but belong to the lingua franca used between the Chinese and the Europeans, the so-called Pidgin English. *Pamischu* is 'permission', *luksi* means 'look see', *pisi* stands for 'piece', for the Chinese do not say 'one man, two men' but *one piece man*, *two piece man*; *bei an bei* is English 'by an by'. (von Hesse-Wartegg 1898: 10, author's translation)

No such bilingualism was found in other German colonies. Official attempts to replace Swahili with a kind of Pidgin German by means of gradual relexification miscarried and, in the absence of any important role of German in Samoa, the local Pidgin English remained immune to its influences.

Relexification can occur not only in the case of competing prestige languages, but also between 'indigenous' and imported lingue franche. An as yet not fully understood case is that of Hiri Motu and its relationship to Papuan Pidgin English (see Dutton forthcoming). Although mission and government in the central districts of Papua favoured the use of a simplified Motu (Police Motu), Pidgin English appears to have been the most common language for expatriate–indigenous contacts in the eastern and western parts of this colony. Because of the high regional mobility of the government agents and the developing plantation and mining economies, a significant number of Papuans were exposed to two prestige lingue franche. Indications are that for a long time both coexisted and that only after the Second World War, with the growing importance of the Motu-speaking capital Port Moresby and adverse reactions against Pidgin English by educators and officials, did Police (Hiri) Motu eventually take over. It appears that in at least some cases this transition occurred in the form of relexification, as is evidenced by a small body of mixed Pidgin English–Pidgin Motu texts, particularly those of a recording of a Papuan Nanai Gogovi from the Gulf of Papua, made during the Second World War. They include (data from Dutton forthcoming):

ai faia traim traim
we (excl.) fire try try
'we kept trying to fire [the guns]'.

memero matamata ia sikulu dekenai ia aut, ia gaukaraia
boys new they school at they out they manufacture.
'New boys who were at school had to leave and go into the work force'.

dina lau stati
day I start
'I started (to go) in the daytime'.

namba wan be Taunisvolo
number one is Townsville
'Townsville is first'.

wadaeni seken, Bulesben
okay second Brisbane
'Brisbane was second'.

A detailed discussion of these and others is found in Dutton (forthcoming).

The case studies just discussed appear to lend support to the classical version of the relexification theory, which traces other European pidgins to Portuguese Pidgin of West Africa. Relexification is most likely to have occurred in Ouidah (Juda or Ajuda) in Benin (former Dahomey), where for several centuries a Portuguese, French and English fortress and slave depot coexisted.[7] The full sociolinguistic context is not yet known. However, we do know that at least some slaves were kept for a considerable period and that there was some exchange between the different depots. Slaves from Ouidah were sent to many parts of the world, including the West Indies and the French plantations in the Indian Ocean. Some of these slaves probably already spoke a partially relexified Portuguese Pidgin; others may have shifted their linguistic allegiance after deportation. Yet others may have understood little, if any, European-derived pidgin. The picture that emerges here is a complicated one. Relexification in many cases may have been an individual strategy for learning a more useful pidgin. It is not clear to what extent it was a social strategy, nor what its relative contribution was in the formative years of various pidgins.

The role of relexification in creole formation and development can be twofold:

1 creolization may have occurred with partially or totally relexified former pidgins;
2 relexification may have occurred after creolization.

In both instances, the notion of creolization is not directly linked to that of relexification, nor is it indeed a necessary component. Whereas relexification does not by definition change the complexity of grammar, creole formation certainly does. Let us examine the creoles of Surinam in the light of such considerations. Writers such as Voorhoeve (1973: 133–45) and Hancock (1984) have adduced considerable evidence for relexification processes involving Sranan and Saramaccan, but probably not Djuka, a third creole of Surinam.

Table 4.1 Thompson's representation of the similarity in function and encoding of tense aspect and modality in Surinam and other creoles

Markers	*Durative*	*Perfective*	*Contingent or future*
Cape Verde	ta	ja	lo
Indo-Portuguese	ta, te	ja	lo, di, had (*neg.* nad)
Macao, Malacca, Java	ta	ja	logo (*neg.* nadi)
Philippine Spanish creoles	ta	ya	de, ay
Papiamentu	ta	taba	lo
Saramaccan	ta	bi	sa
Sranan Tongo	de	ben	sa
Jamaican	a, da	ben, min, mi	
Haitian	ap	te	a
Dominican	ka	te	ke

Source: Thompson 1961: 110.

Table 4.2 A lexico-statistical comparison of Surinam creoles

Origin	*English*	*Portuguese*	*Dutch*	*African*	*Total*
Sranan	118	7	25	4	154
Ndjuka	116	5	20	3	144
Saramaccan	72	50	6	6	134

Source: Huttar 1972.

Their investigations were stimulated by the observation that the creoles of Surinam shared most of their grammatical structures, but differed considerably in lexical composition. The similarity in function and encoding of tense aspect and modality in the Surinam and other creoles was stressed in Thompson's seminal article on relexification (1961) and his representation is shown in table 4.1. A lexico-statistical comparison of the Surinam creoles by Huttar (1972) bore out the second point (table 4.2).

Voorhoeve (1973) added evidence from synonyms, pointing out that there were hardly any of different lexical origin in Sranan, but a substantial number in Saramaccan. They include:

Saramaccan	*Sranan*	*Etymology*
bée	bére	/E belly
baika	—	/P barriga
buuu	brudu	/E blood
sangá	—	/P sangrar, sangue
diíngi	drí i	/E drink
bebé	—	/P beber
hói	óri	/E hold
panjá	—	/P apanhar
lósu	lóso	/E louse
piójo	—	/P piolho
pói	póri	/E spoil (and /P podri?)
lot	—	/E rotten (see also in ND)
pondi	—	/P podri
piíti	príti	/E split
latjá	—	/P rachar

E = English, P = Portuguese.

Voorhoeve concludes that Saramaccan and Sranan have the same linguistic origin, West African Pidgin Portuguese.[8] The Saramaccan or Bush Negro Language retained much of this Portuguese heritage, since it was removed from English influence at an early stage of relexification by escaping maroons. As I read Voorhoeve's arguments, it is not clear to me whether we are dealing with a split at a pidgin or a creole stage, but from the sociolinguistic history given it would seem to be the former. If this is so, then it would provide the needed explanation for the lexical differences between the two languages and the many synonym pairs in Saramaccan.[9] It would not account, however, for many of the grammatical similarities of Sranan and Saramaccan, as creolization and hence large-scale grammaticalization presumably only occurred after the split. It would also fail to account for grammatical similarities between the two creoles and Ndjuka, which developed, according to Voorhoeve, out of a later, possibly unrelated, Pidgin English.

Change in lexical affiliation after creolization may have occurred in a number of other instances, such as Papiamento, a Spanish-based creole with an alleged Portuguese creole ancestor, or the Spanish creoles of the Philippines, where it is still an ongoing process (see Molony 1973). The study of such cases, though irrelevant to an understanding of the creolization process in a narrow sense, may help us to see certain language-mixing processes in a clearer perspective. The kind of relexification processes occurring in present-day Philippine Spanish creoles such as Chabacaño are gradual, partial and involve a number of lexifier languages, in particular English and Tagalog. It also appears that they affect marginal (in the sense of less frequently used, as against a basic Swadesh list-type core) areas more than central ones. In the words of Frake (1971: 232), these refer to dimensions such as 'lesser magnitude, shorter distance, worse evaluation, female sex, younger generation or plurality'. The same type of relexification is also found in numerous creoles. It appears, although hard data are somewhat difficult to come by, that the kind of relexification operating in the transition from one pidgin to another typically affects the central areas of the lexicon as well.[10]

To sum up the discussion on the relexification hypothesis, the following tentative conclusions are proposed:

1 Relexification can occur at different stages in the development of pidgins and creoles.
2 Both gradual and abrupt relexification appears to have been involved in the history of many pidgins and creoles. However, there is no indication that *all* these languages are related in this way.
3 Relexifications appear to account for a number of cases where pidgins developed from other stable pidgins without a significant preceding jargon stage. Relexification cannot account for all instances of pidgin formation, however.
4 The process of relexification appears to be of minimal relevance to creole formation, although it is often found in subsequent later creole development.

This means that the relexification hypothesis is insufficient as an all-embracing explanatory parameter for pidgin and creole formation. However, because it can create similarities between apparently unrelated languages, a detailed knowledge of its role in the history of individual pidgins and creoles is essential, if they are to be used for the study of linguistic universals.

Universalist theories

The view that the linguistic nature of pidgins and creoles is universally motivated is not a recent one. It was inherent in Coelho's work on Portuguese creoles as well as in that of Lenz on Papiamento (1928). After many years of intensive study, Schuchardt, in his late writings, also appears to favour universalist explanations. Discussing the development of plurals in Saramaccan and other creoles, he comments:

> Creole dialects have not yet been fully appreciated for their general linguistic significance. They are customarily regarded as products of very peculiar or extreme mixture, but what distinguishes them is, rather, if I dare say so, their universal linguistic features. (Schuchardt 1979: 73)

Such initiatives remained unexplored for a long time and resurfaced only with renewed interest in linguistic universals in the wake of transformational generative grammar. Perhaps the most exciting development was Heine's demonstration (1973, 1975) that pidgins that were apparently quite unrelated to those based on European languages shared many of their structural properties. The discussion of universals has been hampered by insufficient attention to two questions:

1 The crucial question at what point in the development from jargon to creole universal forces will have been most likely to have occurred.
2 The identification of universals at surface and deeper levels of grammatical organization.

The first point involves two separate issues: the ability to resort to linguistic universals; and the susceptibility of emerging or developing languages to such forces. With regard to the former, there has been considerable disagreement. In the wake of assumptions and findings during the early days of transformational generative grammar, it was usually assumed that access to linguistic universals was restricted to children before the critical threshold of puberty and hence of no importance in the formation of pidgins by adults. This is expressed thus by Naro (1978): '"pidginization must involve adults who no longer have inward access to the *faculté du langage*", the innate language acquisition device that defines the constraints of natural languages'. This argument is also employed by Bickerton (1976), who rejects claims by scholars such as Kay and Sankoff (1974) that pidgin speakers are able to use their *faculté de langage* to select a universally motivated base grammar. Bickerton (1976: 176) points to a considerable body of evidence from a number of jargons to support his view that 'obviously, if pidgin speakers did have the power to reduce their language to some kind of universal base, this power would have to be exercised at the beginning, rather than the middle or end, of the pidginization process'. This assumed hypothesis is not supported by data from early Hawaiian Pidgin English, which, according to Bickerton (ibid.), 'showed internal differences so gross that it is possible to determine the ethnicity of the speaker from written texts and on grounds of syntax alone. The theory that pidgin speakers have access to universals cannot, therefore, derive any support from empirical studies.'

As noted earlier, unstable jargons are very much subject to individual communication strategies, including transfer, resort to linguistic universals and others discussed by Meisel (1983). For relatively homogeneous groups, such as Japanese plantation workers in Hawaii (cf. Nagara 1972), transfer would seem to have been perfectly viable, as universal solutions become necessary mainly in heterogeneous communities. The fact that adult speakers have access to universal strategies does not imply that they must make use of them.[11]

Bickerton, however, who does not agree with this, sees universals as appearing principally in one context: that of creolization of a jargon or undeveloped pidgin. Thus he explains the already mentioned similarity of grammatical systems in creoles the world over in terms of an innate blueprint which surfaced intact whenever the child's language acquisition device failed to find adequate data (cf. Bickerton 1981). Inadequate input is associated with early pidgin-speaking plantation communities, where the data consist of the itself unstable and communicationally inadequate pidgin and a number of different vernaculars such as are spoken by members of the older generation. Without wishing to commit myself to the unlearnability of pre-existing parental vernaculars, I am in agreement that universal strategies are indeed likely to be resorted to in such a situation.

Progress in the area of pidgin and creole universals has long been hampered by the assumption that universals must necessarily be of a static type ('unrestricted independent' in Greenberg's terminology). Thus the universal that no pidgin has a copula was regarded as disconfirmed by the discovery that some pidgins had a copula. The limitations of this view were first made explicit by Heine, who dynamically characterized linguistic universals in African pidgins. Speaking of their shared properties, he observes:

> The common denominator in all these changes seems to be a shift from language-specific to what we feel justified in calling 'universal' grammar: the process of pidginization tends to eliminate all the features by which languages are distinguished and to replace them by features that can be assumed to be present in all languages – either implicitly or explicitly. Operations like the 'stripping' of late syntactic rules and the establishment of one-to-one correspondences between underlying and surface structure items are manifestations of this process.
>
> The extent to which languages have been affected by this process varies considerably. (Heine 1975: 13–14)

It is not quite clear from this quotation whether Heine conceives of universals as a static endpoint to which individual pidgins approximate to a greater or lesser extent, or whether he is referring to an implicationally ordered dynamic development. It is this latter view which has emerged as the most viable hypothesis in recent years.[12] In this model, it would be claimed for a construction such as plural marking that its presence or absence does not define a language as a pidgin or creole, but that, if it emerges at all, it will always appear with nouns in subject position that refer to human beings, then be extended to other grammatical positions (direct object, indirect object, after prepositions, in that order) and degrees of animateness. We are thus arguing in terms of Greenberg's implicational universals.

The assumption at this point, although necessary empirical confirmation is not available, is that the implicational hierarchies underlying pidgin and creole development are the same. In the case of an emerging creole, the endpoint of development would be reached much faster, however, than in an expanded pidgin, where the process can go on over many generations of speakers.

The identification of universal processes and units also needs to be considered in the light of differing theoretical stances. There are two principal approaches to the study of linguistic universals. The first is the Greenbergian approach (cf. Greenberg 1963), which is based on the comparison of surface characteristics of a large number of languages. Examples (from Greenberg 1963) are:

Universal 34: No language has a trial number, unless it has a dual. No language has a dual, unless it has a plural. (This is an unrestricted implicational universal.)

Universal 42: All languages have pronominal categories involving at least three pronouns and two numbers. (This is an unrestricted independent universal.)

Universals of the Greenbergian type can be easily falsified with evidence from new languages, as has been done for universal 42 by Laycock (1977a: 33–41).

A second approach to linguistic universals is that of Chomsky (e.g. 1965) and other transformationalists. It consists of postulating a small number of abstract universal principles, which are said to enable children to learn any language. Examples include the following:

1 The grammars of all languages have a category VP (verb phrase). (This is a substantive universal.)
2 The semantic component interprets syntactic deep structure. (This is an organizational universal.)
3 If the phrase X of category A is embedded within a larger phrase ZXW, which is also of the category A, then no rule applying to the category A applies to X, but only to ZXW. (This is the A-over-A principle, a formal universal discussed by Chomsky 1968: 27–47.)

It should be noted that these are universals of formalization and that their alleged status as mental realities is largely removed from empirical verification. Both Greenberg's and Chomsky's approaches to universals are deficient in a number of ways:

1 As suggested by Bickerton (1981), they compare languages consisting of mixtures between cultural and (biologically founded) natural grammar, that is, systems which are strictly speaking not comparable. At best, one will obtain a mix between natural universals and others based on cultural and other factors.[13]
2 Both types of universals are static, that is, based on fully developed adult grammars. They are therefore difficult to relate to findings from pidgin, creole and child language development.

To consider the first point, genuine natural universals would be expected in one instance: that of rapid creolization of an unstable jargon, the context considered by Bickerton (1981). The fact that older creoles and adult pidgins violate a number of such universals can be regarded as irrelevant to our understanding of the natural roots of human language. Genuine counterexamples are also found in young creoles, however, an instance being Bickerton's claim (1981: 52–3) that they have no category VP.

Such an argument raises a number of serious questions, in particular that of the ability of young children to acquire languages that have deviated considerably from the postulated natural basis.[14] Sranan, for instance, violates Greenberg's near universal[15] number 18: 'When the descriptive adjective preceded the noun, the demonstrative and the numeral, with overwhelmingly more than chance frequency, does likewise'. In Sranan, however, as pointed out by Koefoed (1975: 8 ff), the descriptive adjective precedes the noun, whereas the demonstrative pronoun follows it. Sranan is an old creole and its present-day grammar may have been preceded by one where universal no. 18 was not violated. The source of the violation could have been language mixing that resulted from continued substratum influence on this language. Again, it would be interesting to see if Sranan-learning children start off with both adjectives and demonstratives before the noun.

The initial hope, then, that because of their relatively young age, creoles would not have developed far enough away from their natural base to make them useless for surface comparisons of the Greenbergian kind, is not fully justified. Creoles, and in all likelihood pidgins as well, may be closer to such a universal base, but they do not provide direct access.

The argument just given implies that direct access is barred because of the historical changes undergone since these languages came into being. There is also a second reason: that the development leading to a pidgin or creole, rather than the endpoint of such a development, should be taken as the basis for comparison in universals research. It can be expected that the change from a less to a more complex system of verbal communication will progress along universally preprogrammed lines, particularly in those situations where the target language is relatively inaccessible and where there are great pressures for communication. As yet, only partial studies of the internal development of some pidgins have been made (an interesting summary is given by Sankoff 1979) and no direct studies of the development of a first-generation creole out of a jargon are available. Those who have put forward claims in this area, such as Bickerton (1981), have had to rely on indirect evidence.

Comparative evidence on pidgin and creole development remains scarce and the hypothesis of a single, language-independent expansion programme is too restrictive. However, it would seem wise to put forward a strong claim and revise it as needed, and the evidence suggests that linguistic universals to date are the most satisfactory explanation of the origin of pidgin/creole structures. A developmental universalist hypothesis has no difficulty in accounting for observed differences between 'synchronic' grammars of different pidgins: they are seen as reflecting different stages in linguistic development. However, before the emergence of developmental models, such differences strongly militated against universalist proposals and enhanced the plausibility of two major theories of pidgin and creole formation, which will now be discussed.

Common-core theories

Among the various explanations of pidgin and creole formation put forward by Robert A. Hall in various places, the idea that pidgin grammar is the core common to the grammars of the languages in contact attracted the largest number of followers. The structural resources of a pidgin language seen by Hall (1961: 414) are shown in figure 4.1. Such a view appeared highly plausible, especially in a climate where behaviourist learning theories prevailed. The intersecting hachured area can be interpreted as that of learning facilitation in a contrastive view of second-language learning. It is not easy to see how it could relate to first-language development, however. Thus pidgin learners take the easiest way out by concentrating on those structures that are learnt with the least effort. However, there are some very serious objections to such an explanation. First, the areas of facilitation may turn out to be those parts of grammar that have least communicative relevance. Second, the common-core model is totally static and ignores the fact that at different points of linguistic development a different core would obtain. As pointed out by Posner

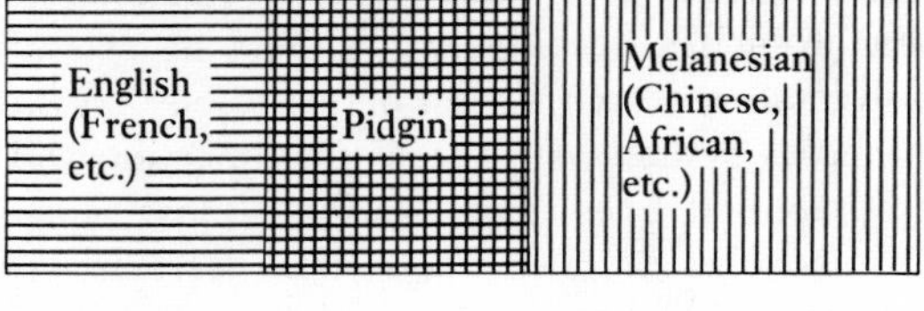

Figure 4.1 Structural resources of a pidgin language (from Hall 1961: 414)

(1983), there is an unfortunate tendency to compare the present-day standard variety of the lexifier language rather than earlier dialectal stages and/or informal varieties. Indigenous languages are equally bound to change over time. Thus, in the case of the formation of Tok Pisin, English has undergone only minor changes, whereas one of its major indigenous parent languages, Tolai, has changed dramatically over the last few decades. Third, this view assumes that the speakers of the pidgin resulting from such language contacts are perfect bilinguals (that is, have equal access to all systems involved), as what is common to two languages can only be established once they are fully known. In fact, at the time that pidgin grammars come into being, access to the lexifier language often is very limited. Finally, there is a growing body of factual counterevidence. The available literature on pidgins and creoles abounds with examples of constructions that cannot be assigned to any identified parent language.[16]

Thus, the pursuit of the common-denominator model does not appear to be a very promising one, although identification of grammar across systems, just like the identification of lexical items across languages, may have been one component in their grammatical development. As regards creoles, the fact of withdrawal of model languages excludes a common-denominator explanation for their grammatical structures during their formative years. Again, identification of structures across languages may be a factor in their subsequent linguistic development.

Substratum theories

The idea that pidgins and creoles combine the lexicon of one language (typically the superstratum – that is, the socially dominant) with the grammar of another (typically the substratum or socially inferior) has been around for a very considerable time. In the field of early creole studies, it is associated with names such as Lucien Adam (writing on French creoles), Herskovits (writing mainly on English-based Caribbean creoles) and Schuchardt in his early years of writing. The reasons for appealing to substratum explanations are varied. They include:

1 the desire to demonstrate that there are mixed languages and that Stammbaum (family-tree) models of language relationship therefore stand in need of revision;
2 the desire to demonstrate linguistic and cultural continuity for Black Caribbeans of African origin;
3 the study of changes in naturalness and internal consistency under conditions of language contact and borrowing.

Although each of these goals is worth while in itself, amazingly little progress has been made in the area of substratum studies over a long period of time, the main reason being the almost total absence of a well-designed model for language mixture. I have discussed the issues involved in a number of places (e.g. Mühlhäusler 1980a, 1982a, 1985) and I will only mention some arguments here.

Mechanical mixture versus linguistic compounds

One of the most common exercises in substratum research has been to identify lexical items or grammatical constructions directly with those of a source language. Thus the lexical item *kavale* 'car, carriage' in Samoan Plantation Pidgin English would be traced to Samoan *ta-avale* 'carriage'; Jamaican Creole *nyaka-nyaka* 'very pretty' would be traced to an African substratum; or *happy-happy* for 'very happy' in the same language to the English item 'happy' and an African construction of iteration. In all these examples, substratum and superstratum features can be separated in a mechanical way. Indeed, the very use of the word 'stratum' suggests that geological rock strata provide the basis for substratum theory (see figure 4.2).

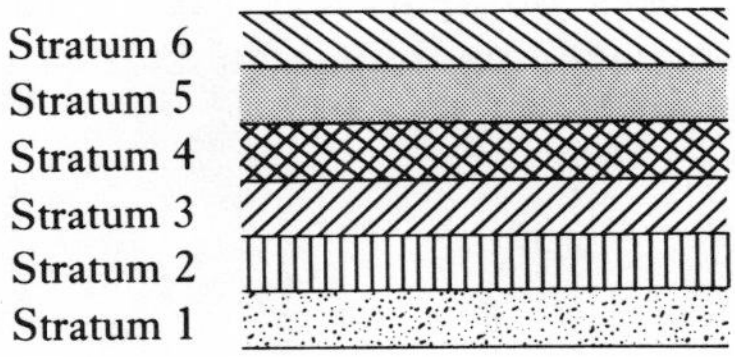

Figure 4.2 The stratum view of language mixing

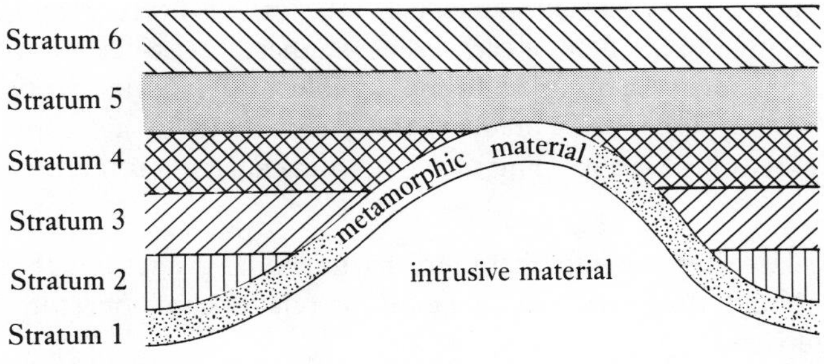

Figure 4.3 The metamorphic view of language mixing

However, there is no reason to expect that substratum elements can be isolated in an easy mechanical way in all instances. To return to our geological metaphor, there is a second possibility: metamorphosis of pre-existing material as a result of a volcanic intrusion, as in figure 4.3. In this instance, only some of the original and some of the intrusive material can be directly identified. The remainder, the metamorphic material, is very much in the nature of a chemical compound: that is, it is unlike either of the contributing elements. Linguists have progressed very little in their understanding of such material and, until they do so, claims as to substratum influence will remain restricted to a subset of potential cases.

'Borrowing grammatical rules'

Whereas borrowing in the area of the lexicon, including cases of lexical syncretism, appears to be relatively easy to describe, the same is not true of the area of grammar. Let me illustrate these problems of establishing substratum influence with a practical example. Most attributive adjectives in Tok Pisin appear before the noun. A small group, however, appear after the noun (so-called postmodifiers), including:

botol bruk	broken bottle
tok giaman	untrue talk
banana mau	ripe banana
han kais	left hand
het kela	bald head
graun malumalu	swampy ground
ples nogut	bad place
wil pas	stuck wheel
tok tru	true talk
buk tambu	holy book

Wurm suggests that Tok Pisin postmodifiers reflect substratum influence from Tolai:

> The appearance of adjectives of different classes preceding or following the nouns which they determine attributively is a typical feature of the Austronesian Tolai which shows the phenomenon uniquely amongst New Guinea Austronesian languages. It may well have entered Pidgin from this source. (Wurm 1977b: 515)

There are a number of problems with this suggestion. First, it is not clear what grammatical rule is involved here. If it was simply the rule that 'some, but not all, attributive adjectives appear postnominally', then one could point to a similar rule in English, manifested in, for instance, *money galore*, *president elect*, *court martial*, etc. This rule would support a superstratum grammar view as well as a substratum and a common-core view. We must go on to examine the adjectives affected in both English and Tolai, and it then becomes clear that those adjectives that appear postnominally in English do not do so in Tok Pisin.

Influence from Tolai could manifest itself in two ways: either in the form of a different word order with a newly borrowed item of Tolai origin (thus conforming to the often held principle that 'ordering of syntactic constituents can be borrowed only if the phonetic form of at least one member has also been borrowed'); or in the form of calquing. Let us examine both possibilities against the historical evidence available.

The only items of Tolai origin in the list of postmodifiers are *mau* 'ripe' and *malumalu* 'swampy'.[17] The former word is documented long before the latter, and thus seems to be the best candidate for triggering off a new word-order rule in Tok Pisin. However, as pointed out by Mosel (1980), 'Tolai *mao* "ripe" appears before the noun and not after it as in Tok Pisin'. As regards *malumalu*, it does not belong to the group of Tolai adjectives that can appear postnominally, and furthermore seems to be an intransitive verb for most Tolai speakers.

The explanation that the new word order is a result of direct substratum influence is thus disconfirmed by the data. The second possibility is indirect influence or calquing. This possibility is alluded to by Mosel (1980), who points out that both Tolai *tuna* 'true' and Tok Pisin *tru* are postmodifiers (Tok Pisin has a variant *trupela*, however). The available historical evidence suggests that *tru* was not the first adjective to appear postnominally. The only postnominal attributive adjective mentioned in Brenninkmeyer's grammar is *nogut* 'bad'. He writes:

> If the adjective appears after the noun, it becomes predicative and is linked to the subject by means of
>
> *he* = *he is*, as in *Pig he fat, boy he nice . . .*
> *banana he 'mao', kaikai he no tan . . .*
>
> Exceptions: No good which followed the noun without the *he* and *save* 'intelligent, wise'.
>
> Man no good
> Man save
> Boat no good
>
> (This appears to have developed in the defective pidgin of beginning learners of the language.) (Brenninckmeyer 1924: 10, my translation)

The corresponding Tolai adjective *kaina* 'bad' is only found before nouns, however. This clearly indicates that the rule emerged in Tok Pisin without any direct or indirect support from either Tolai or English. The fact that further adjectives were subjected to it subsequently may have something to do with substratum influence. What is important, however, is that in most cases there are very significant differences between Tolai and Tok Pisin adjective ordering, as documented in detail by Mosel (1980).

One is reminded of Bickerton's more general statement on the role of substratum influence in pidgins and creoles (1979: 3): 'Although there are here and there some sweeping similarities which tease you and provoke you to go on with the search, you never find any language which has quite the same kinds of structures as the creole language does.'

The location of substratum influence

A recurrent argument in this book has been that pidgins and creoles must be seen as dynamically developing and changing entities rather than as static systems. As regards the determination of substratum influences, nothing is more misleading than a simple static comparison between two languages. Let me illustrate this point with the example of reduplication, a construction seldom found in European lexifier languages and therefore typically assigned to substratum influence. In his thesis on Miskito Coast English Creole (1978), Holm considers a number of semantic shifts brought about/associated with reduplication, including:

1 continuation of action, as in *krai-krai* 'constantly crying';
2 intensification of meaning, as in *big-big* 'very big';
3 accumulation (of small things), as in *bomp-bomp* 'a skin rash'.

For all of these, he cites numerous parallels in African languages spoken in the areas from where Misquito creole speakers originated. At the same time, he dismisses the idea that English baby talk might have been involved.

Steffensen notes that iteration is associated with children's speech in languages as diverse as Zuni, Arabic, Marathi, Spanish and Japanese:

> It is precisely because reduplicated forms are *not* associated with children's speech in . . . many African languages that the latter would seem more likely sources for the phenomenon in creoles than would English. The European association is likely to have contributed to the old, simple-minded characterization of creoles as a kind of baby-talk. (Steffensen 1979: 120)

In spite of the initial plausibility of Holm's arguments, there are some serious problems. First, he operates with a purely synchronic analysis. He does not indicate whether reduplication developed in the creole's pidgin predecessor, during creolization itself or later, perhaps even under the influence of American Indian languages. His argument also leaves another question unanswered: why is it that precisely the same type of reduplication is found in Tok Pisin of Papua New Guinea. An initial explanation in agreement with West African substratum influence is that Tok Pisin, like Misquito Coast Creole, may have developed out of an older Portuguese pidgin, heavily influenced by West African languages. This explanation is excluded on empirical grounds, since the development of productive patterns of reduplication in Tok Pisin only occurred in the 1950s, many years after its formation and stabilization. Moreover, a detailed comparison between Tolai (the main substratum language during formation and stabilization) and Tok Pisin carried out by Mosel is rather sobering:

> The divergencies between Tolai and Tok Pisin suggest that the general idea underlying reduplication in Tolai on the one hand and in Tok Pisin on the other is different. Apart from intensifying reduplication, in Tolai all instances of the second type of reduplication have in common that they express some kind of imperfective aspect, while in Tok Pisin the only function of word level reduplication is to signal some notion of plurality . . . Thus substratum influence of Tolai upon Tok Pisin can be excluded as far as verbal reduplication is concerned. (Mosel 1980: 114)

A type that appears to be a good candidate for substratum influence is reduplication to signal plurality and/or distribution, as in *makmak* 'many spots or rash' or *talinga talinga* 'lots of mushrooms (in different places)'. This construction is found in a number of other creoles, but commenting on reduplicated plurals and Chinese substratum influence in Macanese (Portuguese Creole of Macau and Hong Kong), Coelho cautions:

> The facts accumulated by us show clearly that the essential characteristics of these dialects are everywhere the same regardless of differences of race, climate, distance, or time. It is in vain to seek in Indo-Portuguese, for example, any influence of the Tamil or Sinhalese. The formation of the plural by reduplication of the singular in the Macao dialect can be attributed to Chinese influence, but this process is such an elementary one that little can be established by it. (Translation quoted from Reinecke 1937: 18)

A developmental comparison of Tolai and Tok Pisin echoes these remarks. The use of reduplication for plural marking is highly productive in Tolai, and during intensive contacts between Tolai and Tok Pisin around 1910, two lexical items appear to have been formed in Tok Pisin under Tolai influence: *sipsip* 'sheep' and *meme* 'goat'.[18] However, in spite of access to Tolai, no more plural reduplicatives appeared, and it is only in some very recent creolized varieties of Tok Pisin far removed from Tolai influence that reduplication as a productive process of plural formation re-emerged. A static synchronic comparison between such advanced forms and Tok Pisin and Tolai indeed suggests close parallelisms. However, to postulate substratum influence on the basis of such evidence would be quite misleading.

We can now return to the question: at what point in their formation are pidgins and creoles susceptible to substratum evidence? Let us discuss this stage by stage.

The jargon stage. Individual strategies for cross-language communication are dominant at this stage and they include transfer of structures belonging to the speaker's first language. However, the very nature of unstable jargons also restricts the usefulness of the transfer strategy. As pointed out by Meisel:

> if Bickerton is right and at the time of HCE [Hawaiian Creole English] development, HPE [Hawaiian Pidgin English] was still a jargon, this would mean that it was little more than a list of lexical items and irregularities, lacking systematicness and structural regularities. And in this case, quite logically, it does not make much sense to talk about transfer of L1 syntax. Instead – and this would partly apply to stabilized pidgins too – what looks like syntax (substratum or superstratum or creatively generated) is rather the result of pragmatic principles, e.g. topic-comment order, initialization of information which is useful to 'set the stage' for the following proposition, and so forth. This is in accordance with claims to the effect that the 'pragmatic mode' precedes the 'syntactic mode', ontogenetically as well as phylogenetically. (Meisel 1983: 31)

It would seem desirable to examine the data discussed by Bickerton (1981) and Labov (1971b) to determine whether transfer from substratum languages is indeed as prominent as they claim.

The presence of substratum influence at the jargon stage is unconnected with a second point, that of the continuity of transmission of jargon grammar, which is low, as jargons are to a significant part invented and reinvented by individuals. Consequently, however strong substratum influence is at the jargon stage, it is unlikely to be of great import for subsequent stabilization.

The stabilization stage. Stabilization, or tertiary hybridization, involves the gradual elimination of individual solutions and the establishment of social norms. At the same time, it is the beginning of a transition from a pragmatic to a syntactic mode of verbal intercourse.

The first aspect means that speakers from a number of different substratum languages are involved. In some cases these may be typologically similar or indeed belong to a single Sprachbund, influencing the emerging pidgin. This fact may account for some of the structural differences between developmentally comparable pidgins such as Chinese Pidgin English, West African Pidgin English or Melanesian Pidgin English. The more different their linguistic background, the less likely is substratum influence, and the more speakers will rely on universal strategies.

As regards the second aspect, we are faced with the general principle that only those constructions that fit into the developing grammar of a pidgin can be borrowed.[19] Let me illustrate this with data from the development of causatives in Tok Pisin.

Early Tok Pisin used either lexicalized causatives, such as *kill* 'to kill' or zero derivation as in:

masta raus mi	'the European threw me out'
mi raus	'I was thrown out'

The first morphological causatives in Tok Pisin, documented around 1910, are calques from Tolai, an instance of substratum influence. Compare:

	Tolai		*Tok Pisin*
mat	'to die'	save	'to know'
vamat	'to kill'	meksave	'to inform'
maranga	'to be dry'	pas	'to be stuck'
vamaranga	'to dry'	mekpas	'to fasten'
		nois	'to shake, quiver'
		meknois	'to shake something'

The examples illustrate that Tolai *va-* is identified with Tok Pisin *mek-* but the Tolai construction, in spite of its great productivity, simply did not catch on. Instead, Tok Pisin speakers developed their own convention for morphological causative marking. They used the transitivity marker *-im* (which had become firmly established in the language) to signal causatives, in the following order: with intransitive stative verbs; with intransitive non-stative verbs; with adjectives; and with transitive verbs. Morphological causatives calqued from Tolai appear to have become lexicalized because they conflict with a natural developmental hierarchy underlying causativization.

One is led to conclude from this and similar evidence that the chance of constructions from a substratum language being available at the right time and fitting into an independently given programme of pidgin expansion[20] is relatively low. Consequently one would not expect great substratum influence at the stabilization stage.

The expansion phase. What goes for stabilization also appears to go for subsequent expansion. What can be borrowed from other sources is determined by the independently operating developmental programme. In fact, as grammaticalization increases, the syncretic capacity of an expanding pidgin decreases: the more tightly structured and systematic the pidgin becomes, the more likely it is that borrowing will lead to dysfunctional development. Expanded pidgins are particularly vulnerable when exposed to their former lexifier language. The cost of borrowing from a prestige superimposed variety thus is high.

Creolization. We have distinguished earlier between different types of creolization, according to whether a first language is developed out of a jargon, a stable pidgin or an expanded pidgin. As regards the latter two cases, little carry-over of substratum influence can be expected in the formative years of a creole, because little was encountered in the models.

When it comes to the formation of a creole out of a jargon, two obstacles – one social and one linguistic – are encountered. Bickerton (1981) and some other researchers are confident that, in this type of creolization, access to a substratum vernacular must have been very limited, mainly because of the profusion of different first languages spoken by the creolizing children's parents. However, we can suspect that, in at least some cases, children also acquired a second language side by side with their creation of a creole, and that, particularly if typologically similar languages were involved, carry-over of substratum grammar cannot be excluded. However, in the absence of a proper theory of language mixing, this is difficult to confirm.

Bickerton also stresses the limitations of borrowing for a developing system, in this case a first-language creole:[21]

> at any given stage in that development, the language could only incorporate rules of a certain type, and would have to reject others. Indeed, presence in the input may not even be a necessary, let alone a sufficient, condition since the first creole generation could well have devised such a rule for itself. (Bickerton 1981: 50)

Note that this feature of creole development is very similar to first-language development in children: parental input is ignored or accepted only when it can be accommodated in their developing grammar.[22] Eventually, in 'normal' first-language learning, children must deviate from their natural tendencies and acquire the caretakers' model. Because of the absence of socially or linguistically viable models, creolizing children have considerably more freedom to impose their solutions.

We do not yet have enough observational data to test claims in this area. Particularly serious is the absence of data on the change from pragmatic to grammatical modes of communication in first-generation creole speakers and of data concerning the influence of the first generation on the second.

Subsequent creole development. The discussion of substratum influence at the different stages of pidgin/creole development suggests a more general principle: mixing is disfavoured when languages develop from less to more complex systems, at least it is constrained in that only those elements that fit the expanding grammar can be borrowed from outside. It would appear that the obstacles to mixing are greatest after the transition from pragmatic to grammatical modes of verbal communication, that is, greater with expanded pidgins than stabilizing ones.

Contrary to what has often been said, from Sapir onwards, about language mixing with fully developed systems, that they only borrow what is in agreement with their internally motivated drift and that borrowing thus merely accelerates developments that would occur without outside contacts, it appears that 'finished' systems are much more open to outside influence than developing ones. One of the reasons for this may be that they are typically used by adults, who employ mixing for indexical (particularly social) purposes. In adult speech, the system-destroying abnatural results of mixing are tolerated because of their social benefits. Cultural solutions thus take over from natural ones.

As regards creoles, the natural solutions developed by the first generation of children often lead a very precarious existence. They are replaced by abnatural solutions as well as by further natural developments as in any other language. I will return to this in the next chapter.

In summary, then, it would seem that the role of substratum influence has often been overestimated because of:

1 deficient methodology, such as the lack of developmental perspective and the readiness to classify any similarity between a pidgin or creole and an indigenous language as substratum influence;[23]
2 no proper distinction between the formation and subsequent development of pidgins and creoles.

It can be meaningfully discussed only with regard to individual developmental stages. An important explanatory parameter is also the social benefits and linguistic disbenefits of borrowing and mixing.

Substratum influence and components of grammar

The idea that different parts of grammar are not all equally susceptible to borrowing and mixing is an old one. In creole and pidgin studies, it is already implicit, for instance, in the following quotation from Schuchardt's Saramaccan studies:

> However, we must consider that, if initially the influence of African languages on Black English was only able to exert itself within the framework indicated thus far (the syntax), then this restriction was subsequently voided: namely, at the point when the slaves not only spoke creole with the Whites, but also when they spoke it among themselves, though without having lost their mother tongue, which was readily refreshed by constant importation from Africa. It is during this period that we have transfer of African words. (Schuchardt 1979: 75)

As a general principle, it can be postulated that the more arbitrary an area of grammar, the more readily can languages borrow from one another. With regard to the formation of developmental continua such as the pidgin–creole continuum, this implies that substratum influence will be most pronounced in the areas of lexical semantics, prosodic phonetology, some segmental phonetology, and pragmatics. On the other hand, superstratum influence will be strongest in lexical form and segmental phonetology.[24] Syntax, inflectional morphology and derivational morphology are relatively independent of substratum or superstratum influences.

This means that findings to the effect that substratum languages are the principal source of creole semantic structures (Huttar 1975) cannot be extended to the syntactic component and that, in the areas of syntax and morphology, linguistic universals will be the main source of structural expansion, irrespective of whether this expansion takes place with second-language pidgin speakers or first-generation creole speakers.

This hierarchy is confirmed by recent research in second-language learning (interlanguage). With regard to syntax and morphology, Meisel (1983: 30 ff) suggests that even within these components there are areas of greater and lesser susceptibility to transfer. He observes that:

1 omission of normally obligatory elements (verbs, subject pronouns, articles, etc.) cannot be explained with transfer, or at least not with transfer alone;
2 bound morphology is never transferred; in the case of free morphology, it is concerned with instances of lexical transfer;
3 syntactic transfer is most likely to occur in areas where syntax and semantics are interwoven, for example, relative ordering of two elements where one modifies the other (examples would be adjective–noun sequences, compound nominals expressing possession, part-of-relationships, etc.).

It is anticipated that further research will expose additional principled limitations to borrowing and that consequently the role of substratum influences, at least during pidgin and creole formation, will be shown to be quite restricted.

Some notes on superstratum influence

The model of the lexifier language available to the developers of pidgins and creoles, as already mentioned in the discussion of nautical jargon and baby talk theories, may indeed have been quite different from the standard languages of today and even those of their times. Some very pertinent remarks are found in Posner's review of books dealing with French creoles (1983). In discussing Lefèbvre and colleagues' analysis of Haitian creole French (1982), she writes:

> What is surprising, in a work hailing from Montreal, is that modern standard French is usually contrasted with creole, rather than the non-

> standard varieties that more plausibly formed the basis on which Haitian creole developed. For instance the deictic particle *la*, postposed not only to nouns and noun phrases but also to clauses, prepositions and adverbs is seen by Claire Lefèbvre as a noun determiner that has been reanalyzed as a clause determiner, possibly under the influence of West African languages like Ewe or Yoruba. Yet it may be only a step from documented Canadian usage, in which an unaccented phatic *là* 'there' appears in a whole set of contexts, including at the end of subordinate clauses not introduced by the *que* complementiser that is obligatory in modern Standard French . . . A historical linguist is more interested in the process by which what seems to be discourse usage in Canada, may have become a syntactic rule in Haiti, rather than whether *la* is dominated by X or $\bar{X}$ or $\bar{\bar{X}}$. (Posner 1983: 195)

Posner's example raises the more general problem of observational and descriptive adequacy in pidgin and creole studies. Usually the grammars used as the basis of comparison between pidgins or creoles, on the one hand, and sub- or superstratum languages, on the other, are believed to be descriptive. Creolists are generally aware that many older grammars are highly prescriptive and they tend to make allowances for this fact. However, I feel that the extent of prescriptivism in grammar making is very much underrated. Pronouns provide an interesting example, because the pronoun systems of many pidgins and creoles differ markedly from those found in the descriptions of their European

Table 4.3 English personal pronouns

			Personal Pronouns	
			Subjective case	*Objective case*
1st person	singular		I	me
	plural		we	us
2nd person	singular		you	you
	plural		you	you
3rd person	singular	masculine	he	him
		feminine	she	her
		non-personal	it	it
	plural		they	them

Source: Leech and Svartvik 1975: 260.

lexifier languages. A grammar of English with clearly descriptive aims is Leech and Svartvik (1975). Table 4.3 shows their account of English personal pronouns. However, this table hardly represents the ways in which present-day native speakers of English use personal pronouns, or indeed as they would have been used when speakers of other languages were exposed to the English model in the formative years of pidgins and creoles. With regard to the pronoun *we*, the following observation is made in an empirical study by Wales:

> the general flexibility of personal pronouns, often over-lapping with one another, to express a wide range of references, with varying degrees of generalization, (ii) the tendency for even generalized references to be discourse-oriented, and speaker-oriented in particular, (iii) the frequent conflict, as a result, between surface form and ostensible reference on the one hand, and deeper reference, heavily biased towards egocentricity, on the other. (Wales 1980: 25)

What this implies, among other things, is that *we* is frequently used to address second persons in both singular and plural, as in:

we want to eat our food now	(e.g. nurse to patient)
we heard in our last lecture	(lecturer to students)

We certainly cannot be sure that *we* or its counterpart in other European lexifier languages was not used in this second-person function, particularly at a time when the directive function of the language was a dominant one. Consider Taylor's statement on first and second-person plural pronouns in some West Indian creoles:

> The pronouns of 1st and 2nd persons plural are both *nu* (or *n'*) in Haitian Creole, *unu* (*un* or *u*) in Sranan; and while French *nous* and Dutch *ons* offer plausible models for 1st plural, extension of meaning to 2nd plural cannot be regarded as 'gradual modification'. (Taylor 1963: 811)

However, in the light of my previous observations, we certainly cannot be confident that the non-distinction of pronouns was not already in the linguistic input to creolization. What is claimed to have been introduced from substratum languages, as a result of faulty learning or internal development, thus may have been in the input. It certainly should not come as a surprise that certain pragmatically governed regularities of lexifier languages eventually became grammaticalized in later pidgins and creoles.

Conclusions

We have now examined the most prominent theories of pidgin and creole origins, and must return to the question of their explanatory power. Disregarding questions of detail, such as the precise nature of the superstratum model, the formation as well as the subsequent development of pidgins and creoles is determined most strongly by the following three forces: universals of development; substratum influences; and superstratum influences. We have reason to believe that their respective influence is dependent on the developmental stage of a pidgin and creole as well as on a number of social factors. It is for this reason that any single-cause/factor explanation will not suffice, if we look at a pidgin or creole as occupying a stretch rather than a point in time. Single-cause theories also ignore the important possibility that there may be a conspiracy between the different forces. Most notably, one can expect combinations of:

1 superstratum and universal tendencies;
2 substratum and universal tendencies;
3 substratum and superstratum;
4 all three factors.

Such combinations can occur at all levels of grammar.

With regard to borrowed vocabulary, it is not sufficient to establish cognates; one must also analyse the possible sources of the various kinds of lexical information (cf. Fillmore 1971: 370–91). This point can be illustrated using the Tok Pisin item *bel* 'belly, pregnant, seat of emotions'. The phonological shape of this item can be related to both Tolai *bala* 'belly, seat of emotions' and English *belly*. It is strange that the Tok Pisin form does not have a CVCV structure; the reasons for this are not known at present.

The semantic information 'belly' can be traced to both English and Tolai, whereas the meaning 'seat of emotions' can be traced to Tolai and the semantics of numerous languages spoken in the area of New Guinea. The meaning 'pregnant' appears late in the development of Tok Pisin. One may be dealing with a universally motivated metaphorical expansion.

At the level of grammar, let us consider a recent claim by Dalphinis that the absence of a copula in West Indian creoles demonstrates their African roots:

> In the deletion (ø) of the 'copula', we again find extreme similarity between the West Indian Creole Languages and African Languages of West Africa. For example:
>
> | | |
> |---|---|
> | Jamaican Creole: | [im ø dred] – he *is* a Rasta |
> | St Lucian Patwa: | [i ø fu] – he *is* mad |
> | Yoruba: | [omi ø tutu] – the water *is* cold |
> | | [ejawɔmi ø atata] – my wife *is* beautiful |
> | Twi: | [o ø bɔdam] – he *is* mad |
> | | [insjo ø aw] – the water *is* cold |
> | | [eje ø fefefe/ejefe] – she *is* beautiful |
> | Central Ibo: | [wagnjim ø maramma] – my wife *is* beautiful |
> | | [mmiri ø ɔji] – the water *is* cold |
> | | [ɔ ø baraba] – he/she/it *is* rich |
>
> It is therefore not surprising that a literal word-to-word translation of many West African Languages would give close approximations to West Indian Creole Languages. (Dalphinis 1982: 10–11)

This explanation ignores the much more likely explanation of a conspiracy between universal processes, simplified input and substratum factors (cf. Ferguson 1971 for the former two factors). Where these factors coincide, the cognitive cost for those in the business of developing a pidgin or creole is least, and it is for this reason that pidginists and creolists should be on a constant look-out for such developmental conspiracies and the linguistic syncretisms resulting from them.

5

Linguistic Development of Pidgins and Creoles

> I think it can easily be argued that the fundamental problem for linguistic theory is to understand . . . how linguistic structures evolve, come into being and change into new (sub) systems and thereby to learn what the true nature of language is.
>
> (Bailey 1982: 25)

Introduction

Development is of supreme importance, as has been emphasized repeatedly in this book. Pidgins and creoles should be regarded as dynamically evolving and changing systems, not as states or a sequence of states. When it comes to applying such desiderata to real linguistic description, however, a number of problems are encountered. First and foremost, there is the almost total absence of systematic longitudinal studies for any span of the pidgin–creole continuum, and the consequent need to reconstruct non-documented or ill-documented aspects of language development from whatever data are to hand. Such reconstruction is usually based on the idea that language development is uniformitarian, that is, a steady development in one direction, rather than a sequence of discontinuous developments alternating between progressive and regressive phases.[1] The suspicion that traditional methods of linguistic reconstruction may be less than optimal for pidgins and creoles has been expressed by a number of scholars (for example, Dutton 1980; Hoenigswald 1971) and should constantly be kept in mind when reading this chapter. Second, to make the description of creole and pidgin development possible, a number of concessions have to be made. These include separating the dimensions of restructuring and development, in spite of the fact that actual developments are probably more realistically described as a product of these two (and possibly additional) factors. Finally, although I have attempted to do justice to inter-individual and intra-individual variability, none of my observations is based on controlled sampling and therefore they may not always be representative. All these limitations are unavoidable, given the enormous amount of data to be considered and the small number of researchers working in the field.

I am not convinced, as is Bickerton (1981), that there are any ideal paradigm cases of pidgins and creoles, and that a great deal of labour can be saved by simply considering those.[2] Although acknowledging the need for deductive theorizing in our field, I have chosen to offer mainly inductive generalizations on the basis of as extensive and representative a body of data as possible.

In outlining the development of pidgins and creoles, I will refer to the following key notions. *Structural expansion* is defined as those additions to a system of verbal communication that increase its referential or non-referential potential. It is roughly synonymous with the processes of grammaticalization and addition of lexical resources. Its counterpart, *reduction* in structure, or *impoverishment*, comprises those processes that lead to a decrease in the referential or non-referential potential of a language. *Simplification* means that certain areas of language are made more regular, in the sense that rules apply to a greater number of items or structures. The notion of simplification is a problematic one (see Mühlhäusler 1974; Meisel 1983), because we can determine local, but rarely global simplification of grammar, and also because it is not synonymous with naturalness.[3] It remains to be investigated how greater regularity contributes to greater learnability of pidgins. *Complication* means the opposite of simplification; that is, the loss of rule generality. Again, no obvious link with loss in naturalness of a language has been established. *Restructuring* means the use of different devices to achieve the same referential and non-referential effects. Note that these devices refer to lexical and grammatical properties of pidgins and creoles, but not to paralinguistic or pragmatic ones.

The last point takes us to another problem: the assumption that grammaticalization processes can be studied in isolation from pragmatic and cultural information. In the absence of sufficient information, this assumption will have to be taken as the basis for our present discussion. However, I shall attempt to point out areas where pragmatic considerations determine the direction of grammaticalization. The organization of this chapter is determined by the following parameters:

1 developments at separate developmental stages in the life of pidgins and creoles;
2 developments in different components of grammar.

The jargon stage

Jargons, as we have already said, are individual solutions to the problem of cross-linguistic communication and hence subject to individual strategies, the principal ones being lexicalization or holophrastic talking; pragmatic structuring; grammaticalization by transfer; and universals. In most documented cases, combinations of these strategies have been observed. Cultural and personality factors appear to determine which strategy is favoured. An interesting observation regarding holophrastic talking is found in Zöller (1891):

> There are three stages in penetrating foreign languages. The first and lowest stage which we in educated Europe hardly know, but which is observed more often than the second stage in communication between the white man and the members of the coloured races, merely comprises a more or less limited knowledge of the vocabulary. (Zöller 1891: 419; author's translation)

It seems that this strategy is limited to the very earliest period of interlingual contact and viable only in an extremely limited domain. A possible example is that of labour recruiting in the Pacific in the nineteenth century,[4] as exemplified in the following conversation reported by Ribbe:

> 'Me like boys' the white man says to the black man, 'plenty kaikai (food)'. 'No fight (corporal punishment)?' asks the black. 'Yes, plenty kaikai and no fight', the white replies. 'What you pay me?' the owner of a slave or a village chief asks. 'One fellow anikow (an axe)' the recruiter replies. (Ribbe 1903: 223; author's translation)

In this exchange, at least some of the utterances used by the indigenous speakers are probably remembered in toto. Candidates are *What you pay me?* in the above text and phrases such as *aidono* 'I do not know', *orait* 'it is all right', or *gutwan* 'this is good' in others. In another trade jargon, the Sino-Russian mixed language of Manchuria (Jabłońska 1969), Chinese *tuo-shao Ch'ien* 'what is the price' is reduced to *dôščen*.

The fact that rudimentary communication in terms of holophrastic and very basic grammar (mainly two-word utterances) also occurs nearer home was documented by Harding (1983), in her analysis of the language used between health visitors (H.V.) and mothers (M.) from Asian countries who now live in the Birmingham area. Examples of such conversations are:

H.V.: HUSBAND WORK↗
M.: yes
H.V.: FACTORY↗
M.: factory yes
H.V.: ALL DAY↗
M.: yes all day so:=
H.V.: SO YOU ON YOUR OWN↘
M.: yes
H.V.: BABY.ALL RIGHT↗
M.: all right

H.V.: MILK.ALL RIGHT/
M.: all right

Harding demonstrates the operation of numerous discourse structuring devices (such as the provision of the most likely answer in the above examples). Thus, although most of the linguistic norms of Standard English are replaced by a very different foreigner talk version, the majority of the conversational conventions are upheld. This suggests that one should look at the communicative effects of such jargons as well as their lexical and grammatical inventories. Thus particular attention has to be paid to Ferguson's (1977: 30 ff.) categories of 'clarification processes' and 'expressive and identification processes'. Without these, mechanical rule simplification and shedding or morphological complexities will not result in a communicatively efficient jargon.

The context-dependency of jargons has been known for a long time, as is illustrated in the following discussion of an Eskimo trade jargon:

> Take as an instance the jargon sentence Kĭm-mĭk ka'i-lĭ pi-cū'k-tū (see vocabulary for meaning of words). If it were in answer to 'Why are you whistling?' it would mean 'Because I want the dog [e.g., my dog, his dog, the dogs, your dogs] to come'. If it were in answer to 'Why do you want Jim?' it might mean 'Because I want him to bring a dog [his dog, my dog, etc.] to me.' If it were in answer to 'Why are you locking the door?' it might mean 'Because the dogs keep trying to get into the house.' If in answer to 'Why did Jim go to Fort Macpherson?' it might mean 'Because he wants to get dogs there' – and so on, world without end. It will therefore be understood that the translations given for the illustrative sentences in the body of the vocabulary are but a few among the many possible meanings of the word combinations used. (Stefánsson 1909: 221–2)

The contribution of pragmatic context is particularly easy to see in the areas of tense and iconic word order. Labov (1971a) has presented a well-argued scheme for the development of tense in pidgins. He points out that, in the initial stages, particularly those where no communal grammar exists, there is a very strong tendency to give the overall time reference paragraph-initially. The following passage of Hawaiian Pidgin English, spoken by Max, a native speaker of the Philippine language Ilocano, illustrates this:

> Well . . . in the Filippine, this now . . . you see, he die in three hours . . . and then he come back a--*live* again . . . Three hours die, after three hours, come back live, he talk--tell the story about.

This text also illustrates the second aspect, that narrative sequencing rules are iconic of the sequence of real events reported. It is assumed that this is the most natural strategy and therefore favoured. Thus English 'if' clauses, which can appear either initially or in second place, are typically rendered by juxtaposed sentences of the type:

Samoan Plantation Pidgin English:	
no mani, no kam	If I have no money I won't come
Hiri Trade Language (Kerema):	
Aie, na nava pene na navai. Rae imo.	Gee, I fish some I eat. Insides good 'If I could only eat some fish I'd feel a lot better'.
	(Dutton 1983b: 90)

In later stages of pidgin development, grammatical markers tend to be introduced, thus reducing the need for strict clause ordering.

Substratum influence appears most likely when only two languages are involved (secondary hybridization); when these two languages are related, thus inviting cross-linguistic identification; and when individuals are not concerned with correctness in the target language. Both Cocoliche, the Spanish–Italian jargon used by Italian migrants in Argentina (see Bauer 1975: 78–83; Whinnom 1971), and the Italian–Portuguese contact language of Brazil (cf. Hall 1966: 18) meet these requirements.

Cocoliche and congeners differ from other jargons in that they are not substantially simplified in lexicon and grammar (a consequence of the similarity of the contact languages and the strong social integration between their speakers), and that many of the transfer processes appear to have no communicative function. Compare the following Cocoliche examples from Whinnom (1971):

1 The treatment of grammatical number: the singular form *il pantalone* 'trousers' rather than Standard Italian plural is chosen, because of Spanish *el pantalon*;
2 Spanish gender is used with Italian nouns, as in *la latte* 'milk' and *la miele* 'honey' (in both cases instead of Standard Italian masculine).

As there are no social norms, and as individuals change their grammars with growing integration into the Spanish-speaking host community, one can only point to salient interference phenomena found with 'typical' migrants. It remains to be seen what insights can be gained from the study of such targeted interlanguages of closely related languages.

Substratum influence in makeshift jargons involving unrelated or distantly related languages appears to be more revealing for our purposes. We shall look briefly at the ways it is manifested at different levels of grammar.

Pronunciation has often been singled out as that area where substratum influences can make themselves felt most freely. However, in the case of jargons one must distinguish between departures from the lexifier language due to substratum influence in production; mishearing and other perceptual difficulties; and universal (natural) tendencies in pronunciation. Often, variant pronunciations are found in single texts, indicating that different strategies are used by the same speaker. The extent of such variation can be seen from statements relating to two South-East Asian varieties of jargon English: varieties spoken in Hong Kong and American Japanese Military Jargon. Regarding the phonology of the former, Luke observes:

> The phonetic values of segments show a great deal of variation from those which resemble the external norms of British and American English to those which show clear signs of influence from the Cantonese phonological system. 'Sorry', for instance, may be variably realized as [sɔri], [sɔwi], and sɔ:li:], and possibly some other shapes. (Luke 1983: 4)

Similar observations were made by Goodman about English–Japanese Jargon:

> A rather simplified but essentially accurate statement of the phonological process of EJ-Pidgin would be that it contained a nearly perfect set of diaphonic correspondences and a few diaphonic compromises. The English speaker using the Pidgin employed English phones almost entirely and occasionally modified them slightly in what he considered the direction of corresponding Japanese phones. The Japanese speaker of the Pidgin employed Japanese phones in the same way. Where the corresponding phones of the two languages exhibited a close phonetic similarity, little difficulty existed. But where corresponding phones were phonetically very dissimilar, both speakers seemed to learn quickly the correspondences. (Goodman 1967: 51)

Examples given include the changes in the pronunciation of 'baseball': It is:

> an English loan-word completely asimilated in Japanese; phonemically, its diamorphs are English/beysbol/ and Japanese/besuboru/. In EJ-Pidgin, either of these is an acceptable and comprehensible pronunciation, and the two words illustrate certain basic diaphonic correspondences. English /r,l/ correspond to Japanese /ř/ which is a retroflex flap vibrant with occasional lateral release. English /ey/ corresponds to Japanese /e/. (Goodman ibid.)

Both statements are reduced in their theoretical importance by the application of a phonemic basis for cross-linguistic comparison. Although it is obvious that jargon-speaking individuals develop strategies for identifying sounds across systems, we do not know whether this is done for phonological reasons or for the more likely (though difficult to define) reasons of phonetic similarity. The view that jargon pronunciation simply constitutes the most simple or natural way of pronouncing another language certainly is not borne out, for instance, by data from Chinook Jargon, where Thomason (1981) observes that we have considerable evidence pointing to the fact that English speakers of the jargon recognized its complex phonology, including glottalized stops and dorsal fricatives, and in at least some cases made a considerable effort to learn them. In 1882, one contemporary observer, Gill (quoted from Thomason 1981: 311), explicitly states that 'The pronunciation of these words can only be thoroughly learned by conversation with the Indians, whose deep gutturals and long-drawn vowels are beyond the power of our alphabet to represent.' At the same time, some English speakers considerably distorted the pronunciation of Chinook Jargon forms. It appears that mutual understanding between whites and Indians could be attained, however, once the latter had become accustomed to the mispronunciations of the former, a situation comparable to many other jargon contexts.

Reliable recordings of jargon texts are hard to come by, but the following text, written by a Rarotonagan missionary in the New Hebrides in the 1880s, can be taken to be a good representation of the processes under discussion here.

> Misi kamesi Arelu Jou no kamu ruki mi Mi no ruki iou Jou ruku Mai Poti i ko Mae tete Vakaromala mi raiki i tiripi Ausi parogi iou i rukauti Mai Poti mi nomea kaikai mi angikele nau Poti mani Mae i kivi iou Jamu Vari koti iou kivi tamu te pako paraogi mi i penesi nomoa te Pako Oleraiti
>
> Ta. Mataso.
>
> Mr Comins, (How) are you? You no come look me; me no look you; you look my boat, he go Mae today. Vakaromala me like he sleep house belong you, he look out my boat. Me no more kaikai, me hungry now, boat man Mae he give you yam very good; you give some tobacco belong me [dative], he finish, no more tobacco. All right.
>
> Ta, Mataso.
>
> (From Schuchardt 1889a; 1979 edn: 10–11)

Note the following points. First, substratum influence is most likely in cluster simplification by means of epenthetic vowels, the 'confusion' of l and r, and the avoidance of final consonants. Second, perceptual difficulties are reflected in the loss of unstressed syllables, as in *arelu* for 'how are you'.[5] Finally universal factors, or more likely a conspiracy between universal factors and substratum influence, are evidenced by the predilection for CVCV word structure and phonological reduplications, such as *tete* for today.

In all the examples discussed so far, the simplification of word structure by means of vowel epenthesis has figured prominently, and this phenomenon has long been regarded as an excellent candidate for substratum language influence. Thus, speaking of the early Beach-la-Mar varieties of New Caledonia in 1883, Schuchardt writes:

> I will not go into the phonetic details, but the following forms are readily explicable as derivations from Polynesian or Melanesian phonological

> structure: *esterrong* = *strong*, *esseppoon* = *spoon*, *essaucepen* = *saucepan*, *pellate* = *plate*, *coverra* = *cover*, *millit* = *milk*, *bock-kiss* = *box*, etc. It is a well-known fact that the New Zealanders particularly reshape foreign words beyond recognition. (Schuchardt 1979 edn: 24)

However, these may be only partial similarities. Comparisons of English loan-words in Tok Pisin's principal substratum language Tolai with their cognates in early Tok Pisin reveals some surprising differences. The following is adapted from Mosel (1980: 19)

Tolai	*Early Tok Pisin*	*English source*
palet	plet, pelet	plate
tarautete	trausis, tarausis	trousers
galat	glas, galas	glass
tito	stua, situa	store
bulititon	buluston, bluston	bluestone
torong	sitirong, strong	strong
patiket	bisket	biscuit

Even more surprising is the absence of cluster simplification by means of epenthetic vowels in Pitcairnese. Although in its substratum language, Tahitian, consonant groups do not occur, in Pitcairnese, 'there is no aversion to – or rather an abundance of consonant groups' (Ross 1964: 143). Ross expected to find forms such as Tahitian *totoni* (> stocking), but found none. Does this mean that vowel epenthesis was not employed in the English–Tahitian jargon which preceded Pitcairnese?

Epenthesis has been associated with increasing the naturalness and simplicity (preferably both) of a jargon. However, lexical evidence from languages that developed out of earlier jargons, particularly a survey of the Surinam creoles by Smith (1977a), suggests that highly complex rules are needed to convert, for example, English lexical items into the corresponding epenthesized items of Sranan. They may indeed reflect different strategies by different groups of speakers, and can thus be seen as a continuation of the unsystematic processes of language simplification and adaption of the jargon phase. Most recently, vowel epenthesis has received renewed interest within the comparison of first-language acquisition and pidginization, in connection with the hypothesis that adults begin to develop their second language in the same way that they developed their first. This view is attacked by Aitchison (1983), who claims that, although cluster reduction is found in both child language and early pidgins, the former achieve this by means of consonant deletion, the latter by means of epenthesis. Aitchison's view is supported mainly with evidence from well-established stable pidgins, which moreover have remained in contact with their lexifier language. For the earlier jargon stage, it can be observed that next to forms with epenthetic vowels, which are easier to perceive for speakers of the target language and therefore reinforced, one finds some evidence of language-learning strategies that parallel those of young children. Thus, in the Sino-Russian jargon of Manchuria, 'when Chinese pronounce words of foreign origin, the consonant clusters found in such words are eliminated either by means of inserting a vocalic element between the consonants or through the simplification of the consonant cluster itself' (Jabłońska 1969: 139). Again, in a number of early texts in Melanesian varieties of Pidgin English, examples of cluster simplification by means of omission such as *tesen* 'station', *tima* 'steamer' or *sos* 'church' are widely found. Very much the same point can be made by comparing Boni, one of the eastern maroon creoles of Surinam, with Sranan. Whereas the former contains numerous examples of cluster simplification by means of omission, the latter, probably because of longer contact with English, appears to prefer the retention of clusters, or epenthesis. Compare the following words (data culled from Smith 1977a):

Boni	*Sranan*	*English*
toosi	trusu	thrust
dingi	dringi	drink
feele	frede	afraid
koosi	krosi	clothes
beeni	breni	blind
goon	gron	ground

There are, without doubt, many more such cases of natural universal phonological strategies. The identification of cognates after such processes have occurred constitutes a considerable problem, however. Let me illustrate this with the example of Tok Pisin *abus* 'animal, edible meat'. For this form, until recently, no etymology had been established. However, on hearing my own daughter refer to her soft toy animals as *abus*, it occurred to me that the Tok Pisin form had probably been derived from the English one by means of a number of straightforward phonological processes, including:

1 the identification, because of perceptual similarity, of (l) and (u), *animals* thus becoming *animus*;
2 the loss of the least-stressed syllable, resulting in *amus*;
3 the replacement of a nasal consonant by a homorganic stop, resulting in *abus*.

The form *abus* probably survived because it looked like an item borrowed from a native vernacular. Had it looked more like English, its chances of survival would have been diminutive.

In this survey of jargon grammar, most attention has been paid to phonology. The syntax of such languages is typically governed by pragmatic principles and some transfer of substratum grammar. The widespread absence of syntactic rules and an almost total lack of morphology account for the frequently used attribute 'grammarless' when referring to such languages. Jargons certainly afford interesting insights into the role of syntactic patterns in the communicative process.[6] This leaves us to investigate the lexical and semantic properties of jargons. Much has been written about the composition of jargon lexicons. One view is that there appear random macaronic mixtures of two or more languages; a second view holds that the lexicon of a jargon is typically derived from one language only. Actual empirical support can be found for both views, although the latter is much better documented.

Genuinely mixed lexicons appear to be restricted to the very first stages of contact between two partners, in particular situations where neither is socially dominant. In 1883, Schuchardt (1979 edn: 19) referred to trade languages on New Caledonia and other Pacific Islands consisting of 'a mixture of New Caledonian, Chinese, English, and French words, e.g.: *tayos lookout belong faya* "friend, look out for the fire", *bon jour, tayo* "good day, friend"'. Sino-Russian of Manchuria is said to consist of approximately two-thirds Russian and one-third Chinese lexical material, and in Russonorsk we find considerable lexical variation. Neumann (1965: 222) reports that both Russian *drugoi* and Norwegian *ander* can be used for the ordinal number 'second', and that for 'good' we find two Norwegian-derived (*g* and *bra*) and two Russian-derived (*dobr* and *xoros*) forms. More recently, Clark (1979: 30 ff.) presented a long list of examples from mixed jargons found in the Pacific in the early years of European contact. They include:

Ah, karhowree sabbee lee-lee, ena arva tee maitai!	'Ah, the white man knows little, this *ti*-liquor is good!'
homi pickeninnee wow	'Give the child a nail'
Tungata tihi no good	'A thief is not good'
me tickee tickee	'I saw it'
etiketica no henerecka	'A chief never deceives'
me, tamaree . . . plenty kanaka Martair	'When I was a boy, there were many people at Ma'atea'
Why you no like to stay? Plenty moee-moee – plenty ki-ki – plenty whihenee – Oh, very good place Typee.	
Captain, he come to New Zealand, he come ashore, and *tihi* all my potatoes . . .	

Mixture was also found within individual lexical items, particularly in the form of lexical encounters of hybrids. Thus, in the ad-hoc jargons developed in the dealings of American soldiers with German natives in West Germany after the Second World War, a clear preference for words that can be identified across both languages is exhibited (Amsler 1952). Examples include:

item	*form*
gest	English guest, German Gaest(e) (plural)
wine	English wine, German Wein
beer	English beer, German Bier
drink	English drink, German Trink

It appears that the usefulness of such mixed jargons is very limited when one of the partners is mobile, and after a while such mixed jargons become replaced by varieties based on the dominant language, with the occasional substratum word thrown in. In fact, it is in the lexicon that stable conventions begin to develop first. To take Jargon English as an example, we can distinguish different regional conventions, following Clark (1979):

1 *Worldwide lexical conventions*: for example, *along* (comitative), *been* (past anterior), *by and by* (future, posterior), *him* (third-person pronoun), *piccaninny* (child), *plenty* (plural, quantifier), *savvy* (to know), *suppose* (if), *too much* (much, many);
2 *Sino-Pacific features*: *allsame* (like, as if), *catch* (to get), *fellow* (adjective marker or noun classifier), *got* (have), and *stop* (to be located, exist).

Such lexical features were spread by the highly mobile traders, whalers and sandalwood cutters. In addition, members of this group used whatever other words of their own language appeared useful for establishing contact with new groups. In the case of multiple contacts of one group with many others, then the most mobile language naturally becomes the lexifier language of a jargon.[7]

In the case of trade jargon in border areas between groups that are not mobile, the change-over from a lexically mixed to a more lexically uniform language appears to be associated with factors such as the relative cultural or political dominance, and in whose territory the language is predominantly used. To illustrate the former factor, we find, for instance, that in the Russian–Chinese contact language of Kjachta (described by Neumann 1966), the lexicon was almost exclusively composed of Russian items, or that the military pidgins developed between American troops and the Japanese (see Goodman 1967) or the Thai (see Gebhard 1979) are lexically entirely English.

The second factor is particularly strong in the so-called tourist jargons. Thus the rudimentary language developed between German tourists and Turkish peasants described by Hinnenkamp (1982, 1983), the medieval pilgrim's jargon spoken in Rome, and the many individual jargons spoken by early missionaries and travellers in exotic countries typically exhibit the lexical dominance of the language spoken by the host community. With modern mass tourism and cocacolonization of the Third World, this picture has changed somewhat and English- and German-derived jargons are found in many places.

Often things are not as simple as just outlined. There are many documented cases of a number of different jargons coexisting in a very small geographic area. Thus, in Fiji, English-based, Fijian-based and Hindi-based rudimentary jargons coexisted for a considerable time (see Siegel 1982), as did Motu-based and English-based jargons in Papua (see Dutton forthcoming).

Turning to the size of the jargon lexicon, we find a very low type–token ratio and also a very low number of lexical types. Thus Dutton estimates that for the two Hiri trade languages, a lexicon with about 300 entries appeared to have been sufficient (1983b: 94), but he points out that individual variation had to be expected. The dominance of individual strategies and the non-permanence of a jargon's lexicon outside its small core are also emphasized in the following observations on Japanese Jargon English (Goodman 1967: 54):

> it seems that the lexicon of a reasonably well established pidgin is particularly characterized by its capability for temporary extension. Americans and Japanese, both proficient in the pidgin to the extent of possessing a sense of diaphonic correspondences and a basic grasp of vocabulary and syntax, time and again stipulated new vocabulary items according to the needs of very specific situations. These items did not remain in the permanent lexicon.

The difficulties of accurately determining the size of the lexical inventory are illustrated by the case of Jargon English in the Pacific. All observers appear to agree that, compared with the lexical resources of its principal lexifier language, the inventory of lexical bases found in Jargon English was diminutive. Churchill's remarks (1911: 12) that 'we find the irreducible minimum which is felt to underlie all the refinements of vocabulary' may be regarded as representative of many similar statements. Estimates as to the precise number of lexical items have been made only for the early stabilized Pacific pidgins, although they may be taken as an indication of the number of lexical bases found in Jargon English as spoken by the Pacific Islanders. The lowest estimates are those for the New Hebrides. Speiser (1913: 9) claims that the 'mutilated English' spoken there contained hardly more than fifty words, although Jacomb (1914: 91) puts the figure at 'no more than a hundred words'. Genthe (1908: 10) suggests around 300 lexical bases for Samoan Plantation Pidgin spoken in the 1880s, whereas Churchill (1911), 'who unfortunately drew his vocabulary from various printed sources instead of setting down the words he had actually heard used', gives about 300 words (Reinecke 1937: 764).

The very small lexical inventory should be seen in conjunction with the very general meaning of most lexical items, a consequence of the context-dependency of jargons, and their being governed by pragmatic rather than grammatical rules. The generality is expressed, more than anything else, by the use of the same form in numerous grammatical classes and functions. This freedom from lexical specification, as Silverstein (1972a: 381) refers to it in his discussion of Chinook Jargon, 'can increase the "information" of each unit. A great part of the lexicon of Chinook Jargon is in fact made up of "words" both semantically and grammatically ambiguous, in a far less systematic way than e.g. English, with its zero deverbative and denominative formations.' The tendency towards categorial multifunctionality is also encountered in all the jargons I have examined to date. A long list of relevant quotations is given in Mühlhäusler (1974: 104 ff.).

Next to generality of meaning, the small set of lexical items in jargons is recycled to serve a wider field of reference by means of rudimentary circumlo-

Table 5.1 Examples of circumlocutions from different jargons

Jargon	*Circumlocution*	*Gloss*	*Meaning*
Chinese–Russian jargon of Kjachta	Uma konecajlo	sanity finished	mad
	ruka sapogi	hand boots	gloves
	jazyka meda	tongue honey	skilful orator
Chinese Pidgin English[a] (Ehlerding 1936)	big fellow quack quack makkee go in water		goose
	top-side-piecee-heaven-pidgin-man		bishop
	big-fellow master-lady makee fightum black boxee, black boxee makee cly		piano
Beach-la-Mar (nineteenth-century Pacific Jargon English) (Churchill 1911)	suppose me kitch him grass he die		to pick flowers ('kitch' from catch)
	coconut belong him grass not stop		he is bald (there is no grass on his coconut)
	big fellow master too much		governor
	he all bone got no meat		he is thin
	pickanninny stop along him fellow		egg (little one is inside)

cution. Because of the absence of fixed rules of syntax and word formation, such circumlocutions are often very unstable. Some examples from different jargons are given in table 5.1. Such examples of the linguistic nature of jargons underline their unsatisfactory character as a means of verbal communication. In the absence of stable shared codes between interlocutors, messages frequently got distorted and one can only guess at the degree of understanding found in jargon situations. It certainly cannot be assumed that non-verbal aids employed at the same time eliminated all ambiguities.

Jargons are unstable both linguistically and socially. Moreover, they are not transmitted in any consistent way from speaker to speaker or generation to generation, but invented in an ad-hoc fashion. I hesitate to use Hymes's (1971: 70) term 'pre-pidgin continuum', since what preceded the crystallization of pidgins is by no means a continuous process of grammaticalization and conventionalization. The tertiary hybrids that emerge from the encounter of secondary jargons are qualitatively different languages.

Stabilization

Stabilization of a pidgin is the result of the development of socially accepted language norms. Such norms develop when none of the languages in contact serves as a target language. Whinnom suggests (1971: 91–115) that stable pidgins are unlikely ever to have arisen out of a simple bilingual situation. Instead, they owe their stability to the fact that a jargon (secondary hybrid) is used as a medium of intercommunication by people who are not speakers of the original lexifier language.

The social conditions under which pidgins acquire stability have already been outlined in chapters 3 and 4; we shall now concentrate on their linguistic/structural properties. Generally speaking, stabilization implies the gradual replacement of free variation and inconsistencies by more regular syntactic and lexical structures. In the former area, a pragmatic mode of speaking begins to give way to a grammatical one, whereas in the latter lexical dependency on outside resources is supplemented with internal means of lexical expansion. Most important, the new grammatical devices are independent of a speaker's first language or other individual language-learning strategies. Thus a stable pidgin acquires a stable language community and social norms to which its members conform. Grammatical stability develops gradually and is achieved at different times in different parts of grammar.

As regards the linguistic forces shaping stabilization, language-independent solutions appear to be favoured. This is understandable, because the lexifier language tends to be socially or otherwise remote, and the very fact that stabilization occurs in a highly heterogeneous linguistic environment prevents the adoption of solutions characteristic of any single group of speakers. Put differently, in the absence of sufficient overlap and agreement among the speakers of the various jargons in such a situation, universally motivated solutions need to be adopted. The two facts, that there is a qualitative difference between an earlier and a later stage in the development of a language, and that there is a prevalence of universals in the later stage, would seem to be sufficient reason for studying this process in great detail. In reality, very little has been done, and some pidginists/creolists have not regarded the distinction between jargon and stable pidgin as one deserving great attention: the two stages are often lumped together and compared jointly with creoles, which develop at a later stage.

The phonological component

Of all parts of grammar, those of pronunciation and phonology remain the least stable in stabilized pidgins. The different processes of restructuring the superstratum and substratum systems are carried out only to the extent that communication is not impaired. As long as there is sufficient structural and contextual redundancy, pronunciation and phonological rules can differ quite significantly from group to group and speaker to speaker. Within such a general setting, I have tried to isolate those properties that are most salient in stabilized pidgins. They include the small inventory of sounds, the effect of phonological distinctions in substratum languages, tonal distinctions, phonotactics, derivational shallowness and tempo.

Small inventory of sounds.[8] The small size of the sound inventory of pidgins, particularly when compared to their lexifier and substratum languages, is caused by the elimination of many marked sounds and also by the reduction in the number of phonological contrasts. The former process typically involves the grouping together of a number of marked sounds in the lexifier language under a single sound in the pidgin. For instance, in the Pidgin Zulu (Fanakalo) used between Zulus and speakers of non-Bantu languages, the three Zulu clicks are usually replaced by [k]. In the various Pidgin Germans I have studied, there is a very strong tendency to replace [ç] and [x] by [k], and in Pidgin French, the rounded high front vowel [y] is replaced by its unrounded counterpart [i].

Typical of the relationship between English and various Pidgin Englishes is the realization of [s], [ʃ] and [tʃ] as [s], as in Tok Pisin *san* 'sun', *sem* 'shame' and *sok* 'chalk', or the replacement of [ð] and [θ] by [d] and [t] respectively, as in Cameroonian Pidgin English *den oto* 'their car' (> *them*). These observations pertain to a widely scattered set of pidgins, many of them apparently unrelated. Thus, in a survey of African Pidgins, Heine (1975: 3) observed:

1 The number of vowels tends to be reduced to five. None of these pidgins, however, has less than five vowel phonemes.
2 Distinctive vowel length tends to be lost.

3 Palato-alveolar fricatives tend to be replaced by alveolar fricatives.
4 Voiced fricatives tend to be replaced by voiceless fricatives.

This general picture is also confirmed by data from indigenous pidgins spoken in the Pacific. Chinook Jargon, however, appears to provide counterevidence (discussed by Thomason 1981: 305) against the claim that pidgins exhibit maximally unmarked phonologies. Different groups of speakers appear to have proceeded different distances along the path of 'naturalization', and variability persists even after many years of use.

Effect of phonological distinctions in substratum languages. The analysis of the phonologies of stabilized pidgins soon disperses the notion that they are simply the lowest common denominator of the phonologies of the languages in contact, judging from the small body of comparative work available (in particular, a recent study on Tolai and Tok Pisin by Mosel 1980). During the very first years of Tolai involvement with Tok Pisin, substratum influence was found. Commenting on the Blanche Bay Tolai, Schnee remarks:

> One and the same Pidgin-English word is pronounced quite differently by natives from different regions, depending on whether the consonants of a word are found in the kanaka language in question or not. In the dialects spoken in the Blanche Bay (near Herbertshöhe) the consonants c, f, h, s, z as well as the English th are missing. Since, in addition, most of the natives find it difficult to pronounce consonants in sequence, many words are mutilated to a degree that they become unintelligible. (Schnee 1904: 304; my translation)

A few years later, however, social norms for pronunciation had developed in Tok Pisin that overruled substratum influence.

Mosel (1980: 24) mentions that 'the phoneme /s/ which is absent in Tolai, has been introduced as a separate phoneme in the Tolais' pidgin. Secondly, Tok Pisin exhibits the distinction between lax and tense vowels which is absent in Patpatar Tolai languages.'

The fact that both production and perception of Tok Pisin sounds cannot be explained just in terms of substratum influence is also borne out in a more recent investigation of the Tok Pisin spoken by native speakers of Usarufa (Bee 1972).

Tonal distinctions. In his survey of African pidgins and creoles, Berry writes:

> Peculiar to the African pidgins would appear to be the simplification of tonal systems. The extreme of simplification in this respect (which only occurs perhaps when large numbers of non-Africans have had a significant role in the formation of the pidgins) is the replacement of tone systems by one of stress. (Berry 1971: 527)

Implicit in the above quotation is the view that tone will survive whenever the majority of users are speakers of a tone language. Thus Manessy (1977: 133 f.) mentions that in Sango the three punctual tones of Nghandi-Sango-Nyakoma have been preserved, since this language is used virtually exclusively by speakers of tone languages. Confirmatory evidence for this principle[9] comes also from Vietnamese Pidgin French (Liem 1979), where five tones are encountered.

Liem does not mention whether or not native speakers of French have also adopted these conventions. Presumably, they emerge only among speakers of different local languages. The situation is probably comparable to Chinese Pidgin English where, among native speakers of European languages, no tonal distinctions are made.

Phonotactics. There appears to be a strong tendency in most stable pidgins, whatever their sub- and supertrata languages and whatever their jargon predecessors, to favour open syllables and words of the canonical shape CVCV. Double obstruent clusters, in particular, are rarely encountered. The two morpheme structure rules postulated by Mary Johnson (1974) for English Proto-Creole may well be 'universals of pidginization' (Johnson 1974: 128).[10]

There is a second tendency, independently observed by a number of researchers, that to have a bisyllabic word structure. Thus, Heine writes:

> African-based pidgins tend to have a syllable-per-word ratio of around 2.00. Fanagalo, for example, has been found to have a ratio of 2.01 whereas Zulu, its source language, has 3.09. Kenya Pidgin Swahili has a ratio of 2.32 as opposed to 3.01 of Standard Swahili. In the texts examined, 53.0 per cent of the Fanagalo words and 53.6 per cent of the Kenya Pidgin Swahili words are bisyllabic whereas the percentages of bisyllabic words in Zulu and Standard Swahili are 27.7 and 30.4, respectively. (Heine 1975: 4–5)

I have made similar observations for Tok Pisin (see Mühlhäusler 1979). The restriction on word length is one of the main reasons why word-formation processes such as compounding and derivation are relatively rare in early stabilized pidgins.

Derivational shallowness. Although stable pidgins exhibit a great deal of free variation in their pronunciation, conditioned variation and phonological rules are rare. We can explain this by referring to the two principal causes for phonological rules in language:

1 they reflect language change and diversification over time;
2 they reflect strategies for the optimalization of production (sometimes referred to as 'natural' phonological processes).

Because of the relatively shallow time depth, time-related linguistic changes (such as emerge in transmission from one generation to another) do not play a major role. Their role is further diminished by speakers strongly favouring strategies optimalizing perception, aiming at the invariance of linguistic forms and a one-to-one relationship between meaning and form.

> In fact, it seems a useful working hypothesis, doubtless overstated, that phonology in pidgin languages consists only in a set of systematic phonemes which provide underlying representations that are the same as their surface representations. There are no phonological rules that accomplish deep alternations such as those in *good*, *better*, *best*, or the less deep alternations such as those between the first vowels in *nation, national*; that is, there are no such alternations to be accounted for. (Kay and Sankoff 1974: 62)

One should remember, however, that pidgin speakers have the ability to communicate across varieties, which probably involves some structured phonological rules.[11] In sum, then, the phonological systems of pidgins exhibit strong tendencies towards simplification and increase in naturalness, the principle of one form, one meaning being dominant. Ease of decoding is also promoted by one last factor to be mentioned here, the tempo at which pidgin discourse proceeds.

Tempo. Related to the absence of phonological rules is the matter of tempo. An interesting case study involving the comparison of a vernacular (Buang) and a pidgin (Tok Pisin) is that by Labov (1971a: 24 ff.). Using Sankoff's field data, he established some significant differences between fluent Buang and fluent Tok Pisin.

In the following text involving language shift, the seven Tok Pisin lexical words took as long to articulate as the preceding eleven Buang phonological ones:

> Ngàu ti ˆngmndó, bái ol ˆi kòt strét lòng ˆyú.
> 'You're the only one sitting down, they'll take you straight to court'.

At present, comparative material on this point is not available, but one can expect to find that pidgins are generally articulated at a slower rate of delivery than vernaculars.

Generally speaking, it would seem that the more basic a pidgin, the more important is its decodability and the more likely its speakers will resort to strategies that allow for the maximum amount of naturalness of encoding, without affecting the more important need for ease of decoding. Wherever there is conflict between the former and the latter, considerations of decodability will carry the day.

Inflectional morphology

> One feature which is virtually universal to these languages generally classified as pidgins and creoles is the drastic reduction of morphological complexity and irregularity.
> (Goodman 1971: 253)

The claim of universality of this phenomenon is supported by evidence from many often unrelated pidgins. A few quotations will illustrate how widespread the phenomenon is:

> That inflection is the commonest casualty in the contact situation seems true of both European and African pidgins. The massive reduction of the Bantu nominal prefix system in Fanagalo and other indigenous African pidgins parallels the less striking losses of gender, case and number distinctions in European pidgins. (Berry 1971: 527)

On Pidgin Sango of the Central African Republic, Berry writes: 'Pidgin Sango can best be described as a dialect of vernacular Sango, simplified by the loss of most of its morphology' (ibid.: 521). Reinecke (1971: 51), on Vietnamese Pidgin French, states that 'Except for a few isolated forms standard French inflection has been dropped and has not been replaced by new formations as in many creole dialects.' Further examples, as well as some critical remarks on this phenomenon, are given by Samarin (1971: 125 ff).

The loss of inflectional morphology can be accounted for by two factors. First and foremost is the principle of ease of decoding, or one form = one meaning. Inflectional complexities such as are found in the lexifier languages of many pidgins would make them virtually unlearnable in the situational context they are acquired. Some simplifications of inflections may have been present in the model given to pidgin speakers; one consistent property of foreigner talk registers is the reduction of inflectional variants.[12] A second factor is the relatively low level of grammaticalization in early stabilized pidgins. In particular, grammatical categories peripheral to a message tend to disappear: tense, number and aspect are typical victims. Where these categories are expressed, this is usually done by separate free forms rather than affixes.

The principal functions of inflectional morphology across languages are:

1 to signal relationships between words in utterances;
2 to add 'accidental' information such as tense, case, number, etc. to words;
3 to signal word-class membership.

Are such functions necessary in the pidgin language? As regards the first function, word-order conventions typically take order from morphological signalling. Additional morphological encoding thus would increase the linguistic complexity of a pidgin, reducing its learnability.

A second reason for the absence of morphological signalling of grammatical relationships is that pidgins are only weakly grammaticalized in their early stages of development. Instead, syntactic relationships are derived from pragmatics. As fixed grammatical relations are rare, one cannot expect a significant degree of morphological encoding of such relations.

As regards the second function, in pidgins the traditional grammatical categories (accidents) are typically signalled by free forms such as paragraph or sentence-initial adverbials for tense and aspect. Affixes thus would merely express redundantly what is already expressed by means of free adverbials and again increase complexity.

As regards the third function, most observers seem to agree that there is little fixity of word classes and, in view of the ease with which words can be functionally shifted from one environment to another, overt marking of grammatical (rather than pragmatic) class membership does not appear to increase the communicative efficiency of the language. There are, however, some exceptions to this general principle. Nouns that can be agents are considerably less susceptible to categorial shift. They are also much more likely to become morphologically signalled, as can be seen from the presence of special affix-like agent classifiers in a number of pidgins, for example, *tauna* 'person' in Hiri Motu or reflexes of 'man' or 'fellow' in various pidgin Englishes. Thus Hall (1966: 109–10) observes that in pre-twentieth-century Chinese Pidgin English *-fele* was suffixed to numerals with animate nouns. Subsequently, the marker *-pisi* (from English 'piece') was generalized from inanimates to both animates and inanimates. Apart from numbers, *-pisi* also appears to have been attached to some other prenominal determiners.

The use of *-fellow* as a word accompanying nouns may have spread to the Pacific. However, no documented early texts exactly parallel the Chinese Pidgin model and there is very considerable variation from place to place. In Pacific Jargon English, this element was found variably in a number of positions in the surface structure of sentences, such as following nouns, preceding nouns and following adjectives. It was found with both animate (preferably) and inanimate nouns, as examples of the type *fellow belong open bottle* ('corkscrew') demonstrate. English speakers continued to use this item in the meaning 'fellow' and its metaphorical extension 'thing'. With indigenous speakers, however, a gradual reinterpretation can be observed, leading to *fellow* becoming an affix marking the word-class 'attributive adjective'. The stabilization of such a convention took a considerable time,[13] and during the stabilization period a number of interpretations emerged, only to be discarded later. Ongoing stabilization can be observed in Samoan Plantation Pidgin English, data for which are given by Mühlhäusler (1978b). In this pidgin, we find a great degree of variability in the conventions underlying the use of *-pela/-fela*. However, once Samoan Plantation Pidgin had been transported back to New Guinea by returning labourers, stabilization took place. In Tok Pisin, as recorded after 1900,[14] the use of *-fela/-pela* is restricted to two environments:

1 As a marker of monosyllabic attributive adjectives as in:

tupela lapun	'two old men'
smolpela dokta	'the little doctor, medical orderly'
gutpela kaikai	'good food';

2 As a marker of plurality with the first and second-person pronoun *mipela* 'we' (exclusive) and *yupela* 'you' (plural). The form *empela* 'they' is found in a very small number of sources, but is generally replaced with the *em ol* plural inherited from Samoan Plantation Pidgin.

The solution encountered in Tok Pisin differs from that found in related Melanesian pidgins such as Solomon Islands Pidgin and that of Pidgin Englishes further afield. The development of firm conventions for the use of *-pela* is seen best as a sequence of reinterpretations and restructurings of earlier variable material. English speakers, it appears, were important providers for its grammar at an early stage. Local languages, in particular Tok Pisin's principal substratum language Tolai, appear to have been of no influence. Mosel (1980: 63) categorically states: 'the use of the suffix *-pela* does not go back to Tolai substratum influence'. The case of *-pela* further illustrates the importance of reanalysis as a factor in the grammatical development of pidgins.

A last category which is widely signalled in pidgins is the distinction between transitive and intransitive verbs.[15] Signalling transitive verbs by means of an affixed *-m*, *-im* or *-it* appears to have developed independently in a large number of English-derived pidgins.[16] As in the case of *-pela*, fixed conventions emerge after much fluctuation in earlier stages. The distinction between transitive and intransitive verbs is also signalled in several Romance pidgins as well as in some 'indigenous' ones. A comparative longitudinal study of this phenomenon would seem to be an urgent priority, given the interest of scholars in acquisition studies and theoretical linguistics.

To sum up, the absence of morphology can be seen as the result of promoting greater ease of decoding, simplification of the target (lexifier) language and impoverishment. It also relates to the low level of grammaticalization found in early stabilized pidgins. Yet another factor is the wider problem of borrowing inflectional morphology; because inflections tend to be weakly stressed, they are often filtered out or ignored during borrowing.

Pidgins, as we have seen, can develop inflectional morphology again. It appears that the marking of grammatical word classes is one of the first functions of emerging morphological conventions. As pidgins develop further, many other categories can be added, as will be demonstrated below.

Syntax

The functions of inflectional morphology and syntax (word order) are seen by many linguists to be complementary: what is expressed by word order in one language may be expressed by inflections in the next. This view has led many pidginists to the belief that the scarcity of inflectional morphology in pidgins is compensated for by firm-word order conventions and other syntactic devices.

In real spoken pidgins, the alleged fixity of word order is much less in evidence, and the loss of information resulting from word-order fluctuations is made up by pragmatic and textual information. Nevertheless, when compared with their source languages, pidgins tend to have a considerably reduced number of basic utterance structures. Let us now consider some of the syntactic properties that have figured prominently in recent discussion of pidgin universals.

SVO word order. Linguists tend to distinguish between sequence of surface elements and order at deeper levels of syntactic patterning. In most languages, transformational processes of deletion, addition and permutation are seen as accounting for the difference between sequence and order. In pidgins, where transformations are rare, a much more direct link between the two levels is occasionally postulated and the most basic word order is identified as SVO. It is certainly remarkable how widespread this SVO word order is in apparently quite unrelated pidgins. Heine (1975: 9), for instance, remarks:

> In most Bantu languages, the object pronoun precedes the verb whereas all known Bantu pidgins have the opposite order. Thus, Standard Swahili
>
> *ni-ta-m-piga* 'I shall hit him.'
> (I-Future-him-hit)
> becomes in Kenya Pidgin Swahili *mimi na-piga yeye*
> (I-Aorist-hit he)

For Pidgin Fijian, Siegel (1983b: 11) notes that the variable word order of Standard Fijian, with its alleged preference for VSO, is reduced to a single SVO order in Pidgin Fijian. In contrast to Turkish, where the direct object precedes the verb, it is found after the verb in the pidginized Turkish described by Hinnenkamp (1983: 6). A clear predilection for SVO order is also observed in all pidgin Englishes I have had the opportunity to study.

A particularly interesting case is that of Chinook Jargon. Thomason writes:

> When we turn to the syntax we find at once a consistent feature in all the Indian sources that is hard to account for unless we assume the existence of a grammatical norm for CJ. This is the regular SVO sentential word order pattern, which, as was mentioned above, is not found as a statistically dominant word order in any Indian languages in the Northwest.

> Many of the languages, like Chinook, have SV word order as a stylistic possibility, but the dominant, basic word order in most of the languages is VSO. (Thomason 1981: 333)

However, in spite of the wide distribution of SVO word order, there are a number of counterexamples in 'indigenous' pidgins and more may be discovered as these languages become better known. There seems to be a preference for OSV in Hiri Motu,[17] and Sreedhar's data on Naga Pidgin (1977) suggest an SOV basic word order. There is need for more empirical research, especially using larger samples of naturally occurring speech. My own suspicion, based on the observation of a large body of data on Pacific Pidgin Englishes, is that the notion of fixed word order would be weakened by such research. Nevertheless, the apparent tendency towards SVO word order certainly deserves closer investigation.

Invariant word order for questions, commands and statements. The relationship between word order, on the one hand, and questions, commands and statements, on the other, is by no means a straightforward one, even in languages such as English, where interrogative order is typically paired with questions, declarative order with statements, etc. (see Schegloff 1978). In fact, as can be seen from child language studies and conversational analysis, the job of asking questions is, on the whole, quite separate from that of producing interrogative patterns. It is therefore not surprising that in pidgins the 'luxury' of different word orders is seldom found.[18] Compare the following utterances in Tok Pisin and Hiri Motu:

Tok Pisin (SVO)	*Hiri Motu (OSV)*	*Gloss*
yu klinim pis	gwarume oi huria	you are cleaning the fish
yu klinim pis[19]	gwarume oi huria[19]	are you cleaning the fish?
yu klinim pis	gwarume oi huria	clean the fish!

Similar findings pertain to all the pidgin languages I have investigated to date.

Grammatical categories (qualifiers of propositions). The need to express possibilities, contingencies and similar ideas is met by qualifiers. Kay and Sankoff's statement that in a pidgin such 'propositional qualifiers will appear in surface structure exterior to the propositions they qualify, or not at all' (1974: 64) is confirmed by the data available for a sizeable number of stable pidgins. Not all sentence qualifiers are equally likely to appear at the periphery, however. Thus, only very few pidgins exhibit sentence-external negators, one such pidgin being South East Australian Aboriginal Pidgin as spoken in the early days of contact (between 1788 and 1850). Examples of the use of the negator bail include:

Bail Saturday tumble down white fellow, bail Jingulo tumble down white fellow, bail me tumble down white fellow.	It wasn't Saturday who killed the white man, nor Jingulo nor I myself.

(*Sydney Gazette*, 2 January 1828; adapted from Dixon 1980: 70)

In many other pidgins, the negator usually comes before the verb phrase, as in the following English-derived ones:

Chinese Pidgin English:	man no can stop	the man cannot stop
Bislama:	oli no save mekem	they do not do it
West African Pidgin English (Cameroon):	dem no bi lak dat	they're not like that
Nigerian Pidgin English:	im no de sing	she does not sing

A grammatical category that typically occurs sentence-externally is that of tense/time. In fact, some linguists have argued that the grammatical category of tense is lost, and that its semantic notions are best described as being expressed lexically by means of adverbials, which typically occur at the beginning or end of sentences or texts. Examples illustrating this point include the pidgin of the south-west Pacific. thus, in Plantation Pidgin Fijian (Siegel 1983b: 7), 'time relationships are indicated either by context or by . . . temporal adverbs which come either sentence initially or before the VP marker *sa*'.

In Samoan Plantation Pidgin English (Mühlhäusler 1978b: 67 ff.), in contrast to its successor Tok Pisin, the signalling of tense and time is fairly undeveloped. In many instances, the lack of linguistic information must be made up by reference to contextual factors. Most typically, however, tense and aspect can be expressed optionally by means of adverbs or aspect markers. Adverbs used for this purpose are generally found at the beginning of a paragraph and not repeated with every instance of the verb.

Mi stap long Fiji wan faiv yia PIPO. Mi go long ples mekim suga bilong as.	'I was in Fiji fifteen years ago. I went to this place to cut sugar for us.
Plenti Indian fella wokim de. Plenti Yuropin i wokim long suga . . .	Many Indians were working there. Many Europeans were employed in the sugar industry . . .

The best-known example of tense encoding in a pidgin (because of the writings of Labov 1971a and Sankoff and Laberge 1973) is the use of *baimbai* in Tok Pisin. The dramatic changes occurring in this part of grammar during the expansion of Tok Pisin will be discussed below.

Lack of number distinction in nouns. There is a widespread absence of number distinctions in nouns in the majority of pidgins surveyed. However, in some of them optional number distinctions (mainly between singular and plural) can be expressed by quantifiers or numerals, and there is also a strong tendency for nouns referring to animates and humans to be marked for number in a redundant fashion. Let us consider how number is expressed in selected pidgins.

According to Heine (1975: 8), in Kenya Pidgin Swahili: 'In those cases where the number distinction singular/plural is retained with human (or animate) concepts but not with non-human (or inanimate) concepts [sic.]. This holds for both nominal as well as pronominal expression of number.' In Chinese Pidgin English, no formal means of indicating noun plurals other than optional use of quantifiers is found. In the Lingua Franca, according to Schuchardt (1979 edn: 28–9), the 'substantive has one form for the singular and plural'. Finally, Manessy states for Pidgin Hausa:

> In vernacular Hausa, the formation of the plural of nouns is a very complex process involving a dozen suffixes and diverse modifications of the noun stem: partial or total reduplication, vowel alternations; furthermore, several plural forms may correspond to the same singular form. In the vehicular variety the plural is obtained by the adjunction of *deyawa* 'much' to the singular form. (Manessy 1977: 140)

Pronoun systems. The pronoun systems of stabilized pidgins in all likelihood illustrate the minimal requirements for pronoun systems in human language. When contrasted with the preceding jargon stage, they further illustrate the crystallization of an ordered part of grammar out of chaos. With regard to the English jargons of the Pacific, for instance, the following observations characterize their early beginnings:

1 Many utterances appear without any overt pronoun, where such a pronoun would be expected in Standard English. An example is:
  Now got plenty money; no good work (1840) 'now I have lots of money so I do not need to work'.
2 Proper nouns or nouns are used instead of pronouns:
  Kanaka work plenty 'we shall work hard'.
3 There is considerable variation in the forms standing for the same concept. Thus 'I' appears as *me*, *my* and *I*; 'we' as *us*, *we*, *me*, *my* and *I*, and so on.
4 No consistent norms are found for distinguishing between singular and plural pronouns.

Stabilization involved different solutions in different pidgins. The minimal one appears to be that of Chinese Pidgin English, where we have three pronouns (first, second and third person) with no number distinction.

The system of Samoan Plantation Pidgin has eliminated most of the fluctuations found in its Pacific predecessors, with the exception of variation in the third person singular. The difference between subject and object forms in the plural, but not the singular is an interesting violation of a universal principle that marked categories make fewer distinctions than unmarked ones. However, such abnatural solutions appear to be tolerated in several pidgins (see Kœfoed 1975), and this is not the place to discuss their implications for linguistic theory.

The Samoan system is also interesting in that we can observe a solution for marking plural pronouns which was not borrowed from either its substratum or superstratum language: the use of the quantifier *ol* (> English *all*) as plural marker in pronouns. This is what the stabilized pronoun system looked like:

Subject forms

Person	*Singular*	*Plural*
First	mi	mi ol
Second	yu	yu ol
Third	em, him, hi	emol, himol

Object forms

Person	*Singular*	*Plural*
First	(bilong) mi	(bilong) as
Second	(bilong) yu	(bilong) yu ol
Third	(bilong) em (him)	(bilong) dem

In addition to these forms, a number of fossilized forms of English pronouns are found in expressions such as *aiting* 'it seems to me', *aidono* 'I don't know', *yes aidu* 'yes', and *maiwot* 'my word!' Such forms indicate that the Melanesian plantation workers were exposed to some kind of Standard English during the formative period of this language.

Subsequently, in Tok Pisin, where pressure from Standard English was greatly reduced, the distinction between subject and object forms of the pronouns was abandoned. At the same time, the plural marker *-ol* was restricted to the third person, and the form *-pela* (from English fellow) was adopted as a plural marker instead. Again, this possibility was already inherent in the highly variable jargons preceding Samoan Plantation Pidgin and Tok Pisin. The resulting system in early Tok Pisin thus looked like this:

Person	*Singular*	*Plural*
First	mi	mi-pela
Second	yu	yu-pela
Third	em	em ol

Stabilization once more is manifested as the restriction of variability and approximation to paradigmatic univocity.[20]

Prepositions. There appears to be a major typological difference (discussed, for instance, by Givón 1979) between languages that make use of prepositions and others that express the same relations by means of verb chaining. In the case of European-derived pidgins, a large repertoire of prepositions is found in the lexifier languages; however, very few of them get adopted in the stable pidgins derived from them. The reason for this appears to be twofold. On the one hand, the rules governing the choice between different prepositions can be extremely complex. On the other hand, the semantic or functional load of many prepositions is negligible. Consequently, in accordance with the more general principle that in pidgins semantically full lexemes tend to be more important than grammatical words, the number of prepositions encountered in most pidgins is diminutive. Let me illustrate this with a few examples.

Taking the case of Pidgin German (guest-worker German), Clyne (1968: 136 ff.) remarks: 'the choice of preposition causes considerable difficulties for both bilinguals and learners of German as a second language . . . Those few guestworkers who used prepositions at all, tended to select the wrong ones.' The lack of prepositions is also in evidence in the pidginized varieties of German spoken on Ali Island in New Guinea (examples from Mühlhäusler 1977a: 58–70):

Früher ich war Alexishafen.	Earlier, I worked *in* Alexishafen.
Wir muss gehen unsere Boot.	We must go *to* our boat.

Hollyman (1976) provides some examples from New Caledonian Pidgin French:

la nuit, moi porter kai-kai	At night, I shall bring food
lui a'iver son village	He arrived at his village

Likewise, in Vietnamese Pidgin French (Liem 1979):

battre lui moi	beat him for me
monsieur couper couteau	he uses the knife to cut
madame aller autobus	she went by bus
monsieur aller Nha-Trang	he went to Nha-Trang

The principal stable pidgins of the Pacific are characterized by a one- or two-preposition system of grammatical relations, although some of them acquired additional marginal prepositions by means of borrowing. In the one-preposition systems, *long* (from English 'along') is the most common form; in the two-preposition systems, a reflex of *belong* meaning 'for, possessive or purpose' is added. The choice of *belong* is of particular interest, since it is not a preposition, but a verb in English. As pointed out by Clark (1979: 16), Chinese and South Seas Pidgin English reanalysed English sentences containing *belong* in quite different ways. According to Hall:

> In a number of instances pidgins and creoles show a drastic restructuring of various words, in their assignment to different functions from those they had in the languages from which they came . . . In South Seas Pidgin English we find /bɪlon/, clearly from the English verb *belong*, but functioning as a preposition meaning 'of, for' . . . We find /blon/ in Chinese Pidgin English, too, but this time as a copulative verb equivalent to our 'be'. (Hall 1966: 79)

Clark suggests that on the basis of some data given by Hall, in particular:

dæt belong mai	'That is mine'
dis pensil belong yu	'This is your pencil'

a case could be made for the origin of the Beach-la-Mar preposition *belong* in Chinese Pidgin English. However, he argues that historical continuity is not the most likely explanation:

> Thus if South Seas BELONG is directly related to its Chinese cognate, reanalysis of the above type of predicate may have been the critical step in the radical change of function. More likely, however, is that the two represent independent generalizations in two different directions from the BELONG + NP type of predicate, which has a direct English source (This belongs to me). (Clark 1979: 16)

So far we have considered the more superficial aspects of prepositions in stabilized pidgins. There are a number of important principles involved here, some of which have been discussed by Traugott (1976). Most noticeable is that the splitting up of the semantic space covered by prepositions proceeds in a unitary fashion in both first-language and pidgin development. It is hoped that Traugott's important hypothesis is examined with further longitudinal data from pidgin development in order to establish the universality or otherwise of this phenomenon.

Lack of derivational depth. The distance between surface and deep structures is defined by a number of grammatical operations. For single (simple) sentences these include: rearrangement, deletion, addition and agreement. In the pidgin languages surveyed, such operations are either absent or only minimally present. Thus the same word order is used for statements, questions and commands; the second person singular is not deleted (as in many lexifier languages) in the imperative forms (typical Pidgin English for 'go!' is 'you go'); special grammatical additions such as dummy verbs are not added; and inflectional morphology promoting grammatical agreement is absent. Rules of grammar tend to be few, and those that are found are context-independent rather than context-sensitive. Lack of derivational depth is also seen from a second property, the scarcity of complex sentences in pidgins. Again, in most pidgins surveyed, the only complex sentences permitted are those that do not impinge on the direct mapability of deep structures onto surface structures, that is, conjoining. Embedding, on the other hand, is extremely rare and, in most pidgins, emerges only during the later stages of grammatical expansion. This is true of pidgins with no apparent historical links.

Consider the Koriki and Elema trade languages. Dutton (1983b: 90–1) observes: 'Complex ideas are expressed in both HTL(E) and HTL(K) by juxtaposing simple sentences or by introducing the second sentence with the word for 'okay' in each language.'

The absence of embedding in pidginized varieties of Swahili is commented upon by Scotton as follows:

> What is actually missing are the relative constructions and other forms of subordination which mark complex sentences in the Standard dialect. The result is an 'abbreviated' syntax consisting mainly of content words, with the listener left to make the connections. (Scotton 1969: 101)

The data from Papuan Pidgin English are typical for the range of functions covered by simple juxtaposition in early stabilized pidgins. They include the following (data from Mühlhäusler 1978a):

1 Simple conjoining of sentences or parts of sentences, with the actions occurring in the following sequence:

    He take knife, he go fight Otapeg, another boy, run up, he throw knife away

  or

    you watch, me fellow go bush, I leave you inside house.

2 Concatenation can also express the conditional conveyed in English by 'if', for example:

patrol no longwe, very good, patrol longwe tumas, no very good.	'if the patrol is not far away that's good, if the patrol is far away that's bad.'

3 Temporal relationship ('when') between two statements can be conveyed as follows:

(mi)sik, mi sindaun	'when I was sick I stayed at home'.

4 Concatenation can also express a causative relationship, as in:

    Kiwai man no kill him two boy belong you, I big man.

5 Relativization:

    one fellow name Mat he go burn down my house
    people stop along Sydney go look see picture
    that pigeon he been sing out my name, I plant him.

It will be demonstrated later how such conjoined constructions can be reinterpreted and become the point of departure for embedding in more fully developed pidgins.

The form taken by wh-question words. In most lexifier languages of pidgins, the forms corresponding to English *who?*, *where?*, *when?*, etc. are expressed by single words. However, in pidgins across the world, analytic expressions are favoured. Consider the small sample in table 5.2.

Table 5.2 The form taken by wh-question words in various pidgins

Language	*Form*	*Gloss*	*English*
Kenya Pidgin Swahili	saa gani	hour which?	'when?'
	siku gain	day which?	'when?'
	titu gani	thing which?	'what?'
	namna gani	kind which?	'how?'
	sababu gani	reason which?	'why?'
Fanakalo	ipi-skati	where-time?	'when?'
	yini-ndaba	what-matter?	'why?'
Samoan Plantation Pidgin English	wat man	what man	who?
	wat nem	what name	what?
	wat taim	what time	when?
	wat ples	what place	where, whence whither?
Chinese Pidgin English	hú máen	who man	who?
	hwá sajd	what side	where?
	háw fæšən	how fashion	how?
	hwá tajm	what time	when?

A number of creoles contain similar question pronouns, presumably reflecting a carry-over from a previous pidgin stage (see Bickerton 1981: 70–1). Note, however, that in at least some pidgins (for example, the Lingua Franca) no complex question pronouns were found.

Anaphoric pronouns. A construction that is extremely widespread across pidgins (though absent in some, such as Chinese Pidgin English) is the use of anaphoric pronouns that may eventually become generalized predicate introducers. Thomason (1981: 335 ff.), when writing on Chinook Jargon, notes that a construction involving a pleonastic pronoun is absent in most of the languages spoken by users of Chinook Jargon, but found with most speakers of the Jargon, as in (p. 336):

t'alap'as pi lilú łaska məłayt iht-iht łaska haws
coyote and wolf they live one-one they house

In the various English-based jargons preceding stabilization of plantation pidgins in the Pacific, an anaphoric pronoun was variably present in most areas, although there was very considerable inter-individual and intra-individual variation.

Examples from Samoa and New Caledonia, recorded by Schuchardt's informants in the 1880s, include:

boat he capsize, water he kaikai him	the boat capsized and sank
plenty bullamacow he stop	there were lots of cattle
coconut belong mi too much sore	my head is sore

At the time, there was an almost categorical absence of anaphoric pronouns when the subject was a pronoun, reflecting a similar restriction in English.

As stabilization occurred, a number of new conventions emerged: there was a movement away from English grammar, and partial incorporation of the grammatical conventions of the substratum languages. An interesting example is afforded by the data on early Tok Pisin (some such observations have also been made in Sankoff 1977).

The movement away from English grammar is exemplified by two features: first, the generalization of *he* to referents which are female or neuter (Schuchardt still had examples such as *Woman she finish thing me speak him*); and second, the fact that *i* (rather than *he*) very gradually begins to appear after the third-person pronoun *em* and in a very few cases after other pronouns as well.

The use of *i* in Tok Pisin appears to have been reinforced by the fact that Tolai had a similar construction.[21] As in English, Tolai used different forms of the pronoun for different kinds of subjects. However, with third-person singular subjects, the anaphoric pronoun *i* was used and it is this accidental encounter with English *he* which may have promoted the rapid stabilization of *i*, first as a generalized anaphoric pronoun for singular and plural subjects, and subsequently as a predicate marker.

We have surveyed nine syntactic constructions that have been identified as salient for stabilized pidgins. In a number of cases, it was specifically noted that there was no apparent input model for such constructions and that, moreover, very much the same solutions appear to emerge wherever pidginization occurs and whatever the lexifier languages. Although we do not have full knowledge of the psychological and neurolinguistic processes underlying pidginization, it certainly seems that adults have retained the capacity to develop consistent grammatical structures out of rather inconsistent input, a claim frequently denied by those who operate in terms of a critical threshold model of language acquisition.

Stabilization in syntax, as indeed in other components of grammar, first and foremost implies a reduction of variants. The solutions found tend to conform to the general prnciples of syntagmatic and paradigmatic univocity and derivational shallowness. Of the many solutions that appear consistent with such requirements, only a small subset is actually encountered, suggesting universal limitations on the possible form of pidgins at this state.[22]

The lexicon

Stabilization in the lexicon manifests itself in a number of ways, including the emergence of norms as to what constitutes a lexical item of the language, the crystallization of preferred norms of lexical variants, and the development of lexical field structures. Apart from such general traits, there are a number of more specific similarities in the lexicons of stable pidgins.

The lexicon of a stable pidgin is further shaped by a number of constraints, including considerable pressure for one form = one meaning encoding; pressure to maximize the usefulness of a very limited lexical inventory; and the absence of processes of derivational morphology. We shall now consider these factors.

Emergence of norms

Jargon lexicons have a very small stable core and a large variable area, as any item of the lexifier language and most items of the substratum languages are potential words. This freedom of lexical choice is restricted considerably in a stable pidgin. First, only a very small part of the lexicon of the lexifier language is selected as the basis of the derived pidgin. Consider Fijian, where more than 80 different words for different kinds of cutting exist. Siegel (1983b: 12) observes that in Plantation Pidgin Fijian 'there are only two words for cutting: *ta* and *musu* (SF [Standard Fijian] *tā*-ya and *musu-ka*). This one-to-many relationship between a single lexical item in the pidgin and a larger number of synonyms and near-synonyms in the lexifier language is equally characteristic of other pidgins. Compare:

Pidgin German of New Guinea	Standard German
kaput	zerrissen, zerbrochen, zerplatzt, zerschlenzt, zerfetzt, schadhaft, durchlöchert, etc. 'broken'

Spanish	Trade Spanish of the Piñaguero Panare (Riley 1952)
matar 'to kill'	matándo 'to kill, die'
parar 'to stop, stay'	parándo 'to stop, stay, live at, be with'
kitar 'to remove'	kitándo 'to remove, discard, abduct'

Not only is the number of actual pidgin items highly restricted, but there are also conventions as to the lexical information found with each such item, namely:

1 a standard pronunciation (with some latitude in acceptable variants);
2 a standard range of meanings;
3 conventions regarding the grammatical status of a word;
4 conventions as to its social acceptability.

The lexical information that is acceptable in a pidgin can be very different from that associated with its cognate in a lexifier or substratum language. Let us consider examples for each of the above categories.

First, we will consider conventions for pronunciation:

Language	*Lexical item*	*Source*	*Gloss*
Tok Pisin	kisim	English catch + im	to catch, obtain
Tok Pisin	bruk	English broke, broken	to break, broken
Tok Pisin	umben	Tolai [ubene]	net
Fanakalo	bulughwe	Afrikaans [brøx]	bridge
Fanakalo	sikwelete	Afrikaans [skølt]	debt
Fanakalo	tshisha	Zulu [isa]	to burn

A somewhat special case are instances where two words of the lexifier language have become one in the related pidgin. Examples are reported from a wide range of languages. In Plantation Pidgin Fijian, for instance, inalienable nouns are typically borrowed from Fijian, together with the third-person singular possessive pronoun affix *-na*, as in the examples given by Siegel (1983b: 13):

tamana	'father'
tinana	'mother'
ligana	'hand'

French creoles, and it would seem that this is inherited from their pidgin predecessors,[23] often have nouns with reflexes of a former French article. Some such nouns, with their French etymon, are mentioned by Bollée (1980). Of particular interest is Bollée's observation that, in different varieties of creole French, different nouns are thus marked, suggesting different developmental traditions for these languages. Compare:

French	*Haitian Creole French*	*Seychellois*	*Gloss*
queu	ke	lake	tail
cloche	kloch	laklos	bell
cou	kou	likou	neck

The same phenomenon is observed in Vanuatu English-derived Bislama, which borrowed extensively from French during the years of the French-English condominium. Examples include *lafet* 'feast' (> French la fête) and *lasup* 'soup' (> French la soupe).

That word and morpheme boundaries of the lexifier language are often ignored in the derived pidgin is finally illustrated by a sample from Tok Pisin:

Tok Pisin	*From English*	*Gloss*
baimbai	by and by	'soon'
nambis	on the beach	'beach'
tudir	too dear	'expensive'
lego	let go	'to let go'
sekan	shake hands	'to make peace'
bilinut	betelnut	'betelnut'
simbum	jib-boom	'jib-boom'
kolta	coal-tar	'tar'
trausel	tortoise shell	'tortoise'

Second, whereas in the jargon phase conventions for the meaning of lexical items were often lacking and miscommunication was rife as a result, there is far more agreement about meaning in a stable pidgin, particularly in the core areas of the lexicon. These meanings can differ considerably from those of the lexifier language, as is illustrated in the following examples:

Language	*Item*	*Meaning in pidgin*	*Meaning in source language*
Samoan Plantation Pidgin English	holimpas	to rape, hold tightly	to hold fast
	pisup	tinned food, bully beef	pea soup
Cameroonian Pidgin English	kontri	home area, maternal village	country
	stik	tree, stick, guava	stick
Fanakalo	stronmani	circus	English: strong man

Words from substratum languages can equally be changed, as can be seen with the following Tolai loan-words in Tok Pisin:

Tolai		*Tok Pisin*	
mao	'ripe banana'	mau	'ripe, mature'
tubuan	'old woman, mask of old woman'	tubuan	'wooden mask, carving'
ubene	'fishing net'	umben	'net (in general)'
virua	'victim, human flesh'	birua	'enemy, warrior'
kabag	'white lime'	kambang	'lime'
pagagar	'to be open'	pangangar	'to be in position for copulation (of female)'

A tendency, observed in many pidgins, is that of more powerful words from the lexifier language to acquire an attenuated meaning in the corresponding pidgin. Typical of this tendency is the widespread use of *too much* in the meaning of 'much', or the choice, in the Lingua Franca, of *cunciar* 'to tackle, perpetrate' instead of *fasir* 'to do' to convey the latter. Another example comes from the Chinese–Russian pidgin of Kjachta, where the word for 'to hit, beat' is derived from Russian *pokolotit* 'to give a sound beating', rather than *bit* 'to beat'.

Third, the grammatical class membership of words of the lexifier language is often changed in the pidgin. Examples of this phenomenon include South Seas Beach-la-Mar *hariap* 'quickly' and *tasol* 'but' (from that's all); the use of the Elema adjective *eka* 'bad, poor' to mean 'sickness' or 'to be unhappy' in the Elema Trade language; and the use of the English noun *heap* as a quantifier 'many, plenty' in American Red Indian Pidgin English.

Finally, as regards the social appropriateness of words, considerable differences may exist between a pidgin and its lexifier language. Many words that are rude in the latter are perfectly acceptable in the former. Consider the following examples from Tok Pisin:

Tok Pisin	*From English*	*Meaning in Tok Pisin*
bagarap	buggered up	tired, ruined
sit	shit	leftovers, faeces
kan	cunt	female genitals
as	arse	seat, buttocks, origin, cause

In these and many other instances, the norms of pidgin lexicons differ from those of the lexifier language, thus demonstrating their linguistic independence.

Lexical field structures

So far we have described the lexicon as a socially sanctioned list of irregularities, and for most pidgins this list-like nature is indeed a dominant characteristic. However, there are signs in some areas of the lexicon of some tighter field-like organization of lexical material, particularly in domains that are dominant for the users of a pidgin. Such lexical fields are typically neither a calque from substratum languages nor directly borrowed from the lexifier language, but an amalgam developed out of the special communicative needs of pidgin speakers. Unfortunately, little research has been carried out on this topic, and I must draw on my own studies of Tok Pisin.

An example of such a developing semantic field is that of enumeration. Many number systems are found in the geographic area of Papua New Guinea, and decimal systems are widespread in the Melanesian languages spoken in the area where Tok Pisin stabilized. This facilitated the adoption of the English system of counting, though not without certain changes. Reed observes:

> The system of enumeration in pidgin is a clear example of linguistic syncretism under the impact of culture contact. And we may also observe herein significant cultural adjustments by the natives toward European institutions of economics and finance. The cardinal numbers from one to ten are patently of English derivation: won, tu, tri, for, faif, sĭkĭs, sĕfĕn, et, nain, and tĕn; but with numbers above ten, the native pattern of grouping numbers more frequently occurs. Thus eleven is wonfela ten won, twelve wonfela ten tu, and so on to twenty, which is tufela ten. (Reed 1943: 282)

A second example is that of kinship terms. It appears, however, that stable conventions existed only for central kinship terms, whereas considerable latitude was – and still is – found with the more peripheral ones. Although a number of items appearing in this field have English cognates, their semantic information has been restructured:

Tok Pisin	*Central meaning*
tumbuna	'grandparent, grandchild'
papa	'father'
mama	'mother'
kandare	'maternal uncle or aunt'
smolmama	'paternal aunt'
smolpapa	'paternal uncle'
brata	'sibling of the same sex'
susa	'sibling of the opposite sex'

One form = one meaning

The requirement that there should be one form for one meaning is one that is frequently violated in the older languages. Reasons for this include the borrowing of incompatible suppletive items, pressure for stylistic flexibility, and conflict between strategies promoting optimalization of production and others optimalizing perception.

The requirement that one form should express one meaning and vice versa is violated in two ways:

1 one form stands for a number of meanings (homophony);
2 one and the same meaning is expressed by a number of forms (synonymy).

Whereas the former is found frequently in stable pidgins, synonymy or near synonymy is rare. The reason would seem to be that some homophony is of little consequence, since disambiguation can occur by means of textual and contextual information. Thus the fact that *sip* in Tok Pisin can mean 'sheep', 'ship', 'jeep' and 'jib' is unlikely to result in any major communicative disasters. The presence of synonyms, on the other hand, constitutes a considerable cost, particularly at a stage where propositional rather than connotative dimensions of meaning are dominant.

The requirement of one form = one meaning also relates to recurrent semantic components.[24] One example of such recurrent elements is the negative in antonym pairs. Examples of pidgins encoding antonyms by means of adding an equivalent of 'no' to the base form are numerous. Two languages illustrate this:

Tok Pisin	*Gloss*	*From English*
no kamap	to be absent	come up

nogut	bad	good
no inap	deficient	enough
no hatwok	easy	hard work

Fanakalo	*Gloss*	*Literal translation*
hayi figile	absent	has not come
hayi muhle	bad	not good
hayi bona	blind	not see
hayi saba	brave	not fear

Another recurrent element is the male and female animates expressed by putting an equivalent of 'man' or 'woman' before the base noun. Examples are documented for a number of pidgins including:

Samoan Plantation Pidgin English	*Gloss*	*Translation*
man hos	male horse	stallion
wumen hos	female horse	mare
man pik	male pig	boar
wuman pik	female pig	sow
Cameroon Pidgin English		
wuman fawul	woman fowl	hen
wuman got	woman goat	nanny goat
man fawul	man fowl	rooster
Hiri Motu		
boroma tau	pig man	boar
boroma hahine	pig woman	sow
boromakau tau	cattle man	bull
boromakau hahine	cattle woman	cow

As a final example, the semantic feature (+ human) is very frequently expressed by means of an affix translating as 'man'. Although some suppletion is encountered with the most frequently used words for persons, more peripheral terms tend to be morphologically perspicuous, usually considerably more so than in the related lexifier language. Examples include:

Hiri Motu	*Gloss*	*Translation*
diba tauna	know person	expert
hadibaia tauna	teach person	teacher
hereva gauna	say person	subject of conversation

Tok Pisin	*Gloss*	*Translation*
kaisman	left man	left-handed person
kamman	come man	new arrival
loman	law man	generous person
masman	march man	marcher

Similar examples were found in virtually all the pidgins I have examined.

Maximum use of a minimum lexicon

Although pidgins are considerably less powerful in terms of their referential potential than their lexifier languages, nevertheless they have developed mechanisms to extend a highly restricted lexical inventory. This is done primarily by letting the syntactic component do some of the work of the morphological and lexical components in related lexifier languages. The principal mechanisms are the use of syntactic paraphrases and circumlocutions; the use of grammatical categories such as aspect to distinguish between meanings; the use of multifunctionality, that is, the same word is used in a multitude of grammatical functions; and the generation of verbs from nouns.

In contrast to the long-winded jargon circumlocutions, stable pidgins often have phrase-like formulas for the description of new concepts. An interesting case is Hiri Motu, which has a formula of the type *0–V – gauna* 'a thing for doing something to an object' as in:

Hiri Motu	*Gloss*	*Translation*
kuku ania gauna	smoke eat thing	pipe
lahi gabua gauna	fire burn thing	match
traka abiaisi gauna	truck raise thing	jack
godo abia gauna	voice take thing	tape recorder

The use of grammatical categories to distinguish between meanings can be illustrated by the Tok Pisin aspect markers, *pinis* (completion) and *nating* (frustrative):

painim/painim pinis	to search/to find
boilim/boilim pinis	boil/sterilize
rere/rere pinis	to prepare/ready
indai/indai pinis	to be unconscious/to be dead
bagarapim/bagarapim pinis	to damage/to destroy
hukim/hukim pinis	allure/catch with a hook
promis/promis pinis	to promise/to keep a promise

Nating can be found in a number of collocations. Its meaning is more difficult to recover and some contextual information is usually needed. Depending on the context, *pusi nating* can mean (inter alia) 'a desexed cat', 'a stray cat', 'a very weak cat' or 'a cat without a pedigree'. Other examples include:

bun nating	'very thin, skinny'
kuk nating	'to cook vegetarian food (no meat)'
sik nating	'a minor disease'

A very similar picture is found in Hiri Motu. Compare:

Hiri Motu	*Gloss*	*Translation*
bada/bada vadaeni	big/big completion	big/grown up
kaukau/kaukau vadaeni	dry/dry completion	drying/dry
dika/dika vadaeni	bad/bad completion	bad/rotten
mase/mase vadaeni	die/die completion	about to die/dead

Jargons feature looseness of grammatical class membership, but, because of the lack of grammatical conventions, this cannot be exploited in a systematic fashion. Once grammatical class membership can be deduced from an item's position in a sentence, however, considerable savings can be made. The widespread use of the third mechanism, multifunctionality, in pidgins can be seen from the following quotes for a large number of diverse languages. Jacobs, describing Chinook Jargon, states:

> It should be remembered that in (Chinook) Jargon elements are indiscriminately verbs, nouns, adjectives, or adverbs depending on their meaning and the ability an element of a given meaning has to serve as another form of word. (Jacobs 1932: 40)

Goodman, on Japanese Pidgin English, writes:

> Another key process in the syntax of English–Japanese Pidgin is the use of many words in a variety of grammatical functions. This process is closely related to and probably inseparable from the semantic tendency towards abstraction. (Goodman 1967: 53)

Wurm and Harris write about Hiri Motu:

> The predicates of such simple sentences often consist of words which we have called bases, and which can be translated by English verbs, adjectives or nouns. (Wurm and Harris 1963: 3)

The prominence of this phenomenon has been remarked on by a number of pidginists; for example, Wurm (1970: 8) writes: 'A characteristic feature of Pidgin is the presence of many universal bases, i.e. words which can function as nouns, noun and verb adjuncts, intransitive verbs and transitive verbs . . . The functional possibilities of pidgin bases are fundamental to the grammar of Pidgin.'

One observer, Voorhœve (1962: 241–62), went so far as to calculate the actual savings derived from the multifunctional use of lexical items:[25] 'there exists a certain relationship between the size of the vocabulary and the complexity of the grammar' which is optimal in pidgins and creoles. 'Now, if we introduce two grammatical rules into our hypothetical language, to distinguish, for example, between verbs and non-verbal words, then this means that the number of words can be reduced by a half.' Further on (p. 242), Voorhœve claims that 'compared with a model language containing *X* words and *X* rules, creole languages have X/p (*X* divided by *p*) words and $Y + p$ (*Y* plus *p*) rules. The reduction in the number of words is far greater than the increase in the number of rules.' In reality, the saving achieved is much less, particularly in stable as against expanded or creolized pidgins. Contrary to the idea that early pidgins are characterized by overgeneralization and optimal application of grammatical rules, such rules as shifting lexical items from one grammatical category to another are often underutilized and restricted by constraints. When considering multifunctionality in early Tok Pisin, for instance, one is struck not only by the absence of numerous mathematically possible forms, but also by the fact that restrictions on productivity appear to have been inherited from substratum sources.

Although the use of one and the same lexical item in a number of functions may constitute a considerable gain in simplicity, one of the less desirable consequences is a violation of the principle of one form = one meaning.

Finally, most pidgins surveyed exhibit a considerable shortage of verbs. One way of obtaining new verbs is the generation of verbs from nouns. A second way, and one which involves explicit signalling of the category verb, is to employ a phrase of the type 'to make' + N. Examples of this construction are documented for a number of unrelated pidgins, for example:

1 Pidgin German (cf. Hinnenkamp 1983: 7):

foto machen	'to make photo'	to take a photograph

2 Hiri Motu:

laulau karaia	'to make picture'	to take a photograph
durua karaia	'to assistance make'	to help
hera karaia	'to decoration make'	to adorn

3 Tok Pisin:The construction is widely found in Tok Pisin of the 1920s, but appears to have virtually disappeared by 1930. Examples include:

mekim hos	to make horse	to saddle
mekim krismas	to make Christmas	to celebrate
mekim pepa	to make paper	to write, sign a labour contract
mekim man	to make man	to marry a man
mekim siga	to make cigar	to smoke

Examples for Chinook Jargon, as well as a more general discussion, are given by Silverstein (1972a: 602 ff.).

We have now surveyed the principal internal means by which stable pidgins expand their lexical resources. It should have become obvious that word formation at this stage is very restricted and pidgins therefore have to rely on external borrowing for most of their lexical expansion.

Sources of lexical borrowing

Pidgins at an early stage of development are constrained in two ways: their internal word-formation mechanisms are still underdeveloped, and borrowing from outside systems is made difficult by a number of linguistic and social factors.

As regards the linguistic factors, there is an oft-expressed belief that any word of the lexifier language is also a potential word in the related pidgin (this view was expressed, for instance, by Mafeni 1971: 103). This, however, is not quite the case, because:

1 pidgins tend to have a marked preference for bisyllabic or at least short words;
2 pidgins have more rigid phonotactic restrictions on consonant clusters than their lexifier languages;
3 the boundary between lexicon and syntax is different in the two languages.

Thus, pidgins have fairly tight internal structures, which make borrowing difficult. Long and morphologically complex words of English, such as uneducated, specialization, information, select committee, citizenship and archbishop, will tend to violate these conditions for optimal word length, particularly after clusters have been split up by means of epenthetic vowels. *Sipesialaisesen* or *sitisensip* (both documented as recent loans in Urban Tok Pisin) are very strange-sounding items in a pidgin and a potential source of misunderstanding.[26] Moreover, they are unacceptable bases for further word-formation processes, such as compounding or derivation.

Without wishing to go into detail, it should be conceded that there are principled linguistic barriers to borrowing in pidgins. Generally speaking, the less complex and/or the more regular a system, the less it is susceptible to outside influence.

Apart from such internal barriers to borrowing, there is the question of access to potential sources of new vocabulary. Stabilization (or tertiary hybridization) takes place at a time when the lexifier language is relatively withdrawn. In fact, the most clear-cut examples are those where it was almost fully withdrawn, as with Cameroon Pidgin English and Tok Pisin under a German colonial administration. At the same time, it typically occurs in the context of considerable linguistic diversity among the speakers of substratum languages, diminishing the chance of any single language becoming the obvious source of innovations. It may be for this reason that pidgins are typically lexified from the languages of socially dominant groups.[27]

Differential social status is also reflected in a second way: typically, the core vocabulary is borrowed from a single main source, whereas more marginal (statistically less frequent, more specialized) items tend to be borrowed from substratum languages. Let me illustrate these general observations with examples.

According to Cole (1953: 4 ff.), the lexicon of Fanakalo consists of about 70 per cent Zulu vocabulary; the remainder is borrowed from Afrikaans or English. Again, the core vocabulary is almost exclusively derived from Zulu.

More than 90 per cent of the lexicon of Samoan Plantation Pidgin English and virtually all its central lexical bases are derived from English. A small number of words is borrowed from Samoan and, in its later years, a handful of lexical items of New Guinea origin were added by Melanesian plantation workers recruited from there.

Tok Pisin differs from its Samoan predecessor in two regards: first, the considerable element of local languages in non-central domains of communication, and second, the heavy reliance, in its early years, on German as a lexifier language. Again, the lexical core of the language remains uniformly derived from English.

The vast majority of lexical items in present-day Hiri Motu are derived from Motu, with a significant borrowed element in the more marginal areas of the lexicon from English and Tok Pisin. However, there are indications of a more lexically mixed earlier stage (discussed in Dutton forthcoming), signalling the close contacts between the semi-official Papuan Pidgin English and Police Motu which existed in the 1920s and 1930s.

In Vietnamese Pidgin French, Reinecke (1971: 50) writes that 'remarkably few Vietnamese words are used in Pidgin French. Not a single Vietnamese word appears in Swadesh's 200 word list . . . Most of the Vietnamese words in Pidgin French are names of foods and plants.'

The above data illustrate the very strong tendency of present-day pidgins to be lexically affiliated to one main language. However, such synchronic evidence must not be taken to mean that more mixed lexical systems were not found at earlier stages of stable pidgins.

Stabilization: a summary

Although I am fully aware that stabilization and the crystallization of stable pidgins are dynamic processes, the data at hand make a description in dynamic terms difficult. We often find ourselves in the unenviable position of having to argue about developments from the perspective of a plateau or endpoint reached. None the less, I hope that the following general characteristics are truly salient, if not universal elements of the development of stable pidgins:

1 the reduction of variability found in preceding jargon stages;
2 the establishment of relatively firm lexical and grammatical conventions;
3 the development of grammatical structures independent from possible source languages.

Moreover, when compared to their lexifier languages, one finds that:

4 subsequent to their stabilization, pidgins are unintelligible to speakers of the lexifier languages;
5 when compared, pidgins are partially characterizable as reduced and simplified versions of their lexifier languages;
6 the reduction in form is accompanied by a reduction in function: the most immediate victim of such functional reduction is stylistic flexibility.

Stable pidgins are thus in many ways quite restrictive systems, incapable of filling the needs of first-language communicators and inadequate even for some of the requirements of their second-language users. Although they have acquired some linguistic autonomy, their potential for internal growth remains restricted, as is borrowing from outside sources. However, in the narrow social context, in which they tend to be institutionalized, pidgins are a highly efficient means of communication.

It has been noted over and over again that pidgins with no shared history exhibit amazing similarities in their structural make-up. Such evidence provides necessary, but by no means sufficient support for the view that people appeal to innate linguistic universals when under pressure for communication, such as is found in a pidgin situation. An alternative view would seek to relate pidgins to more general pragmatic and problem-solving capacities found with human beings. In the absence of more detailed observations, particularly longitudinal studies, we shall have to postpone judgement on this matter.

The expansion stage

The notion of expanded or extended pidgin was formally introduced by Todd, although it was implicit earlier in distinguishing basic stable pidgins from expanded ones. Todd writes:

> Clearly distinguishable from this type of pidgin is what I call an 'expanded' or 'extended' pidgin. This is one which develops in a multilingual area, which proves extremely useful in inter-group communication and which, because of its usefulness, is extended and utilized outside the range of its original use . . . They differ from restricted pidgins in that,

> in them, we see the emergence of new languages with the potential to grow and spread or to disappear if their usefulness as a means of communication comes to an end. (Todd 1974: 4)

The underlying assumption is that adult second languages can be elaborated to the extent that they become comparable with creoles and other vernaculars. The notion of expansion relates to increases both in the communicative functions and domains and a pidgin's referential and non-referential power.

Since it takes place only in special external circumstances, the number of expanded pidgins is relatively small. Clusters of expanded pidgins are located mainly in the linguistically highly heterogeneous areas of West Africa and Melanesia. Typically, they accompany increased geographic mobility and inter-tribal contacts, generally as a result of colonial policies. The best-known expanded pidgins are Tok Pisin and West African Pidgin English (particularly the Cameroon variety). Others include recent varieties of Hiri Motu, Bislama, Solomon Islands Pidgin, Sango and some varieties of Torres Straits Broken. To the best of my knowledge, longitudinal studies of these languages have not been made, and we thus have to rely on occasional observations about their growth.

The importance of expanded pidgins to linguistic research is twofold. First, they illustrate the capacity of adults to drastically restructure existing linguistic systems; secondly, they call into question such dichotomies as first and second, primary and secondary, native and non-native language. The structural changes to be discussed in the following sections highlight not only the considerable complexity of expanded pidgins, but also the ordered fashion in which new constructions are added to existing simpler grammars.

The phonological component

The phonology of expanded pidgins has attracted relatively little attention, especially concerning development. However, some generalizations are still possible. Phonological expansion is manifested in the following areas:

1 a steady increase in phonological distinctions;
2 the emergence of phonological rules;
3 the increasing use of former free pronunciation variants for stylistic purposes.

I will now illustrate these points with data from Nigerian Pidgin English, Torres Strait Broken and Tok Pisin.

The increase in phonological distinctions. Stable pidgins were characterized by a small inventory of distinctive vowels and consonants, as a rule considerably reduced in comparison with their lexifier language, and also smaller than the speaker's substratum phonological inventory. Additions to this inventory typically involve taking over distinctions from the lexifier language (and it is therefore difficult to draw a clear-cut distinction between development and restructuring at the phonological level), although substratum and adstratum languages may provide additional material.

West African Pidgin English, Torres Strait Broken and Tok Pisin all appear to have had a five-vowel system during early stabilization, in all cases:

i				u
	e		o	
		a		

After some time, this was replaced by seven-vowel systems; in the case of Nigerian Pidgin (Mafeni 1971: 107–8) and Tok Pisin, the inventory was:

i						u
	e				o	
		ɛ		ɔ		
			a			

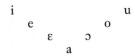

Torres Strait Broken had distinctive vowels in the central area (Dutton 1970: 145). Vowel length was not distinctive in any of the three pidgins. More recent varieties of coastal Tok Pisin have replaced the seven-vowel system by a ten-vowel system, which is being restructured by some speakers to include contrasts in vowel length. Torres Strait Broken, where contact with English appears to have been more intensive, has a twelve-vowel system, involving both quality and length contrasts, as demonstrated by Dutton (1970: 145).

The consonant systems of the three pidgins under discussion are again considerably more extensive than those found at earlier developmental stages. They still differ from their lexifier language in the exclusion of certain highly marked sounds (in particular, certain sibilants and forms of *th*). Nigerian Pidgin English has a number of sounds not found in English (including labiovelar [kp] and [gb] as well as a palatal [ɲ]). The consonants of both Tok Pisin and Torres Strait Broken at first sight appear to be a subset of the English consonant system. However, their phonotactic properties, as will be shown shortly, can differ.

When comparing earlier stages of Tok Pisin with expanded varieties, we find that, irrespective of a Tok Pisin user's native language, a number of distinctions absent from earlier Tok Pisin are now widely made. These include a distinction between [s] and [t], [p] and [f], and [l] and [r], in that order. The consonant system of expanded Tok Pisin can be summarized as shown in table 5.3 (less common distinctive consonants are given in brackets). One can anticipate that the bracketed consonants become distinctive for more and more speakers as the language develops. Apart from having more distinctive sounds, expanded pidgins also use existing sounds to a greater degree. Thus, whereas in older

Table 5.3 Consonant system of expanded Tok Pisin

		Labial	*Labio-dental*	*Dental*	*Palatal*	*Velar*	*Laryngeal*
Plosive	Unvoiced	p		t		k	
	Voiced	b		d		g	
Nasal	Voiced	m		n		(ŋ)	
Fricative	Unvoiced		f				
	Voiced		v				
Sibilant	Unvoiced			s	(š)		
Affricate	Unvoiced				(č)		
	Voiced						
Trill	Voiced			r			
Lateral	Voiced			l			
Aspirate	Unvoiced						(h)

varieties of Tok Pisin distinctive sounds tended to be restricted to the most natural environments, in extended Tok Pisin distinctions are upheld in more difficult environments, this being illustrated by word-final nasals.

The emergence of phonological rules. Pidgins, and second languages in general, are governed by strategies for the optimalization of perception, that is strategies promoting the ideal of one form = one meaning and one meaning = one form. Thus rules that promote the ease of production tend to be suppressed in the early stages of development. It is only in a community of fluent second-language speakers that such rules have a chance of gaining wider acceptance.

There are two types of phenomena subsumed under the label of 'phonological rules': phonotactic restrictions; and rules that delete, permutate or add phonological information of base forms. As regards the former, a highly limited set of possible syllable and word structures was found with stable pidgins. Of particular interest are consonant clusters. Mafeni states, for Nigerian Pidgin English, that (1971: 108) 'The generalised formula for Nigerian Pidgin syllable structure is: /$C_{so-2}VC_{o-2}$/ and /N/ where the subscript figures indicate the possibilities in terms of number of elements, for that place of syllable structure.' Speakers of more developed varieties, on the other hand, admit the following syllable structures (Mafeni ibid.): 'Conservative speakers tend to avoid clusters altogether, however, either by dropping one member of the cluster as in *pún* – one pronunciation of the word *spún* (spoon) – or by vocalic intrusion, as in the case of *sìpik* instead of the more anglicized pronunciation *spik*.' Clusters with three consonants are found only with speakers of restructured anglicised varieties of the language. Very much the same observations can be made for Tok Pisin. In early forms of this language, we find a very strong preference for a CVCV word structure. Words containing three or more syllables and syllables containing consonant clusters are very rare. However, a longitudinal study of the Tok Pisin lexicon clearly shows a recent quite dramatic increase in lexical items that violate these conditions. Thus early records suggest that English 'straight' became either *tiret* or *sitiret* in Tok Pisin. Records around 1930 report *steret*, whereas in most recent times *stret* is found. The role of epenthetic vowels in such forms is discussed by Pawley (1975).

In sum, it appears that development in the area of phonotactics is manifested as a gradual relaxation of the many restrictions so characteristic of earlier pidgins. As regards other phonological processes, very little is known at present. However, it seems evident that the relaxation of phonotactic restrictions must be seen as a precondition for the existence of phonological processes that result in a phonologically more complex output. In most cases, phonological rules result in variants and thus increase the load of the decoder. As long as the majority of them are second-language speakers, the degree of phonologically conditioned variation can be expected to remain small.

Recent developments in the phonology of Tok Pisin illustrate the operation of rules separating underlying from surficial forms. A first example is the rule reducing vowels in unstressed syllables. Thus the adjective ending *-pela* of earlier developmental stages of the language is reduced to [pəla] or [fəla] in allegro varieties of present-day expanded Tok Pisin (cf. Lynch 1979), and the earlier future marker *baimbai* is frequently reduced to *babai*, *bai* or *ba* (see Sankoff and Laberge 1973).

A second example concerns voiced plosives. Whereas older varieties of Tok Pisin reflect the Melanesian practice of pronouncing the sounds [b], [d] and [g] with a strongly nasalized onset (making them sound like [mb], [nd] and [ngg] respectively), Tetaga (1971) demonstrates the decline of this practice among younger speakers. He observes that the use of prenasalization is now regarded as a marker of social backwardness and employed mainly as a stylistic device by younger speakers. This, then, takes us to a third aspect of phonological development.

The use of variants for stylistic purposes. There are two principal sources for the emergence of registers of style in a developing pidgin: borrowing from external sources; and backsliding, that is, the use of developmentally earlier forms in special stylistic functions. A comprehensive picture of these processes is given by Wurm and Mühlhäusler (1983), and only some brief comments on the second aspect will be made here.

For instance, in addition to the above-mentioned stylistic use of prenasalized consonants in Tok Pisin, proficient younger speakers also can be observed to ignore their usual distinction between [s] and [t], [p] and [f], and [l] and [r], and to insert epenthetic vowels when speaking to less advanced speakers or when portraying a hillbilly mentality. No systematic observations on phonological backsliding in any expanded pidgin are available at present, however.

Inflectional morphology

Although all the expanded pidgins examined here remain fundamentally analytic languages, there are signs in at least one of them, namely Tok Pisin, that inflectional devices are beginning to make an appearance.[28] For most speakers, the transition from free morphemes to affixes has not been completed and there remains a considerable amount of variability. Let us consider some of the developments encountered.

First, the full stress-bearing *hia* 'here' of earlier Tok Pisin, in constructions such as *dispela man hia* 'this man here', has been changed to unstressed *ya*. This form has come to convey either emphasis or 'noun previously referred to in a text' (that is, it has moved in the direction of a definite article as in *man ya* 'this man, the man') (more details in Sankoff and Brown 1976).

Second, one of the best-documented instances of developing inflectional morphology is the transition from sentential adverb to verbal prefix in the case of the so-called future marker[29] *bai* (discussed, for instance, in Sankoff 1979; Sankoff and Laberge 1973). In Tok Pisin, the earlier form of *baimbai* was not only gradually reduced phonologically, but also has come to be used redundantly, has moved from sentence-initial to preverbal position, and in some instances has become a prefix. Although this appears to have begun with second-language speakers, it is particularly common in creolized varieties of Tok Pisin. Compare the first sentence, spoken by a middle-aged speaker from a remote rural area, with the second, recorded by Sankoff of a young speaker in an urban area:

Bai em kam bek na i stap na kaikai na kisim wara.	'She will come back and stay and eat and fetch water.'
Pes pikini ia *bai* yu go long wok, – *bai* yu stap ia na. *bai* yu stap long banis kau bilong mi na *bai* taim mi dai *bai* yu lukautim.	'You, first son, will go and work in, – you'll remain here and you'll stay on my cattle farm and when I die you'll look after it.'

A further example illustrates both redundancy and shift to a preverbal position:

Bihain ol man bai stap wantaim het-man bilong ol.	'Afterwards the people will stay with their leader.'

A third form in Tok Pisin that has undergone phonological condensation (to *sa* or *se*) and is now being prefixed to verbs is the habitual marker *save*. Again, affixation is a variable feature and encountered principally in informal allegro speech of younger speakers. A longitudinal study of yet another example of affixation, the clitization of anaphoric pronouns, has been discussed by Sankoff (1977).

It is likely that similar examples of morphological expansion occurred in other pidgins, although unfortunately it is often not possible to determine at which stage. For example, in the case of Sri Lanka Portuguese creole (discussed by Smith 1983), the development of a number of affixes may have occurred prior to creolization. As in the case of Tok Pisin, the data discussed by Smith suggest a dual process of phonological reduction of stress-bearing full words and their gradual shift into a position close to the verb. Thus the verbal prefix *lo-* 'future' is derived from the Portuguese adverb *logo* 'soon', *ta-* 'present progressive' derived from the auxiliary *esta* 'present progressive', and the *ja-* 'past' prefix relates to *ja* 'already' in the lexifier language. Although it is difficult to reconstruct developments in Sri Lanka Portuguese Creole, the ongoing expansion of languages such as Bislama, Hiri Motu and Solomon Islands Pidgin English may provide interesting data for generalizations on morphological expansion.

The syntactic component

The three most important aspects of expansion in the syntactic component are the sources of grammatical innovation; the ability of adult second-language speakers to drastically restructure their grammar; and parallels between pidgin expansion and other forms of language development. Observations of many pidgins suggest the following general properties of syntactic expansion:

1 Syntactic innovation appears to be language-internal and derived from universal principles of language development. Borrowing is a minor factor and restricted by general principles.
2 Dramatic growth can take place in the absence of creolizing children.
3 There are significant parallels between pidgin expansion and other kinds of second-language and, to a lesser degree, first-language development.

Observations on the longitudinal development of number encoding in Tok Pisin will illustrate these points. In Tok Pisin, number marking for nominals emerged as follows. In the jargon stage, there was no formal means of marking plurality.

In the stabilization stage, *ol* (from English 'all') is used as a plural pronoun. In the following text, spoken by a very old speaker near Dagua, plural is indicated only with the first pronoun of a sentence, otherwise the third-person singular pronoun *i* is used. With some nouns, plurality is implied by the context:

Siaman i kamap. Nambawan samting bipo dispela graun no gat masta. I no gat masta. Ol i raun nating i kamap long Wallis, i kamap.

'The Germans arrived. At first this land had no Europeans. It had no Europeans. *They* (predicate marker) sailed about and *they* arrived on Wallis, *they* arrived.'

It is significant that this method of plural marking is not found in either Tok Pisin's lexifier languages or its principal substratum language, Tolai.

In the early expansion stage, plural was redundant with pronouns and animate nominals, indicated by means of *ol* or various quantifiers, as in the following text spoken by a middle-aged speaker from near Maprik:

Mi toktok long *ol* pipol insait long *ples*, toktok long *rot* o long *skul* samting . . . *Ol* i no bin wok long helt, nogat, *ol* i save sindaun nating. Na *ol* i no save troimwe *pekpek* long bus. *Ol* i save sindaun wantaim *ol pekpek*.

'I speak to the people in the villages, I talk about the roads and . . . schools and so on . . . They didn't do anything about their health, they . . . just sat around. And they did not use to throw away their excrement(s) in the bush. They used to live with their excrement(s).'

The forms *pekpek* and *ol pekpek* illustrate the variable use of plural *ol* with inanimates. This feature, together with the redundant use of *ol* together with other quantifiers, characterizes the following stage.

In the late expansion stage, the following examples were recorded with young second-language Tok Pisin speakers:

olgeta mipela *ol* man
'all we' (inclusive) pl. man = all us men
ol wanwan tasol *ol* i stap na *ol* Erima *ol* sampela *ol* man tu ol i dai
'(pl.) a few only they stayed and (pl.) Erima people (pl.) man also they died.'
na planti *ol* bikpela *ol* man *ol* i dai olgeta.
'and many (pl.) big (pl.) man they died entirely.'
(And only a few Erimas were left and some of them also died, and a large number of 'big men' were lost).

As regards point (3) above, namely parallels with second-language development in more structured (targeted) teaching contexts, my own non-representative collection of data from German learners of English suggest a comparable development. Thus, in spite of the fact that both languages have plural marking in all grammatical environments, learners appear to be inclined to omit English plural markers with inanimate and abstract nouns, particularly in oblique cases and after prepositions. My data on another pidgin, Torres Straits Broken, again suggest that the emergence of plural marking takes the path outlined for Tok Pisin. Whether this is due to some innate developmental programme or the result of more general pragmatic factors (what is pragmatically important is more likely to attract morphological markers than what is not) cannot be decided here. The absence of substratum and superstratum influence in the development remains significant, however.

A second construction illustrating grammatical expansion is that of causatives. This example also illustrates the transition from a lexical to a syntactic and eventually morphological way of encoding the same message.[30] The development of causative encoding in Tok Pisin and its immediate predecessor occurred as follows.

During the jargon stage only a few lexicalized causatives, such as *kil* 'to kill' and break 'to break', are found. The absence of periphrastic and morphological causatives can be accounted for by developmental factors. The fact that one is dealing with a one-word or two-word grammar at this stage means that constructions of the type *mekim* NV 'to cause N to do what is expressed by V' are automatically excluded, in spite of the fact that such periphrastic causatives were found in most, if not all, of the linguistic systems in contact. The lack of morphological causatives can be explained in terms of the general principle that inflectional and derivational morphology are late developments; that is, they are the first victims of language contact and the last features to be restored.

As the language develops, more lexicalized causatives such as *cut* 'to cut', 'to cause to be cut' and *move* 'to cause something to move' are added. The first instances of periphrastic causatives are found in Tok Pisin's direct predecessor, Samoan Plantation Pidgin English (cf. Mühlhäusler 1978b). Examples include:

yu mekim sam wara i boil	'bring some water to the boil'
mi mekim kabora ia drai	'I dried the copra'

As sentences with simple embeddings become increasingly common, so the use of periphrastic causatives becomes more widespread. By around 1900, the idea of causativity could be unambiguously encoded and, assuming that simplicity of expression and optimal decodability were the main forces in the development of pidgins and creoles, one would expect the development to have ended here, as it appears to have done in other expanded pidgins examined, such as West African Pidgin English and Torres Strait Creole.[31]

The structural expansion during the expansion phase is characterized by a drastic increase in referential potential during its first half and by a significant increase of non-referential potential in later years. The development of morphological causatives is an instance of the latter type of expansion, for, as we have seen, the referential demands of Tok Pisin speakers were fully met by the periphrastic construction. This is rather similar to the development of tense marking discussed by Labov (1971a). In present-day Tok Pisin, morphological causatives are stylistic variants of the equally widespread periphrastic causatives.

The first morphological causatives made their appearance in the late 1910s and early 1920s, at a time when contact with Tolai was intensive. A result of this contact was a number of morphological causatives of the type: prefix *mek* + V. This must be regarded as a direct calque of Tolai *va* + V. Compare:

Tolai		*Tok Pisin around 1920*	
mat	'to die'	save	'to know'
vamat	'to kill'	meksave	'to make know, inform'
maranga	'dry'	pas	'fast, obstructed'
vamaranga	'to make dry'	mekpas	'to fasten, tie up'
		nois	'to shake, tremble'
		meknois	'to make tremble, shake'

In spite of the productivity of this pattern in Tolai, it did not catch on in Tok Pisin, and the above examples are the only ones found today. Their status is that of lexicalizations. The reasons for this absence of carry-over from Tolai seem obvious. In the development of morphological causatives, non-stative verbs (*nois*), adjectives (*pas*) and transitive verbs (*save*) should occur later than with + stative verbs. The new calques are premature, since they do not fit in with the developmental tendencies of pidgin language.

The use of the same lexical base in a number of grammatical functions (zero-derivation) is a widespread phenomenon in pidgins and creoles (cf. Mühlhäusler 1978d) and is also used for causativization in English, as in:

to walk a horse	= to make a horse walk
to burp a baby	= to make a baby burp
to start a car	= to make a car start

Although this method is used in some related Pacific pidgins and creoles (for example, Torres Straits Pidgin), it is not found in Tok Pisin. Instead, the transitivity marker *-im* is used to signal causativization.

The first morphological causative ending in *-im* is found around 1910, *rausim* 'to throw out' derived from *raus* 'to be outside' (from German *raus*). By 1927 we get a number of additional lexicon entries pertaining to the context of giving and receiving orders in a colonial setting. They include:

bek	'to be back'	bekim	'to return something'
boil	'to boil'	boilim	'to boil something'
hariap	'to be in a hurry'	hariapim	'to make someone hurry'
lait	'to be bright'	laitim	'to light something'

The above four items violate the postulated developmental hierarchy. In the mid-1930s, a number of stative intransitive verbs underwent morphological causativization:

slip	'to sleep, be horizontal'	slipim	'to make lie down'
stret	'straight'	stretim	'to straighten'
orait	'all right'	oraitim	'to mend, repair'
pinis	'finished'	pinisim	'to finish'

Shortly afterwards, the first morphological causatives are derived from true adjectives (that is, those belonging to the small set that can appear in attributive position). They appear in the following order:

bikim	'to make big, enlarge'
kolim	'to make cool'
sotim	'to shorten'
switim	'to make feel pleasant'
truim	'to make come true'
raunim	'to make round'
stretim	'to straighten'

From the early 1960s onwards, more and more non-stative verb bases underwent causativization. The pattern appears to be on its way towards full productivity.

noisim	'to make noise'
sanapim	'to make stand up, erect'
pundaunim	'to make fall down'
wokabautim	'to make walk'
pairapim	'to make belch'
gohetim	'to make advance'

The first causative derived from a transitive verb base was found in 1973:

dokta i dringim sikman 'the doctor makes the patient drink'

The outcome of such expansion must be seen against the wider grammar of which it is part. Thus, after the development of a number of tense and aspect categories, the distinctions one can make in languages such as West African Pidgin English and Tok Pisin are very much comparable to those of English. Compare the following:

English	*Cameroonian Pidgin English*[32]	*Tok Pisin*
she goes to market	i go maket	em i go long maket[33]
she is going to market	i di go maket	em i wok long go long maket
she has (just) gone to market	i don go maket (naunau)	em i go long maket pinis em i bin go long maket
she went to market	i bin go maket	em bai go long maket (em laik go long maket)
she will go to market	i go go maket	

In addition, Tok Pisin can express aspectual distinctions that are not grammaticalized in English.

In addition to the development of compulsory encoding of grammatical categories, syntactic mechanisms of embedding are also introduced during pidgin expansion. In many cases, reanalysis of conjoined construction leads to the establishment of conventions for embedding. Again, data of a longitudinal type from languages other than Tok Pisin are not available. However, the endpoint of development reached in languages such as West African Pidgin English, Torres Straits Pidgin or Hiri Motu is usually comparable to stages identified during the expansion of Tok Pisin, suggesting that this process is highly constrained. More details can be taken from a useful overview of this phenomenon by Sankoff (1979). Generally speaking, one finds that:

1 with increasing age, expanding pidgins become grammatically more complex in that embedding and even multiple embedding are commonly encountered in the speech of younger speakers;
2 there is a growing tendency to mark embedded sentences by such means as relativizers and complementizers;
3 markers of embedded structures originate by means of reinterpreting existing forms;
4 there appears to be a natural order in which complex sentences emerge in a developing pidgin; however, many details remain ill understood.

I will illustrate these points with data on the development of complementation in Tok Pisin. This construction was not borrowed or calqued from either substratum or superstratum languages, but instead developed internally by means of reanalysing or expanding the use of existing material. The principal sources for complementizers were:

1 sentence adverbials *olsem* and *baimbai*;
2 prepositions, that is, *long* and *bilong*;
3 verbal concatenation as in *se*.

Two of these, *baimbai* and *olsem*, were encountered in a letter written in 1913:

mi laik *pabai* iu givemi log en	I want you to give it to me
mi tokiu *olsem* mi laik save tok bolog iu	I am telling you that I want to know your opinion

Subsequent to the reanalysis of sentence adverbials as complementizers, we find that prepositions are also used for this purpose. The data to be discussed shortly lend support to the 'localist hypothesis' that 'the extension of the use of cases from marking local and concrete relationships to their use in marking abstract or syntactic relationships' (Washabaugh 1975: 6) is a regular and universal process.[34]

The historical development of this particular type of complementation appears to be one in which the formal marking of the embedded sentence has developed very gradually. In the earliest grammar of Tok Pisin (Brenninkmeyer 1924), only complementation without complementizers is documented, as in:

i gut yumi go   It is good for us to go, let us go

As late as 1970, Wurm (p. 77) wrote that 'noun clauses in Pidgin have no distinguishing characteristics, and precede (as subject) or follow (as object) other clauses without a conjunction'. It must be taken into consideration, however, that Wurm is referring to Highlands Tok Pisin, which in some ways is less developed than the corresponding coastal varieties.

The earliest example of the use of the preposition *long* as complementizer that has come to my attention is found in Hall (1943: 62):

kiap i no laik long mi long mekim taim   the patrol officer does not want me to get myself indentured

It would be a gross over-simplification, however, to state that more and more instances of the *long* complementizer are encountered as the language develops. In actual fact, a large number of intervening factors, some of which are discussed by Woolford (1979), are also operative. First, *long* is used differentially after different verbs, as the data in table 5.4 (Woolford 1979: 115)

Table 5.4 Percentage use of long *preceding the complements of* laik, laikim, giaman *and* tokim

Speaker	*Age*	*Laik* 'want' (intr.)	*Laikim* 'want' (trans.)	*Giaman* 'pretend'	*Tokim* 'tell'
G	50	0 (0/17)	0 (0/4)	100 (3/3)	50 (1/2)
P	35–40	0 (0/13)	100 (1/1)	100 (1/1)	50 (1/2)

indicate. Second, there may be social and sex-preferential differences. Third, the range of *long* is encroached upon by other competing complementizers in the speech of some users of Tok Pisin. The technical aspects of *long* grammaticalization are discussed by Woolford (1979) and will not be repeated here.

A last Tok Pisin complementizer, *se*, is of particular interest, as it has parallels in numerous other pidgins and creoles. The development of English *say* into *se*, a 'complementizer following verbs of saying, believing etc.', appears to have taken place in the following stages. First, *se* becomes collocationally restricted, that is, it is used only together with other verbs of similar semantic content,
as in:

em i tok i se   'he said, was saying'

Second, the *i* joining the two verbs is dropped, because of the semantic similarity of the concatenated verbs:

em i tok se: mi laik kam	'he said: I want to come'

Third, sentences in which the speaker is non-coreferential with the agent of the reported event neutralize the distinction between direct and indirect speech:

em i tok se papa i gat sik	'he said: the father is ill' 'he said, that the father was ill'

Finally, *se* is reinterpreted as a complementizer following certain verbs, rather than as an independent verb in concatenation. Conventions for the treatment of pronouns in the embedded sentence are introduced at the same time:

em i tok se em i laik kam	'he said that he'd like to come'

In Tok Pisin, *se* is only found after a very small number of verbs. However, in another pidgin, Cameroonian Pidgin English, its use has been extended to such a degree that 'la proposition introduite par *se* peut se trouver après n'importe quel verbe' (Féral 1980: 279).[35]

A solution paralleling that of Tok Pisin and West African Pidgin English is also in evidence in pidginized varieties of Quechua (Muysken 1975). Whereas the particle /ñispa/ is used to introduce quotations in Standard varieties of Quecha, in pidginized forms of this language the related particle /nisha/ 'is used to complement verbs of saying and asking, but moreover, verbs of believing, wondering, wanting' (ibid.: 13).

The fact that pidgins often develop strikingly similar solutions to the same problem of grammatical expansion has led observers to postulate historical relationships between them, where in fact we are dealing with independent development. An interesting example is the case of the relativizer *we* (English where?), which is found in, among other pidgins, West African Pidgin English, Bislama, Solomon Islands Pidgin English, Tok Pisin, Queensland Kanaka English, Krio, Torres Strait Broken and Northern Territory Kriol.

With present-day evidence only, applying the criteria of comparative linguistics would suggest that a relativizer *we* was already present in some as yet ill-described proto-pidgin English. However, data of a longitudinal kind do not support such a hypothesis. Thus, when Dutton carried out fieldwork in the late 1960s in the Torres Straits, he failed to elicit relativizers (cf. Dutton 1970: 146), whereas in 1978 I had few problems in obtaining a relativizer *we* used not only for spatial and temporal relative clauses, but also to refer to animates. In Tok Pisin, *we* was not documented until the early 1970s, that is, many years after contacts between German West Africa and German New Guinea had come to an end. An implicational analysis of my own data suggests a development of the type:

1	ples we em i stap longen	'the place where he lived'
2	taim we em ikam (longen)	'the point in time at which he arrived'
3	man we i stap long ples	'the people who live in the village'
4	samting we mi bin lusim tingting longen	'something which I forgot'

Speakers who use the fourth version will also use *we* in the preceding contexts, but not vice versa. It would seem that a similar development accounts for the emergence of the relativizer *we* in other pidgin Englishes. This case clearly serves as a warning against reliance on the traditional comparative method in pidgin linguistics.

The case of West African Pidgin English *we* may have a different story, that is, its origin may well be traceable back to Krio constructions such as (Jones 1971: 82):

Da kau we no get tel, na God go dreb in flai.	(literally, 'That cow which does not have a tail, it is God who will drive away its flies')
Da buk we yu bin gi mi, a don los am.	(literally, 'The book which you gave me, I have lost it.')

The development of relativizers again illustrates that there are only a very small number of sources for this construction. Next to a reanalysis of a form of 'where',[36] we find a form corresponding to 'who', as in English, or a form corresponding to 'that'. All these solutions are found, incidentally, in the development of Tok Pisin, although some of them have not been successful. Whereas these examples illustrate the development of grammar through the reanalysis of existing grammar, some observers have also pointed to a second source for new grammar, namely pragmatic factors. An example, again relating to relativization in Tok Pisin, is the development of the emphatic marker *ya* (from English here) from a locative adverbial to a bracketing device at the beginning and end of relative clauses (Sankoff and Brown 1976).

In surveying these and other aspects of the syntactic development of pidgins, one can clearly see the movement away from a stage where surface sequence was determined by pragmatic factors to one of considerable discrepancy between surface sequence and grammatical order. Grammaticalization of this type certainly increases the overall complexity of a pidgin. However, at the same time it allows for stylistic variation, for devices which emphasize and de-emphasize aspects of meaning and structures beyond those found within simple sentences. It seems remarkable that such complexities appear to be the necessary accompaniment of functional expansion and that, moreover, the sources of functional expansion are very similar across languages. Unfortunately, the data base discussed here is rather limited, and it is hoped that more comparative longitudinal studies will become available soon.

The lexical component

It was argued that syntactic development served the principal function of increasing the stylistic flexibility of a developing pidgin. One suspects that lexical expansion is geared towards increasing the referential potential of a pidgin as it is used in new domains or functions. Although much of lexical expansion is related to this aim, a surprising amount of lexical development appears to serve mainly stylistic requirements.

Lexical expansion is manifested in two ways: either as borrowing from external sources, typically indigenous languages in the absence of the lexifier model, or as the development of language-internal devices of word formation. The reliance on these mechanisms appears to be unevenly spread among expanding pidgins. Although some pidgins (such as Hiri Motu) have a fairly limited word-formation power, others (such as Tok Pisin) have developed a considerable array of derivational devices. An example of an expanding pidgin that relies almost exclusively on borrowing is Sango (described by Samarin 1961 and Taber 1979). The process of lexical modernization of this language is seen by Taber as follows:

> But it obviously is in desperate need of new vocabulary. We have already seen that the few morphological processes known to tribal Sango have been lost in pidgin/creole Sango, so that the usual processes of derivation and compounding are unavailable. Some terms can be created syntactically in the form of phrases, especially noun-plus-modifier phrases, which are common in the language. But for many concepts and cultural items, Sango must look beyond its own limited resources. Whenever someone wants to talk about a republic, or a hypodermic needle, or school, or a truck, or politics, he quite automatically turns to French. (Taber 1979: 192)

As a consequence, in a large collection of text samples, more than 51 per cent of the lexical types in Sango were found to be of French provenance. It is interesting to note that a token count gives quite different results:

> The 508 French types account for only 6.8 per cent of the tokens, that is, 6.8 per cent of the running text. The Sango types account for 91.3 per cent of the tokens (1.9 per cent are proper words, which are ignored in this study, even though they would be an interesting subject for study in themselves). Sango types occur on an average 69 times each, while French words occur only 5 times each. Of the 508 French types, 205, or 40 per cent, occur only once each in the corpus. (ibid.)

Equally interesting is the observation that a large number of recent loans are not needed to increase the referential power of Sango, but merely add to its stylistic flexibility. On average, 17 per cent of all French loans had perfectly good Sango synonyms (see Taber 1979: 194). Similarly heavy reliance on French is also found in other African pidgins, such as pidginized forms of Fula (cf. Noss 1979).

The reverse case, that of European-derived pidgins borrowing from local vernaculars during their expansion, is illustrated with data from Pacific Pidgin Englishes. Such borrowings are often found in the more peripheral areas of the lexicon, and furthermore tend to refer to marked rather than neutral or unmarked meanings. Unlike borrowing from prestige superimposed languages, which is dependent on social factors, borrowing from indigenous sources often depends on regional preferences.[37] Thus, during the expansion of Tok Pisin in the 1930s, a number of lexical items were borrowed by different regional varieties, including:

1 the New Ireland region

Tok Pisin	*Gloss*
pudel, pudelim	'heap, to heap'
tapak	'leprosy'
talambar	'picture'
ramitim	'to kiss, to lick'
palar	'flat'
pirpir, pir	'story'

2 Manus Island

bulukai	'sago boiled with water'
burukin	'dish'
burumbut	'to tread on'
kaur	'bamboo'
kauvas	'friend, gift'

3 New Britain

varkurai	'court case, debate'
vinamut	'silence, peace, retreat'
kukuvai	'umbrella'
kulkulup	'cup, drinking vessel'
vivingul	'flute, to play the flute'

Few of these have survived. The relatively low status of indigenous forms is seen from the following estimates of their proportion in a number of contemporary Pacific Pidgin Englishes:

Bislama	90% English,	5% indigenous,	3% French
Tok Pisin	77% English,	16% indigenous,	7% German and other
Solomon Island Pidgin	89% English,	6% indigenous,	5% other

As indicated above, the pressure for new lexical material is lessened by the development of word-formation devices in a number of pidgins. Generally speaking, this proceeds along the following lines:

1 Jargon stage: there is no productive word formation.
2 Stabilization stage: circumlocution is used to express new ideas; there are a very small number of compounds at word level.
3 Early expansion stage: there is an increase of word-level compounds. As a rule the surface structure of derived lexical items is relatively close to their putative deep structure.
4 Late expansion stage: there is a strong tendency to derive word-level rather than phrase-level lexical items. There is also an increasing discrepancy between lexical surface structures and related deep structures, and lexical programmes become increasingly productive.

As regards the origin of new lexical patterns of word formation, two views can be noted. One, which was proposed, for instance, by Camden (1979) for Bislama, and by Sreedar (1983) for Naga Pidgin, suggests that calquing of indigenous word-formation patterns is the principal source. Another view (proposed by Mühlhäusler 1979) suggests development independent of external sources. This latter view is supported by the observations that many pidgins develop no word-formation devices where numerous such devices are found in contact languages, and that the emergence of word-formation appears to follow certain universal lines. Thus, as the expansion of a pidgin proceeds, we can observe:

1 the development of more and more abstract patterns of word formation;
2 a development from phrase-level to word-level derived lexical items;
3 a tendency towards greater derivational depth.

The endpoint of this development may well be a word-formation component that looks similar to one found in a substratum language or, indeed, looks like a common core of substratum and superstratum word formation, as in Bislama (Camden 1979: 54): 'while the Bislama lexical structure looks basically English to a native speaker of English, it also looks basically Tangoan to a native speaker of Tangoan'. However, during the stages leading up to this endpoint, considerable discrepancies may have existed, as can be seen in Mosel's detailed comparison of Tok Pisin and Tolai word formation (1980). The three tendencies mentioned above can be illustrated with some longitudinal data from Tok Pisin.

The emergence of more abstract patterns. The emergence of compounds is a good illustration of this principle. In the initial phases, syntactic compounds (in Bloomfield's terminology 1933: 233) – that is, compounds that reflect syntactic surface structures – are the only ones permitted. Examples include the type adj. + N (for example, *blakboi*) related to a syntactic phrase adj. + N. The emergence of fixed collocations of this type can be observed as early as the jargon phase, where we find:

big food	feast
white man	European

although an increasing number of such examples are recorded after 1900 in both Tok Pisin and the closely related variety of Samoan Plantation Pidgin. The most common word-level compounds in use at the time include:

blakboi	black indentured labourer
nuboi	freshly indentured labourer
olboi	labourer having served a three-year term
waitman	European

A great increase of compounds of this kind is found in Borchardt (1926), who lists the following:

biknem	fame
bikples	mainland
blakboi	native labourer
bluston	antiseptic
haiwara	flood, tide

and several others. Many more words following this pattern have been added since. It is interesting to observe that this type of compound does not exist in Tok Pisin's principal substratum language, Tolai, and that, moreover, most of the Tok Pisin compounds have no English cognate, which suggests development from internal resources. It is also interesting that pidgins with only limited word-formation powers, such as West African Pidgin English or Pidgin Naga, have comparable compounds; for example, Naga *kala borol* 'black bee' and *ori poka* 'white ant'; Torres Strait Broken *waitpis* 'white fish', and *bikfist* 'celebration, big feast'; or West African Pidgin English *deiklin* (from day clean) 'dawn'.

Adjective and noun compounds are also found as exocentric compounds, and it is with these that substratum influence is often cited as the major factor in their emergence. Thus Mafeni, in commenting on the two principal ways of word formation in Nigerian Pidgin English, remarks:

> The second important method of word-formation is the kind of compounding known as calquing, utilising English loan-words in combination according to the pattern of compounds to be found in Nigerian languages; stròng-héd or tròng-héd (stubborn), big áy (greedy), lòngà-trót (i.e. 'long throat') and bòtòm-bèlé (vagina), òpùn-áy (boldness, wisdom, or to browbeat) are a few examples which spring readily to mind.

Briefly, therefore, although English has supplied the vast majority of

> the items that make up the Nigerian Pidgin lexicon, the various substrates also supply vocabulary items (however few) as well as the more important processes by which the English loan-words are made to acquire new or additional meanings. (Mafeni 1971: 106)

Similarly, Camden, in discussing the word-formation component of Bislama and comparing it with Tangoan, a Vanuatu vernacular, points to close parallelisms between the two languages: e.g.:

> In Tangoan, a noun phrase occurs consisting of a head noun followed by a second noun which modifies it. The second noun may indicate purpose or characteristic of the head noun, particularly its species or the type of materials used in its construction.
>
> In Bislama, a noun phrase occurs consisting of a head noun followed by a second noun which modifies it. The second noun may indicate purpose or characteristic of the head noun, particularly its species, or the type of material used in its construction.
>
> Thus haos prea 'house prayer' ('a house for prayer'), boks tul 'box tool' ('a tool box') where the second noun indicates purpose, lif kokonas 'leaf coconut' ('a coconut leaf'), lif aranis 'leaf orange' ('an orange leaf') where the second noun indicates species, haos kava 'house sheet metal' ('a house with a galvanised iron roof') where the second noun indicates material. (Camden 1979: 85)

Compounds exhibiting such a word order are not found in other expanding pidgins, such as Pidgin Naga (Sreedar 1983), but they do occur in Tok Pisin, where Tangoan influence was certainly never experienced. As pointed out by Mosel (1980), compounds of this type in Tok Pisin were found before contact with Tolai and, on the basis of my own data, appear to have become highly productive only after contact with Tolai had come to a virtual end. A substratum language may thus have reinforced an ongoing development, but certainly cannot be regarded as its only source.

Greater restraint with regard to deducing origins from rough parallelisms is found in Hancock's studies of lexical expansion (1975, 1980). In the latter study, in particular, Hancock points to the relatively large set of language-internal sources of lexical innovation, when compared to external borrowing (1980: 67). Compounding, it is concluded, is a language-internal process. The best argument against the substratum view of the origin of new compounds is developmental/longitudinal; thus, although a comparison of a developed pidgin with substratum languages may reveal many similarities, the word-formation patterns of the substratum languages were not readily borrowed by the pidgin at earlier stages, when they were maximally accessible. Hancock's (1975) remark that 'Calquing, or adoption-translation, was probably not widely employed as a method of augmenting the lexicon during the early period' is explained by the fact that no transfer of lexical structures is possible unless a developing pidgin is ready for them. That is, abstract asyntactic or exocentric types of compounding cannot be borrowed in the early stages of pidgin development.

This argument also relates to a second form of word formation, reduplication, which, in the view of many, though not Hancock, is the paradigm case of substratum influence. Thus Mafeni, writing on the expansion of Nigerian Pidgin English, observes:

> The contribution of African languages to the lexicon of Nigerian Pidgin may, however, not be fully appreciated if we consider only direct borrowings from these languages; of far greater importance are the various processes of word-formation which it has adopted from the substrates. There are two principal ways in which Nigerian Pidgin increases its lexicon apart from the direct borrowing of lexical items. The first, which we have mentioned above, involves the phenomenon of reduplication as a method of word-derivation. In this way new words may be formed either as intensives of the words from which they have been derived, or with completely different meanings from them. (Mafeni 1971: 106)

Data from several pidgins contradict this view, which has been expounded, for example, by Thompson (1961).

Although there are a number of reduplicated forms in many pidgins, in almost all instances these are fully lexicalized rather than members of a productive word-formation paradigm. The role of reduplication in pidgins such as Papuan Pidgin English, Chinese Pidgin English, Pidgin German of New Guinea or Japanese Pidgin English is minimal, and Reinecke, discussing Vietnamese Pidgin French (1971: 51), observes that 'Reduplication, prominent in many pidgin and creole languages, is lacking in Tay Boi, even though it is virtually the only morphological feature of Vietnamese', thus providing interesting evidence against the substratum view of origin.

A comparison between reduplication in Tok Pisin and Tolai, carried out by Mosel concludes:

> Tolai and Tok Pisin have only a very few types of reduplication in common. Since we have already found out, that the types of verbal reduplication shared by both languages result from two different though related and partly overlapping concepts, there are only three other types of reduplication left which correspond to each other:
>
> 1 the reduplication of nouns denoting plurality,
> 2 the reduplication of cardinal numbers by which distributional numbers are derived,
> 3 the reduplication of adverbs denoting intensity.
>
> But these types of reduplication are too common to prove substratum influence. (Mosel 1980: 11)

To this, it must be added that those instances of parallels between the two languages were late to emerge (that is, they did not emerge before the 1950s), a long time after close contacts with Tolai had come to an end. It is true that there are some cases of reduplication calqued from Tolai, but such calques tend to be restricted to individual lexical items and have not resulted in productive morphological patterns. Much of the argument about substratum influence would become unnecessary if the distinction between isolated calques and borrowed patterns were made. As regards the latter, we appear to be unable to relate their development to any external source.

From the available evidence, it can thus be tentatively concluded that the expansion of derivational morphology follows language-independent lines and that there is a gradual change from patterns closely related to syntactic surface structures to others which are less transparent, a development also reflected in the change-over from phrase-level to word-level formation of new lexical items.

Change in size level. The formation of new lexical items during the stabilization phase of pidgins often takes the form of lengthy circumlocutions, and for a long time phrase-level lexical items were preferred to word-level ones. The reasons for this general tendency are, among others, limitation on word length in less developed pidgins and their general derivational shallowness. The replacement of older phrase-level items with shorter word-level ones is illustrated with some examples from Tok Pisin. For example:

Form recorded before 1985	*Form recorded in 1975*	*Gloss*
lam wokabaut	wokabautlam	'hurricane lantern'
manki bilong masta	mankimasta	'servant (male)'
mekim hariap	hariapim	'to speed someone up'
hatpela wara	hatwara	'soup, hot water'
mani pepa	pepamani	'paper money'
wara bilong skin	skinwara	'sweat'

It is quite clear from these examples that English influence was only marginally involved here, if at all. It is also noteworthy that the downward shift in size level occurred many years after the cessation of contacts with Tok Pisin's principal substratum language, Tolai. We are thus dealing with language-internal development. A detailed case study will illustrate the gradualness of this process, proceeding by way of lexical diffusion rather than generalization or overgeneralization. Thus, in Tok Pisin, lexical phrases of the form *man bilong Vint* expressing 'someone who usually does what is referred to by the verb' are documented in reasonable numbers for the mid-1920s, including:

Tok Pisin	*Gloss*
man bilong singaut	'noisy person, beggar'
man bilong slip	'sleepy, lazy person'
man bilong stil	'thief'

The only word-level items at this point are *sutman* 'policeman' and *sutboi* 'indigenous hunter'.

For the mid-1930s, the authors of the *Wörterbuch mit Redewendungen* remark (p. 53) that '-man as the suffix of verbs forms agent nouns' (author's translation). However, only a few word-level items are listed:

Tok Pisin	*Gloss*
wasman	'watchman'
sikman	'patient'
daiman	'dead, dying man'
stilman	'thief'

Phrase-level items listed in the *Wörterbuch* include:

Tok Pisin	*Gloss*
man bilong toktok	'talkative person'
man bilong save	'wise, knowledgeable person'
man bilong pait	'warrior, fighter'
man bilong pret	'fearful person'

No additional word-level items are documented until 1957. At this stage, Mihalic lists the following additional examples:

Tok Pisin	*Gloss*
saveman	'wise person'
trabelman	'troublesome person, fornicator'
lesman	'lazy person'

Other forms are only documented as phrase-level items.

Mihalic (1971) lists some new word-level items:

Tok Pisin	*Gloss*
holiman	'a saint'
sinman	'a sinner'
paniman	'a joker'

My own observations confirm that the trend towards word-level derivations continues and that a number of items which were recorded as phrase-level items in Mihalic (1971) are now being supplemented by word-level items, examples being:

Tok Pisin	*Gloss*
paitman	'fighter, warrior'
pretman	'easily frightened person'
bilipman	'believer'

Increased depth of lexical derivation. In the lexicon, as in other components of grammar, expansion increases the distance between surface structures and related deep structures. In the lexicon, this is associated both with the above-mentioned tendency towards asyntactic compounds and with the relaxation of a convention barring recursive application of word-formation rules. Let me illustrate this point briefly.

Although a number of different ways of word formation are encountered in expanded Tok Pisin, there is one powerful restriction to their use: only one lexical programme can be applied to a lexical base at any given time. This means, among other things, that:

1 No instrumental verbs can be derived from nominal compounds. Thus, although there is a form *saripim* 'to cut with a grassknife' derived from *sarip* 'grassknife', no form **grasnaipim* can be derived from *grasnaip* 'grassknife'.
2 No intensifying reduplications can be formed from denominalized verbs. Thus, whereas *kilkilim* 'to hit with force' can be derived from *kilim* 'to hit', no form **brumbrumim* can be derived from *brumim* 'to sweep', since this is a complex lexical item (that is, a verb derived from the lexical base *brum* 'broom').
3 No compounds involving more than two components are found. Thus, whereas *man* 'man' plus *meri* 'woman' can be combined to form *manmeri* or *meriman* 'people' and whereas *sikman* or *sikmeri* 'patient' are documented, no form **sikmanmeri* 'sikpeople' is permitted.

A number of progressive second-language speakers of Tok Pisin have begun to ignore these limitations and now produce some of the above-listed asterisked forms. Unfortunately, I have no comparative data for other expanding pidgins, but it is hoped that one is dealing with a general tendency.

One can conclude from the evidence presented here that new methods of extending the lexicon from internal resources can emerge within expanding pidgins without substratum or superstratum influence. Moreover, we have seen that influence from or borrowing of substratum material is restricted to those items that can be accommodated in the developing patterns of lexical enrichment: as the initial creativity of pidgins increases, so does their syncretic capacity.

The development of stylistic flexibility

Implicit in much of what has been said so far is the observation that the grammatical expansion process observable in pidgins is not aimed primarily at increasing their referential power, but at providing stylistic choice. This is achieved through reduction rules in the phonological component, the parallel development of morphological and syntactic devices encoding the same meaning, or through the emergence of extensive synonymy or near-synonymy in the lexicon.

The sources of this increase in stylistic flexibility are a complex mixture of language-internal and -external factors. First and foremost, they reflect a development of expanding pidgins away from being a mere medium of communicating denotational information to one for expressing a number of personal emotions. Put differently, there is a growing need for encoding the indexical dimensions of language, such as group membership, politeness or sex. Next to this, we find an expansion of the language resulting from its use in new media (radio, print) and its use as a form of art.

In discussing emergent stylistic differences, it should be remembered that there is no easy one-to-one correspondence between form and stylistic application; the same formal means can be used to achieve different stylistic effects and different forms may be employed for the same effect.

The effect of a pidgin's use in a new function, in this case that of playing a verbal game, is illustrated by the use of riddles in Cameroonian Pidgin English. Todd (forthcoming) points out that the reason for the emergence of riddles in this pidgin is the lower age at which it is learned, for riddles are seldom asked by adults. Riddles, like Pidgin English proverbs, jokes and folktales, are very much an urban phenomenon, associated with the growing number of intertribal marriages. In spite of this ongoing detribalization, urban riddles preserve the fundamental insights of a pre-urban society. This is reflected in the fact that many of them are calqued on a vernacular model. The following examples are given first in Cameroonian Pidgin English, then as a morpheme-by-morpheme gloss, and finally in Todd's translation:

Tɔri wei mek man krai ivɛn fɔ i mama i haus
Story rel. make man cry even for he mama he house
Something that can make one cry even when one is perfectly safe

Smok fɔ faia
Smoke from the fire

Tudei nɔting no dei fɔ haus, tumɔrɔ haus di fulɔp
Today nothing no loc. for house, tomorrow house prog. full + up
Today the house may be empty but tomorrow it will want for nothing

Pua bɔi wei i di go skul
Educated poor boy

A second type of linguistic play found in expanding pidgins is the use of poetic metaphors. The reader should be reminded that, in earlier developmental stages, the distinction between metaphor and literal meaning was not well defined and that social conventions for literal meaning emerge only late in pidgin development. Thus the use of such expressions as:

bel bilong mi i hevi	my belly is heavy	I am sad
bel bilong mi i isi	my belly is easy	I am contented

in Tok Pisin are metaphorical expressions from the point of view of target language speakers, but not for indigenes. Distinct from such phenomena is the deliberate creation of metaphors to achieve certain poetic effects. This activity, named *tok piksa* 'picture talk' or *tok pilai* 'play talk', is found in a number of domains: for instance, in connection with drinking. This act is referred to by *tok piksa* terms such as *botomapim* (to turn bottoms up = to empty a glass), *kapsaitim* (to turn over, upside down = to drink hurriedly), *drink paia* (to drink fire = to drink alcoholic beverages). *Tok piksa* references to some drinks on offer in Papua New Guinea include *meri buka* ('Buka girl'), a type of rum so called because of the black (Buka people are very black) girl on the label; *grinpela man* (green man = beer in a green bottle); and *braunpela man* (brown man = beer in a brown bottle). A term sometimes used to refer to intoxicating liquor in general is *spesel mailo* 'a special type of Milo (a malt drink)'.

A similar drinking vocabulary, involving considerable use of metaphorical speech, is found in Cameroonian Pidgin English (see Todd 1979). In her analysis of a narrative concerned with drinking, she isolates a number of deliberate metaphors:

> /mi a bi smɔl man we di tek kɔp/ meaning literally 'I'm a little man who habitually takes a cup' but implying: 'I'm very fond of a drink'. (Todd 1979: 285)

Realizing this, the listeners are prepared for other references to drinking and for the idiosyncratic code associated with it. Taken out of context:

/i nak bɔtu fɔ ma hed/

could imply 'he hit me on the head with a bottle', but here it means 'he put a bottle in front of me, implying that I could help myself'. In the text, we have three terms for a large bottle of beer:

/kiŋsai/	< English 'kingsize'
/ɔdine/	< French 'ordinaire'
/ŋgɔŋgi/	probably in many of the vernaculars, certainly used in Lamso, often in the form /ŋgaŋgi/

On seeing the bottle, the speaker tells us:

/a di krai . . . a krai ɔntɔp i finiʃ/

which, out of context, would mean 'I'm crying . . . I cry on top (over) it until it is finished', but here it implies 'I drank very slowly, savouring the delights of every mouthful until it was finished'.

Yet another example of emerging verbal poetry are proverbs. Whereas proverbial expressions are only now emerging in Tok Pisin, they appear to be firmly established in West African (particularly Cameroonian) Pidgin English. Todd (1979: 289) not only demonstrates the viability of proverbs in this language, but also shows the close similarities between proverbial expressions in Krio and Cameroonian Pidgin English, thereby supporting an argument that the latter is a continuation of Krio. Examples illustrating these two points include:

C. bad buʃ no de fɔ trowe bad pikin K. bad bus nɔ de fɔ trowe bad pikin	No matter how bad a child is his parents will not want to get rid of him.
C. dʒam pas dai mɔŋki tʃɔp pepe tɔk se na ndʒakato K. we ɛleja mit mɔnki i jit pɛpɛ, i se na dʒakato	When a monkey is hungry he eats pepper and calls it garden eggs

C = Cameroon Pidgin English   K = Krio

Language games are not just related to the structural properties of a particular pidgin, but also to the very choice of the pidgin language in the first place. Thus, in a recent discussion of Cameroonian Pidgin English in Urban Duala, Pradelles de Latour (1983) observes that two linguistic games of 'making fun' and 'making secret' are typically performed in pidgin, mainly because compulsory marking of honorifics and certain indexical rules of speech use found in local African languages do not exist in Cameroonian Pidgin English. Thus, for the function of 'making fun':

> there is a voluntary obliteration of the differences between generations, statuses and sometimes even sexes (a father can address his daughter as he would his son): 'Jean-Marc, yu kam tchop?' (b), (meaning: with me) a father asks his 8 year-old son, as he would a person his own age. 'How papa, yu tchop ol di tin, yu no lif mi som tin?' (c), says a son in Pidgin, and the father laughs. It would be absolutely unthinkable for this young boy to say such a phrase in Bangwa or for the father to accept such a comment in his language.

The same relaxation of traditional bonds of obligation is encountered in the use of Cameroonian Pidgin as a language for 'making secret':

> 'If your father is there and you don't want him to hear, it's O.K. to use Pidgin', says a young man. In this example among others, Pidgin appears as the means of telling something to someone in such a way, that those not involved will not understand what it is all about. But, contrary to a certain logic that would advise both partners concerned by the message to step aside from the group, it seems that it is precisely in the midst of family members or friends that one feels the urge to transmit a confidential message: one must add that the harmless and far from urgent nature of such exchanges is striking to the observer.

In Tok Pisin, comparable uses of language are expressed in terms of special stylistic registers of the language itself. Thus secret varieties of Tok Pisin exhibit a number of structural devices not found in everyday language. Backslang or *tok mainus* is used to refer to taboo areas in communication and exclude outsiders from access to a conversation between initiates. So, for instance, *kepkep* is used as a euphemism for *pekpek* 'to defecate' and *supsup* for *puspus* 'to have sexual intercourse'. Aufinger (1948–9) reports from a plantation context the warning *alapui wok, atsam i mak* standing for *iupala* (in standard orthography: *yupela*) *wok, masta i kam* 'you (pl.) work, the master is coming'. Aufinger suggests that the practice of pidgin backslang developed as a result of the introduction of writing.

Substitution of lexical items is also widespread in secret varieties. *Tok bokis* describes a linguistic register which involves the replacement of lexical items by others whose meaning and/or form are conventionalized within a large or small group of speakers, rather than being predictable from lexical conventions concerning metaphorical shift or lexical derivation.

A particularly rich field for the study of *tok bokis* are the various Melanesian cargo movements. For example, according to Schwartz (1957), some *tok bokis* items used by the followers of the Paliau cargo movement on Manus Island were *kastem haus* (custom house), referring to a shed for receiving and handling goods in trade with other villages; *mep* (a map = graveyard); *orait* (all right, healthy = to be equal to the white man in terms of knowledge, goods, etc.); *star* (star = turnstile in the village [having reference to heaven]).

I recorded some *tok bokis* terms from members of the Pele cargo movement in the Yangoru-Dreikikir area of the East Sepik Province. For example, *gaten memore* (memorial garden = cemetery); *kandere* (maternal uncle = someone who has died and will give money to the living); *wok* (work = the Pele movement); *rot bilong kandere i pas* (the uncle's road is obstructed = the dead body fails to provide money).

The use of Tok Pisin backslang illustrates an important point in the discussion of stylistic diversification: the dependence of linguistic structures on the medium in which they are used. Spelling and pronouncing words backwards appears to be crucially related to the institutionalization of Tok Pisin as a written medium. The use of pidgins in the media can also be related to the emergence of numerous other phenomena. One of the main effects of writing pidgin languages is that they have been, wittingly or unwittingly, moved closer to their lexifier language. Thus spelling often approximates to Standard English usage in Tok Pisin:

Phonetic spelling	*Written convention*	*Gloss*
go kwap	go goap	go go up
daun tampilo	daun daunbilo	down down under
torowe	troimwe	to throw away

Deliberate policies of the editors of influential Tok Pisin newspapers have had other effects. In the *Rabaul News*, many loans from English were introduced in the late 1940s, and in the largest present-day publication, *Wantok*, certain syntactic constructions, such as the use of subordinate-clause bracketing in relative embedding, are encouraged. Many idiomatic expressions for beginning and concluding letters have also emerged. Broadcasting has led to yet other innovations. In Tok Pisin, the past marker *bin*, and the use of the pronoun *yumipela* 'we' (inclusive or exclusive) (discussed by Siegel 1985: 8166) have been significantly promoted by radio announcers, as have many new lexical items such as *stopwok* 'strike' or *raneweman* 'refugee'.

Our understanding of the stylistic resources of pidgins is far from complete, and registers such as baby talk, public speaking or family interaction remain unexplored. It is hoped that there will be more studies of pidgin registers and their origin and use, and that modern techniques such as video-recording will be employed to gain a fuller understanding of the great communicative potential of expanded pidgins.

The expansion stage: a summary

The study of expanding pidgins suggests that the differences between first and second languages may be very tenuous. Innovations such as are produced by second-language speakers, principally adults, have been shown to be comparable both to the linguistic changes and elaborations produced ontogenetically by children acquiring a first language, and to the processes found in historical changes of 'normal' languages. What distinguishes expanding pidgins is the enormous speed at which such qualitative changes occur. West African or Melanesian varieties of Pidgin English today are very different from varieties spoken fifty years ago, and intelligibility between expanded pidgins and their related lexifier languages seems to be generally absent.

The study of pidgin expansion often seems to suggest a unidimensional progression from less complex to more complex systems. This, as the evidence presented here shows, is an oversimplistic view. Different pidgin speakers introduce competing solutions to certain communicative problems and as a consequence, we find considerable variability, including inter-individual variation. In addition, a detailed study of expansion often reveals unsuccessful innovations by individuals and subgroups. The general impression gained, although this needs to be corroborated by more comparative studies, is that the overall process of expansion is narrowly constrained by a number of developmental principles (such as the one which says that less marked constructions should precede more marked ones). As a result, borrowing from external sources, be they of the substratum or superstratum type, is relatively limited, particularly in the earlier stages of expansion.

The study of expansion also suggests that repair of referential deficiencies is not a major factor in language growth, particularly not towards the end of expansion. Much more important is the introduction of stylistic flexibility, variation and choice. As the requirement for ease of perception becomes less important, more choice and greater distance between superficial and underlying structures is introduced.

Creolization

Creoles, as was pointed out in chapter 1, are commonly regarded as pidgins that have become the first language of a new generation of speakers. It should by now be abundantly clear, however, that there are numerous difficulties with this simple formula. Recent work on creolization, in particular the discussion triggered off by the appearance of Bickerton's *Roots of Language* (1981), has done little to clarify the problem.

A major distinction, though one not always made, is that between the linguistic innovations accompanying the first-generation creation of a creole and subsequent changes over a longer timespan. Whatever the latter may tell us about general properties of linguistic change, it is unlikely to shed light on the former. One should thus distinguish two types of questions regarding creoles:

1 what are the linguistic correlates of initial creolization?
2 what are the sources for subsequent structural expansion?

Regarding the former, Valdman has observed:

> The expansion of linguistic functions served by a creole is accompanied by a set of processes subsumed under the term creolization: (1) relative stabilization of variation; (2) expansion of inner form; (3) complexification of outer form. While the corresponding mirror-image process, pidginization, has received detailed attention, creolization has remained by and large ill described. (Valdman 1977a: 155)

Regarding the latter, different views are found, falling roughly into the universalist and substratum camps, which have already been discussed.

The linguistic documentation of creolization is extremely sketchy. Particularly distressing is the lack of longitudinal studies. Most creolists rely on the comparison of the endpoints of creolization rather than the ongoing processes. Although this methodology has resulted in some highly interesting insights into common creole grammar, it is methodologically suspect. One fact, which is becoming more widely acknowledged,[38] is the lack of any reliable documentation of the transition from a rudimentary pidgin to a first-generation creole, and there are now voices that maintain that any creolization will draw on the resources of earlier elaborated pidgins.

The study of the actual process of creolization only began a few years ago (with Sankoff and Laberge 1973) and has concentrated mainly on syntax and semantics. Other aspects of grammar still await study, as does the area of pragmatics. The picture of creolization presented here is therefore an abstraction and in need of further substantiation.

The phonological component

The fact that pidgins were second languages and learnt, in most instances, by adults imposed considerable restrictions on their phonological flexibility. Generally speaking, all phonological processes favouring production at the cost of perception were discouraged. At the same time, segments and sequences that were difficult to produce were avoided. Both phenomena are reflected in the phonological systems of many creoles. Their relative phonological shallowness, when compared with languages such as English, appears to be due mainly to two factors: first, the need to communicate with second-language speakers for some time after initial creolization, and second, the short life-span of these languages. The most comprehensive case study of the sound system of a creole that arose out of an undeveloped jargon is that of Pitcairnese. Useful information on Hawaiian Creole English is given in Bickerton and Odo (1976). The Pitcairnese data are particularly useful in testing two of the main claims as to the origins of the phonological systems of creoles: namely the retention of earlier pidgin forms, and substratum influence. According to the hypothesis of the retention of earlier pidgin forms, one would expect a highly simplified shallow phonology, characterized by the absence of difficult sound and sound sequences. This does not hold for Pitcairnese, although occasional lexicalized exceptions such as *mema* 'mainmast' or *ko* 'because' suggest the existence of an earlier pidgin.

Substratum influence in the phonologies of creoles has been a second favourite explanation. Thus Le Page (1960: 18, quoted by Rickford 1977) appeals to the 'process of translation by West African ears' when discussing cluster simplification in Jamaican, and, more recently, Holm (1980: 56) traces a number of Bahamian pronunciations to West African origins. A study of the Pitcairnese data, however, does not suggest such close parallelisms, even if we heed Ross's (1964: 142) caution that 'In Pitcairnese philology, it is always necessary to keep in mind the possibility of a linguistic feature existing at the Settlement being replaced, partially or entirely, under later English influence.'

Counter-evidence against substratum influence comes from four sources. First, regarding the evidence from consonant clusters, Ross states:

> In Tahitian, consonant-groups do not occur, and all words end in a vowel. It might, perhaps, have been expected that Tahitian influence would have been strong enough to modify English words in Pitcairnese to make them conform with these rules. In fact, this has not happened.

> In Pitcairnese, there is no aversion to – rather an abundance of – consonant groups. (Ross 1962: 143)

Second, vowel length is distinctive in both English and Tahitian; however, Ross's data seem to suggest that it is non-distinctive in Pitcairnese. Third, the voiced stops [b], [d] and [g] are absent in Tahitian, whereas they are widespread in Pitcairnese. Finally, with regard to voiceless stops, in Tahitian [k] appears as a variant of [t] only, whereas in Pitcairnese the two sounds distinguish forms. It appears that the presence or absence of sound or sound combinations in the substratum language is not a very powerful factor in the formation of Pitcairnese.

In discussing the phonological processes leading to the establishment of another creole, Krio, we are hampered by two factors: first, inadequate knowledge of the external history of the language (it would seem to be over-simplistic to describe it as a simple continuation of a pre-existing pidgin); and second, the lack of very early documentation of pronunciation. Jones (1971: 70–1) points out that 'it may very well be that many words reverted to their English forms because of the continuing and increasing contact between the two languages, in a situation where its exclusive use in education confers a superior status on English'. Jones appears to suggest that the phonology of Krio is best understood by appealing to African substratum languages spoken in the same area. As with Pitcairnese, Krio does not distinguish long and short vowels. Compare:

English	*Krio*
mill	mil
teeth	tit
wool	wul
move	muf

Jones (1971: 72) remarks: 'The Krio vowel system is thus more akin to that of many African languages than to English.' With consonants, cluster simplification again is an outstanding trait of Krio. Some examples illustrating this phenomenon include:

English	*Krio*
straight	tret
strength	trɛnk
scratch	krach
scrape	krep
ground	gran

However, cluster reduction is far from categorical, and in at least one case the Krio cluster is more complex than the corresponding English one. Compare (Jones ibid.):

English	*Krio*
beans	binch
ants	anch
fence	fɛnch
rinse	rench

Rickford discusses the problem of clusters and substratum influence in more detail in the context of tracing Black American English to its creole roots. He dismisses claims that creoles are direct continuations of earlier simplified pidgins, by drawing attention to the systematic variability found with phonological phenomena in creole. Thus:

> While consonant cluster simplification by itself might be considered 'simpler' in some articulatory sense, it is difficult to see how a system in its application is contingent on a host of subtle factors could be considered 'simpler' than one in which simplification is either categorically present for all final clusters (the case in some West African creoles?) or categorically absent (more nearly the case in Standard English). (Rickford 1977: 199–200)

He further points out that there are few neat parallelisms between cluster presence and deletion in English-based creoles and West African languages and that:

> in any case, in view of the widespread occurrence of some form of consonant cluster simplification in other dialects of English (both in the United States and elsewhere), arguments for substratal influence in this case might seem very strained. (ibid.)

The various English-based creoles of Surinam illustrate how complex cluster 'simplification' can be. As regards the English word-final clusters *-nd* and *-nt* alone, the variants shown in table 5.5 have been recorded by Smith (1977a: 27) for these languages.

The following observations can be made about the data in table 5.5. First, it is virtually impossible to argue about creole origins on the basis of synchronic comparison of present-day creoles. Second, both the starting points and development of cluster treatment can be different for different creoles based on the same language. Third, in the case of Sranan, cluster simplification appears to be a more recent process, that is, one that took place after contacts with the substratum languages were severed. Present-day Sranan appears to exhibit more similarities with West African languages than Sranan spoken at the time of West African slave trade. In conclusion, in the absence of longitudinal data, as well as very good socio-historical information, claims as to strong substratum influence in creole phonologies appear to be dangerous.

If the notion of substratum influence seems problematical with sound

Table 5.5 Variants of English word-final clusters -nd *and* -nt *in the Surinam creoles*

English	*Sranan*	*Older Sranan*	*Boni*	*Djuka*	*Saramaccan*	*PSC*[a]
bend	béni		béni		béndi	béndi
send	séni	*sendie* (1798)	seni	sende	(*sendi* 1778)	séndi
find	féni	*finde* (1780)	féni	fénde	fén(d)i	féndi
blind	bréni		béeni		. . .	beléndi
mind?	. . .				mɛni	
want	wáni	*wandi* (1780)	wáni	wani	. . .	wánti
		wan (1780)	wã			wán
sand	(Dutch)		sandi (Dutch?)	(Dutch)	sándu	sándu
hand	ánu	*hanoe* (1798)	ana anu	ána	. . .	hán(d)a/u
stand	tan	*tan* (1780)	tã		tán	tán
want		*wan* (1780)	wã		. . .	wán
ground	gron	*gron* (1780)	goon	goón	goón	gorón
hunt	ónti	*hoendi* (1780)	hónti	hónti	hóndi	hhnti

[a] I remain doubtful as to the feasibility of reconstructing proto-creoles. In this particular case, the appearance of more complex clusters appears not to be a case of retention of proto-forms, but the result of convergence with the lexifier language.

Source: Smith 1977a: 27.

sequence and phonotactic restrictions, it becomes almost impossible to prove in the case of phonological rules. All we can say is that rules of phonological condensation that are not found in an earlier pidgin can appear in the creole of the following generation. An example is the condensation of Hawaiian Pidgin English *wen*. Pidgin speakers of this language, according to Labov (1971a: 57 ff.), only have two variant pronunciations: [wən] and denasalized [wəd]. For creole speakers, considerably more variability exists:

> Alternating with the full form [wɛn] are reduced forms [wən] and [wn], [ɛn], [n] and [ŋ], [wə] and [w]. The lone nasal consonant usually assimilates its point of articulation to a following consonant. The lone glide can be particularly difficult to hear: it may be reduced to a feature of rounding on a vowel or consonant. (Labov 1971a: 57–8)

Examples given include:

> So they wen walk [dew·ɔk] pas' the bridge.
> We wen looking [w:nlukin] for the guy Malcolm, eh.
> I wen go [a°ŋgo] kick one of 'em.
> So I went look [al:uk] by the door.

Next to such reduction of full lexical items, phonological reduction processes are particularly common with grammatical markers such as tense, aspect, number or category markers. The most detailed studies of this phenomenon relate to creoles that developed from expanded pidgins, such as Tok Pisin and Guinea Bissau Creole Portuguese (Kriol). This is understandable, as there would have been few forms to condense in a tenseless, aspectless and numberless jargon. The phonological condensation of the Tok Pisin irrealis (or future) marker *baimbai* to *bai* (discussed above) is paralleled by a similar development in Bissau Kriol. Kihm writes:

> There is in Kriol a complex TA [Tense–Aspect] marker *or* combination TA marker + auxiliary, *na bin*, where *na* is punctual and *bin* is homophonous (identical?) with *bin* 'to come', meaning 'punctual future', i.e. that such and such a thing will take place at such and such a time, explicitly stated or part of shared knowledge:
>
> (9) amañan n na bin kunpra arus 'tomorrow I will buy some rice'
>
> For (9) children quite often say:
>
> (10) amañan n nin kunpra arus 'id.'
>
> where *nin* can be pronounced either [nʌiŋ] or [niŋ]. The phonological derivation is clear: deletion through fricativization of intervocalic /b/ is a fairly regular process in BK in 'small' atonic words. The grammatical result is the creation of a new, fully grammaticalized TA marker which, having no link to any other lexical item, can now enter into the speakers' competence with nothing but its grammatical 'meaning'. (Kihm 1983a: 9)

Developments such as these appear to have their beginnings with adults, but are accelerated in communities of first-generation creole-speaking children.

A major reason for this kind of contraction seems to be the pressure for a more natural morphological system (in the sense of Mayerthaler 1978), where semantically less important information is signalled by means of phonologically less prominent forms.

In summing up what little we know about the role of phonological restructuring in creolization, it appears that there is a strong tendency towards both phonological and morphological naturalness. As regards the former, my own observations on Tok Pisin creolization suggest that the pronunciation of children can indeed be very different from that of second-language adults. Recordings made of children playing were virtually unintelligible to their parents, primarily, it would seem, because of their more 'advanced' phonology. However, older children typically conformed more closely to the norms of adult second-language speakers. This means that many of the expected introductions of natural phonological processes actually occur in creolization, but are later filtered out for communicative reasons. This process is comparable to children in other societies learning to conform to adult standards by suppressing many of the natural processes encountered in early child phonology.

Table 5.6 Development of words of structure C Liquid V(c) in Sranan, Djuka, Boni and Saramaccan

English	*Saramaccan*	*Saramaccan (1778)*	*Boni*	*Djuka*	*Sranan*	*Sranan (19th century)*	*Sranan (1798)*	*Sranan (18th century)*
split	piíti	plitti	piíti	príti	príti	priti 1844	prietie	plitti 1781
sleep	—		siibi	siíbi	sríbi slíbi	sríbi 1855 slíbi 1855	sliebie	sliepe 1718 slibi 1780
play	pɛɛ́	pre	peé	peé	prej	pleh 1844	pley	pree 1780
fly (n)	(feéi)		fée	feefée	frejfrej			vly 1765F
fly (v)	—		fái	fee	frej	flei 1844	fley	
blow	bɔɔ́	blo/bro	boo	boó	bro	blo 1856 bro 1855	bloo	
clothes	koósu	krossu klossu	koóši	koósi	krósi	klōsi 1844	kloosie	klossi 1780
black	baaka	blakka brakka	baáka	baáka	bláka bráka	blákka 1855 brákka 1855	blaka	blakke 1780 blaka 1765F

Many questions concerning creolization of the phonological component remain unanswered. Of particular interest, and undocumented to date, would seem to be the question whether new words are spontaneously created by children to make up for the numerous lexical gaps allegedly found in their pidgin or jargon model. If this indeed occurred, it could provide badly needed evidence in the area of universals of sound symbolism (cf. Taylor 1976).

Once creolization has occurred, creole phonologies can continue to change, due to internal pressures or outside borrowing. Although such subsequent changes do not help us to understand the nature of creolization, their study is important in determining what is genuinely universal in creole formation. All too often universals are derived from the comparison of arbitrarily chosen later stages of creole development.

This point can be illustrated with two examples, one from Surinam and one from Indian Ocean varieties of French. Smith (1977b) gives a detailed survey of the fate of the English *liquids* subsequent to creolization in Sranan, Djuka, Boni and Saramaccan. For words of the structure *CLiquidV(C)* (ibid.: 33), the complex picture of development shown in table 5.6 can be seen. Of particular interest in Smith's paper is the observation that tonal distinctions in Djuka are not so much a take-over from African substratum languages, but apparently the result of a historical development:

> In Djuka however there took place a sort of tone-spreading when the unstressed/low toned syllable followed the stressed/high toned syllable and the subsequent syllable began with a liquid:
>
> bátala
> bátara
> bátala
> bátála
> bátáa
>
> This preserved the original structure of the word, or at least the memory of the original structure of the word. (Smith 1977b)

The complexity of Surinam creole treatment of liquids is surpassed by the problems facing the linguists studying final-vowel truncation in the French creoles of the Indian Ocean (Baker and Corne 1982: 49–78). Both Réunion and Ile de France (Mauritius) creole lose their final vowels in certain conditions: that is, they sometimes have a long form ending in [-e], sometimes not: for example, *kon kone* 'to know'. The phonological and syntactic, though not semantic environments for the final-vowel truncation rule are similar, if not identical, in both creoles. However, whereas a synchronic comparison would lead to the conclusion of shared origins, longitudinal evidence makes this unlikely. Thus, when studying older texts of Mauritian creole, it is found that final-vowel truncation is a highly variable phenomenon, particularly in the

Table 5.7 Short and long forms in early Mauritian creole (contexts +NP, +V, +LOC)

Date	*Approximate occurrence (%)*
1805	40
1818	83.3
1828	6.9
1818–38	23.7
1835	9.3
1855	53.4
1867	39
c. 1860	100
1878	79
1885	97
1880–8	98

Source: Adapted from Baker and Corne 1982: 71.

speech of non-Africans. This is evident from the data in table 5.7, adapted from Baker and Corne (1982: 71). Corne concludes the investigation of this phenomenon with the following remarks:

> Although the evidence is not conclusive, there is a clear implication that the FVT [final-vowel truncation] rule appeared initially in 'slave' Creole, while 'master' Creole used long forms. This is obviously an oversimplified view, since Whites had at all times access to French morphology and syntax . . . while the exposure of non-Whites to French would have been highly variable. The picture then is that of a morphosyntactic rule being gradually adopted and gaining a semantic value quite absent from any variety of French. (Baker and Corne 1982: 72)

To this it must be added that the development of the various semantic regularities governing final-vowel truncation occurred long after contacts between Mauritius and Réunion had become insignificant and contacts with other French creole-speaking areas in the New World had been severed.[39]

Inflectional and derivational morphology

The only studies of the ongoing appearance of inflectional morphology in a creole are those of Tok Pisin. Generally speaking, there appears to be no qualitative difference between the developments in expanded second-language Tok Pisin and creolized Tok Pisin. Instead, creolization merely continues and generalizes ongoing changes. Comparative data from other creoles would be particularly welcome.

Let me illustrate these observations with the example of plural marking in creolized Tok Pisin.[40] Arguing from what is widely maintained in the theoretical literature on creolization, I set up the following hypotheses:

1 plural marking will become categorical in all environments, that is, it is semantically determined;
2 the position of the plural marker in the noun phrase will become fixed;
3 differences in surface form will always be associated with differences in meaning;
4 semantic plural will be marked in parts of the sentence other than the noun phrase.

None of these predictions was borne out in full. Moreover, it appears that different solutions to the problems of plural marking are found in the three creolized varieties of Tok Pisin examined: that is, those of Malabang (Manus Island), Yip (on the Keram River) and urban Lae (data recorded by Sankoff and Laberge 1971). Unfortunately, the texts examined were not of sufficient length for a detailed syntactic analysis such as the one undertaken here, and elicitation and formal interviews were only used in Malabang. However, the following generalizations can be made with confidence.

First, plural marking remains variable for all creolized varieties examined; the only instance of categorical plural marking was that of animate subjects in Malabang Tok Pisin. None the less, plurals without *ol* are in the minority in all semantic environments of the varieties examined. My own feeling is that the trend towards a categorical marking of the semantic plural is blocked by the fact that *ol* is a relatively stressed free-standing formative and not an unstressed affix.

Second, my data suggest that the position of *ol* in the noun phrase is not fixed in creolized Tok Pisin and that variation is found not only across creolized varieties in different localities, but also within the speech of individual speakers. However, the favourite form is the one in which *ol* appears at the beginning of a noun phrase. Compare the following data:

1 Speakers from Yip aged between 8 and 12 years:

ol adj. N	*adj. ol N*	*ol adj. ol N*
ol dispela lain	dispela liklik ol tumbuna	ol narapela ol tumbuna
this group	those little grandchildren	the other grandchildren
ol planti dok many dogs	olgeta ol pis all the fish	

2 Speakers from Malabang (first-generation Tok Pisin speakers, aged 25–35 years):

ol dispela lain	dispela ol man
this group	these people

ol faivhandet masalai five hundred spirits	bikpela ol man big men
ol lokal pipel the local people	

3 Speakers from Lae (children recorded by Sankoff in 1971):

ol adj. N	*adj. ol N*	*ol adj. ol N*
	ol dispela man 'these men'	ol dispela ol man 'these men'
sampela ol man 'some men'	ol sampela man 'some men'	

More fixity is found with some prenominal modifiers, such as *olgeta* 'all', which is followed by *ol*, and *lokal* 'local', which is always preceded by *ol*. It is not clear to me to what extent the position of *ol* is linked to certain lexical items.

Third, although the principle of one form, one meaning is realized to a greater degree in creolized Tok Pisin than in other varieties, I have not been able to find any consistent difference in meaning between, for instance, *ol sampela man* 'some men' and *sampela ol man* 'some men'. I would predict, however, that unless speakers settle for one of these alternatives, a difference in meaning will develop in creolized Tok Pisin.

Finally, the prediction that plurality will be marked in parts of the sentence other than the noun phrase is partly fulfilled in Malabang creole Tok Pisin, where a kind of agreement between plural noun subjects and reduplicated verbs is developing. Examples of this construction are:

ol pikinini i pilaipilai	the children are playing

as against:

wanpela pikinini i pilai	a child is playing
*wanpela pikinini i pilaipilai	a child is playing
planti man i lainlain	many men were lined up
ol manmeri i bungbung	the people gathered

In conclusion, the following generalizations can be made about morphological developments in Tok Pisin's creolization phase:

1 the differences between non-creolized and creolized Tok Pisin are slight rather than drastic;
2 although there is a definite tendency for rules to become more productive (and less restricted by environmental conditions), the endpoint of maximum simplification has not yet been reached;
3 the amount of redundancy found in creolized Tok Pisin is not significantly greater than that found in late expanded Tok Pisin.

Most creoles, it appears, still have not acquired any significant inflectional categories and those that have, like some Portuguese-based ones, may have acquired them some time after creolization, in which case their change from isolating to inflectional languages is comparable with that in other full languages. Creoles for which the absence of inflectional morphology has been explicitly stated include Guayanese Creole French (Fauquenoy 1974), Krio, the English-based creoles of the Caribbean, and many more. In those cases where inflectional categories have developed, this typically involves condensation of pre-existing fully stressed markers of grammatical categories, as in Tok Pisin. Thus:

> where Mauricien Creole has *Mo te apre manzo* for 'I was eating', the usual representation of the Haitian equivalent is *Mtap manže* (Faine 1939). In the French Creole of the Antilles, we have a future marker *ke*, which seems to have been derived from the durative marker *ka* with *ale*; *ka* + *ale* → *kale* → *kao* → *ke*. (Labov 1971a: 60)

As these condensations are typically optional and characteristic of fast-spoken language, their representation in available grammars of creoles is often sketchy.

Therefore the emergence of inflectional morphology does not appear to be a necessary feature of creolization, although the fact that it subsequently emerges in many creole studies suggests considerable inter-speaker variation in the use of condensed and affixed grammatical markers, thus casting doubt on the idea that the transition from isolating to inflectional creoles follows any universally preprogrammed path.

As regards the development of derivational morphology or word formation, more information has come to light in recent years, in particular on English-based creoles such as Krio (Jones 1983), Sranan (Sebba 1981; Voorhœve 1981), and the Australian creoles (for example Steffensen 1979). More comprehensive surveys were made by Hancock (1980) and Allsopp (1980). We must again distinguish between cases where some word-formation processes are found in the preceding pidgins and those where the pidgin is lacking in derivational morphology. We must also distinguish developments accompanying creolization with first-generation speakers from subsequent developments.

The only documented case of a creole that has developed from an expanded pidgin which already had word formation worth mentioning is that of Tok Pisin. The principal difference between second-language expanded and first-language creolized Tok Pisin was found to lie in the following areas:

1 existing derivational rules are generalized (that is, made fully productive);
2 derivational processes can apply recursively;
3 some derivational morphology is borrowed from local vernaculars.

The following examples will serve as illustrations. First, we will consider the derivation of causative verbs from intransitive verbs and adjectives. Only a small number of forms are encountered in most second-language varieties of the language. In creolized Tok Pisin of Malabang, this rule has become virtually exceptionless; new forms encountered include:

Malabang Tok Pisin	*Gloss*
wara i STINGIM ol plang	'the water makes the planks rot'
dispela kaikai i SWITIM maus bilong mi	'this food gives my mouth a pleasant taste'
meri i BONIM pikinini	'the woman gave birth to a child'
em i wok long RAUNIM diwai	'he is busy making a piece of wood round'
meri i SMATIM em yet	'the girl dolled herself up'

It is interesting to note that Malabang Tok Pisin now exhibits the same lexical productivity in this area as Tok Pisin's original principal substratum language, Tolai. A static comparison of the two languages would suggest direct substratum influence.

Second, a major increase in Tok Pisin's lexical power is caused by the relaxation or abolition, in the creolized varieties I studied, of the constraint on multiple derivation. Instead, recursive application of derivational rules yields numerous new forms such as:

1 the derivation of abstract nouns from derived verbals:

huk	huk	huk
'hook'	'to go fishing'	'fishing'
kuk	kukim	ol Hailans i gat narapela KUKIM bilong saksak
'to boil, cook'	'to cook something'	'the Highlanders have a different COOKING METHOD for sage'

2 the derivation of abstract nouns from reduplicated verbs:

holim	holholim	paip i gut long HOLHOLIM bilongen
'to hold'	'to grasp, hold fast'	'the pipe is good with regard to its HANDLING QUALITIES'
lukim	luklukim	meri i gut long LUKLUKIM bilongen
'to look, watch'	'to gaze, stare'	'the girl is really very good looking'

3 the reduplication of derived verbals:

smok	smokim	smoksmokim
'so smoke'	'to smoke (coconuts)'	'to smoke thoroughly'
sak	sakim	saksakim
'bag'	'to fill in bags'	'to fill many bags'
krugut	krugutim	krukrugutim
'crooked'	'to crush'	'to crush to little pieces'

It is important to note that many of the changes in the lexicon do not relate to an increase in referential power of the language, but provide new linguistic styles.

Finally, borrowing of derivational affixes from a local language is illustrated with the following set: creolized Tok Pisin of Manus Island has developed a new variant way for expressing concepts, previously expressed by complex lexical items in the second-language varieties:

Second-language Tok Pisin	*Malabang-creolized Tok Pisin*	*Gloss*
Manusman	pomanus	'a true Manus man'
Manusmeri	pimanus	'a true Manus woman'
man bilong smokim paip	popaip	'a pipe smoker'
man bilong smokim brus	pobrus	'a cigar smoker'
spakman	pospak	'a habitual drinker'

Other studies of derivational morphology in creoles are not developmental. To date there is no evidence that a powerful derivational lexicon develops within a single generation of children to make up for the numerous lexical deficiencies of their input language. However, it is possible to make a number of observations. These relate to the origin of word-formation processes in preceding pidgins; the role of substratum languages; and the overall power and regularity of creole lexicons. Many writers have asked whether there are any aspects of creole derivational morphology that set them apart typologically from other languages. The two areas singled out most frequently are multifunctionality and reduplication, which are both said to be present in creoles to a greater extent than in other languages, due to the fact that creoles continue a trend already noticeable in their pidgin predecessors. With regard to multifunctionality, Voorhœve (1981: 26) explicitly states: 'subsequent grammatical expansion in a creolization process does not offer incentives to create semantically empty affixes. This may explain why multifunctionality seems to be more frequent and more regular in Pidgins and Creoles than in the model language.' Unfortunately, he does not illustrate the actual process of expansion. A study of multifunctionality in Sranan (Sebba 1981) suggests that, although this process is extremely common, it is also subject to a number of fairly complex restrictions: for example, no nouns can be derived from benefactive or position verbs. The presence of such restrictions, as well as differences from restrictions in the lexifier language, make the suggestion of direct pidgin ancestry less attractive. However, only a longitudinal analysis could answer the question.

Reduplication in creoles again has often been traced back to preceding pidgins. Thus, Thompson argues:

> The amount of iteration which takes place in Creole languages is striking. We must, however, guard against according this phenomenon too much importance. Not everyone who says 'sí, sí, señor', 'ay, ay, sir' or 'oh, la la' is a Creole speaker. Iteration is common to many languages and the part it plays in the formation of pidgins could, alone, explain its vigorous presence in the Creoles. (Thompson 1961: 11)

However, as already pointed out, productive reduplicative processes are not widespread in pidgins, and indeed are almost lacking in creoles such as Seychellois (Bollée forthcoming). The data presented in studies on Northern Australian Kriol again suggest no direct link with a pidgin antecedent, although Steffensen suggests:

> It will be claimed that semantically-motivated reduplication in the Australian creole is similar to that found in other English-based creoles, including Jamaican, Krio and Pidgin English of West Cameroon, a fact providing some support for the genetic relationship of these languages. In the case of adjectivals, the process is similar to that which has been described for an Aboriginal language, showing a syntactic influence of the substratum languages. These two sources of reduplication clearly parallel the two sources of the language. (Steffensen 1977: 603)

In sum, then, creoles are qualitatively different from documented pidgins spoken previously. Lack of longitudinal studies prevents us from determining whether there has been an abrupt break or whether these differences reflect a gradual drifting apart.

The influence of substratum languages on creole word formation has often been advocated. Again, with the data we have, it is difficult to draw any firm conclusions. Where more detailed studies exist, such as with reduplication in Seychellois and Australian creoles, direct substratum influence is seen as a very minor factor. It is true that many creoles exhibit a certain amount of transparent calques such as the ones given by Hancock (1980: 81):

Tobagonian CrE	ha:d-e:z 'stubborn' (<Afr., 'hard' + 'ears')
Trinidadian CrE	kʌt-ai 'to turn away one's glance'
	lɔŋ-ai 'to be covetous'
	da:k-ai 'poor vision'
	mɔ:tə-pɛsl 'pestle' (all < Afr.)

Papia Kristang CrPtg	kumi-bɛntu 'stroll' (<Malay makan aŋin)
	mai-pai 'parents' (<Malay ibu-bapa)
	olu-di-pɛu 'ankle' (<Malay mata-kaki)

However, such calques typically are lexicalizations rather than the basis of productive processes of word formation. In fact, I have yet to see hard evidence to convince me that substratum languages have played an important role in the development of word formation in any creole. I should add that younger creoles appear to be even less affected than older ones, suggesting that similarity of the derivational lexicons of languages such as Krio and West African vernaculars is the result of prolonged language contacts rather than the process of creolization or even creole development over time.

A cursory examination of the lexicons of a number of creoles suggests that they are neither very regular nor very powerful. The cumulative impression is one of numerous competing developments, a high degree of lexicalizations or semi-productive processes, and a continued reliance on borrowing from outside sources. This, however, can only be a tentative conclusion, and I am well aware of DeCamp's brilliant demonstration (1974) that the full extent of productivity in a creole language cannot be recovered by conventional methods of fieldwork.

As yet, the change-over to a system with a derivational lexicon has been described only for an expanding pidgin (Tok Pisin in Mühlhäusler 1979). How first-generation creole speakers in instances of more abrupt creolization cope with their lexical needs remains ill understood. With regard to the potential sources for new word-formation patterns, we should keep two things in mind. First, the discontinuities in the transition from pidgin to creole make direct expansion of a pre-existing pidgin an unlikely explanation for many creole languages. Second, it is by no means clear that creoles have the syncretic capacity to borrow derivational morphology from substratum or other outside systems.

In the light of these observations, a gradual development out of internal resources, comparable to that encountered in Tok Pisin, seems more likely. In this view, new derivational regularities would result from surface analogy, reanalysis of pre-existing structures and rule generalization. Linguistic evidence from a number of present-day creoles suggests that these processes take place over many generations and that, in most instances, they remain a long distance away from the theoretically possible optimal endpoint.[41] It is only in those cases that have been subject to active language engineering (as, for instance, Bahasa Indonesia, Swahili or Afrikaans) that anything like full productivity has been reached.

Syntax

Almost all recent discussion of creolization has centred around syntactic observations. Most important are Bickerton's suggestions that a number of widely found aspects of creole syntax are indeed innate or bioprogrammatic. This issue is still being hotly debated and cannot be dealt with in full here.

It again seems best to distinguish between creoles that have arisen out of expanded pidgins and others that have developed out of unstable jargons, and between developments accompanying creolization and those occurring later. Recent studies of Tok Pisin and Australian Aboriginal Kriol, both of which developed out of expanded pidgins, have suggested considerable syntactic variation within even small groups of creole speakers, or indeed individuals. Thus Koch (1984) found that relative clauses in Central Australian Aboriginal Creole were introduced by a number of different relative markers, including *we* (> English *where*), *wanim* (> English *what name*), *who* and *what* as in (data from Koch 1984):

we just got a lot of kurtungurlus *who* work for them	(Peter J 95)
and some of them kurtungurlu been pass away	(Peter T 75)
pewelerrenge *what* 'im talk kurrkurr kurrkurr nighttime	(Sam 5. 30 a)
etenetene *where* him jump (an insect)	(Sam 5. 32)
alpalhe ('fur string') *where* they cut'm from rabbits	(Sam 5. 32)
Euro – they *where* they live along hill	(Peter T 101)
nytveypere *wanim* flying, nighttime	(Sam 5. 31)

These forms appear to have coexisted for some time without streamlining of relative marking. Similar findings for Tok Pisin were arrived at by Aitchison (1983). Differences were found within a small group of females living at a hostel in Lae, the second largest town in Papua New Guinea, and these differences did not disappear even with members of the same family. In addition to different language-internal solutions to the problem of relative markers, some group members had also borrowed grammar from Tok Pisin's lexifier language English, rendering the distinction between creolization and decreolization a difficult one to maintain.

Supporters of the bioprogram theory of creole syntax would argue that such variation in the pidgin–creole complexes is symptomatic of the gradual transition from second to first language. Children who are exposed to minimal jargon input would presumably have fewer structures to reanalyse, and hence would have to appeal to innate solutions. However, this theory leaves unexplained several points:

1 the obvious qualitative differences between creoles such as Hawaiian Creole English and their jargon or pidgin predecessors;
2 the syntactic similarities between creoles world-wide;
3 the fact that such similarities arose without apparent historial links and without shared substratum languages.

I will deal with these points in turn.

First, Bickerton's Hawaiian Pidgin and Hawaiian Creole English show numerous documented qualitative differences. Speakers of the former appear to have at their disposal an extremely rudimentary syntax, idiosyncratic and generally devoid of grammatical markers. Speakers of the latter have acquired, within a very brief time, a relatively complex creole syntax. Bickerton (1984: 177) argued that 'such structures can only have been acquired by processes inaccessible to pidgin speakers'. Why second-language pidgin speakers never learnt the more sophisticated language of their offspring seems strange, particularly as no such aversion to learning is found with Tok Pisin or the Australian Aboriginal Creoles. The reasons would seem to be social (having to do with their bilingualism, the social networks they operate in and so forth), rather than a mental inability to learn more complex structures as adults. If indeed the creole of the children is such a 'natural' system, it should surely be one that is highly learnable. Another consideration with regard to the generational language differences is that Bickerton does not have data to show at what age and in what order the creole constructions were acquired.

Second, there is considerable disagreement as to the world-wide similarities of creole structures, although 'the hypothesis of the structural interdependence of creoles with different lexical components' (Hellinger 1979: 332) remains popular. I have recently had the privilege of examining data from a hitherto virtually unknown creole, Unserdeutsch, a German-based creole of Papua New Guinea, which appears to be a case of an insufficient jargon turning into a creole within one generation. A comparison of this creole and Tok Pisin, which was also used by Unserdeutsch speakers with Bickerton's bioprogram features, reveals some major discrepancies, however. Using the features singled out by Bickerton (1981) as diagnostic of biogrammar, the following observations were made.

1 *Movement.* Rules move focused constituents to sentence-initial position. Such rules are found both in Tok Pisin and Unserdeutsch, for example:

Nur ein Name i konnte ni finden.
Only one name I could not find.

2 *Article.* The definite article is used for presupposed-specific NP; an indefinite article for asserted-specific NP; and zero for non-specific NP. Unserdeutsch does not appear to follow this system (nor does Tok Pisin), as can be seen from the following utterance:

I lesen Buch   I read a (particular) book

According to Volker (1982: 37), 'reflecting perhaps the lack of articles in Tok Pisin, the use of either article is optional and in many sentences, Vunapope Germans omitted an article where this would not have been possible in English or Standard German'.

3 *Tense–modality–aspect system.* Neither Tok Pisin nor Unserdeutsch appear to fit into Bickerton's suggested universal framework for creole languages. Like southern dialects of German (spoken by the majority of the German mission workers), Unserdeutsch has only one past tense, in addition to present and future tenses. Like Tok Pisin and English, but unlike High German, it signals the distinction between durative and non-durative aspect. The important distinction in Tok Pisin between inception and completion, on the other hand, is not found in Unserdeutsch.

4 *Realized and unrealized complements.* The data available to me do not permit any definite statements on this point, although it appears that the evidence is negative rather than positive.

5 *Relativization and subject copying.* Whereas Tok Pisin conforms to the universals postulated by Bickerton in this area of grammar, Unserdeutsch does not. The most common relative pronoun appears to be *wo*, as in:

Der Mensch, wo is am bauen de Haus, hat gehauen sein Finger.
The man who was building a house hurt his finger(s).

6 *Negation.* Neither Tok Pisin nor Unserdeutsch conform to the conditions for negation in creoles laid down by Bickerton.

7 *Existential and possessive.* Whereas the same lexical item is used to express existentials (there is) and possessives (have) in many creoles and in Tok Pisin, Unserdeutsch does not have this construction. This is surprising, since the Tok Pisin model (*mi gat mani* = I have money, compared with *i gat mani* = 'there is money') was available and southern German dialects also have this feature (*es hat Geld* = 'it (e.g. the child) has money' or 'there is money').

8 *Copula.* In Unserdeutsch, the copula is conspicuous by its presence and, what is more, it is inflected for person and tense.

9 *Adjectives as verbs.* Adjectives are used as verbs in many creoles and in Tok Pisin, but not in Unserdeutsch. Other changes of grammatical category are observed in this language, however: in particular, abstract nouns may become verbs or adjectives. It would seem that the presence of a verb–adjective distinction is closely connected with the presence of a copula in Unserdeutsch.

10 *Question forms.* Like Tok Pisin and all other creoles, Unserdeutsch shows no difference in syntactic order between questions and statements; for example:

Du will drinken Kaffee
Do you want to drink coffee?
or You want to drink coffee.

In spoken discourse, differential intonation patterns are often used to distinguish questions from statements.

11 *Question words.* Whereas question words are typically polymorphemic in the creoles considered by Bickerton as well as in Tok Pisin, Unserdeutsch has a mixed system. Compare:

Standard German	*Unserdeutsch*	*Tok Pisin*	*Etymon gloss*
warum	was, warum	wa(t)nem	why?
welche	was fuer	wa(t)nem	what (e.g. time)?
wieviel	wieviel	hamas	how many?
wer	wer	husat	who?

12 *Passive equivalents.* Unlike virtually all other known creoles, including Tok Pisin, Unserdeutsch has a fully developed passive construction. It is basically the same as that found in English, using the formula copula + past participle + *bei*, as in:

Der Chicken war gestohlen bei alle Rascal.
The chicken was stolen by the rascals.

The above information has to be considered in the light of available linguistic models at the time when Unserdeutsch came into being. The models in question are Standard German (taught to the speakers at school), (New Guinea) Pidgin German (a very rudimentary pidgin) and a newly stabilized Tok Pisin. Table 5.8 indicates the presence or absence of Bickerton's features for

Table 5.8 Presence or absence of various features in available linguistic models at the time when Unserdeutsch came into being

Feature	*Hawaiian Creole*	*New Guinea Pidgin German*	*Tok Pisin*	*German*	*English*	*Unserdeutsch*
1 Movement	+	–	+	+	+	+
2 Definite article	+	–	–	–	–	–
3 Tense, etc.	+	–	–	–	–	–
4 Complements	+	n.a.	–	–	–	?
5 Relativization	+	–	+	–	?	–
6 Negation	+	–	–	–	–	–
7 Existential	+	+	+	+	–	–
8 Copula	+	0	+	–	–	–
9 Adjectives	+	–	+	–	–	–
10 Questions	+	n.a.	+	–	–	+
11 Question words	+	–	+	+ –	+ –	+ –
12 Passive equivalent	+	n.a.	+	–	–	–

n.a Not applicable, no evidence
0 Variable presence
\+ Categorical presence
– Absence

these languages. This table clearly demonstrates that Unserdeutsch drastically differs from Bickerton's ideal creole, whereas Tok Pisin, as used by second-language speakers, exhibits considerable overlap with Bickerton's diagnostic features. At the same time, it reveals major structural differences between Unserdeutsch and the two input languages – pidgin and 'standard' German. Similar differences are also found in Pitcairnese (cf. Le Page 1983b).

Finally, in the light of such findings, the question of origins for creole syntactic structures must be asked again. The fact that both Pitcairnese and Unserdeutsch developed out of pidgins unrelated to those that have been the base of most other creoles could be taken as an indication that the structure of a creole is linked, in an as yet ill-understood fashion, to its pidgin precursor. However, some qualitative differences remain to be explained.

More historical research is needed into the diffusion of creole grammar. The fact that some of the Portuguese speakers working on the Hawaiian plantations in the nineteenth century had been recruited from the creole-speaking Cape Verde Islands may well account for the wide distribution of some of Bickerton's creole features.

The degree of access to the target language must also be further researched. The fact that the lexicon of most creoles appears to have been drawn largely from the socially superordinate lexifier language suggests that this access cannot have been as limited as is often made out. Lexical borrowing can be expected to have considerable repercussions in the syntactic component. If, for instance, the difference between causative and non-causative verbs is fully lexicalized in the lexifier language, then the emergence of productive rules for causative formation is likely to be slowed down or prevented. Many speakers of European-based creoles have been exposed to standard forms of the lexifier language in the classroom or on mission stations.

Access to substratum languages is another area of dispute. Supporters of the bioprogram generally admit the availability of substratum languages as potential models, but are quick to point out the various factors that make them unattractive to children. In the absence of any first-hand data on creolization of jargons, I would prefer to postpone judgement on this.

Even if it should turn out that first-generation creole speakers were maximally cut off from syntactic input, such conditions would be necessary rather than sufficient components of a bioprogram explanation. In a recent review of Bickerton (1981), Foley (1984) has spelt out the functionalist alternative. In discussing the alleged bioprogrammatic nature of the SVO word order of creoles, Foley points out that this is the most likely solution to the problem of variable word order in the pidgin stage for simple functionalist reasons. Since creole-speaking children do not develop inflectional morphology:

> without inflections to mark the subject or object of a sentence, word orders like SOV or VSO are problematic because the order of the subject and object may not be altered without changing the meaning of the

> sentence, but such languages tend in fact to use such rearrangements heavily to signal the relative importance of the subject or object. The word order SVO avoids this problem by using the positions on either side of the verb to indicate subject and object, and movement of the object before the subject, as in *John, I saw yesterday*, causes no interpretation problems because the subject is the immediately preverbal noun. Note that in this explanation there is no need to appeal to an innate bioprogram which specifies SVO word order. The restricted input plus the constraints imposed by human communicative needs determine this preference. (Foley 1984: 337)

These matters remain unresolved. It seems obvious, however, that a great deal more has to be learnt about creole syntax, before a final judgement can be made.

I have already mentioned the lack of longitudinal studies of creole syntactic development, and there are few reliable guidelines for distinguishing between developments during and subsequent to creolization. That such subsequent development has played a major role in many of the present-day creoles is well known. The relative isolation in which some of them have developed does not appear to have slowed down their rate of internal change. A detailed discussion is beyond the scope of this book, but a few cases will serve to highlight the strong parallels between pidgin expansion and changes in later creole development.

As pointed out by Voorhœve and Kramp (1982: 11), Bickerton hardly acknowledges the possibility of syntactic change in creoles other than for change motivated by decreolization under the influence of a dominant language. If it is true, however, that many internal developments subsequent to creolization spring from the 'need to differentiate basic concepts' (ibid.: 12), then they are well worth considering.[42] Voorhœve and Kramp follow up a number of developments in Sranan, including the creation of a future marker, changes from an aspect-centred to a tense-centred system of verbal modification, and the development of new prepositions. A particularly interesting case is the development of three-place verbs. Sranan, as recorded in the late eighteenth century, had the following phrase structure (PS) rules (Voorhœve and Kramp 1982: 3):

1 S → NP AUX VP
2 VP → V (NP) PP
3 PP → *na* NP

These rules provide for a maximum of two arguments per verb.[43] In later texts, however, strategies for adding a further argument to verbs are encountered, among them the use of the all-purpose preposition *na*, as in:

ju gi assranti na Bakkra? Did you give brutality to a white man?

It appears that the development of *gi* into a three-place verb proceeded in stages. In the early texts it can only be a three-place verb, if the third argument is pronominal. Later any NP is permitted. This kind of change is difficult to categorize and certainly involves more than a reanalysis of existing linguistic structures.

A similarly 'spontaneous' development involves the Jamaican interrogative form *duont* (Roberts 1977: 101–8), meaning 'isn't that so?'; this is a relatively recent form. It is unusual because of its phonological shape (final-consonant cluster); its not being used as a social marker; and its functional differences with pre-existing tags in both Jamaican Creole and Standard English. Thus it is not simply a new form used in an old function,[44] but a sign with new form and function.

Other documented examples of creole development most frequently take the form of syntactic reanalysis. A very common example is the emergence of complementizers out of prepositions (Nichols 1976; Washabaugh 1975). Nichols notes the close parallel of this development in the expanded pidgin Tok Pisin and the creole Gullah.

A number of changes in the history of French-based creoles are discussed by Valdman (1977a: 155–89), including phonological condensation of grammatical markers and changes with verbal and nominal modifiers. Among the latter, Valdman (ibid.: 164) discusses the development of an older system, illustrated in Mauritian Creole for *lisjē* 'dog':

$$\left\{ \begin{matrix} \text{Indef} \\ \left\{ \begin{matrix} \text{Poss} \\ \text{Dem} \end{matrix} \right\} \text{(Pl)} \end{matrix} \right\} + \text{N} + \text{Def}$$

Singular		Plural
en lisjē	Indef	lisjē
lisjē-la	Def	ban lisjē-la
mo lisj̃	Poss lsg	mo ban lisjẽ
sa lisjē-la	Dem	sa ban lisjẽ-la

into a new one, which adds a plural marker identical with the third-person plural pronoun. A further development is the shift of the demonstrative from a preposed to a post-nominal position in some French-based creoles; this is summarized, for instance, in Haitian Creole (ibid.: 168) as follows:

$$\text{Indef} + \text{N} + \left\{ \begin{matrix} \left\{ \begin{matrix} \text{Def} \\ \text{Poss} \end{matrix} \text{(Deictic)} \right\} \text{(Pl)} \\ \text{Dem+Def} \end{matrix} \right\}$$

Singular		Plural
ju liv	Indef	liv
liv-la	Def	liv-jo
liv-sa-a	Dem	liv-sa-jo
liv-li	Poss 3 sg	liv-li-jo
liv-la-a	Deictic	liv-la-jo
liv-li-a	Poss+Deic	liv-li-a-jo

Valdman arrives at his conclusions primarily by comparing different French creoles and only occasionally relying on longitudinal evidence for individual creoles. In view of the above-mentioned unsuitability of the comparative paradigm for creole studies, his conclusions must be interpreted with care. In fact, recent studies by Baker (in Baker and Corne 1982: 210–11) clearly disconfirm Valdman's suggestion that the Mauritian system is a conservative one. A detailed longitudinal examination of the plural marker *ban* (> French *bande* 'bunch') makes this abundantly clear. The fact that *ban* is found in Mauritian and Réunion, as well as all the minor Indian Ocean creoles, does not warrant the conclusion that these creoles all derived from an ancestral language containing this form. Although the count noun *ban* 'group, shoal' is attested in Mauritian Creole from the middle of the nineteenth century, it was not used as a pluralizer until about 1880. As regards Réunion Creole, Baker (ibid.: 211) remarks that 'The earliest examples of /ban/ as a plural marker I have yet found in RC are in Fourcade (1930). In that text, /ban/ occurs with some frequency and thus can scarcely then have been a new feature of RC.' One can therefore only agree with his conclusions:

> It seems clear from the above that /ban/ alone did not function as the plural marker at the beginning of the nineteenth century in any Indian Ocean Creole but had acquired this status in MC by 1885 at the latest. Whether this was a Mauritian innovation – a distinct possibility on the available evidence – or not, remains to be determined. However, one can at least conclude that the presence of a grammatical (or lexical) item in all the Indian Ocean Creoles does *not* prove that this was a feature of eighteenth-century RC. (ibid.)

In conclusion, longitudinal accounts of creole expansion – both for the process of creolization itself and for subsequent developments – would seem essential. The short-cuts taken by many scholars in the past appear not to lead to the insights they had hoped for and have often produced a quite unrealistic picture.

Lexicon and lexical semantics

Although much has been said about the lexicon of individual creoles, comparative studies and those using up-to-date lexicological techniques are rare, as is reliable information as to the point in time at which lexical items entered a creole. Many of the traditional studies only consider the relative proportion of substratum and other 'foreign' lexical material, concluding mainly that the European element is dominant. Thus, Sylvain (1936: 136) refers to Trinidad French Creole as 'une langue Ewé à vocabulaire français'. A recent study of the same language by Aub-Buscher (forthcoming) also concludes that, after considering all foreign loans, 'a solid residue of 90% of entries in a Trinidad French Creole glossary has its origin in the central or dialectal French of past centuries'.

Foreign loans are categorized according to semantic domains. In the case of Trinidad French Creole, these include (data adapted from Aub-Buscher forthcoming):

1 Magic and traditional religion, for example:

obja	magic	Eik, Twi
wãga	magic spell	Duala, Mbondu, Bolo Songo, Sama
dẽge	sorcerer's sleight of hand	Ngombe

2 Traditional ways of food preparation:

akra	fritter	Yoruba, Igbo
tõtõ banan	mashed green bananas	Twi
kuku	corn	Ewe

3 Polite names for body parts:

pumpum	female genitals	Twi
lolo	penis	Ewe (?)
bõda	buttocks	Bambara, Kongo

4 Local fauna:

tiktak	large ant	Bulu
kõgowi	sort of millipede	Kongo
kulu (bwa)	termite	Kanuri
kungala	frog	Kongo
zẽglẽtẽ	sea bird	Ewe, Kongo

Other domains, such as local flora, fish names and diseases are typically of Amerindian origin.

Regarding the European part of the lexicon, a number of creolists have painstakingly traced its elements back to regional or social varieties of the lexifier language. One example is Holm's (1981) analysis of the Misquito Coast Creole English vocabulary. Some of the numerous British English dialect words that Holm identified in this creole include those shown in table 5.9.

Recently, there have been a number of innovative attempts to gain a better understanding of the contribution of non-European languages to the vocabulary of the so-called European-based ones. An important consideration is that of Edwards (1974: 5): 'The factors which determine that the phonological form from one heritage will be adopted by pidgin speakers are sometimes distinct from the factors which determine the origins of the semenic, symbolic, and emotional content for any given lexeme.' Thus lexical items should not be regarded as undividable wholes, but capable of accommodating different types of lexical information from different sources. In the case of many 'multi-level syncretisms', the shape of a lexical item is similar to that of the related

Table 5.9 Origin of British dialect words in Miskito Coast Creole English

Dialect words	*Region*
arm-hole 'armpit'	1 456 8
at 'to'	1 4
atween 'between'	G1 3
ax 'ask'	G1 3
baby (of eye) 'pupil'	3
back 'carry on back'	8
backways 'backwards'	4
bawl 'shout, cry'	1 4 89
belly-work 'diarrhea'	4
bank 'estate, farm'	4
best 'had better'	G1
blow 'breathe; rest'	34
booboo 'bogeyman'	34 6
bro 'male peer'	7
brogues 'stout shoes'	1 34
dodge 'follow stealthily'	34
drudge 'dredge'	1 9
drugs 'dregs'	9
drownded 'drown'	1 456
duff 'raisin cake'	1 89
evening 'afternoon'	1 5 7
fall 'fell (timber)'	1 89
fass 'meddle, disturb'	1 34
favor 'resemble'	G1
first 'immediately'	45 9
for 'to (+ verb)'	1 4 9
from 'since (conj.)'	1 3
frowzy 'musty'	G1 3
full 'to fill'	34
gal 'girl'	G 78

G General; 1 Ireland; 2 Wales; 3 Scotland; 4 North England; 5 West Midlands; 6 East Midlands; 7 East Anglia; 8 Home Counties; 9 West of England
Source: Adapted from Holm 1981: 47.

European language, whereas semantic or syntactic-categorical information may be traced back to substratum languages. This idea was taken up by a number of scholars, including Givón (1979) and Mühlhäusler (1979), and tested against data from various creoles. It appears that the extent of non-European influence on lexical semantics is fairly extensive and that the traditional method of comparing undivided cognates for lexical comparison is insufficient. A major attempt to determine the extent of substratum semantics across a wide range of creoles was made by Huttar (1975). He examined the degree of correspondence of lexical semantics between the Surinamese creole Djuka and 43 other languages with respect to 20 lexical roots. The results are:

> 1 The major factor we may call 'linguistic substratum'. This label subsumes the total linguistic background (genetic, areal, and contact phenomena) of the native speakers of non-European languages involved in the initial contact situation that produced a pidgin. It does not include extralinguistic cultural background.
>
> 2 A second factor that appears important enough to merit further investigation is the role played by language contact after the original pidginization period.
>
> 3 The nature of creoles themselves – arising from pidgins not only by expansion of vocabulary, but also by extension in meaning of existing vocabulary items – plays at most a minor role. (Extension of meaning occurs in pidgins as well.) This pidgin–creole factor is clearly less significant than factors 1 and 2. (Huttar 1975: 694)

This suggests that the lexical semantics of the source language is modified to a considerable extent in related pidgins and creoles, and that resulting differences are due principally to substratum influence; that language mixing is particularly common at the lexical level (disconfirming earlier views as to the relative lexical purity of pidgins and creoles); and that, moreover, substratum structures must have been available both during and subsequent to the creolization process.

That substratum influence is not haphazard and restricted to single lexical items is seen by the apparent continuation of lexical field structures from substratum languages in later creoles. This is obviously what can be expected in the case of a gradual transition from a pidgin to a creole, as, for instance, in the case of Australian Kriol. Sandefur (1981: 256) illustrates this with Kriol kinship terms, where the lexical forms of English have been paired with meanings typical of Aboriginal kinship systems:

dedi from 'daddy' refers to 'father and father's brothers'
mami from 'mummy' refers to 'mother and mother's sisters'
anggul from 'uncle' refers to 'mother's brothers'
andi from 'aunty' refers to 'father's sisters'
greni from 'granny' refers to 'mother's mother and her brothers and sisters; sister's daughter's sons and daughters'
meit from 'mate' refers to 'spouse and spouse's brothers and sisters'
gajin from 'cousin' refers to 'mother-in-law and her brothers and sisters'

Lexical field structures of substratum languages are also encountered in creoles that allegedly emerged over a much shorter period, such as Jamaican Creole English and Djuka. In both these languages, a West African system of day-names and names for persons born on a specific day is preserved. Kahn (1931: 171) remarks:

> This method of naming children after the day in the week on which they were born seems to have been brought over from the Tshi-speaking people in Africa. The similarity is easily recognized after consulting the following table, compiled by Mr Charles de Goeje.

	Male		*Female*	
Born on	*Djuka*	*Tshi*	*Djuka*	*Tshi*
Sunday	Kwassi	Kwassi	Akwasiba	Asi or Akwasiba
Monday	Kodjo	Kwadjo	Adoea or Adjoba	Adua
Tuesday	Kwamina, or Kwabina	Kobina, or Kwabina	Abena or Akoba	Abena or Arabat
Wednesday	Kwakoe, or Quakoe	Kwaku	Akoea	Akua
Thursday	Jaw	Know, yow, or Akhor	Jaba	Awbah, Awybah, or Yawa
Friday	Koffi, or Koffay	Kwaffi	Afida	Yah-awfua
Saturday	Kwassi	Kwassi	Amba	Anenimwah

DeCamp (1967) reports the same phenomenon for Jamaica and other creole-speaking areas of the New World. DeCamp supplements his observations on substratum influence with remarks on the development of name-giving in Jamaican creole over the last two hundred years, thus illustrating the numerous changes that occur in creole lexicons subsequent to their creolization.

The West African system of name-giving appears to have gradually died out and was obsolete by the end of the nineteenth century. The reasons given by DeCamp include social changes as well as the fact that most of these names underwent semantic deterioration. The word *quashie*, for instance, which originally meant 'male person born on a Sunday', and its female counterpart *quasheba*, had come to mean the following (1967: 145):

quashie

1 a Negro, especially of low class
2 a fool, idiot, stupid man
3 a gullible country-bumpkin
4 an irresponsible ne'er-do-well
5 a dirty, filthy man
6 a stubborn, pig-headed man
7 a half-full breadfruit

quasheba

1 a prostitute
2 a foolish, ne'er-do-well woman
3 typical name for a mule

DeCamp also follows up the history of the names given to African slaves by their European owners:

> his Christian name, (if he was baptized) was given not by his parents but by his owner, and it was often chosen as casually, sometimes as whimsi-

> cally, as are the names we bestow on dogs and parakeets. Classical names were the most popular, with *Venus*, *Bacchus*, and *Chloe* among the most frequent. In naming or renaming an adult slave, it was sometimes considered a good joke to name an exceptionally stupid man *Plato* or *Socrates* or to name a sexually promiscuous woman *Diana*. Slaves also were named in honor of, or as an insult to, public figures. The fact that a large number of slaves were named *Pitt* does not indicate that the slave-owners endorsed the policies of the Great Commoner; it is more likely comparable to the case of a Republican acquaintance of mine who bought his children a pet skunk and named it Lyndon Johnson. (DeCamp 1957: 143)

Again, for understandable reasons, these naming conventions have long been replaced.

An area where retention of substratum language is particularly intense is that of exclamations, interjections and related phenomena. A recent article by Cassidy (forthcoming) remarks:

> the great majority of interjections in the Creole are of African origin. In use by slaves these were not necessary to communication, however natural they might be to expression of feelings or emotions. They did not require translation or relexification; their meaning was evident in context, and could even, in different contexts, serve for such related emotions as fear and anger. (Cassidy forthcoming)

Examples from Jamaican Creole English mentioned by Cassidy include:

aóo, aóa (> Twi *áò*,) 'what! why! hey! ay! fie!'
bábwá (> Twi *bóbŭóo*) 'exclamation of astonishment'.

With the advent of theories of linguistic naturalness and markedness, a new instrument for determining the 'foreign' element in European-based creoles became available. An early paper in this category is Frake's analysis of the Spanish-based creoles of the Philippines (1971); his initial findings have since been confirmed by data from other creoles.

As a general principle, in a marked–unmarked pair of the same set, the indigenous forms tend to occur in the marked category. Thus, for Zambuangoeño we find that the less marked singular pronouns are derived from Spanish, and the more marked plural ones are derived from indigenous Philippine languages:

person		
1	yó	kami
1 + 2		kitá
2	tú	kamó
3	? éle	silá

(from Frake 1971: 226). This is also found in numerous other lexical domains, including:

1 adjectives contrasting magnitude (ibid.: 232), such as:

gránde	dyútay	large	small
?álto	pandak	tall	short
lihéro	mahínay	fast	slow
kórre	páta?	fast	slow
mapwérso	malúya	strong	weak
?árde	?amamaluŋ	bright	dim
?apretáo	haluga?	tight	loose
?agúda	mapurul	sharp	dull

2 nouns contrasting sex or age, such as:

byého/a	báta?	old man/woman	child
lólo/a	?apu	grandfather/mother	grandchild
táta/nána	?anak	father/mother	son, daughter
?óhas	talbus	mature leaf	young leaf
plóres	putput	blossom	bud
soltéro	dalága	bachelor	unmarried girl

3 general versus specific names for food items, such as:

komida	kanon	food	main dish
pwerko	lecon	pork	suckling pig
peskao	tulinan	fish	tuna

Different origins for cardinal numbers are documented for a number of creoles and creoloids. An example for Angolar (a Portuguese-based creole spoken by the descendants of maroons on São Tomé) is given by Ferraz:

> The only cardinal numbers in Angolar which are of Portuguese origin are those for 1, 2, and 3 (*'ũa*, *'dosu*, *'tesi*), which occur also in compounds with these numerals. For the rest, the Angolar numerals are of Bantu origin, and are very similar to those of Kumbundu, for example:
>
> | | *Angolar* | *Kimbundu* |
> |---|---|---|
> | 4 | 'kwana | kwana |
> | 6 | sa'mano | samanu |
> | 60 | ma'kyɛ sa'mano | makwi a samanu |
>
> The Angolar numbering system suggests that when the Angolares left the main community, São Tomense may not yet have had more Portuguese numerals than Angolar has. (Ferraz 1974: 185)

Unfortunately, it is not reliably known whether the Angolares took to the interior of the island subsequent to creolization. Evidence on this point could throw light on the question of differential complexity of creoles. In any case, data now available suggest that the indigenous forms were borrowed late (that is, possibly subsequent to creolization), and that substratum influence may not have played a major role during creolization itself. We certainly are again alerted to the fact that static comparisons are not reliable in determining the affiliations of creoles with their numerous contact languages.

Studies that give information as to the precise timing of loans from languages other than the lexifier language are not numerous, but they confirm the principle just mentioned. Thus, in a recent conference paper, Shnukal (1984) remarked on the growing tendency of Torres Straits Broken to adopt grammatical markers and lexical items from the Western Islands language as in:

1 aspect markers – lak, kainɛ, mata, kasa:
Em i go baik gɛn – Lak ɛm go baik (gɛn) 'She went back again'
– Kainɛ em go baik (gɛn)
Em pɔ jan – Em mata jan 'She can't stop talking'
Em i giaman wagbaut – Em i kasa wagbaut 'She's just walking around'
2 intensifiers – mata, mina:
Em i prapa gud man – Em i mata/mina gud man
'He' a very/truly kind man'
3 emotives – gar, jagar:
Em i gud mɛt blo mi – Em mai prɛn gar
'She's my good friend'
Wai, ju go nau – Jagar, ju go nau
'I'm sorry you're going'
4 kin terms – atɛ, aka:
pop, ata – atɛ 'grandfather', aka 'grandmother'

These kind of lexical replacements occur side by side with the increase of the referential power of this creole by adding indigenous forms such as:

nazir – kabar 'trochus'
nasɛm – natam 'namesake'
kipro – kɛkei 'seagull'
ketai – kutai 'wild yam'
goi – pɛdauk 'bald head'
abal – kausar 'pandanus'

Another creole that has undergone significant changes in its later history is Javanese Creole Portuguese, which has been described by Hancock (1972). Here, as in the English-based creoles of Surinam and Papiamento of the Netherlands Antilles, Dutch has made considerable inroads. However, whereas in the latter two Dutch vocabulary is more marginal, in Javanese Creole Portuguese it is found more at the centre of the lexicon, perhaps reflecting its relative weakness *vis-à-vis* other languages spoken in Java in the later years of its life. Lexical replacement in language death situations does not appear to follow the same general principles as with viable vernaculars (see Dressler 1977a).

Changes in the lexicon, particularly lexical semantics, are not only of the unconscious type largely in evidence so far, but may also be due to deliberate human interference. The development of a special Rastafarian lexicon of Jamaican Creole is a good example, as are the numerous lexical innovations introduced by mission bodies or some aspects of the Shelta lexicon (cf. Hancock 1974).

Although much remains to be done in the area of lexical studies, there can be little doubt about the insufficiency of the notion that creoles are a lexical continuation of their European ancestral language.

Conclusions

Studies of creolization have concentrated on what is sometimes called 'hard-core grammar'. Consequently many aspects of these languages remain ill described. Examples of serious gaps in our knowledge include ideophones, discourse grammar, speech acts and many other areas of 'higher-level grammar' and language use. Even if descriptive work in these areas becomes available, we will still have to face the more basic issue of the degree of dependence of creole structures on external contextual conditions.

Recent work in linguistic functionalism (for example, Duranti 1981) has provided interesting support for the idea that the speech situation can crucially influence the language associated with it, and there can be little doubt that environmental/external factors interact with historical and/or biological factors in shaping the nature of creoles. Differences in the referential and non-referential power of creoles, should these become more firmly established, may well turn out to be the result of the special conditions in which they developed. Thus, to name one example, the establishment of turn-taking conventions may be crucially determined by the frequency and quality of caretaker–child interaction (Bruner 1981: 151 ff.), and its absence in a number of West Indian creoles (cf. Reisman 1974) may reflect disruptions in earlier transmission patterns.

The absence of certain sounds from creole phonologies may also be due to similar environmental conditions. As has been pointed out by Edmondson, different linguistic features are affected at very different times in phonology. Thus 'the neural detector for prevoicing will not survive until the thirtieth day of life, whereas the voiced–voiceless detector is more tenacious' (Edmondson 1985: 120 ff.). Further studies of creolization and creoles offer one of the best opportunities to solve a number of the fundamental issues of the linguistic sciences.

Post-pidgin and post-creole continua

The notion of a post-creole continuum was introduced first by DeCamp (1971b) and has subsequently been extended to cover post-pidgin situations. In general terms, by a post-pidgin or post-creole variety we understand a pidgin or creole which, after a period of relative linguistic independence, has come under renewed vigorous influence from its original lexifier language, involving the restructuring and/or replacement of earlier lexicon and grammar in favour of patterns from the superimposed 'target' language.

Recent work in this area (for example, Aitchison 1983; Rickford 1983a) highlights several problems, notably the locus of post-pidgin and creole grammar. Whereas the grammatical structures of stabilized and expanded pidgins and creoles are widely acceptable, post-pidgin and post-creole varieties are often individual solutions, reflecting a speaker's social mobility and social aspirations rather than shared social norms. Depending on one's standpoint, the post-pidgin and post-creole continuum can be interpreted quite differently, as observed by Rickford:

> Note, however, that while the community's 'decreolization' between time 1 and time 4 would undoubtedly involve language acquisition, each new lect serves as an *addition* to the community's linguistic repertoire rather than a *replacement* of any earlier lect. In individual second language acquisition, however, progress along the continuum seems to involve replacement of one interlanguage grammar with another, rather than addition to or expansion. (Rickford 1983a: 5)

It is only in the first sense that one can speak of 'elaboration', as Valdman (1977a) does, when looking at post-creole development. From a different perspective, there are merely changes in individual grammars. Mesolectal speakers, it appears, can be proficient in more lects than basilectal speakers, however, particularly if movement along the social and linguistic continuum involves social or financial benefits.

Further problems with the notion of decreolization include the separation of untargeted and targeted growth of creoles (a point raised by Aitchison 1983; Kihm 1983a; and Meisel 1983), discontinuities in the continuum, and the question of whether such continua reflect any general linguistic principles, such as the development from less to more marked constructions in a fixed sequential order. The principal aim of this section is to present data which may throw light on such questions, rather than proposing final answers. These will be forthcoming only once a more comprehensive theory of language mixing is available.

A last point is of a more terminological nature. Some linguists would like to reserve the notions of depidginization and decreolization for the transition of a pidgin or creole to its original lexifier language. Others have suggested that continua can develop with lexically different target languages, such that, for instance, a former English-based creole may gradually be turned into a Dutch-based one. I believe that there are good reasons for keeping such processes separate, and I shall therefore only consider examples of depidginization and decreolization in the more limited sense.

I shall again look at developments in individual components of grammar. The reader should be reminded, however, that in DeCamp's original model (1971b) the continuum embraced constructions from different levels simultaneously and that the separation into different levels is particularly problematic in continuum situations. The reason for this is that mixing between systems whose components of grammar do not neatly correspond can lead to the disruption of the original organization of a grammar.

Phonology

The separation of internal change from decreolization is particularly difficult in the phonological component, where one cannot apply Bickerton's (1981: 113) formula: 'In spontaneous change, an already existing form or structure acquires a new meaning, function or distribution. In decreolization, an already existing function or meaning acquires a new form or structure', as we are concerned with forms only. As a general rule, phonological changes appear to be triggered off by lexical borrowing and innovations restricted to recently borrowed lexical material. In some instances, rule generalization and hypercorrection is also found.

A case study of phonological developments in a post-pidgin situation is that of Tok Pisin, where, among other things, the following changes have been observed. First, Laycock (1970a: xii) reports that 'some Pidgin speakers who have learnt English add an eleventh (vowel), as a third pronunciation of *o*. This is [ɔ], as in English *court* (Pidgin kot)'. I have found little evidence for a spread of this pronunciation, however.

Second, whereas Laycock (1970a: xv) states that English [dž], as in June, is usually pronounced [s], the English pronunciation is becoming increasingly common, as in *joinim* 'to join', *jeles* 'jealous', *jem* 'germ'.

More dramatic than the addition of such marginal sounds to the sound inventory of Tok Pisin is the ongoing restructuring of a large number of words in the direction of their English etymons, a process which is greatly facilitated by the addition of new consonant combinations, in particular medial consonant clusters. Since medial clusters tend to be restored before final clusters, however, we find new irregularity in Tok Pisin's derivational lexicon as a result. Consider:

Expanded Tok Pisin		*Post-pidgin Tok Pisin*	
bihain	bihainim	bihain	bihaindim
'behind'	'to follow'	'behind'	'to follow'
poin	poinim	poin	pointim
'point'	'to point at'	'point'	'to point at'

Limited access to the English model has meant that cluster restoration occasionally takes the form of hypercorrection, as in *kistim* instead of *kisim* 'to catch', or *justim* instead of *jusim* 'to use'. Changes in the treatment of clusters are also felt in the morphophonemic area of the language. Thus there are now exceptions to the general rule of expanded Tok Pisin that a transitive verb is formed simply by adding *-im* to the intransitive stem. Note that there is as yet no new simple rule in anglicized Tok Pisin, for at least some intransitive verbs can end in a consonant cluster, for example, *rifand* 'to refund' and *koment* 'to comment'. The presence of such consonant clusters affects yet another rule, that of reduplication. Instead of the former *holim* 'to hold', *holholim* 'to hold tightly', we now have *holdim* 'to hold' and *holholdim* 'to hold tightly'.

Another far-reaching consequence of restructuring under the impact of an English model is described by Hall (1956: 95–6). Following Australian pronunciation, Tok Pisin [e] is variably replaced by [aj] in words such as *longwe* 'far' and *nem* 'name'. Because of the frequency of this replacement, a number of back-formations have arisen, including *keke* for *kaikai* 'food', *lek* for *laik* 'to like' and *tulet* for *tulait* 'dawn'. Note that, as a result, a number of potentially annoying homophones have emerged, as *lek* already means 'leg' and *tulet* 'too late'.

For post-creole situations, a number of detailed studies of phonological changes have been made, concentrating again on cluster restoration and the addition of 'hard' sounds to the phonological inventory of creoles. The final-vowel truncation in the Indian Ocean French-based creoles was, as pointed out in the section on creolization (pp. 212–13), a case of independent development. Its disappearance, on the other hand, particularly in Réunion French Creole, is related to the decreolization process taking place under the influence of Standard French. Table 5.10, compiled by Corne (1982: 59), illustrates the gradual decrease in truncated forms as one moves from the basilectal Dos-d'Ane varieties to those of Grand-Ilet.

A similarly extensive data analysis is presented in Akers's paper on consonant cluster restoration in Jamaican Creole (1981). Although Akers succeeds in demonstrating a fairly neat transition from basilectal to acrolectal creole, it is not clear to me that his continuum maps more than a lexical diffusion process.[45] Comparisons with similar processes in other creoles would seem desirable to settle this point.

Table 5.10 Decrease in truncated forms, from the basilectal Dos-d'Ane varieties to those of Grand-Ilet

	Infinitives			*Past Participles*					
Region	*Short* (*No.*)	(%)	*Long*	*Short* (*No.*)	(%)	*Long*	*Total*	*Total short*	*Approximate percentage short*
Dos-d'Ane	62	100	0	17	94.5	1	80	79	99
Ste Suzanne	104	85	18	40	81.5	9	171	144	84
Grand Coude	24	68.5	11	28	78	8	71	52	73
Etang Salé	18	64	10	7	35	13	48	25	52
Grand-Ilet	10	33.5	20	17	63	10	57	27	47.5

Source: Corne 1982:59.

As regards the increase of the meaning distinguishing sounds or phonemes, it appears that, by and large, highly marked sounds appear late in decreolization. The difference between urban (UC) and rural (RC) creole of Haitian French (HF) is characterized as follows by Stewart:

> UC differs from RC principally in being structurally closer to HF in certain ways, so that many of the differences in form which distinguish RC from HF do not hold for UC. For example, the phonemes /y ə ɔ̃ ɥ/, absent in RC, occur in UC with much the same lexical distributions as in HF. The same is fairly true for post vocalic /r/ and, to some extent, for the final clusters /C/, /Cr/, and /st/ as well. (Stewart 1962: 154)

DeCamp (1971b) found, for Jamaican Creole, that the ability to produce interdental fricatives implied the ability to produce all other mesolectal forms.

It is important to keep in mind that mesolectal forms can be unlike either the basilect or their acrolectal target. In many instances, the transition proceeds via a large number of separate pronunciations. Thus Sandefur (1984: 121) reports that the following series is common in decreolizing Northern Australian Kriol:

jineg — jinek — sinek — sineik — sneik 'snake'
buludang — bludang — blutang 'bluetongue lizard'

Kriol speakers regard the middle forms as Kriol proper and those on the left and right as heavy and light respectively. These data also illustrate the enormous task involved in establishing regularities in the ordering of different phonological processes (for example, cluster restoration *vis-à-vis* final voicing).

Inflectional and derivational morphology

An important claim as to the nature of decreolization is that of Bickerton, that there is a concept of 'possible change to grammatical state G_1' which governs the sequence of grammars intermediate between basilect and acrolect. He claims:

> This point is worth stressing insofar as at least some generativists (Lightfoot 1979: 385) appear to believe that there may be 'no formal constraints on the ways in which a grammar may differ from that of the preceding generation, beyond constraints imposed by the theory of grammar, i.e., both grammars must satisfy the limits on a possible grammar of natural language.' This view is almost certainly incorrect, given the facts of decreolisation. (Bickerton 1981: 110)

We shall look at this claim, and the related one that new forms appear first in old functions, using data on plural marking in post-pidgin and post-creole Tok Pisin.

If Bickerton is correct, then

1 English *-s* would have first become attached to those Tok Pisin words that could freely appear with the plural marker *-ol*;
2 *-s*, the acrolectal form, would replace *-ol* in roughly the same sequence that *-ol* developed during the expansion of this language. This process has been discussed in the section on pidgin expansion (pp. 214–15).

However, the data on plural marking in Urban Tok Pisin do not bear out these hypotheses. Instead, they indicate, as has been suggested by Bailey (1977), that mixing of systems of comparable complexity leads to unnaturalness. The first person to draw attention to this phenomenon was Hall (1956: 99–100). Hall documents plural *-s* for the following lexical items:

Tok Pisin	*Gloss*
bepis	babies
des	days
traktas	directors
yams	yams
yias	years
kreps	crabs
mails	miles
pauns	pounds
praisis	prices
silings	shillings
taims	times
wiks	weeks

Although Hall does not provide information on the grammatical environment in which these forms were found, it seems clear that the presence of the plural *-s* is not determined by the degree of animacy of a noun. My own data suggest that the presence or absence of plural *-s* is neither determined by the animacy hierarchy, nor by the grammatical environment, nor, in the case of written Tok Pisin, by spelling. The following examples are taken from letters written in anglicized Tok Pisin. Sentences by the same writer are grouped together:

1	wok bilong kainkain gava*men*	the work of various government officials
	ol man (subject)	men
	wanem gava*men* (direct object) long African kantri*s*	what government officials in the African countries
2	bilong mipela ol meri	of us women
	planti meri wok olsem taipis, post office clerk, nurse*s*, radio announcer na sampela wok moa	many women work as typists, post office clerks, nurses, radio announcers and in other jobs
	ol Pacific Island	Pacific Islanders
3	sampela boy*s* (subject)	some boys
	ol meri skulmanki go long haiskul*s*	the school girls go to the high schools
	long ol boy*s*	to the boys
	olgeta kantri*s* ol i laikim man na meri citisen*s*	all countries appreciate both their male and female citizens
	ol pipol bilong narafelo kantri*s*	people from other countries
	bilong dispela tupela steje*s*	of these two stages
	bipo yu givim kain point*s*	earlier on you gave a number of arguments
	ol skulmeri i save pulimapim spes bilong ol boy*s*	the schoolgirls take up the places for the boys
	putim boy*s* wantaim meri	put the boys with the girls
	hevim seperet haiskuls long boy*s*	have separate high schools for the boys
4	ol gel*s* (subject)	girls
	mipela ol girl (subject)	we girls
	pilai long ol girl	have sexual intercourse with girls

Comparable data are also found in urban Bislama (Charpentier 1983: 8), particularly in official discourse. Again, the data given do not suggest any implicational hierarchy for plural *-s* affixation.[46]

No detailed study of developing plural marking for a creole has come to my attention. However, data on the appearance of a plural *-s* in Krio (Jones 1983) again suggest that it enters the language in a random rather than well-ordered manner.

Data such as these would seem to disconfirm Bickerton's view that decreolization is constrained by factors comparable to those that constrain the expansion of a language.[47] Again, although often the functions are old and the forms new (as in *gavamen* 'government officials', *stafs bilong haiskul* 'the staff of the high school' or *ol bisnisgrups* 'a business group'), there are cases where both form and function are new in mesolectal Tok Pisin. Even then, English grammar may not be the only source.

In summary, one can say that the kind of mixing processes found when two linguistic systems of comparable complexity are in contact are quite different from those resulting from contact between a developing pidgin and other languages. In the former case, borrowing appears to be largely free to increase the unnaturalness of the developing mesolect, whereas in the latter case borrowing is highly selective and restricted by universal principles of language development.

The influence of English on the derivational lexicon of Krio was recently studied by Jones. As with other languages in the post-creole stage, extensive lexical borrowing from the lexifier language is encountered in Krio and 'one of the largest categories of words modern Krio seems susceptible to are, in fact, English words with derivational affixes' (Jones 1983: 3). This is of interest for two reasons. First, although pidgins, especially in the early stages of development, tend to discourage the take-over of long or morphologically complex forms, similar constraints do not appear to exist for extended pidgins or creoles. This again weakens Bickerton's view on the matter. Second, unlike at earlier developmental stages, derivational affixes borrowed along with lexical loans tend to become rapidly productive.

Some of Jones's examples of this type of borrowing include the affix *-a* from English *-er* (as in *runner*, *killer*, *teacher*). It appears that this affix is gradually encroaching on the traditional method of forming agent nouns from verbs (that is, adding the noun *man* person).[48] This agentive suffix has become productive, as illustrated in the following forms:

bɛlà (Temne: *bɛl* + English-type '*-er*') = hypocrite, person who destroys others by evil gossip;
chákà (Fula and Arabic source word *chak* + '*-er*') = drunkard;
bádà (English: 'bad' + '*-er*' – another case of the use of an adjective, *bad*, as stem) = a very evil person.

A second set of examples given by Jones includes the prefix *ova-* from English *over*:

òvàplɔ́s 'over + plus' = more than the mark, too much';
òvàjàyé 'over' + Yoruba 'jaye' = too much happiness.

The affix *-bul* from English *able*, as in *likeable*, etc., forms a third set of examples:

àjáyébùl (Yoruba source: *ajay* + '*-able*') = grossly exaggerated, fantastic, out of the ordinary;
éjébùl (English: 'age' + '*-able*') = of a person 'aged, advanced in years'; Krio speakers may have confused the word 'aged' for this form;
màsmásébùl Krio: *màsmâs* (reduplicated from English 'mash') = 'bribe' + '*-able*' = fertile for shady deals.

Similar processes are probably found in creoles elsewhere. The widely held view that derivational morphology is particularly unborrowable will thus need to be revised in the light of creole evidence.

Syntax

The most detailed studies of post-creole developments are in the area of syntax. One language in particular, Guayanese Creole English, has been described in considerable detail (Bickerton 1975b). Data on other creoles have also become available in recent years and some simple case studies will illustrate the kinds of phenomena and descriptive solutions presented.

The nominative shift in Hawaiian Creole pronouns. In basilectal Hawaiian Creole as well as in child varieties, there is no formal difference between nominative and accusative pronouns. However, as pointed out by Peet (1979: 151), there is a strong 'nominative shift' gradually replacing accusative subject pronouns with their nominative counterparts. The 'nominative shift' has at least one apparent constraint: subjects of copular sentences retain the accusative form longest. Accusative subject pronouns are representative of basilectal Hawaiian Creole, child Hawaiian Creole and 'plantation' pidgin.

Peet obtained much of his data by means of hypno-elicitation, involving hypnotic age regression of Hawaii Creole speakers. The nominative shift takes the form of a gradual replacement over a number of years. Moreover, it is

Table 5.11 Transition from the as *to the* wi *first-person plural pronoun*

Session	*Suggested age*	*As (number)*	*Wi (number)*	*Wi (%)*
1	3	1	1	50
2	4	4	5	56
3	4+	4	39	91
4	5	0	2	100

Source: Peet 1979: 153.

sensitive to the syntactic environment, in that subjects of copular sentences retain the accusative form longer and appear to progress at a different rate for different pronouns. Generalizations should not be made on the basis of a small sample, but the data are certainly suggestive. An example is the transition from the *as* to the *wi* first-person plural pronoun (see table 5.11).

Negation in Guayanese Creole. Rickford (1983a) discusses some interesting aspects of decreolization, using, among other data, information about verbal negation. His summary displays the differential use of the main variants of the negator by three different informants in both spontaneous conversation and formal interviews by an expatriate. Rickford's data suggest that the mesolectal form differs from both basilect and acrolect forms. The first informant appears to operate in terms of two discrete systems rather than a continuum, indicating that mesolectal competence cannot simply be associated with either individuals or society. The presence of an expatriate interviewer, or indeed the formal interview situation, tends to favour the incidence of acrolectal over basilectal forms.[49] Rickford's view that 'speakers in a creole continuum move upwards to higher lects by expanding their linguistic repertoires rather than by replacing one lect by another' is borne out.

Relative markers in Tok Pisin and Australian Kriol. In the section on pidgin expansion (pp. 189–90), a number of language-internal methods of relative marking were discussed, involving various types of reanalysis. The presence of a viable method of relative encoding has not prevented languages such as Tok Pisin from changing these yet again in the direction of their superimposed lexifier language. It appears that the relativizer *husat* 'who' began as a calque from English in written Tok Pisin, particularly in direct translations by both European and indigenous translators. The case of *husat* appears to differ from Bickerton's postulated normal path for decreolization in two ways. First, a new form is not used in an existing function; rather, a pre-existing *husat* 'question pronoun who?' begins to be used in an English function, as in:

opisa em i man husat i gat gutpela trenin	'an officer is a man who has good training'
Mister Paul Langro husat i bin askim sapos gavman i ken rausim tupela bisnisman	'Mister Paul Langro who asked whether the government could deport two businessmen'

Second, it appears that in the course of further development *husat* was no longer restricted to human beings, but extended to grammatical contexts where relativizers such as *we* 'which, that' were previously found. Siegel (1985: 88–9) gives examples, recorded around 1980,[50] for this phenomenon; for example:

Dispela liklik sik bilong Melbon Kap tasol i paulim planti wok manmeri insait long biktaun bilong PNG husat i gat haus bet.	'This "Melbourne Cup fever" has fouled up many working people in the cities of PNG which have horse-racing betting shops.'

Thus we have a development in which type Tok Pisin calques an English function and subsequently reverts to a previous pidgin function. Although it is not necessarily a counterexample to a unilinear view of post-creole development, it certainly underlines the fact that internal and external developments interact in a fairly complex manner.

The Central Australian Kriol data discussed by Koch (1984) differ from Tok Pisin in that here both the English form and the English function were borrowed simultaneously. The same apparently is true for the complementizer *that* in this language.

Verb serialization and prepositions. Most pidgins and creoles have a very small inventory of prepositions. Relationships that are encoded in prepositional phrases in languages such as English typically take the form of verbal chains (cf. Givón 1979), or else are covered by the few existing general prepositions. The addition of new prepositions from the superstratum lexifier language thus will have two effects: first, to reduce the importance of verb serialization, and second, to delimit the areas of meaning of pre-existing prepositions.

The emergence of new prepositions has been documented for many creoles. In Central Australian Kriol, for instance, the existing general preposition *long – longa* and the use of a verb chain of the type *V + got'm* 'with' are both replaced by forms borrowed from English, as in the following examples given by Koch (1984):

> Some here *at* Warrabri . . . some *along* Tennant Creek . . .
> Some *along* Ti Tree Station.
> I grow up *in* Barrow Creek.
> You sitting *in* shade.
> My father sitting *in* this shade . . . *long* this shade.
> You fella go back longa camp *with* you father.
> I b'n come back from camp *long* my brother.
> *With* a spear? . . . 'Goin' back, that man, long 'is camp, *got'm* spear.'

As with borrowed relativizers, the development of prepositions appears to be less neat than one would have hoped for. With Tok Pisin, for instance, borrowed prepositions can follow English in both form and function, as in *ten tu tri*, instead of *ten minit i painim tri klok* ('ten to three'). They can also take English forms used in Tok Pisin function, as in *I no stret long laik bilong pipol ov Papua Nu Gini* ('This is not correct in the view of the people of Papua New Guinea'). In addition, borrowed prepositions can be open to multiple interpretation, as in *ol i pait egens long enimi*, which can be interpreted both as 'they fight prep. prep. enemy', with a complex prepositional phrase as found in traditional Tok Pisin, or as 'they fight V prep. enemy', where *egens long* is interpreted as a verb followed by a preposition appearing after the first main verb. The new form is thus found in two functions simultaneously. Similar cases must be expected for other pidgins and creoles, as the lack of inflectional morphology tends to increase the ambiguity of surface structures.

An investigation of my data on new prepositions in Tok Pisin suggests that their addition does not follow the natural hierarchy for prepositional development postulated by Traugott (1977). This, in turn, suggests a qualitative difference between the ordered grammaticalization of pidgin expansion and initial creolization and the rather unsystematic appearance of new constructions in the post-creole situation.

Our discussion of post-creole developments has been restricted to local phenomena. Little is known about the relative sequence in which such new constructions enter the grammar of depidginizing or decreolizing languages, although in DeCamp's original sketch of a post-creole continuum this was a central idea. There can be little doubt, however, that developments at one level of analysis have repercussions at other levels, as will become obvious in the discussion of lexical borrowing.

The lexicon

Although earlier writers (for example, Todd 1974: 59–60) have suggested that pidgins and creoles can borrow freely from their lexifier languages without structural penalties, more recent observers have found that lexical borrowing can have considerable repercussions on systematic aspects of grammar, and that borrowing involves more than taking over a linguistic sign.

Again, as with syntactic developments, the bioprogram theory provides a strong hypothesis: borrowing is constrained by the principle that borrowed lexical forms first appear in indigenous meanings. Thus Bickerton writes:

> This tinkertoy concept of decreolisation is a radical misconstrual of the processes involved. In fact, creole and superstrate differ, in their structure, at every linguistic level and in every linguistic component, in such a way that simple feature-substitution is out of the question even in such relatively unstructured areas as the lexicon. (Bickerton 1981: 111)

This view is almost certainly too restrictive. Among the data I have scrutinized, there appear to be numerous instances in which new lexical borrowings are introduced in toto or where a new meaning is attached to an existing form. An instance of the latter is the common tendency in pidgins and creoles to impose the etymological meaning onto existing forms. Thus educated urban Papua New Guineans are now found either to avoid items that resemble English expletives such as *bagarap* 'ruined' and *bulsitim* 'to deceive', or to use them in the full awareness of their English connotations. The number of lexical items thus affected is significant, some important examples being:

Lexical item	*Interpretation in rural Tok Pisin*	*Interpretation in urban Tok Pisin*
rabis	poor, destitute	rubbish, worthless
baksait	back	backside
pisop	to depart quickly	to piss off
sarap	to be silent, quiet	to shut up

More important than linguistic or language-internal constraints on lexical borrowing in post-pidgin and post-creole situations are social ones, in particular access to the target language (which often remains limited) and the social functions of prestige borrowing. Some interesting general observations on these two points are made in Samarin's paper on lexical developments in Sango, a creolized pidgin spoken in the Central African Republic (1966). For many speakers, access to the lexically related prestige vernacular Sango is very restricted. This incomplete knowledge of the prestige system has led to two self-defeating strategies. First, second-language Sango speakers reject a Sango word, if it happens to be a close cognate with a form in their first language. Also, second-language speakers enrich their Sango lexicon by borrowing anything that does not bear resemblance to forms of their first language; for instance, a Banda speaker may use a Gbaya word and a Gbaya speaker may use a Banda word (Samarin 1966: 200).

Incomplete access to the prestige model can also manifest itself in fluctuations in the meanings of recently borrowed forms. Thus the following meanings of *jeles* (> English jealous) were given to me by speakers of urban Tok Pisin in the early 1970s: 'to fight with, to have sexual intercourse with, to tell a secret as well as to be jealous'. Only the last meaning could not be expressed adequately in earlier forms of Tok Pisin. Note also that the new form replaces a number of established lexical phrases (such as *eramautim tok hait* 'tell a secret') and stems (such as *puspus* 'to have sexual intercourse'). Similar examples could be adduced for other depidginizing and decreolizing systems.

Lexical borrowing, it has been suggested, can have repercussions in other components of grammar. This is most apparent in pronunciation, where new sounds are typically borrowed. New lexical items are often suppletive to existing ones, that is, an older solution involving a regular grammatical process is replaced by a borrowed lexical solution. For example, Tok Pisin distinguishes between verbs signalling inception and completion of an action by means of the grammatical markers *laik* 'inception' and *pinis* 'completion', as in:

mi (laik) rere	'I am preparing myself'
mi rere pinis	'I am ready'
em laik dai	'she fainted'

em dai pinis	'she is dead'
ol i painim	'they are looking for it'
ol i painim pinis	'they found it'

This regular grammatical process is being replaced by lexicalization as a result of borrowing the verbs *priperim* 'to prepare', *ankonses* 'to be unconscious, faint' and *luk po* 'to look for' in urban varieties of the language.

Because many of the processes that are encoded lexically in their target languages are encoded by means of regular grammatical processes in pidgins and creoles, extensive lexical borrowing can have far-reaching grammatical consequences.

Conclusions

The concepts of depidginization and decreolization remain insufficiently understood. The data do not suggest a simple unidimensional continuum between a pidgin and creole and a related target language, even if it was possible to separate neatly internal and external factors of development. It also appears that the formula of new forms in old functions is insufficient as a characterization of the total process.

Decreolization, it appears, required catastrophic as well as uniformitarian explanations. Bickerton has done a great deal to illuminate the nature of the latter, but an account of the former is still needed.

Linguistic development of pidgins and creoles: summary

I have attempted to come to grips with the complex phenomenon of linguistic flux and change characterizing pidgins and creoles. The account has been rather uneven in coverage, both as regards the languages considered and the grammatical components for which data were provided. Further problems relate to the conversion of fundamentally static data into information suitable for dynamic description.

The following provisional findings are worth emphasizing, however. First, the changes that can be observed in the development of pidgins and creoles are ascribable to three major factors: internal expansion with changes in complexity, which appears to be governed by universal forces; internal changes with no change in complexity, which, though using processes found across a large number of languages, do not appear to follow any single universal programme; and externally caused restructuring. Second, the structural changes described can, but need not, proceed in a neat linear fashion. In most documented cases, such linearity is replaced by discontinuous developments and other catastrophic events. Third, the shape of pidgin and creole grammars appears to be crucially related to a number of external factors, in particular the influence that individual linguistic strategies can bring to bear on these developments. Fourth, it would seem desirable to distinguish between local developments (taking place without affecting other parts of grammar) and more global ones that affect other areas of grammar. Most available studies only concern themselves with local effects. Finally, given the numerous gaps in observation and description, no explanation for the processes of pidgin and creole development is available at present. For the most part, the data discussed in this chapter are in the process of being explained.

The achievement of a developmental dynamic account of pidgins and creoles is a worthwhile task. I hope, in particular, that detailed descriptions of the development of many more of these languages will become available soon and that a true predictive theory of pidgin and creole development will be possible one day.

6

The Relevance of Pidgin and Creole Studies to Linguistic Theory

> At the present, creole studies has a unique opportunity of contributing to, perhaps even decisively influencing, the development of general linguistics – an opportunity foreseen by Schuchardt nearly a century ago.
>
> (Bickerton 1974: 85)

Introduction

It is often hoped that pidgin and creole linguistics will provide new insights for theoretical linguistics, although these hopes are not universal. Kihm (1983b), for instance, argues that linguists have failed to demonstrate that creoles develop differently from other languages, and that consequently the term 'creole' has no meaning in linguistic typology. Although this is an issue that remains to be settled, pidgins must be regarded as a special case in that they are quantitatively and qualitatively reduced human communication systems, spoken as second languages and acquired by adults. One can therefore expect some significant differences from other languages, including creoles.

However, even if the differences between pidgins and creoles, and between them and other languages should turn out to be negligible, there remain a number of reasons for studying them and relating one's findings to linguistic theory. First, factors that are peripheral or less noticeable in other languages, and hence seem to be irrelevant to linguistic theorizing, are quantitatively prominent in pidgins and creoles. Examples include linguistic variability and rapid change over time. Second, because of their short life-span, developments that can only be postulated for the prehistory of other languages can be retrieved by a careful study of historical sources or even by contemporary fieldwork. Third, because pidgins and creoles arise in a maximally culture-neutral environment, they are paradigm cases of 'natural' languages. Their subsequent development can illustrate the gradual impact of cultural forces on such natural objects. Fourth, an understanding of pidgins and creoles can lead to a more realistic reconstruction of earlier stages of languages and human language. Finally, the study of pidgins and creoles poses special methodological problems, whose solution may enrich linguistic methodology in general.

In the following sections, I shall single out a few areas where pidgin and creole studies have provided particular challenges to linguistic theory. No attempt at an exhaustive statement will be made, nor will theoretical points made elsewhere in this book be repeated in any detail.

The comparative method and the family-tree model of historical relationships

One of the earliest reasons for the scientific study of pidgins and creoles was, as pointed out in chapter 2, their challenge to certain views of language history and relationships, in particular the view that languages are genetically related to a single ancestral language. This relationship, it was argued, could be studied by systematically comparing linguistic material from two or more systems. It seems best, in my discussion, to distinguish between the underlying assumptions and the method itself.

As regards the former, it is held, in the words of Hall:

> (i) that among languages related through having come from a common source, the process of differentiation has always been gradual; and
> (ii) that, among such languages, the relationship has always been 'pure', that is, there has been little or no introduction of structural patterns . . . from any source outside the language family concerned. (Hall 1966: 115)

It is only under those conditions of uniformitarianism and linguistic parthenogenesis that family-tree-like relationships can be postulated. The metaphor of a family tree is powerful one, but there are a number of obvious limitations to it. For instance, family trees in everyday life have one surprising property: they allow one to trace back only one of the two sexes of ancestors. Thus, whereas it is perfectly possible to trace one's grandfather's grandfather's greatgrandfather, it is very difficult, if not impossible, to do the same for one's grandmother's grandmother's greatgrandmother. In other words, family trees are cultural interpretations or artefacts, rather than objective mirrors of reality (particularly since biological fatherhood is much more difficult to prove than biological motherhood).

Family-tree models of languages are similarly selective. It is assumed that languages typically develop by diffusion, more particularly inheritance, which means diffusion from one generation to another. Accordingly, later languages are traced back to one single earlier language, which is positioned directly above it in a family tree; this language, in turn, is traced back to a single node, until the

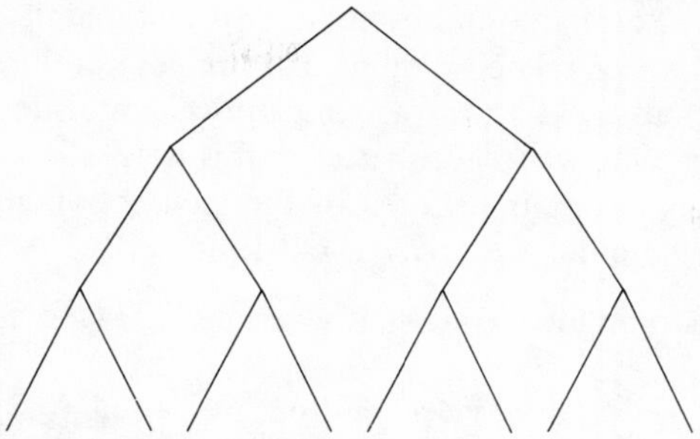

Figure 6.1 The form of the family-tree model

presumed ancestral language is reached. The familiar form of the family-tree model thus is as shown in figure 6.1.

The initial aim of Schuchardt, and other scholars sympathetic to his ideas, was to demonstrate that pidgins and creoles are mixed to such an extent that a single-ancestor model was incapable of accounting for observable data. The matter remained unresolved for many years, mainly because of the inconclusive nature of the data appealed to. Thus, as recently as 1966, Hall dismisses Schuchardt's arguments and defends the family tree as a suitable model for pidgins and creoles:

> But even though all languages are 'mixed', some – to paraphrase Orwell's famous expression – are more 'mixed' than others. We are left with the question whether, in fact, the more mixed languages are so mixed as to invalidate the assumption of genetic relationship, particularly as applied to language of whose history we have no detailed knowledge. In theory, a language might conceivably combine elements from two or more sources so that they were perfectly evenly balanced and so that they would be, therefore, unclassifiable according to our customary assumption. Yet, in practice, such a condition of perfect balance is never found – not even in any of the pidgins and creoles that have been investigated in more detail than say, Schuchardt or Jespersen were able to do, and not even with their (admittedly extensive) carry-overs, in structure as well as vocabulary, from Chinese, Melanesian, African, or other substrata. In Haitian Creole, the proportion of French structure is both greater and more fundamental than that of African-type structure; and the same is true of Chinese Pidgin English, Neo-Melanesian, Sranan, Gullah, etc., in relation to English and the various substrata involved. (Hall 1966: 117)

A similar sentiment is found in Meillet's assertion (1921: 85) that 'what little grammar creole has is French grammar' (author's translation).[1] Hall argues that empirical evidence suggests the feasibility of his approach:

> Even with the data available at present, it is evident that the ancestral form of any given group of related pidgins and creoles can be reconstructed, using the accepted techniques of comparative linguistics, and that the 'proto-pidgin' which we reconstruct in this way shows a reasonable correspondence to certain features of the 'source' language which we already know from other materials. (Hall 1966: 118)

An actual tree illustrating these views is given by Hall (see figure 6.2).

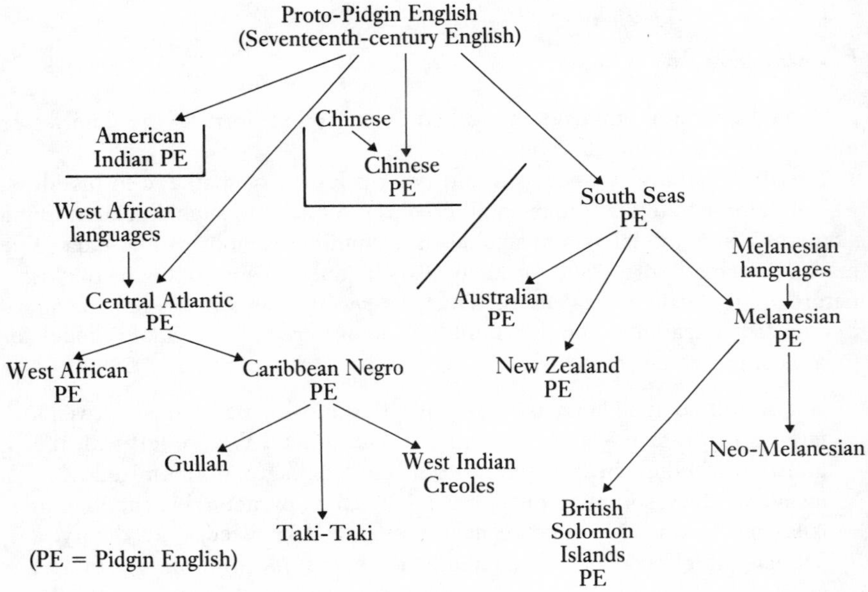

Figure 6.2 Hall's family tree (from Hall 1961: 413)

In chapters 4 and 5, however, I have tried to provide data which make Hall's position quite untenable. They include the observation that, even within lexical items, different aspects of lexical information are derived from different external sources; and also the fact that at least some pidgins and creoles have a highly mixed lexicon, even in the area of basic vocabulary, particularly in their early stages of development. These two points suggest that family-tree construction on the basis of lexical cognation is not feasible. As regards mixing at other levels, I have adduced data to suggest that lexifier languages, generally speaking, do not play an important part in the grammaticalization of pidgins and creoles; and that chance similarities do not warrant any conclusions of genetic affiliation.

More detailed studies of grammatical development in pidgins and creoles have demonstrated that grammar can also be derived by language-internal means, through reanalysis and possibly from universal sources. A simple dichotomy, either superstratum or substratum, thus is not sufficient. A major problem with Hall's view is the simplistic idea that language mixing must be of a mechanical type rather than in the nature of chemical compounding. As yet, we have no reliable identification procedure for linguistic systems resulting from mixture, but we certainly do have enough examples of non-mechanical mixing.

What is perhaps the most serious flaw of the genetic-tree model as applied to pidgins and creoles is that it presupposes identity of languages over time which they simply do not possess. Whether or not a pidgin is a highly mixed system can be answered only relative to a particular developmental stage. Language mixing is a successful strategy in some stages, but not in others. Its success is further dependent on a large number of external factors. Again, mixing is not an instantaneous phenomenon, but in many instances is a prolonged process constrained by the linguistic nature of the systems in contact.[2]

These last remarks lead me to consider the comparative method appealed to in establishing family trees. The usual comparison of arbitrarily chosen language states cannot, as has been illustrated with numerous data, provide any reliable information about historical links. In particular, a comparison of a pidgin and creole with a contemporary form of either a substratum or superstratum language can be totally misleading; a more reasonable basis for comparison would be non-standard varieties spoken at the time when pidgins and creoles came into being. Also, it often turns out (as in the previously discussed cases of causative encoding, relativization and plural marking) that pidgins and creoles become more similar to alleged source languages after a long period of internal development and after all contacts with those source languages have been severed. Consequently, the only way of identifying even plausible areas of borrowing is the comparison of developing systems rather than static ones.

The factual and philosophical reasons why the comparative method is inapplicable to the study of pidgins and creoles will also apply to other languages, and the evidence from pidgins and creoles is thus very much supplementary in nature. Its main importance lies in its promise to lead to new ways of unravelling complex language relationships.

Continuity and discontinuity in language development

A second important question of historical linguistics is: 'In what sense is it possible for a language to undergo changes of the kind familiar from the historical grammars, and yet remain the same language?' (R. Harris 1977: 17). Historical linguists working with 'normal' languages have chosen either to ignore this problem or to propose a number of ad-hoc solutions, including the appeal to continuity of speech communities, intelligibility and geographic boundedness. More recently, linguists working on the description of linguistic continua have been able to show that historical continuity involves the addition of low-level rules to a grammar and that the development from internal resources can be pictured as a continuum composed of implicationally patterned rules.

Occasional mention is made of discontinuities between grammars, but most of these discontinuities are seen to be the result of minor discrepancies between the grammars of successive generations rather than sudden breaks in a linguistic tradition. Very little has been written about this topic since Hockett's important introductory survey (1950), and the assumption that uniformitarian change and gradualness are a precondition for doing historical linguistics continues to prevail (for example, in Lass 1979: 53 ff.).

That discontinuities cannot be theorized away in the case of pidgins and creoles is becoming more widely accepted. Hoenigswald, for instance, has pointed out that:

> More than in the case of natural languages one expects to run into problems of identity from stage to stage. It is difficult enough to be quite sure, both in theory and in practice, when a given ordinary language is a descendant (under change) rather than a collateral relative of a given older language. It has been said that to discover a line of descent is to discriminate what has gotten handed down from mother to infant over the generations from what has passed through other channels. If this is true, the pidgins, with their special mechanism of exclusively secondary transmittal (?) should indeed be troublesome to place on a family tree. And if it is further the case that pidgins are typically born and then again dropped from use in shortlived bursts of activity, the whole linear notion of 'gradual' change is not even a superficially useful approximation to the truth. (Hoenigswald 1971: 476)

These sentiments are echoed in a more recent statement by Markey (1980: 1) that 'pidginization/stratified creolization signals a virtually complete disruption of continuity'. Apart from providing further problems for the adherents of a family-tree model of language relationships, this discontinuity poses very difficult problems for the historian of pidgins and creoles.

The assumption that two documented pidgins spoken at different times in the same area are part of a continuous development is implicit in many historical accounts. Thus, with regard to Hawaiian Pidgin English, we find that whereas Elizabeth B. Carr (1972: XIV) appears to suggest a continuous development from the early seaport jargons (*hapa haole*) spoken around 1800 to present-day pidgin and creole varieties of Da Kine, she has to admit: 'Unfortunately we are without records of the many intermediate stages in this change.' A very different account is given by Bickerton:

> Over the last few years I've been privileged to be in one of the few places in the world where a pidgin language still survives – Hawaii. It survives there for the very simple reason that the Hawaiian pidgin does not date from the first European contact. The first European contact was strictly between English speakers and Hawaiian speakers and produced a language known as hapa haole which is quite distinct from the subsequent pidgin.
>
> Pidgin English really only dates from the turn of the century. (Bickerton 1979: 8 ff.)

A second example is that of West African Pidgin English of the Cameroons. Whereas Schneider (1974: 22) and Féral (1980: 11–49) trace present-day Cameroonian Pidgin English back to the broken English used in the first European trading posts and settlements, Todd (1979: 289 ff.) proposes, supported by some very convincing evidence, that its links with the pidginized forms of English spoken before 1850 are very slight or non-existent, and that instead we are dealing with a second-language version of Krio (and hence ultimately West Indian Creole), which was introduced after 1850. In both instances, any attempt to reconstruct missing intermediate stages would seem ill advised.

Discontinuities in the development of pidgins and creoles are not restricted to such extreme cases. More often, we find partial discontinuities resulting from factors such as (in the case of pidgins) changes in established patterns of second-language transmission, sudden shifts in the functions and domains in which a language is used, or dramatic changes in the composition of the pidgin-speaking population. In the case of creoles, discontinuities arise through repidginization resulting from the large-scale influx of new second-language speakers, sudden changes in the superstratum language, splitting up of speech communities under conditions of marooning or manumission and so on. Most of these factors are encountered with Tok Pisin, the language whose history I have studied in most detail. In the hundred years of its history, we find a number of significant breaks in the composition of the speech community, including the decline in the importance of European speakers, the severing of the links with Samoa, the decline of the plantations and compartmentalization into regional and social varieties; several changes in the substratum and superstratum languages, including the change from English to German and back to English again, the decline of Tolai, and the growing importance of speakers of non-Melanesian languages, in particular Highlanders; and a number of changes in social functions, mainly a development from a master–servant language to an indigenous lingua franca to either a regional lingua franca or creole. All these external factors have left traces in the linguistic development of Tok Pisin. It is possible to identify at least three, and possibly five, qualitatively different and mutually only partially intelligible varieties with no discernible transitional varieties linking them.

The discontinuous developments of pidgins and creoles are not marginal accidents, but, in all likelihood, constitutive of their nature. If this assessment should turn out to be correct (and I have given many more details in Mühlhäusler 1984a: 118–34), then this will provide a considerable challenge to historical linguistics. As in the case of mixed systems, the available uniformitarian models of description will have to be supplemented with catastrophe models of linguistic change.

Systematicity and rule-governedness

Linguistic theory tends to treat languages as closed systems governed by a finite set of grammatical rules. Both notions are applicable to standardized written languages, but, as has often been pointed out, are problematical for the description of everyday spoken discourse. The solution favoured by creolists is to replace static systems of the conventional type with dynamic implicationally ordered ones such as have been developed by Bailey, Bickerton and DeCamp. However, even if large areas of grammar can be shown to be governed by such implicational scales, the fact remains that an even larger part of grammar will remain impervious to such treatment.

The question of systematicity in pidgins and creoles has been dealt with in detail by Labov (1971b: 447–72), in an article that has not stimulated sufficient discussion, however. Labov points to both the logical possibility of unsystematic areas of language and adduces a considerable body of supportive data from pidgins and creoles. He stresses the important role of system-eroding hypercorrection and hyper-creolization, as well as the fact that mixing of linguistic systems can lead to ill-integrated results. Although speakers of all pidgins and creoles have considerable skills in repairing their languages, one cannot assume that they are all equals in terms of 'systematic adequacy'.[3]

In previous chapters, some examples of unsystematic linguistic behaviour have been discussed, in particular in connection with jargons. Variability was seen at both the interpersonal and intrapersonal levels. However, communication problems are also encountered at developmentally much later stages.

It would seem that creolists should give up the notion of an ideal speaker who knows the system of his/her language and that of a linguistic system located in some collective mind. In the case of all the pidgins I have looked at, and probably with many creoles, such an assumption would not seem to be a useful abstraction, but a falsification of the nature of the subject matter. What is needed is a serious study of non-ideal pidgin or creole speakers and their problems in day-to-day communication. Misunderstandings of this kind, it will be rightly objected, are not unique to pidgins and creoles. There have been numerous voices (for example, Harris 1982; Reddy 1979) stating that the conduit metaphor of communication falsely suggests that successful exchange of messages is unproblematic. However, the dangers of such a view may well become much more obvious, if data are selected from communication involving culturally, racially and socially widely different interlocutors, as with pidgins and creoles.

Nature and nurture in linguistic structures

One of the main insights of semiotics, but one which is often unheeded, is that the notion of naturalness is extremely problematic. As put by Vico in 1725 in his *The New Science* (quoted from Hawkes 1977: 14), 'human beings are habituated to and made to acquiesce in a man-made world which they nevertheless perceive as artless and "natural"'. More recently, in writings on the philosophy of science, the claim has been made that 'shifts in the notion of what a thing does "naturally", that is, if left to its own devices, are the stuff of which scientific revolutions are made' (Reddy 1979: 296). Consequently, and not surprisingly, there is widespread confusion in linguistic circles between what is 'normal' and what is 'natural', reinforced in the more recent past by the sloppy use of the term 'natural language' within transformational generative grammar.

The debate about the naturalness of linguistic systems has recently been revived by Bickerton's suggestions that the grammar of creole languages is maximally natural in that it is shaped by an innate bioprogram rather than historical forces. This hypothesis, if worked out in further detail and if shown to be correct,[4] could have some interesting implications for general linguistic theory. It would suggest that languages can differ qualitatively in their distance from the natural foundations of language.[5] Bickerton's theory suggests an extremely simple solution for determining this distance:

Language X minus Endpoint of grammatical development of first-generation creole equals Cultural grammar

The debate as to whether languages are works of man or works of 'God', which many linguists believed was settled in favour of the latter, is open again. One can foresee far-reaching consequences not only for the study of historical linguistics, but also for the discussion of linguistic universals, as has indeed been pointed out by Bickerton (1981).

Qualitative differences between linguistic systems

The suggestion that languages may differ in their distance from their natural foundations inevitably leads to the problem of equality among linguistic systems. Although this has been a taboo topic for many years, it does not deserve to be one.[6] Whinnom's pertinent remarks (1971: 108 ff.) on this matter certainly deserve to be taken very seriously. In one sense, the topic can easily be diffused: pidgins are second languages for people who speak another 'full' language and therefore need not be of the same complexity or cultural appropriateness as other languages. We have seen that they have the capacity to grow more complex as they are put to new functional uses. In the early stages of their development, it is their very simplicity which makes them so suited to their communicative functions.

The complexity of creoles is a very different matter. After discussing the relative adequacy of medieval Spanish and Latin, Whinnom concludes that there are similar differences in creoles:

> There may be some reason to suspect that the creole-speaker is handicapped by his language. Creolists have had a hard enough struggle to justify the respectability of their discipline, and modern linguists are rather more sensitive than nineteenth-century linguists to patronizing and despective attitudes to creole languages (partly because of a well-intentioned but mistaken failure to distinguish between attitudes to languages and attitudes to speakers of those languages); but, without wishing to spark an emotionally loaded discussion, I feel that someone should venture the suggestion that modern linguists may have been dangerously sentimental about creole languages, which, with only a few notable exceptions, constitute in most communities a distinct handicap to the social mobility of the individual, and *may* also constitute a handicap to the creole speaker's personal intellectual development. (Whinnom 1971: 109)

At present, we lack the criteria to answer this question. My own work in this area (e.g. Mühlhäusler 1982b) has led to the following tentative conclusions as to what questions might be profitably asked:

1. Why do all languages (including older creoles) give up most of the postulated bioprogram/natural categories? Is there any disadvantage to a system based closely on such fundamentals of human communication?
2. How can one find culture-free determinants of qualitative language differences? What may be a cognitive advantage in one culture may be a distinct disadvantage in the next one.
3. There is ample evidence that older cultural languages also block or impede cognitive processes. How can the respective 'damage' caused by different linguistic systems be assessed?
4. What is the relationship between cognitive and social adequacy?

Answers to these and similar questions should be based on the linguistic skills of polylectal speakers or speech communities, not on grammatical descriptions of abstract competence. Moreover, since the boundary between verbal and non-verbal communication differs from culture to culture, a mere comparison of the verbal repertoire seems futile. What needs to be studied is the full set of communicative skills available to speakers of creole and other languages.

It would also be dangerous to generalize from the perceived inadequacies of a communicative system to inadequacies of average members of a speech community. I expect that the differences in communicative skills within a language community would outweigh those across languages.

Insights from language planning, philosophy of language, language pathology and the study of what Ullmann (1957: 122) has labelled 'semantic pathology' should be combined with empirical research to throw light on these matters. The resulting findings are likely to be important in two areas: social and educational planning and historical linguistics. If there are determinable qualitative differences, these are likely to be one of the major causes of linguistic change.

Language learning, pidgins and creoles

Qualitative differences between languages have been most reliably demonstrated in the area of learnability. This factor has received considerable attention in recent years for the following three reasons. Research into the nature of second-language learning has revealed the operation of apparently language-independent learning hierarchies. Bickerton (1981) has claimed strong parallels between first-language acquisition and creole formation. In fact, he regards many early acquisition errors as reflections of a bioprogram. Finally, the question of a critical threshold for language acquisition has received renewed attention.

In view of the vastness of the issues involved, only a small number of points can be covered in this chapter. In particular, I have decided to leave aside the area of interlanguage studies, referring the reader instead to recent summaries (for example, Corder 1976; Meisel 1983; Wode 1977). I do not wish to suggest that there should not be the closest co-operation between pidginists/creolists and interlanguage researchers; however, I do consider that pidginization and creolization can be regarded as the unmarked case of language acquisition and should therefore be studied before acquisition in contextually more complex situations.

A question I would like to investigate in more detail is the correspondence between pidgin development and child language acquisition. Before this question can be answered, one has to locate the areas of grammar and points in time at which such parallelisms are most likely to occur. As regards the former, it is not likely that the emergence of lexical semantics will be parallel, as the first domains and functions of pidgins differ very significantly from those of child language. As regards the latter, the basis of comparison cannot be arbitrarily isolated states, but only dynamic development. Both child language and pidgin development are maximally culture-free in their initial phases, and a comparison of very early grammatical development is therefore the most promising enterprise.

The search for parallels is further affected by the model of language acquisition employed; this, in turn, depends on whether one regards languages as either static or dynamically developing entities. Most existing models are of the replacement type: that is, earlier developmental stages are replaced by increasingly more complex ones, until at last adult grammar is acquired. That earlier stages are considered lost is manifest in the concept of instantaneous acquisition of language, postulated as a useful abstraction within transformationalist generative grammar. The alternative, the retention model, states that earlier stages of acquisition are not lost, but retained, either by a simple addition of developmental strata or else by way of fusion and mixture. A useful discussion is given by Ochs (1979). Support for this view comes from the fact that developmentally earlier stages of language are available.

As regards the relationship of these two models to the question of parallels between child language acquisition and pidgin development, one should note that, whereas in the replacement model the existence of foreigner talk registers and pidgins alike is described in terms of deviation from an ideal endpoint, in the retention model the structures of such varieties are related to the ability of adults to regress to developmentally earlier stages. Pidgins in their early stages could then be seen as conspiracies between language-specific regression and universal (possibly bioprogrammatic) tendencies.

The question of alleged parallels has been dealt with recently by Aitchison (1983). Her strategy is to pick out salient features of pidgins and to discuss their status in pidgins and child language respectively. The problem with this is that her pidgin data are of a static type, typically representing stabilized, mildly standardized varieties. As my own data are developmental and, in general, relate to the earlier jargon phase, my conclusions are quite different from hers. Let us turn to some of her diagnostic constructions.

1 *Reduction in the number of phonological contrasts*. This characteristic, according to Aitchison, is found in both pidgins and child language, with the important difference that in child language the number of contrasts eliminated is vastly greater, such as seriously to impair comprehension. My own data on jargons suggest that homophony is equally rampant in the earliest stages of pidgin development, and moreover, that strategies for overcoming its disadvantages appear to be comparable in children and adults. Thus, at the age of 2, my bilingual daughter had a word [daks] deriving from both German *Dachs* 'badger' and English *ducks*. It meant any soft cuddly toy animal. A similar

extraction of common meaning, or folk etymologizing, is also found in many pidgin homophones. Thus English *bandage*, *fence*, *banish* and *punish* are all realized as Tok Pisin *banis*, meaning 'to put something around something else, thereby constraining someone or something'.

2 *Simplification of consonant clusters*. According to Aitchison, in child language clusters are typically simplified by deletion processes, whereas in pidgin the same aim is achieved through epenthetic vowels. This, as has been pointed out several times in this book, is simply not supported by the data:[7] for example, in Cameroonian Pidgin English *pun* ('spoon') or Vietnamese Pidgin French *sam* ('chambre', 'room').

3 *Paradigmatic univocity*. This term, introduced by Hjelmslev, means that a stable relationship obtains between a content and an expression-level unit. Such a relationship is reported for many pidgins: for example, for most African pidgins by Manessy (1977). However, data suggest that this is not a characteristic of initial pidginization. Thus, in early Papuan Pidgin English, one finds considerable variation in the encoding of personal pronouns. For the first person singular, for instance, the forms I~me~my for subject and object position coexist. For some speakers, the difference between *me* and *I* is felt to be one between subject of transitive sentence and subject of intransitive or object of transitive sentence (that is, it behaves like an ergative system); for others, it is simply a case of free variation, as in the story told by Eka Kave of Sinaka Settlement outside Port Moresby (see p. 80 above). That text also constitutes a counterexample to the next assertion made by Aitchison (1983).

4 *Syntagmatic univocity*. By this we understand two phenomena: first, the replacement of analytic by synthetic constructions; and second, fixed word order. Eka Kave's story, with its variable word order for interrogative structures, is not consistent with the first phenomenon. As regards the second, Aitchison finds that there is little evidence that children impose analytic constructions onto their speech to any great extent, implying that in pidgins this is common practice. However, although this is generally so for stabilized or expanded pidgins, this is not the case for earlier phases. The reader will remember that plural encoding in Pacific Jargon English was achieved not by a single analytic device, but by means of a whole array of strategies, including dependence on textual or contextual information, the use of a number of quantifiers such as *plenty*, *too much*, *all* or *altogether*, by occasional transfer of superstratum or substratum morphology, and by the iconic process of reduplication. The many competing strategies were eventually streamlined during stabilization.

Aitchison mentions other salient features, none of which in fact characterize the early phases of pidgin formation. One must conclude, then, that differences between child and adult language acquisition have not been demonstrated for the early stages of pidgin development,[8] although one must remember that what has been examined are local developments in small areas of grammar rather than the sequence in which such developments occur relative to one another.

The question of parallelisms between child language and pidginization is of interest not only because of the descriptive convenience which would result from its confirmation, but also because it relates to the more general issue of child and adult learning.

The critical-threshold hypothesis

The critical-threshold hypothesis of language learning suggests that the ability to acquire or drastically restructure human languages dramatically declines after puberty, as does the ability to relearn language lost under pathological conditions. This hypothesis suggests fundamental differences between pidgin development in adults and first-generation creolization in children. This is precisely what is argued by Bickerton (1984: 175). Pidgins are seen as haphazard ill-structured systems whose grammar (and lexicon in some cases) closely parallels its users' substratum language. Evidence for this view is indeed found in the language of very old speakers of Hawaiian Pidgin, on which Bickerton bases his views on pidgins. His data are problematic for two reasons, however. They represent the speech of elderly speakers, whose capacity in a second language can be expected to have deteriorated considerably (cf. more general remarks by Clyne 1977). Second, even if no significant deterioration had occurred, Bickerton's data seem to refer to the jargon stage, when a number of individual language acquisition strategies, including transfer, can be expected, as has been pointed out above.

It is difficult to disconfirm conclusively Bickerton's claim that expansion in first-generation children proceeds differently from pidgin development, as his data only represent the endpoint and not the development itself. However, this endpoint would appear to be perfectly attainable by adults. For instance, of the areas of grammar distinguishing Hawaiian Creole English from its pidgin predecessor, the four where it shows 'substantial identity' with *all* other creoles (existential possessive, adjective as verb, questions and passive equivalents) are also shared with Tok Pisin, as is the copula encoding, which is present in *many* creoles. Bickerton's remark (1981: 72) that 'the degree of identity is quite remarkable when we consider that HCE shares none of the substratum languages of the other creoles' is not more remarkable than the observation that, in the case of Tok Pisin, such apparent recourse to universal bioprogram grammar was taken by second-language-speaking adults. In fact, adults and children appear to behave very much in the same manner: when there is no input, or highly conflicting input, they will turn to their bioprogram. When there is sufficient input, they will try to incorporate it into their developing system, even if it involves having to commit a large number of unnatural linguistic acts.

The crucial factor therefore is not a speaker's age, but discontinuity of transmission resulting in insufficient access to a pre-existing model. Similar or identical expansion of linguistic systems will be encountered in three situations: first, where the target is maximally remote, that is, in cases of both untargeted first-language acquisition (first-generation creole) and untargeted second-language acquisition (pidgin). The second situation is where the resulting system is a social rather than an individual solution. In the case of a pidgin developing in a highly multilingual environment, the strategy of transfer is highly restricted and the developmental sequences thus appear to be the same. It is also interesting to observe that natural interlanguage grammar is most likely to emerge where learners find themselves in a natural discourse setting (rather than in the classroom). The third situation in which similar expansion of linguistic systems will be found is where we are dealing with the early stages of language acquisition.

Discontinuity in transmission has both positive and negative effects, in that it encourages the selection of certain types of solutions, while discouraging or blocking others. If it is the case that certain features and rules can only be acquired if learners are exposed to them during a narrowly defined period of time, the likelihood that such features will figure in a pidgin or a creole is remote. However, in order to make sense of this, the global notion of critical threshold will have to be abandoned in favour of a much more detailed account of the critical time for learning individual features and constructions. Pidgins and creoles can be used as a heuristic tool here, since it is precisely those features that are absent in these languages that are likely to be subject to some time-limit on their learnability.

The notion of critical threshold is also linked to another issue, that of the independence of grammar from external factors. In a model of language that treats grammar as an independent variable (that is, independent of other possible innate cognitive skills), observed surface differences between L1 and pidgin development are highly significant. However, if grammar is seen as developing to serve a number of functions, such as making requests or establishing social bonds, it can be expected that the sequence in which such functions become important to language learners also influences grammatical development. The order in which children acquire new functions differs quite significantly from that found in adult second-language acquisition and pidgin formation. All this means is that the activation of certain linguistic developments is dependent on the presence of specific environmental factors, rather than on different cognitive abilities of children and adults.

Simplification and simplicity

Although these two terms often describe the linguistic nature of pidgins and creoles, what is meant by them has remained obscure. Three earlier attempts at defining these notions have been made by Agheyisi (1971), Mühlhäusler (1980c) and Meisel (1983).

Studies in the area of interlanguage (for example, Corder 1976; Traugott 1977: 132–62) have also drawn attention to the insufficiency of the notion of simplification in some pidgin and creole studies. The latter points out that:

> The natural semantax hypothesis suggests that a large number of linguistic phenomena often called 'simplification' do not in fact involve processes of simplification . . . The result of acquisition may be an internalized system simpler from a comparative point of view than others' systems, but in itself it is not simplification. (Traugott 1977: 153 ff.)

Uncertainty appears to be due to the following reasons:

1 the confusion of second-language learning strategies with the outcome of a structural comparison;
2 the failure to distinguish simplification and impoverishment;
3 the lack of observational data about the first stages in the pidgin–creole life-cycle;
4 discrepancies between folk views and technical description;
5 confusion of descriptive simplicity with learnability or naturalness.

I would refer the reader to the above-mentioned authors as regards interlanguage and related issues, and begin my discussion of the matter with the second reason.

Although impoverishment involves the loss of referential or non-referential potential of a language, simplification is neutral with regard to a language's expressive power. Simplification only refers to the form of the rules in which a language is encoded, indicating optimalization of existing rules and the development of regularities for formerly irregular aspects, for example, grammaticalization of the lexicon. Simplification is a dynamic concept. It expresses the fact that as one moves along a developmental continuum, more and more regularities appear. Its opposite, complication or increase in irregularity, is basically the result of restructuring following language contact. It is thus found on the restructuring continuum. It appears that impoverishment and simplification are inversely related: as the referential and non-referential power of a language increases, so its content must become more structured. A basic jargon used to exchange information in a limited contextual domain does not need structure. In its initial phase, it is little more than a list of phrases or lexical irregularities. We thus get the following picture:

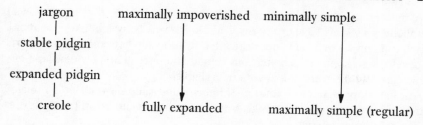

jargon	maximally impoverished	minimally simple
↓	↓	↓
stable pidgin		
↓		
expanded pidgin		
↓		
creole	fully expanded	maximally simple (regular)

It has been held by a number of authors that simplification is most vigorous during the actual formation of a pidgin – that is, in its jargon phase. Empirical studies of incipient pidgin systems (such as Bickerton and Odo 1976; Mühlhäusler 1979; Silverstein 1972a) reveal a different picture. Silverstein (1972a) stresses two aspects of jargon grammars, namely their being drastically reduced and their structure being definable only in terms of a speaker's first language. Mühlhäusler (1979) finds less evidence for substratum influence, at least in the derivational lexicon and in syntax; he presents jargon as almost entirely lacking in grammatical regularities. Such evidence suggests that degrammaticalization and impoverishment, though not simplification, are symptomatic of the formative stage of a pidgin (cf. also Labov 1971b). This is related to the more general principle that regularities are less necessary to organize a small inventory of items than for a large one. In addition, it reflects the gradual decrease of context-dependency as pidgins develop into more complex systems.

My use of simplicity in this technical sense has been criticized by Meisel (1983), who, among other things, points to the discrepancy between what learners describe as simple and what counts as simple for the creolist. Examples mentioned by him include the reduction of morphology and the disappearance of grammatical function words. It would seem that non-linguists apply the term simplification to the overall system of verbal and non-verbal communication, whereas my technical definition considers the generality of rules for the verbal system only. I am prepared to concede that this may be a dangerous abstraction. However, in the absence of descriptive devices capturing the entire communication process, it would seem to be defensible. It certainly seems to be supported by observations that even expanded pidgins are considerably easier to learn than older languages of comparable expressive and referential power.

It should not be forgotten that the relationship between grammatical description and mental processes is not a simple one and that the use of the term grammar to describe both, as is customary within transformational generative grammar, is quite misleading. The fact that a grammatical process in one language can be described in simpler terms than a comparable process in another language is only one of the factors that determines its learnability or 'simplicity for the learner'. Considerations of naturalness, token frequency, and associations outside the system under consideration are equally likely to play a part.

A final point raised by Meisel (1983) relates to the fact that my notion of simplicity is a strictly local one. This, I admit, is a very severe limitation, but one which can only be overcome once the inter-relationship between different parts of developing grammars is better understood and once genuinely developmental accounts of different languages are available.

A satisfactory characterization of simplicity and simplification thus remains wanting, but this should not stop us from discussing this notion in the context of pidgin and creole studies.

The diagnosis of earlier creolization

Whereas the notions of simplicity and simplification are concerned with synchronic systems, there is an equally lively debate on the next question – whether or not it is possible to diagnose an earlier creole stage on the basis of contemporary (synchronic or shallow diachronic) evidence. This question has been asked of several languages and language families, including the Melanesian group (cf. Lynch 1980), English (cf. Bailey and Maroldt 1977) and American Black English Vernacular (cf. Rickford 1977). A principled discussion of this problem is also given by Cassidy (1971) and Southworth (1971).

Unfortunately, in discussing this question, a number of writers do not distinguish between creolization in the sense of 'highly mixed language' and creolization in the sense of 'lexically related, but drastically restructured language, the result of major discontinuity in transmission'. I feel that this distinction is an essential one, as we have ample reason to believe that mixture over a long period of time involving two or more full languages has results that are different from mixture involving complexity-changing systems, such as developing pidgin.[9] Whereas in the former case abnatural or polysystemic solutions can be expected, the result of the latter tends to be a relatively homogenous, integrated system. The question of prior creolization should therefore be restricted to discovering major discontinuities in earlier language stages.

From the above-mentioned general articles, in particular Rickford (1977), it emerges that the following four identification procedures are most commonly appealed to:

1 information from external history;
2 simplification of grammar;
3 admixture from substratum languages;
4 divergence from the dialects of a lexically related language.

To these another, still much debated, is added either explicitly or implicitly:

5 typological similarities with known 'genuine' creoles.

In most instances, researchers require a conspiracy of three or more of the above factors before seriously considering the possibility of prior creolization. Even then, no absolute certainty can be gained, as can be seen from a brief investigation of the relative merit of the above parameters.

With regard to the first parameter, the best-known case of creole development is that of the Caribbean and it has been widely accepted as the paradigm case. Three scholars, Alleyne (1971), Grimshaw (1971) and Mintz (1971), have sketched some of the socio-historical conditions that accompanied the development of pidgins and creoles in this region. They provide a useful basis for comparison. Thus Southworth argues, with regard to the situation of mixed languages in the Indian subcontinent:

> It seems . . . that the co-existence of interdependent but distinct hierarchically arranged social groups was a characteristic of all the Caribbean slave communities, as well as other situations which have given rise to European-based pidgins (e.g. in Melanesia and the Philippines). This characteristic, which would seem to be a crucial one, is also present in the multi-caste towns and villages of contemporary India, and has been a fundamental feature of society throughout the subcontinent from very early times. (Southworth 1971: 268)

Distinct social groups were also identified as an important factor in creolization by Bailey and Maroldt (1977),[10] and similar discrepancies in power relations were postulated by Dutton (1978) for Austronesian and non-Austronesian 'mixed' languages of south-east mainland Papua New Guinea.

The presence of two distinct social groups speaking different languages would seem to be a necessary, but not sufficient condition for the development of linguistic discontinuity and creolization. Thus other types of language change have been observed under these conditions: for example, the gradual *rapprochement* of two typologically different languages in the case of Kupwar (Gumperz and Wilson 1971), the death of either the dominant or socially inferior language (cf. Aitchison 1981), and prolonged institutionalized bilingualism or dual-lingualism.

The question as to sufficient reasons for assuming prior creolization thus remains to be answered. It would seem that the most promising area of inquiry will lie in establishing discontinuities, catastrophic changes and periods of accelerated change; this will require a knowledge of historical details which is difficult to achieve. What has been said by Rickford about the question of American Black English Vernacular:

> If we are to resolve such possibilities, we will need to sift through a great deal of historical and ethnographic evidence and interpret it with great sensitivity. In any case, until we have the required documentation and analysis, there is little more we can say about the extent to which

> conditions favorable to creolization were present in the United States. (Rickford 1977: 194)

is equally applicable to the more remote processes of the origin of Melanesian, Germanic or 'modern' Romance languages.

Concerning the second parameter, simplification has been adduced as one of the main reasons for Ray's hypothesis of the pidginization/creolization of Melanesian languages and Southworth's (1971) account of the linguistic situation in the Indian subcontinent, among others. There are, however, some major difficulties with the notion of simplicity and simplification. Even if an adequate definition could be found, it is not clear whether such simplification would be retained over a long period of language change. We are, at present, not much further than Rickford was in 1977, when pointing out these and related problems. In particular, his warning against making statements about simplification on the basis of arbitrary comparison of isolated synchronic states should not be ignored:

> We also need to confess that in comparing the *present* form of the standard language with the *present* form of the hypothetical creole, we are implicitly assuming that no major changes have taken place in the relevant features being compared in both languages since the periods at which the original pidginization or creolization might have occurred. Where this assumption cannot be verified, our comparisons to determine simplification might well be meaningless. (Rickford 1977: 195)

It is clear that simplification is not a sufficient criterion for deducing prior creolization, and it is even doubtful whether it is a necessary one.

With regard to the third point, although mixture is regarded by some writers (for example, Bailey and Maroldt 1977; Southworth 1971) as a particularly important criterion, I hope to have made it clear in this book (particularly in the previous chapter) that mixture per se cannot be a reliable indicator of creolization. The reasons for this include the facts that mixing can be the result of long and continuous or brief and sudden encounters; that mixing is not consistently found with different stages and types of pidgins and creoles; and, given no developmental data, natural (internal) developments and the results of mixing are often indistinguishable.

My major hope is that a combination of substratum research and considerations of linguistic naturalness could give us an instrument for postdicting creolization. I have tried to demonstrate in the preceding chapter that although pidgin development and creolization are severely constrained by language-independent developmental 'programmes', decreolization or contact between systems of comparable complexity is much less constrained, and also that the principal constraints for developmental programmes appear to be naturalness hierarchies such as the animacy or accessibility hierarchies.[11] My hope thus is that the traces left by rapid creolization are distinct from those left by gradual contacts between full languages. Let me illustrate this with an example. Lexical mixture in the case of creolization would be a linguistically (though not socially) random process, in that lexical replacement of pre-existing terms does not follow any naturalness or markedness hierarchies. Thus, in Jamaican Creole English, we find *eat* replacing *nyam* and *child* replacing *pikni*. In the case of rapid creolization, we expect all lexically unmarked (most natural) items to come from the lexifier language and a greater or smaller proportion of more marked items from the substratum, as is indeed the case in Philippine Spanish creoles (see Frake 1971).

The process of gradual replacement in the lexicon is also retrievable from synonyms such as may coexist in present-day varieties, and may be supplemented with information about stages in the development of a language where synonym pairs were used in day-to-day communication. One such case is that of Tok Pisin, where traditional lexical items are gradually being replaced with others that bear a closer resemblance to English. Some instances of the multitude of synonym pairs I have observed include:

Tok Pisin	*Gloss*
ol ofisa i bin RISAIN o LUSIM WOK BILONG OL	'the officers resigned or left their job'
em i wok long planim KASANG o PINAT	'he was busy planting peanuts'
em i kisim gut RES o MALOLO	'he takes a good rest'
yumi mas PREVENTIM o STOPIM	'we have to prevent or stop'

The same phenomenon has been reported for Middle English, particularly for the years 1250–1400, when numerous French loan-words were flooding the language. Thus Jespersen reports that an understanding of these new loans was promoted by the systematic use of synonymy:

> A greater assistance may perhaps have been derived from the habit which may have been common in conversational speech, and which was at any rate not uncommon in writing, that of using a French word side by side with its native synonym, the latter serving more or less openly as an interpretation of the former for the benefit of those who were not yet familiar with the more refined expression. (Jespersen 1948: 89 f.)

Such evidence would suggest a gradual relexification of Middle English, rather than an abrupt new start following creolization. At present, our understanding of language mixing remains limited and its usefulness to the task of diagnosing previous creolization is limited accordingly.

Fourth, the notion of divergence from the dialects of a lexically related language has been underutilized because of the compartmentalization of linguistics and the resulting splitting off of dialectology in the days of structuralism. However, in more recent models within the developmental framework (cf. Bailey 1982), this notion has become important again, especially where there is a break in the implicational pattern governing a linguistic process. If such gaps are numerous when comparing two lexically related systems, a major break in continuity, suggesting creolization at some point in the past, is likely. Some actual examples involving American Black English Vernacular are given by Rickford (1977). This criterion is also discussed with regard to Motu and Hiri Motu by Wurm (1964).

Finally, the view that there are certain typological properties that signal prior creolizations is found, for instance, in Lounsbury:

> There is a possibility that gross typological differences reflect, if not thought or culture, then something of the accidents of the social histories of speech communities, as these have created periods and circumstances in which traditional linguistic structures were, one might say, destroyed, and language rebuilt, putting (as Powell and so many others expressed it) 'old materials to new uses'. It may be of interest in this connection that the purest 'analytic' and 'isolating' languages known are the Pidgins and Creolized languages. These have long been the unwanted stepchildren of linguistic science. But it is in these that one can see most clearly something like the first principle in the building of grammar that was posited by the evolutionary typologists. One may note that the historical circumstances that gave birth to the Pidgins and Creolized languages were far more drastic and destructive of continuity of tradition in language than were those that gave impetus to change in the modern 'analytic' Romance vernaculars, or in early modern English. (Lounsbury 1968: 205–6)

The use of typological arguments has indeed been common, as has been pointed out by Rickford (1977: 198). Again, there are numerous problems here. In the first instance, we still have no general agreement as to the grammatical properties of creole-type languages. The so-called bioprogram features used by Bickerton, for instance, may be historical accidents rather than genuine inevitable categories. They certainly do not figure prominently in languages such as Unserdeutsch or Pitcairnese, which, by other criteria, count as creoles. Second, even if creoles were characterized by a recurring set of grammatical properties, this is at best a necessary condition for the creole status of a language, for none of the properties appears to be unique to creoles (cf. Kihm 1983b). Third, creoles change like other languages subsequent to creolization. The direction of change may well be away from those features commonly thought of as being characteristic of creoles. In the absence of typological constancy over time, the criterion of typology is not particularly useful for reconstructing linguistic prehistory.

However, the above statements refer mainly to the local constructions and typological properties commonly used in the creole identification process. Lounsbury's suggestion that disruptive events in the history of languages can leave long-lasting traces is well worth further investigation.

The question of identifying pidginization and creolization in the history of languages thus remains at best partially answered. However, I am confident that a continued study of the development of these languages will provide insights of value to the historical linguist.

Pidgin and creole speech communities

The notion of 'speech community' was relatively uncontroversial until recently. Concern with its usefulness was voiced by a number of contributors to a volume edited by Romaine (1982b) and in a paper by Rigsby and Sutton (1982). For the field of pidgin and creole studies, a critical investigation was made by Labov (1980). The importance of pidgins and creoles for the discussion of this concept lies in the following points.

1 The nature of speech communities is dynamic and changing, rather than a given constant parameter.
2 Pidgins, at least in their early developmental stages, illustrate that communication is possible without any well-defined community.
3 As pointed out by Labov (1980: 370), the range of variation encountered in creole 'communities' is so great 'that the tools developed for the analysis of variation elsewhere, dealing with alternate ways of saying "the same thing" do not apply'.
4 As the description of post-creole phenomena shifts from individual to social grammars, the question of the 'locus of language' (see DeCamp 1974) is of renewed interest.

I will briefly expand on these points.

First, the fact that the composition and boundaries of speech communities can change rapidly in creoles is illustrated by both LePage's studies on Belize Creole (e.g. 1980) and Rigsby's studies on the creole situation in the Cape York area of Queensland (Rigsby 1984). Within a geographically relatively small area, and with a very low number of speakers, we find a highly complex relationship between the social groups interacting and the varieties of speech these people use and identify with. We find Aboriginal creole speakers with no fixed norms, others who identify with the norms of immigrant Torres Straits Islanders, others with their own norms for creole English, and yet others who aspire to the external norms of Aboriginal or white Australian English. To integrate all the linguistic rules into a coherent community grammar seems an impossible undertaking. In conditions where one is dealing with a rapid succession of migration, forced resettlement, culture change and shift in models, no one-dimensional implicational pattern of linguistic structuring can be expected. This, it would seem, is also the message given by the inventor of implicational scaling of linguistic structures, DeCamp, in his discussion of the relationship between language and social networks in Jamaica.[12]

With regard to the second point, one of the reasons why pidgins come into being is the desire of different groups to maintain distance and non-solidarity over a prolonged period of time. The composition of jargon and pidgin-using groups can change rapidly over time, with no continuity of transmission or even grammatical traditions. Although in the very early stages norms for linguistic behaviour are absent, such norms may develop subsequently. Their principal function in languages such as Chinese Pidgin English or the Hiri Trade languages was to enable users of a pidgin to communicate efficiently over a narrow range of topics. It is interesting that in many instances speakers of a pidgin believe that they are speaking the other party's language, not realizing the separate linguistic nature of their lingua franca.

It is true that pidgins can change their social status over time and that social norms for the language may develop even in short-lived communities, such as plantation communities in systems operating with indentured labour. This only underlines the changeable relationship between language and communities of speakers. The same problems of defining clear-cut communities are encountered in post-pidgin and post-creole situations. The extent of compartmentalization remains to be determined, as does the amount of miscommunication and communication breakdown one finds in such communities.

Third, the impossibility of describing variation as deviations from a single norm or in terms of optional rules poses considerable problems for those who wish to maintain the independence hypothesis of linguistic and social structures, a point which has been forcefully made by LePage (1980). However, before an alternative to the independence hypothesis gains wider acceptance, creolists will have to think carefully about the amount of abstraction needed to cope with what otherwise would be too complex to describe.

Finally, linguists have opted variably for locating language either in the individual or in society. It appears that this dichotomy is neither necessary nor useful and that a fresh start should be made, acknowledging the possibility of a gradient between the two poles, at different points on which different grammatical phenomena are located. Progress in this area is unlikely until the conduit metaphor of linguistic communication (see Reddy 1979) is replaced by a more adequate model.

Conclusions

The title of this chapter is perhaps somewhat misleading, since much of what I have discussed here comes under the category 'Is linguistic theory relevant to pidgin and creole studies?' My conclusion is that many of the assumptions shared by present-day theoreticians are challenged by evidence from these languages, including the uniformitarian principle of change; the possibility of atemporal models of description; the separability of linguistic and extralinguistic factors; and assumptions about the nature of the human communication process from Shannon and Weaver to Jakobson. Pidgin and creole languages are, more often than not, the extreme counterexample to general claims. This works both ways. On the one hand, linguists have accepted findings triggered off by pidgin and creole data and revised their theoretical thinking accordingly; a good example is that of implicational ordering in linguistic continua. On the other hand, however, linguists have remained suspicious of creole evidence; it is seen as somehow a freak case for whose sake a general theory of human language should not be changed. The main task facing pidginists and creolists will be to state why their evidence should be regarded as of central concern. Unless this is done, they will find themselves in the situation outlined by Hymes:

> In 1968, it seemed inevitable that attention to pidginization and creolization would unite the linguistic and the social in a specially revealing way. How we underestimated the resourcefulness and creativity of linguists and psychologists! After a decade, the inescapable embedding of pidgin and creole languages in social history remains a theme to be argued for, a topic to be rediscovered. (Hymes 1980: 389–90)

Although this chapter has summarized a number of arguments proposed earlier by my creolist colleagues, it differs in its emphasis on historical and developmental processes, and also on non-optimal and disruptive types of communication.

Given the short period of time and small number of workers concerned with the questions raised in this chapter, the impact of creolistics on general linguistics thus far must give one cause for satisfaction. It also promises that further concern for relating findings from pidgins and creoles to other areas of linguistic inquiry will continue to yield highly interesting results.

7

Conclusions and Outlook

> Almost every detail of the formation, nature and function of the marginal languages is a subject of disagreement. Many baseless or outworn ideas are still current about these forms of speech.
>
> (Reinecke 1937: 40)

Some conclusions

The following conclusions are derived from explicit as well as implicit statements made earlier in this volume. First, pidgin and creole languages, like other human communication systems, are open systems in the technical sense. They are influenced by a large number of internal factors, are liable to change and fuzziness, and are generally ill defined. The general points raised by Hockett (1968: 44 ff.) against Chomsky's views on language seem even more powerful in the context of pidgin and creole studies. These languages, more than any others, reflect the human ability for rule-changing creativity.

Second, available models of linguistic and sociolinguistic description are typically designed for closed systems and, as such, are ill suited to the needs of pidginists and creolists. Whereas the need for abstraction and streamlining in model making is not denied, it is felt that adequate accounts of these languages call for some radical re-thinking. It should be remembered that such models are also needed for other means of human communication, although on a scale of open-endedness pidgins and creoles would rank higher than most of these. Particularly problematic aspects of most available models are the traditional dichotomies of competence versus performance, synchronic versus diachronic or grammatical competence versus communicative competence. Whatever their usefulness has been in linguistic model making, they are of very limited relevance to the study of pidgins and creoles.

Related to the above two points is the observation that the evidence from pidgins and creoles appears to favour the dependency hypothesis: that is, the view that some linguistic structures are to be explained by language-external parameters. Pidginists and creolists are likely to remain at the forefront of those who study the cultural prerequisites to grammatical analysis.[1]

Pidgins and creoles, particularly in their first stages, develop in a maximally culture-neutral context and are therefore maximally 'natural' communication systems. Their naturalness is related to the fact that, under pressure for communication, the least costly solutions tend to be favoured. After their initial crystallization, pidgins and creoles are subject to numerous cultural forces. Thus, the older languages of this group exhibit a mix of cultural and natural grammar similar to that found in other languages. Because of their greater initial naturalness, pidgins and creoles afford highly interesting insights into language universals.

Contrary to many claims, language mixing is not an important factor in many areas of grammar and many developmental stages. Instead, the encounter of languages and communication systems that gives rise to pidgins and creoles tends to result in new systems. To the extent that mixture is involved, it appears to be of the 'chemical compound' rather than 'mechanical mixture' type. At present, the analytic apparatus capable of dealing with non-mechanical mixture is lacking.

Next to solutions reflecting the biological and neurological roots of language, pidgins and creoles also reflect the ability of people to regress to earlier stages of development of communicative behaviour. Such regressive behaviour is particularly strong in initial pidgin formation.[2] The fact that regression is traditionally seen as deviation (performance, or parole in linguistics) has prevented its wider discussion.

For most of their history, pidgins and creoles have been severely misunderstood by laymen and experts alike. These everyday prejudices have exercised a very considerable influence on linguistic thought and continue to be reflected in some scientific writings.

The study of pidgins and creoles has concentrated on relatively few questions. Such questions as were asked reflect its dependence on general linguistics rather than on other disciplines such as anthropology, sociology, literary studies or communication studies. It is hoped that a wider basis can be found for the study of these languages.

The practitioners of the field in most instances have been outsiders. The insider view, which has begun to emerge in the most recent past, may force considerable re-thinking of a number of widely held assumptions.

Finally, contrary to some claims, pidgin and creole studies has a large number of potential applications involving, among others, the fields of second-language learning, cross-cultural and international communication, understanding of social-control mechanisms, and language planning. The minimal financial investment by governments and universities in pidgin and creole research is hardly in tune with the potential (financial and other) benefits one can anticipate.

Conclusions on a number of other issues were more difficult to arrive at, as certain areas still await the attention of pidginists and creolists. It is to these that I will now turn.

The metalanguage of pidgin and creole linguistics

Throughout this book I have drawn attention to instances where our metalanguage and everyday metaphors suggest problematic interpretations of pidgins and creoles. Perhaps the most serious is to regard languages as objects (reifications) rather than processes; this is closely followed by a tendency to locate such objects in a well-defined area of time and space.

The most thorough examination of the metalanguage used in the pidgin and creole field is provided by Tabouret-Keller (1980: 313–27). She draws attention to the fact that a considerable amount of psychological vocabulary has been carried over into pidgin and creole studies, including terms such as need (need for communication), imitation, and identity. Although pidgin and creole linguistics owes a great deal to insights from psychology, there is the danger that such terminological innovations (p. 223) 'may also smuggle into a discipline notions which, if they are isolated from the epistemological interrogation on which they were based, lack vitality and obstruct discussion'.

An equally problematic consequence is that questions of language and cognition have been given considerably more attention than the social forces shaping these languages. This is a serious matter in view of their often brief life-span and the drastic changes in social setting brought about by the advent of independence in pidgin and creole-speaking countries.

Next, I would like to mention the metalanguage derived from the conduit metaphor (Harris 1982; Reddy 1979), that is, the view of human communication models as analogues of technological ones such as telegraphy. Such a model is particularly unsuited to the pidgin situation, where there are notorious discrepancies between the messages sent by the transmitter and those interpreted by the receiver. Moreover, in the critical stages, communication proceeds with no single code and considerable discrepancies between message and signals. The success or non-success of pidgin communication can hardly be explained in terms of simplistic concepts such as 'noise'. The prevailing static models of communication have also tended to deflect emphasis from the dynamic and changing character of both pidgins and creoles. These languages do not just provide examples of how human beings employ a code to its limits, but, more significantly, of how human beings construct and change codes in order to meet certain communicative requirements. Rule-changing creativity, which was traditionally associated with the marginal or secondary areas of parole and performance, should really be the focus of pidgin and creole linguistics.

Martyn-Jones and Romaine have drawn attention to another dangerous metaphor, the container metaphor:

> From the perspective of the history of science, it is perhaps not surprising that the container metaphor should be applied to notions of linguistic competence. Lakoff and Johnson (1980) claim that the container metaphor is a basic one in the human conceptual system, without which we couldn't function or communicate. It has been a dominant mode of conceptualizing human intellectual capacities in other scientific fields. One needs only to think of craniometry as a good example of a literal application of the metaphor, 'the mind is a container'. (Martyn-Jones and Romaine 1984: 11)

This metaphor has been particularly powerful in the discussion of the educational role of pidgins and creoles. Most of those who have argued that a knowledge of a pidgin or a creole prevents children from acquiring the related lexifier language properly were guided by it.

Finally, and related to the container metaphor, there is the gift metaphor, where the transmission of a European language to non-Europeans is seen as an act of giving a valuable present to a group of 'undeserving' recipients. The gift metaphor is particularly dangerous, since it suggests that the only active and constructive partner is the expatriate, and that the role of the indigenes is one of corruption and debasing.

A better understanding of the metalanguage employed by pidginists and creolists is urgently needed, if they are to break out of the limitations dictated by established terminology.

Understanding naturalness

As observed by Reddy (1979: 296), 'shifts in the notion of what a thing does naturally, that is, if left to its own devices, are the stuff of which scientific revolutions are made'. In the history of pidgin and creole studies, there have been a number of views about naturalness in these languages, and it would seem worth while to look at these briefly.

Initially, and until relatively recently, the natural state of both pidgins and creoles was perceived to be that of grammarless languages. What little grammar some of them had was said to have been borrowed from the lexically related superstratum language. This view, that one was dealing with simplified versions of more sophisticated, usually European models, was replaced in the late 1960s and early 1970s by the idea that pidgins and creoles represented some universal deep structure, that they shared most (in the case of pidgins) and all (in the case of creoles) deep properties of human languages, but lacked certain late transformations. Put differently, they possessed all essential phrase-structure rules, but few non-essential transformations. Their grammar was thus optimal rather than deficient or lacking, as in the previous view.

A third view, which is gradually making itself felt, combines the earlier two. In as much as pidgins and creoles are used by actual human beings in highly complex communicative situations, rather than by ideal speaker–hearers in a communicative vacuum, they will always fail to be totally natural. Next to the strategy of reverting to one's biological roots when constructing a new first or second language, many other culture-related strategies enter the formation process of actual pidgins and creoles, most notably strategies of linguistic regression. It is further felt that the emergence of biologically founded grammar, if such grammar should exist at all, is subject to a triggering of social and socio-psychological factors. Put differently, all languages leak, although some pidgins and creoles may leak somewhat less because of their shallow history.

This emergent view also acknowledges that no language is a perfect code. Instead, particularly in the case of incipient pidgins and post-pidgin and post-creole continua, a considerable looseness – and even lack – of structuring can be observed. This lack of linguistic grammar is partially compensated for by greater appeal to non-verbal channels of communication, although in many instances we can simply observe non-optimal communication, a feature widespread in any language, though perhaps more prominent in second languages such as pidgins.

From this third viewpoint, the natural function of a pidgin or creole is to bring about communication. Such communication can be achieved by both verbal and non-verbal means. In as much as there is a biological/natural basis to these, they will be employed in preference to other solutions wherever there is conflict between communicative strategies. Pidgin and creole development is thus seen as involving a wider communicative context. Verbal forms of behaviour are at least partially dependent on and interwoven with extralinguistic and non-linguistic factors. A social vacuum would lead to no language development, rather than the development of ideal natural pidgins or creoles.

In comparing these three solutions, it appears that the former two present self-contained wholes, whereas the latter can only hope to identify some of the pieces that make up our intellectual puzzle. However, as the price for internal consistency is the lack of fit between the model and the real world, the last approach would seem preferable. Although explanations can be given only locally, such explanations at least have the advantage of a reasonable fit with observed reality and/or predictive power in a restricted area. In sum, it is concluded that since pidgins and creoles are never left to their own devices in real life, direct access to naturalness is not given. However, the forces shaping these languages appear to be quantitatively less prominent than in the case of many older languages with a long history of human interference.

Non-expatriate pidgin and creole studies

Pidgin and creole linguistics, for better and for worse, has been dominated almost exclusively by Westerners, typically speakers of the lexically related standard languages superordinate to the pidgins and creoles. Within this tradition, an impressive body of knowledge has been amassed. It would be foolish to ignore or dismiss the contributions of expatriate experts or suggest that they should abandon their work. However, it could be argued that the view they present is subject to a number of limitations, such as are inherent in any work produced by outside observers.

These include the already mentioned limitations imposed by Western metalinguistic and metacommunicative language. Different systems could provide a new and potentially more profitable frame for looking at pidgins and creoles. The change from an entity to a process frame provides an example. Second, the elicitation techniques and field methodology employed by many researchers provide, at best, a partial view of these languages. As has been pointed out in a recent monograph by Duranti (1981), established elicitation techniques may actually distort linguistic data to the extent that they become useless for genuine insights into natively spoken languages. From this limitation, the often heard desire for better, more 'natural' data for pidgins and creoles often follows. However, as the data become increasingly informal, the ability of outside observers to make sense of them decreases. I have called this the 'Labovian Paradox': the better your data, the less you can do with them.

The systematic training of linguists from creole-speaking communities could do a lot to alleviate this situation. Care must be taken, however, to avoid the carry-over of expatriate models into the academia of new societies.

I have argued elsewhere (Mühlhäusler 1983) that there are additional problems even for inside observers. They relate to the more general principle that what is developmentally early is least accessible to introspection and most likely to go unobserved by adult members of a linguistic community. In as much as the early developmental stages of pidgins and creoles are of particular interest to theorists of these languages, we are faced with a very considerable problem. Disregarding evidence, over- and under-reporting, and misinterpretation thus are also likely to occur with inside investigators. These problems can be diminished by appealing to outsiders and by applying more sophisticated experimental techniques, such as hypnosis.

Linguistic experiments

The development of pidgins and creoles takes place within a relatively short timespan. This makes them ideal for testing claims about language development and change. However, as in all social sciences, conditions likely to cast light on the problem investigated do not always present themselves and, in the case of pidgins and creoles, the very rate of development tends to lead to a rapid replacement of some highly interesting early developments. Many theoretical questions can only be solved by either patiently waiting until a new case emerges or else by deliberate experimentation.

As regards the first strategy, pidgins and creoles continue to emerge and/or get known, such that waiting and careful search frequently pays excellent dividends. This point was made in Wurm (1979), where Papua New Guinea, an area with a very high incidence of linguistic encounters, pidgins and creoles, was referred to as a 'linguistic laboratory'. The recent York Conference on Urban Creoles has identified the large urban centres of both the First and the Third World as another such laboratory.

Regarding experimentation, the first explicit suggestions for experiments with pidgins and creoles are those of Voorhœve (1961: 37–60). Voorhœve, like the transformationalists that were to follow him, was concerned with the inadequacies of linguistic corpora, particularly in the syntactic area, and thus suggested a number of systematic elicitation techniques to obtain lacking information. Experiments of this type, because they provide a distorted context, though undoubtedly useful, have to be made with great care, and evidence thus gained will need to be checked continually against 'naturally' elicited materials. Still, large-scale comparative projects involving pidgins and creoles can hardly do without them.

The question of how to recover earlier developmental stages has thus far received two answers: one is that by Peet (1979), involving controlled regression under hypnotic conditions. For ethical and practical reasons, one can expect only limited information from this technique.

A much more ambitious project, attempting to recreate the genesis of pidgins and creoles whilst cutting down socio-historical variable to a minimum, is that by Bickerton (described in Bickerton 1979: 17–22). The experiment did not get the approval of funding bodies and hence little more can be said about its potential use.

It would seem to me that experiments attempting to solve global issues will run into financial problems, raise difficult ethical problems and not achieve the aim of controlling the variables involved. Thus it might be more realistic to devise smaller, self-contained local experiments of the type that have been customary in neighbouring sciences such as experimental psychology.

On funding pidgin and creole studies

The widespread view that pidgins and creoles are marginal languages is reflected in their marginal role when it comes to academic funding. Although it would seem unwise to insist on the establishment of a separate new discipline with separate funding, a case could nevertheless be made for giving more recognition to pidgin and creole research within established disciplines such as linguistics (where this has happened to a limited extent), communication studies, anthropology, psychology and language-learning studies. It seems anomalous that a country such as Australia, where a large number of Aborigines speak at least four distinct pidgins and creoles, should not have a single established academic post devoted to these languages. A similar situation holds in most countries where pidgins and creoles are spoken. Such a situation, although entirely explicable, is nevertheless deplorable. Now that pidgin and creole studies has attained greater academic respectability, the time may have come for more determined promotion, pointing out potential social and financial as well as academic benefits.

Particular attention should be given to informing the wider public of the insights to be gained. There is a continued need for sound popular writings, informed discussion of the prejudices that continue to surround pidgin and creole languages, and a willingness to enter into public debate. It is only once these languages have come to be seen as assets rather than liabilities by a large audience that there will be a genuine chance for expansion of the field.

The primary benefit of pidgins lies in the fact that they enable communication between speakers of different languages. In highly multilingual areas such as Melanesia or West Africa, effective administration would be impossible without the local pidgins. Moreover, they increase co-operation and reduce socially damaging misunderstandings between groups. The dramatic downturn in tribal warfare in Papua New Guinea, for instance, is a direct consequence of a common language, as my informants have pointed out to me many times. It should be noted that pidgins, as second languages, really offer the best of both worlds to their users: they can communicate with outsiders, while continuing to express their own identity through their vernacular. Those in the business of developing an international auxiliary language can learn a great deal from the study of pidgins.

The social value of creoles, in contrast to pidgins, is that of providing a symbol of group identity for displaced and disrupted people, while at the same time providing a certain protection against further disruptive outside influence. A good example is Northern Australian Kriol, which has grown into a marker of Aboriginal identity, following large-scale upheavals in the traditional patterns of communication in the wake of settler, government and mission activities.

This function of creoles is often ignored even by their speakers, and to make it explicit could help to reduce the pressure from related standard languages, which is suffered by many creoles. Recognition of their constructive role in the formation and maintenance of stable societies may well bring social and economic benefits. Instead of labelling them as diseconomies and working towards their eradication, government and education bodies should try to use them for constructive purposes. As long as research on pidgins and creoles remains insufficiently funded, these languages will remain under-utilized resources.

Outlook

I hope that I have succeeded in demonstrating that pidgins and creoles deserve to be taken seriously not only by linguists and sociolinguists, but also by their speakers and the governments of those countries where they are spoken. Whether or not we can learn and profit from the insights afforded by these languages is our choice. It is my hope that this book has helped to show the relevance of this often neglected group of languages to a wide range of linguistic, social and political issues. It will be the task of a new generation of scholars, in particular speakers of these languages, to spread this message and carry out the vast amount of work in the field which remains to be done.

Notes

Chapter 1 Names and Definitions

1 This view is not shared by everybody working on this language. For a comprehensive discussion, see S. G. Thomason's article 'Chinook Jargon in Areal and Historical Context' (1981).

2 The basis for most standard pidgins and creoles developed by missionaries tends to be a conservative rural form of the language, as is illustrated with Tok Pisin (see Freyberg 1975) or Sranan (Voorhoeve 1971).

3 Hall and others take discontinuity as an annoying detail rather than a central question of pidgin and creole studies. How a different view could affect the field is discussed by Hocket (1950) and, more recently, by Mühlhäusler (1984a).

4 Whereas by *linguistic universals* one understands the formal properties of the descriptive systems needed to account for human languages, *universals of language* refers to observable (surface) properties shared by human languages. The difference is discussed in more detail by Comrie (1981).

Chapter 2 The Study of Pidgins and Creoles

1 This view is not shared by everybody working on this language. For a comprehensive discussion, see S. G. Thomason's article 'Chinook Jargon in Areal and Historical Context' (1981).

2 The basis for most standard pidgins and creoles developed by missionaries tends to be a conservative rural form of the language, as is illustrated with Tok Pisin (see Freyberg 1975) or Sranan (Voorhoeve 1971).

3 Hall and others take discontinuity as an annoying detail rather than a central question of pidgin and creole studies. How a different view could affect the field is discussed by Hockett (1950) and, more recently, by Mühlhäusler (1984a).

4 Whereas by *linguistic universals* one understands the formal properties of the descriptive systems needed to account for human languages, *universals of language* refers to observable (surface) properties shared by human languages. The difference is discussed in more detail by Comrie (1981).

5 The consequences for arguments about pidgin and creole origins should be clear: the ability to relate a construction to any single factor's substratum influence, simplified model and universals, is a necessary, but not a sufficient demonstration of the influence of this factor.
6 The colours most commonly given are black and white, red and yellow (presumably reflecting some natural colour hierarchy), mostly with explanations why this should be so. Any Western person can be pushed into providing an explanation, which again is a quite unreasonable request.
7 The entire continuum is called a panlectal continuum or grid. The continuum consists of a number of isolects, which differ from the one immediately above or under them by a single feature.
8 It is for this reason that the model is referred to as a time-incorporating, developmental or quantum model.
9 Read more marked to less marked.
10 I have ignored models within which the description and the use of pidgins and creoles as evidence has been minimal, such as systemic, tagmemic and stratificational grammar.
11 Indeed, it is difficult to see why in the case of creoles the result of a long history of population displacement, social upheavals and cultural mixing should be a smooth linguistic continuum.
12 Thus creole structures of a natural type could be exploited in advertising and political indoctrination, if the view that the most basic (natural) linguistic structures are the ones that have the greatest persuasive force should turn out to be correct.

Chapter 3 The Socio-historical Context of Pidgin and Creole Development

1 The division between language-internal (structural forces) and language-external factors (social, psychological forces, etc.) appears a somewhat arbitrary one and is accepted only for the purposes of pre-theoretical discussion.
2 Bibliographical references on such sign languages are to be found in Reinecke et al., *Bibliography of Pidgin and Creole Languages* (1975).
3 The uniformitarian principle relies on smooth continuous change. It needs to be supplemented, particularly in the case of pidgins and creoles, with the catastrophic principle, which accounts for qualitative changes resulting from sudden discontinuous events.
4 Developmentally earlier stages are a frequent source of stylistic diversification in pidgins and creoles, a phenomenon referred to by some as backsliding.
5 In the most catholic view, internal factors relate to a single linguistic system only. Contact between languages is seen as external influence. It is argued (for example, in Aitchison 1981: 123) that: 'Foreign elements do not of themselves disrupt the basic structure of a language. They merely make use of the tendencies already in the language.'
6 This goes for both European and non-European overseers. Thus, in the case of the Queensland sugar plantations, some of the Europeans had previously served in Ceylon, Natal and the Caribbean. In turn, some of the Melanesian workers were

employed as overseers on plantations in other parts of the Pacific, such as Fiji and Papua. Because of their social position, their language must have served as a model for pidgin development. At present, the full extent of the regional mobility of plantation overseers and workers remains unknown. However, there is no doubt that the pattern begun with Cyprus and the Atlantic creoles (cf. Washabaugh and Greenfield 1983) was continued in most other plantation areas.

7 More precisely, distinguished, as the use of special forms for Europeans was banned in official language in the last days of the Australian administration and has declined considerably since independence.

8 The pre-theoretical term 'semilingual' is often used in the characterization of such speakers. However, as has been pointed out by Martyn-Jones and Romaine (1984), there are considerable problems with this notion.

9 Some of them also learned English as a second language in later life. What I found most astonishing is that informants who claimed to have grown up speaking creolized Samoan Plantation Pidgin English remembered only small fragments of this language.

10 Dual-lingualism (see Lincoln 1975) was probably fairly common in the creole context: children could understand their parents' vernaculars, but never acquired any skills in it because of its limited use. Another interesting case is that of Queensland Kanaka English, where pidgin-speaking parents encouraged their children to learn and speak Standard English even at home (cf. Dutton and Mühlhäusler 1984). Examples involving Northern Australian Kriol are provided by Sandefur (1984: 83).

11 The study of pidgins and creoles is closely concerned with rule-making and rule-changing creativity. Any model of grammatical description catering for rule-governed creativity only would seem to be inadequate for the purposes of pidgin and creole linguistics.

12 Recent work in semiotics has done a lot to dispel simplistic notions of nature. Thus Culler, in his discussion of Barthes (1983: 17), comments: 'His writings attempt to show us how we do it and what we are doing: the meanings that seem natural to us are cultural products, the results of conceptual frameworks that are so familiar as to pass unnoticed.'

13 Although this is certainly untrue for Tok Pisin, there was at least one concrete proposal to introduce an artificial pidgin language into the German colonies, Kolonial-Deutsch (Schwörer 1916).

14 This context includes, among other things, missionary attempts to purify the language, the inclusion of indices signalling differential power of language users, and certain trappings of polite (in the Western sense) speech such as lexical forms for 'thank you' and 'please'.

15 The possibility that incipient creoles are lacking in the referential and expressive power associated with older languages is discussed by Whinnom (1971).

16 This is to be distinguished from *unnatural*, a term which is best reserved for the results of such wilful external interference as the stretching of the neck, manipulation of the nasal cavities or the enlargement of the lips. Unnatural aspects of language cannot be transmitted, but have to be borrowed or reinvented.

17 Such pressure occurs both in a monolingual context where adults are found to

regress linguistically to more natural language, and in multilingual contact situations such as the formative period of a stable pidgin.

18 This finding does not reflect directly on the various solutions to the question as to the locus of language. It certainly should not be taken as support for Saussure's view of language as located in the mind of society. Rather, table 3.1 suggests that there is a continued interchange between social and individual forces. For more on this point refer to DeCamp (1974).

19 I am well aware of the difficulties surrounding correlationalism (Taylor and Mühlhäusler 1982). However, in view of the scarcity of statements on sociolinguistic factors in pidgin and creole formation, the above pre-theoretical classification is the only available basis for comparative statements.

20 The stress here is on *can*. Continued bilingualism or diglossia is another possibility found, for instance, with Northern Australian Kriol (cf. Sandefur 1984). Bickerton (1980: 109) certainly overstates the case when claiming: 'Decreolization is a phenomenon which is found wherever a creole language is in direct contact with its associated superstrate language.'

21 This is partly due to the fact that although an implicational grid with a continuum of lects can be constructed, it may be found that speakers are clustered around the two extremes of such a continuum. The existence of a few individual mesolectal speakers may reflect linguistic principles, but not necessarily social ones. Again, there can be a considerable discrepancy between the perception of speakers (which favours a dichotomous view) and objectively recordable patterns. It is a moot point which of the two, given the aim of 'emic' linguistics, should serve as the basis for analysis.

22 Millenarian type of religious movements centring around the belief that European goods (cargo) are not man-made, but have been obtained from a divine source. An excellent account is given by Lawrence (1964).

23 Pollard (1983: 1) suggests that the roots of the Rastafarian movement lie in the predisposition of the oppressed black poor to accept an ideology that offers a reversion of the social order and a positive self-image. As to Sophiatown Afrikaans, to describe their language purely as an antilanguage (cf. Halliday 1976) would be far too simplistic.

24 We should be aware of the problems of defining the notion of regional dialect of a pidgin or creole. For a discussion, refer back to chapter 1. For the purposes of the present discussion, some of these problems will have to be ignored.

25 Renewed contact with its original lexifier language destabilized Cameroonian in the British-controlled areas more than in the French one.

26 Unlike in most European languages and unlike the analyses proposed by speakers of these languages, Tok Pisin *baimbai* actually stands for 'event taking place after another event', that is, it refers to aspect, not to tense.

27 I do not wish to claim that all earlier material is preserved. As well as cumulative processes, there is probably replacement and as yet ill-understood mixing, which leads to partial restructuring of earlier material. The fact that such developmentally founded polystylism exists is one of the reasons why communication between less and more progressive speakers of the language can occur. It also accounts for the fact that understanding the latter varieties implies understanding the former, but not vice versa.

28 Dutton, in a number of papers and a forthcoming book (1976b, 1983b), has demonstrated that the languages used by the Motuans on the occasion of their hiris (trade expeditions) were pidgins based on Koriki and Eleman, rather than any predecessor of Hiri Motu (Police Motu).

29 Unfortunately virtually no linguistic documentation of this language exists. Some notes are given by Urry and Walsh (1981).

30 Very often such qualitative differences differ from speaker to speaker and region to region within the same pidgin.

31 Mass tourism is not an entirely new phenomenon. Apparently, some form of Pidgin Italian was used by medieval pilgrims making for Rome, and it seems conceivable that other religious centres such as Mecca have similar languages.

32 In contrast to the plantation system, modern guest workers can move more freely, both geographically and socially, in their host community and thus can have considerably more access to the target language. Instead of a stable pidgin, one thus mostly finds unstable interlanguage continua (cf. Meisel 1975).

33 Relexification theory usually traces European-derived languages back to other European-derived languages. However, it seems plausible that Cantonese Pidgin Arabic Chinese may have been involved in subsequent Pidgin Portuguese spoken in this area.

34 It is interesting to note (as described in much detail in Dutton (forthcoming) that in trading with their immediate neighbours the Motuans availed themselves of a simplified (foreigner talk) version of Motu. They appear to have been in no position (unlike the Australian administration and its police force) to impose this language in more remote areas.

35 In spite of its name, the language is a pidgin for many of its speakers.

36 Note, for instance, the variable use of *I* and *me* as first-person subject pronoun, variable word order in interrogatives as in *We i go*? as against *Ai go we*? and the variable absence of prepositions.

37 Arguments against this assumption include the facts that in child language the propositional function emerges last, and that in multifunctional adult discourse one often encounters utterances with no propositional content, but rarely propositions with no other functional connotations.

38 Since Fernando Póo was a Spanish possession and its economy only partially controlled by English interests, the Pidgin English spoken there underwent a fair amount of relexification in the direction of Spanish, as pointed out by Schuchardt (1979: 60).

39 The numerous mission lingue franche in use in Melanesia are discussed in Wurm (1979). For their African counterparts, see Heine (1973).

40 My attempts to pun in this language, for instance, were perfectly acceptable to young speakers, but either misunderstood or discouraged by older ones, particularly those living in traditional villages.

41 This view is also found in many sociolinguistic studies. However, it is difficult to see, particularly if one recognizes the role of human involvement in linguistic structures, why more formal styles should be regarded as less desirable objects of sociolinguistic analysis than informal ones.

42 It could be objected that pidgins are used to discuss issues that do not involve shared

knowledge. This is indeed the case more often than not. However, it should not be assumed that communication between speakers of different cultural backgrounds using a pidgin is always successful. Rather, partial or total communicative breakdown has often been observed, and certain domains and/or functions can simply not be discussed at all.

43 By this I mean that Pidgin English speakers on the plantations of Samoa had access to Samoan, speakers of Fanakalo in South Africa access to Afrikaans and a number of Bantu languages, and so forth. This access can result in borrowing, bilingualism and change of language affiliation.

44 A number of the questions to be raised in connection with discontinuity of pidgins and creoles are discussed in an important article by Hockett (1950, particularly pp. 455–6). None of these questions have been investigated in great detail to date (cf. Mühlhäusler 1984a).

45 However, it must not be ignored that there can be irreconcilable conflict between the two, in which case the preference for productive or perceptive modes of optimalization depends on social factors. Generally speaking, second-language pidgins favour perception-oriented solutions, whereas first-language creoles favour production-oriented ones.

Chapter 4 Theories of Origin

1 This assumption obviously raises a number of questions, particularly that of identifying constructions across languages and between different stages of the same language. Furthermore, it also brings into question the level of linguistic abstraction at which such samenesses are identified.

2 Samarin (personal communication 1984) has brought to my attention that large numbers of West African sailors were employed in other parts of the world, thus acting as possible agents of diffusion of a West African type of pidgin. We thus appear to have reasons for combining a nautical origin with a relexification theory. This point deserves further attention.

3 Secondary foreigner talk in the terminology employed by Ferguson (1975: 2).

4 This simplified Motu is not identical with the various trade pidgins (discussed above) used by the Motuans in their annual hiris (trade expeditions).

5 In the words of Whinnom (1971), it plays a role in the emergence of unstable secondary hybrids, but not in that of stable tertiary ones.

6 Hinnenkamp's observations confirm my own tests, based on Ferguson (1975), as to German speakers' intuitions. Although most of the expected simplifications turn up at one time or another, they appear side by side with ill-motivated lexical or word-order changes and 'normal' German.

7 The Portuguese enclave São Jão Batista de Ayudá survived until 1961, when it was occupied by Dahomey. It is worth mentioning that a considerable number of slaves were shipped to Brazil via this depot until the second half of the nineteenth century. The relationship between Brazilian Portuguese and Pidgin Portuguese and this African Portuguese Pidgin remains ill understood.

8 In the early years of Surinam plantations, most of the slaves appear to have been recruited from the Guinea coast of West Africa, an area dominated by Portuguese slave traders. Later favourite slaving areas were the Congo and Angola areas.

9 For a discussion of the systematic use of synonym pairs during relexification, see Mühlhäusler (1978c).

10 A good illustration is the above quoted incipient Pidgin German of Kiauschau.

11 The principal difference between adult and child language acquisition thus would seem to be that adults have a number of options, a child-like acquisition strategy being just one of them.

12 The argument is that following this developmental hierarchy is the least costly solution in terms of productive and perceptive effort. However, this natural development can be overruled by pragmatic and cultural considerations.

13 A study of such possible factors in pidgin and creole development is made by Koefoed (1975), who adduces the following two additional sources for language universals: universal factors of performance, and general laws or trends of language evolution.

14 Bickerton, in this case, would argue that natural creoles are acquired with greater ease and without the many wrong starts and deviations from target grammar characteristic of the acquisition of older languages. However, no empirical investigation of this point has been made to date, and recent research in child language acquisition (Aitchison 1983) does not seem to bear out this hypothesis.

15 The notions of 'near universal' or 'statistical universal' have often been attacked because they are empirically vacuous. However, they can be used as an initial discovery procedure.

16 One such example is the quite un-English distinction between inclusive and exclusive first-person plural pronouns (*yumi* versus *mifela*) in English-based Tok Pisin.

17 I will ignore *tambu* 'sacred, taboo', as in *buk tambu* 'holy book, bible', because of its phonological properties and the fact that the word is widely found in other Oceanic languages and Pacific pidgins. Moreover, it is not listed as a postmodifier in Brenninkmeyer's grammar (1924).

18 The forms *me* and *sip* are documented in some very early texts.

19 This is true for any developmental system (that is, one that develops from lesser to greater complexity), including child language and second-language acquisition.

20 This developmental programme, or innate syllabus as it is sometimes called in second-language-learning research, appears to be universally motivated. At least, this strong hypothesis is assumed to provide a useful empirical framework for the discussion of pidgin development.

21 Note that Bickerton only speaks for first languages; he appears happy to admit any kind of borrowing for second-language development.

22 At least as far as production grammar is concerned.

23 Linguists suffering from these tendencies are often referred to as substratomaniacs.

24 It is assumed here that the superstrata language typically becomes the lexifier language. I have not considered relexification, as this is dealt with separately in this chapter.

Chapter 5 Linguistic Development of Pidgins and Creoles

1 By this I mean that development achieved at an earlier stage may be erased subsequently only to reappear later.
2 Note that even for Bickerton's paradigm language, Hawaiian Creole English, little or no developmental descriptions are available.
3 In an earlier article (1980c: 21), I suggested that simplification would usually lead to an increase in naturalness. This, it seems, is an unwarranted view, as has been pointed out to me by C.-J. N. Bailey (personal communication). Rule generalization often implies its extension to less natural environments of application and/or rule output of a less natural type.
4 The situation referred to is that of 'pulling' raw recruits, that is labour trade, in newly opened up areas. The labour trade in Melanesia shifted, at a rapid pace, from the Loyalties and New Hebrides in the south to the Solomons and New Guinea in the north.
5 This expression, incidentally, is a good example of holophrastic expressions in jargons.
6 The role of syntax in this process is commonly overestimated. Some more recent observers are inclined to believe that syntax is like the spare wheel on a car, that is, it is used for communication only if other 'wheels of communication' are punctured.
7 There is one notable exception to this principle, namely the different trade languages used by the Motuans of Papua: simplified Motu is used with their immediate neighbours, a trade language with considerable Elema components in dealing with the Elema peoples, and one with a considerable Koriki component for their dealings with this group (see Dutton 1983b: 94 ff.).
8 This heading relates to both the actual sound segments (phones) and form-distinguishing sounds (phonemes). Because of the lack of derivational depth in the phonological component of pidgins, the relationship between phones and phonemes comes close to that postulated within structuralist phoneme theory. The 'phoneme' as a theoretical construct is not accepted by the author, however.
9 This is also one of the few instances where a common denominator view makes the correct predictions.
10 The two rules are $[+\text{consonantal}] \rightarrow [+\text{nasal}] / \underline{\quad\quad} [-\text{sonorant}]$ and
$[+\text{consonantal}] \rightarrow [+\text{sonorant}]\ [-\text{sonorant}] \underline{\quad\quad} [-\text{nasal}]$
11 Next to such rules there will be guesswork, dependence on contextual factors and, in many cases, misunderstandings. For a detailed discussion of cross-lectal communication, see Trudgill (1983: 8–30).
12 Some writers, for instance Coates (1969) in his discussion of German–Italian, have appealed to contrastive factors as a further source of interference. Recent work in the area of interlanguage appears to rule out such an explanation, however.
13 Longitudinal studies for pidgins appear to suggest that crystallization of new grammatical rules is a slow, cumbersome and by no means straightforward affair. These findings parallel recent findings for first-language development in children (e.g. Labov and Labov 1978).
14 There is growing evidence that the principal reason for the emergence of Tok Pisin

in New Guinea was the indenture of New Guineans on the German plantations in Samoa (cf. Mühlhäusler 1978b).

15 Some interesting parallels with first-language acquisition can be observed here. For details see Clahsen (1984).

16 Ms M. Vincent of the University of Hamburg has pointed out to me that the encoding of transitivity is also common in her data on West African Petit-Nègre (Pidgin French), as in *je l'allume le feu* 'I light the fire' (personal communication 1984).

17 Some very early texts of Hiri Motu contain examples of SVO word order, however.

18 This can also be seen as relating to the nature of linguistic input. Although word order in foreigner talk tends to be more restricted than in full languages, there is no clear correspondence between different word orders and different main sentence types.

19 Usually with rising intonation.

20 This expression, coined by Hjelmslev, is used frequently by pidginists and creolists to refer to a constant relationship between a unit at the content level and one at the expression level.

21 In a recent paper, Keesing (n.d.) attempts to demonstrate that in Solomon Islands Pidgin English this construction is due to substratum influence. In the light of the other evidence just considered, this explanation is not fully satisfactory. The question can only be settled once comparative data, similar in scope and quality to those used by Keesing, are considered.

22 It is suggested that the notion 'possible grammar' is a variable one, depending on the developmental stage a first or second language has reached.

23 I am aware of the divergence of opinion as to whether all French creoles developed out of preceding pidgins; however, in at least some cases (for example, the West Indies and Mauritius, but not Reunion), this seems to be a reasonable assumption.

24 Meisel (1983: 14) refers to this as the 'factorization principle'. A discussion of some of the issues involved is given by Dixon (1971).

25 Voorhœve originally based his calculations on a creole (Sranan), but appears to be generalizing to pidgins. In a later article (1981), Voorhœve revises some of his earlier views on the matter. He also considers data from a wide range of pidgins and creoles.

26 There appears to be an as yet uninvestigated principle that longer words tend to invite more communication errors than bisyllabic ones.

27 An example of a pidgin that developed in the context of social equality between European colonists and Australian Aborigines at Port Essington is discussed by Harris (1984). Its lexical composition appears to have been an even mix between the contact languages.

28 This constitutes a counterexample to Todd's view that 'it seems unlikely that modern varieties of English will become increasingly synthetic' (1984: 251).

29 The Tok Pisin future marker, unlike English *will*, signals action taking place after another reported action as well as action taking place after speech event. It is thus better described as an irrealis or posterior marker.

30 This transition from lexicalization to morphological encoding appears to be a general trend in pidgin expansion. It reflects the move away from optimalization of

perception to a state where perception and production are more balanced. It also suggests that the boundary between the different components of grammar is not universally determined.

31 A possible exception is Hiri Motu (see Dutton and Voorhœve 1974: 138), where morphological encoding of causatives is common. However, we may be dealing with a special case of post-pidgin development caused by pressure from the lexifier language.

32 Data adapted from Todd (1979: 283).

33 There are a number of competing constructions, including *em i go long maket i stap* and *em i go long maket i go.*

34 The knowledge that prepositions often develop into complementizers is old, and a thorough discussion of some cases can be found, for instance, in Paul (1970 edn.: 370 ff.) (originally published in 1880).

35 A number of writers, mentioned in Rickford (1977: 212), have postulated an African origin (Akan *se*) for this complementizer. The evidence presented here suggests a conspiracy between substratum and universal forces in pidgin development.

36 This is also found in numerous non-pidgins, for example, Alemannic wo in *Dr Ma wo kumme isch* 'the man who arrived'.

37 For Nigerian Pidgin English this is illustrated by Mafeni (1971: 105).

38 For example, at the pidgin and creoles symposium at the ANZAAS Congress, in Canberra, May 1984.

39 As Corne illustrates (Baker and Corne 1982: 73–8), comparable regularities are also encountered in other French creoles.

40 Remarks on plural marking at earlier stages are given in the section on expanded pidgins (pp. 182–3).

41 This endpoint is to be understood as full productivity and absence of suppletive patterns (cf. Markey 1985).

42 Such evidence would be of particular interest to the question of qualitative differences between languages, as it suggests the possibility that first-generation creoles (those created by children only) may be lacking in important areas of grammar.

43 Cases of verb chaining are ignored for the sake of this argument.

44 This, as will be shown shortly, is the typical property of decreolization processes.

45 To me, his data do not seem to suggest a restoration of clusters starting from the most natural to increasingly less natural phonological environments.

46 An interesting case of decreolization is mentioned by Eersel (1971: 322):

> In December 1967 a young Surinamese poet published a collection of poetry with a subtitle containing *puwemas* 'poems', that is, with an -s suffix for the plural. In an interview with one of his colleagues he declared that he wanted to start a discussion on the need for a plural in Sranan. That is why he introduced it on the title-page of his book! [The book is: *Sibiboesi, Powemas foe Jozef Slagveer*, Paramaribo, 1967]

47 Bickerton (1980: 112) proposes that 'a decreolization change is a natural development when a creole is in prolonged and intimate contact with its related super-

strate'. What duration and type of contact would make decreolization natural is not clear to me.

48 Precisely the same process can be observed in Tok Pisin, where forms such as *woka* and *draiwa* are replacing *wokman* 'worker' and *draivman* 'driver'. However, the *-a* has not yet become productive in urban Tok Pisin.

49 This message should be heeded by those creolists who are under the impression that external factors do not influence grammatical behaviour. A more detailed rejection of this independence hypothesis is given by Duranti (1981).

50 Examples of *husat* with (+ human) antecedents date back to the 1960s and probably even earlier.

Chapter 6 The Relevance of Pidgin and Creole Studies to Linguistic Theory

1 This is discussed in more detail in Kihm (1983b: 76 ff).

2 How these constraints operate in the case of Guinea Bissau Portuguese Creole pronouns has been demonstrated by Kihm (1983a).

3 The criterion of systematic adequacy is employed widely in language planning and language engineering (see, for instance, Tauli 1968).

4 I do not wish to commit myself to the idea of an innate bioprogram. However, even in the absence of such a programme, the fact remains that creoles (and pidgins) develop in a maximally culture-neutral (free) environment.

5 Similarly, from a developmental point of view, by contrasting, say, creole development and first-language acquisition of English, one could deduce the increasing importance of cultural learning over biological acquisition as children grow older.

6 The topic is at present being studied by a speaker of Guayanese Creole, Professor John Rickford of Stanford University (e.g. Rickford 1984). See also Hudson (1983).

7 Recent work on cluster simplification in second-language learning suggests that there remain numerous gaps in the area of observational adequacy of this phenomenon.

8 At least, it has been demonstrated that adults can, and frequently do, adopt the same strategies of acquisition observed in very young children. This is not to say that they do not have other strategies at their disposal; whether natural or cultural strategies are used would seem to depend primarily on social and socio-psychological factors (see Meisel 1983).

9 A detailed account of these differences is given in Mühlhäusler (1984a).

10 Bailey and Maroldt do not assume, however, that creolization here involved the development out of a pre-existing pidgin. Such a pidgin has been identified by Albert (1922). Its role in the formation of Middle English is not understood at present.

11 I am aware of the fact that these are theoretical constructs rather than directly observed facts. Still, within these limitations they are a useful basis for numerous generalizations on language development.

12 The proposition that social networks, rather than the larger speech community, are a likely locus for shared linguistic knowledge has become more widely accepted since Milroy's (1980) research on Belfast English.

Chapter 7 Conclusions and Outlook

1 A more detailed discussion of this topic is given by Silverstein (1977).
2 Some interesting support for this view comes from a recent study of the interlanguage behaviour of Japanese learners of English (Neustupný 1983: 29).

Bibliography

Adam, Lucien. 1883. *Les Idiomes Négro-Aryen et Maléo-Ayren*. Paris: Maisonneuve.
Adler, Max K. 1977. *Pidgins, Creoles and Lingua Francas*. Hamburg: H. Buske Verlag.
Agheyisi, Rebecca. 1971. 'West African Pidgin English: Simplification and Simplicity'. Unpublished PhD thesis, Stanford University.
Aitchison, Jean. 1981. *Language Change: Progress or Decay*. London: Fontana.
—— 1983. 'Pidgins, Creoles and Child Language'. Manuscript, London School of Economics.
Aitken-Cade, S. E. 1951. *So you want to learn the Language: An Amusing and Instructive Kitchen Kaffir Dictionary*. Salisbury: Centafrican Press.
Akers, Glenn. 1981. 'Admissibility conditions on final consonant clusters in the Jamaican continuum'. In Muysken (ed.), 1–25.
Albert, H. 1922. *Mittelalterlicher englisch-französischer Jargon*. Halle: Niemeyer.
Alleyne, Mervyn C. 1971. 'Acculturation and the Social Matrix of Creolization'. In Hymes (ed.), 169–86.
—— 1980. 'Introduction: Theoretical Orientations in Creole Studies'. In Albert Valdman & Arnold Highfield (eds), *Theoretical Orientations in Creole Studies*, London: Academic Press, 1–19.
Allsopp, Richard. 1980. 'How does the Creole Lexicon Expand?' In Valdman & Highfield (eds), 89–108.
Amsler, Jean. 1952. 'Schnuckiputzi, ou La Naissance d'un Sabir'. *Vie et langage*, vol. 59, 71–6.
Anon. n.d. *Wörterbuch mit Redewendungen*, Alexishafen.
Ardener, Edwin W. (ed.). 1971. *Social Anthropology and Language*. London: Tavistock.
Aub-Buscher, Gertrud. Forthcoming. 'Non-Romance Elements in the vocabulary of Trinidad French Creole'. To appear in Gilbert (ed.).
Aufinger, Albert, 1948–9. 'Secret Languages of the small islands near Madang'. *South Pacific*, 3(4), 90–5; 3(5), 113–20.
Baessler, Arthur. 1895. *Südsee-Bilder*. Berlin: Georg Reimer.
Bailey, Beryl L. 1966. *Jamaican Creole Syntax*. New York: Cambridge University Press.
Bailey, Charles-James N. 1973. *Variation and Linguistic Theory*. Arlington, Virginia, Centre for Applied Linguistics.
—— 1977. 'Variation and Linguistic Analysis'. *Papiere zur Linguistik*, 12, 5–56.

—— 1980. 'The Role of Language Development in a Theory of Language'. *Papiere zur Linguistik*, 22, 33–46.

—— 1982. *On the Yin and Yang Nature of Language*. Ann Arbor, Mich.: Karoma.

—— & Harris, R. (eds). 1985. *Developmental Mechanisms of Language*. Oxford: Pergamon.

—— & Maroldt, K. 1977. 'The French Lineage of English'. In Meisel (ed.) (1977b), 21–53.

Bailey, Richard W. & Görlach, Manfred. 1982. *English as a World Language*. Ann Arbor, Mich.: University of Michigan Press.

Baker, Philip. 1982. 'On the Origins of the First Mauritians and of the Creole Languages of their Descendants'. In Baker & Corne, 131–260.

—— & Corne, Chris. 1982. *Isle de France Creole*. Ann Arbor, Mich.: Karoma.

Balint, Andras. 1969. *English, Pidgin and French Dictionary of Sports and Phrase Book*. Rabaul: Trinity Press.

Bateson, Gregory. 1944. 'Pidgin English and Cross-Cultural Communication'. *Transactions of the New York Academy of Sciences*, 2, 187–241.

Bauer, Anton. 1975. *Der soziolinguistische Status und die Funktionsproblematik von Reduktionssprachen*. Frankfurt: Lang.

Bauman, R. & Sherzer, J. (eds). 1974. *Explorations in the Ethnography of Speaking*. Cambridge: Cambridge University Press.

Baumann, Adelbert. 1916. *Weltdeutsch*. Munich: Huber.

Baxter, Alan N. 1985. 'Kristang (Malacca Creole Portuguese)'. Unpublished PhD thesis, Australian National University.

Bee, Darlene. 1972. 'Phonological Interference between Usarufa and Pidgin English'. *Kivung*, 5(2), 69–95.

Bell, Henry L. 1971. 'Language and the Army of Papua New Guinea'. *Army Journal*, 264, 31–42.

Bell, Roger T. 1976. *Sociolinguistics*. London: Batsford.

Berry, Jack. 1971. 'Pidgins and Creoles in Africa'. *Current Trends in Linguistics*, 7, 510–36.

Bickerton, Derek. 1974. 'Priorities in Creole Studies'. In DeCamp & Hancock (eds), 85–7.

—— 1975a. 'Can English and Pidgin be kept apart?' In McElhanon (ed.), 21–7.

—— 1975b. *Dynamics of a Creole System*. London: Cambridge University Press.

—— 1975d. 'Creolization, Linguistic Universals, Natural Semantax and the Brain'. Paper presented at the International Conference on Pidgins and Creoles, Honolulu.

—— 1976. 'Pidgin and Creole Studies'. *Annual Review of Anthropology*, 5, 169–93.

—— 1977. 'Some Problems of Acceptability and Grammaticality in Pidgins and Creoles'. In S. Greenbaum, *Acceptability in Language*, The Hague: Mouton, 27–37.

—— 1979. 'Beginnings'. In Hill (ed.), 1–22.

—— 1980. 'Decreolization and the Creole Continuum'. In Valdman & Highfield (eds), 107–28.

—— 1981. *Roots of Language*. Ann Arbor, Mich.: Karoma.

—— 1984. 'The Language Bioprogram Hypothesis'. *The Behavioral and Brain Sciences*, 7(2), 173–88.

—— & Odo, Carol. 1976. *Change and Variation in Hawaiian English*. Final Report on NSF Project No. GS–39748.

Bley, Bernhard. 1912. *Praktisches Handbuch zur kErlernung der Nordgazellensprache*. Münster: Westfälische Vereinsdruckerei.

Bloomfield, Leonard. 1933. *Language*. New York: Holt, Rinehart & Winston.

Bodemann, Y. M. & Ostow, R. 1975. 'Lingua Franca und Pseudo-Pidgin in der Bundesrepublik'. *Zeitschrift für Literaturwissenschaft und Linguistik*, 18, 122–46.

Bold, J. D. 1961. *Fanagalo: Phrasebook, Grammar and Dictionary*. Johannesburg: Keartland.

Bollée, Annegret. 1977. 'Pidgins und Kreolische Sprachen'. *Studium Linguistik*, 3, 48–76.

—— 1980. 'Zum Projekt eines Dictionaire Etymologique du Créole'. In Bork et al. (eds), *Romanica Europaea et Americana*. Bonn: Bouvier Verlag, 68–76.

—— Forthcoming. 'Reduplication and Iteration in Seychelles Creole'. In Gilbert (ed.).

Borchardt, Karl. 1926. 'Tok Boi Wörterbuch'. Unpublished, Manus.

Brash, Elton, 1975. 'Tok Pisin'. *Meanjin Quarterly*, 34(3), 320–7.

Brenninkmeyer, Leo. 1924. 'Einführung ins Pidgin English – Ein Versuch'. Unpublished manuscript, Kamacham, PNG.

Bright, William (ed.). 1966. *Sociolinguistics. Proceedings of the UCLA Sociolinguistics Conference, 1964*. Janua Linguarum, Series Maior 20. The Hague: Mouton.

Bruner, Jerome. 1981. 'The Social Context of Language Acquisition'. *Language and Communication*, 1(2–3), 155–78.

Buchner, M. 1885. 'Kamerun-Englisch'. *Deutsche Kolonialzeitung*, 2, 676–8.

Camden, William G. 1979. 'Parallels in Structure of Lexicon and Syntax between New Hebrides Bislama and the South Santo Language Spoken at Tangoa'. In *Papers in Pidgin and Creole Linguistics*, No. 2. Canberra: Pacific Linguistics, A–57, 51–118.

Capell, Arthur. 1969. 'The Changing Status of Melanesian Pidgin'. *Monda Lingvo-Problemo*, 1, 102–15.

Carle, Rainer, Heinschke, Martina and Pink, Peter W., Rost, Christel, Stadtlander, Karen. 1982. *Gava* (Festschrift Kähler). Berlin: Reimer.

Carr, Elizabeth B. 1972. *Da Kine Talk*. Honolulu: University Press of Hawaii.

Cassidy, Frederic G. 1966. 'Multiple Etymologies in Jamaican Creole'. *American Speech*, 41(3), 211–15.

—— 1971. 'Tracing the Pidgin Element in Jamaican Creole'. In Hymes (ed.), 202–22.

—— Forthcoming. 'Interjections in Jamaican Creole'. In Gilbert (ed.).

Charpentier, J. M. 1983. 'Le Pidgin, Bichelamar avant et après l'Independance de Vanuatu'. Paper presented at the York Creole Conference.

—— & Tryon, D. T. 1982. 'Functions of Bislama in the New Hebrides and in independent Vanuatu'. *English World Wide* 3(2), 146–60.

Chomsky, Noam. 1965. *Aspects of the Theory of Syntax*. Cambridge, Mass.: MIT Press.

—— 1968. *Language and Mind*. New York: Harcourt Brace.

Churchill, William. 1911. *Beach-La-Mar*. Washington, DC: Carnegie Institution.

Clahsen, Harald. 1984. 'Der Erwerb von Kasusmarkierungen in der deutschen Kindersprache'. *Linguistische Berichte*, 89, 1–31.

Clark, Ross. 1979. 'In Search of Beach-la-Mar'. *Te Reo*, 22, 3–64.

Clyne, Michael G. 1968. 'Zum Pidgin-Deutsch der Gastarbeiter'. *Zeitschrift für Mundartforschung*, 35, 130–9.

—— 1975. 'German and English Working Pidgins'. *Linguistic Communications*, 13, 1–20.

—— 1977. 'Bilingualism of the Elderly'. *Talanya*, 4, 45–56.

—— 1978. 'Some Remarks on Foreigner Talk'. *Proceedings of the German–Scandinavian Symposium on Language Problems of Migrant Workers*, Roskilde.

Coates, William A. 1969. 'The German Pidgin-Italian of the 16th-Century Lanzichenecchi'. *Papers from the Fourth Annual Kansas Linguistics Conference*, 66–74.

Cole, Desmond T. 1953. 'Fanagalo and the Bantu Languages in South Africa'. *African Studies*, 12, 1–9.

Comrie, Bernard. 1981. *Language Universals and Linguistic Typology*. Oxford: Basil Blackwell.

Corder, S. P. 1976. 'Language Continua and the Interlanguage Hypothesis'. In Corder & Roulet (eds), 11–17.

—— & Roulet, E. (eds). 1976. *The Notions of Simplification, Interlanguages and Pidgins and their Relation to Second Language Pedagogy*. Geneva: Droz.

Corne, Chris. 1982. 'A Contrastive Analysis of Réunion and Isle de France Creole French'. In Baker & Corne, 7–130.

Culler, Jonathan. 1983. *Barthes*. London: Fontana.

Curtiss, S. 1977. *Genie: A Psycholinguistic Study of a Modern-Day 'Wild Child'*. New York: Academic Press.

Daiber, A. 1902. *Eine Australien – und Südsee fahrt*. Leipzig: Teubner.

Dalphinis, Morgan. 1982. 'Approaches to the Study of Creole Languages – The Case of West African Language Influences'. *Occasional Papers on Caribbean Languages and Dialect*, 2, 8–14.

Day, Richard (ed.). 1980. *Issues in English Creoles*. Heidelberg: Groos.

DeCamp, David. 1967. 'African Day Names in Jamaica'. *Language*, 43, 137–49.

—— 1971a. 'Introduction: The Study of Pidgin and Creole Languages'. In Hymes (ed.), 13–39.

—— 1971b. 'Toward a Generative Analysis of a Post-Creole Speech Continuum'. In Hymes (ed.), 349–70.

—— 1974. 'Neutralizations, Iteratives, and Ideophones: The Locus of Language in Jamaica'. In DeCamp & Hancock (eds), 42–60.

—— 1977. 'The Development of Pidgin and Creole Studies'. In Valdman (ed.) (1977b), 3–20.

—— & Hancock, Ian F. (eds). 1974. *Pidgins and Creoles*. Washington, DC: Georgetown University Press.

Dennis, Jamie & Scott, Jerrie. 1975. 'Creole Formation and Reorganization: Evidence for Diachronic Change in Synchronic Variation'. Paper presented at the International Conference on Pidgins and Creoles, Honolulu.

Devonish, Hubert. 1983. 'Creole Language Standardization in Guayana: Race, Class and Urban Rural Factors'. Paper presented at the York Creole Conference.

Dixon, Robert M. W. 1971. 'A Method of Semantic Description'. In Steinberg & Jakobovits (eds), 436–71.

—— 1980. *The Languages of Australia*. Cambridge: Cambridge University Press.

Domingue, Nicole Z. 1977. 'Middle English: Another Creole?' *Journal of Creole Studies*, 1(1), 89–106.

Dressler, Wolfgang. 1977a. 'Wortbildung bei Sprachverfall'. In Brekle, H. E. & Kastovsky, D. (eds), *Perspektiven der Wortbildungsforschung*. Berlin: Bouvier, 62–9.

—— (ed.). 1977b. 'Language Death Issue'. *International Journal of the Sociology of Language*, 12.

Ducrocq, Louis. 1902. 'L'idiome enfantin d'une race enfantine'. *Revue de Lille*, 20, 439–58.

Duranti, Alessandro. 1981. *The Samoan Fono: A Sociolinguistic Study*. Canberra: Pacific Linguistics, B–80.

Dutton, Thomas, E. 1970. 'Informal English in the Torres Straits'. In Ramson (ed.), 137–60.

—— 1978. 'The "Melanesian Problem" and Language Change and Disappearance in South-Eastern Papua New Guinea'. Unpublished manuscript, Australian National University.

—— 1980. *Queensland Canefields English of the Late Nineteenth Century*. Canberra: Pacific Linguistics, D–29.

—— 1982. 'On the Frontiers of Contact: Non-verbal Communication and Peaceful European Expansion in the South-West Pacific'. Unpublished manuscript, Australian National University.

—— 1983a. 'The Origin and Spread of Aboriginal Pidgin English in Queensland'. *Aboriginal History*, 7(1–2), 90–122.

—— 1983b. 'Birds of a Feather: A Pair of Rare Pidgins from the Gulf of Papua'. In Woolford and Washabaugh (eds), 77–105.

—— Forthcoming. *Foreigner Talk to National Language: The Origin and Development of Hiri (or Police) Motu, Papua.*

—— & Mühlhäusler, P. 1979. 'Papuan Pidgin English and Hiri Motu'. In Wurm (ed.), 225–42.

—— & —— 1984. 'Queensland Kanaka English'. *English Worldwide*, 4(2), 231–63.

—— & Voorhœve, C. L. 1974. *Beginning Hiri Motu*. Canberra: Pacific Linguistics, D–24.

Eades, Diana. 1982. 'You Gotta Know How to Talk . . . : Information Seeking in South-East Queensland Aboriginal Society'. *Australian Journal of Linguistics*, 2(1), 61–82.

Edmondson, Jerry A. 1984. 'Linguistic Naturalness'. *The Encyclopedic Dictionary of Psychology*. Oxford: Basil Blackwell.

—— 1985. 'Biological Foundations of Language Universals'. In Bailey & Harris (eds), 109–30.

Edwards, Jay. 1974. 'African Influences on the English of San Andrés Island, Colombia'. In DeCamp & Hancock (eds), 1–26.

Edwards, Viv & Ladd, Paddy. 1983. 'The Linguistic Status of British Sign Language'. Paper presented at the York Creole Conference.

Eersel, Christian. 1971. 'Prestige in Choice of Language and Linguistic Form'. In Hymes (ed.), 317–22.

Ehlerding, Carl W. 1936. 'My Speakee You, You Speakee Me'. *Der deutsche Seemann*, 36, 303–6.

Faine, Jules. 1939. *Le créole dans l'univers*. Port-au-Prince: Imprimèrie de l'Etat.

Farrar, Frederic W. 1899. *Language and Languages*. London: Longmans, Green.

Fauquenoy, Marguerite Saint-Jacques. 1974. 'Guyanese: A French Creole'. In DeCamp & Hancock (eds), 27–37.

Feist, Sigmund. 1932. 'The Origin of the Germanic Languages and the Indo-Europeanising of North Europe'. *Language*, 8, 245–54.

Féral, Carole de. 1980. *Le Pidgin-English Camerounais*. Nice: Centre d'Etude des Plurilinguismes.

Ferguson, Charles A. 1971. 'Absence of Copula and the Notion of Simplicity'. In Hymes (ed.), 141–50.

—— 1975. 'Toward a Characterization of English Foreigner Talk'. *Anthropological Linguistics*, 17, 1–14.

—— 1977. 'Simplified Register, Broken Language and Gastarbeiterdeutsch'. In Molony, C., Zobl, H. & Stölting, W. (eds), 25–39.

—— & DeBose, C. E. 1977. 'Simplified Registers, Broken language and Pidginization'. In Valdman (ed.) (1977b), 99–125.

Ferraz, Luiz. 1974. 'A Linguistic Appraisal of Angolar'. In Luiz Ferraz, *In Memoriam António Jorge Dias*, 177–86. Lisbon: Instituto de Alta Cultura.

Figueroa, John J. 1971. 'Creole Studies'. In Hymes (ed.), 503–8.

Fillmore, Charles J. 1971. 'Types of Lexical Information'. In Steinberg & Jakobovits (eds), 370–92.

Fishman, J. A., Ferguson, C. A. & Das Gupta, J. (eds). 1968. *Language Problems of Developing Nations*. New York: John Wiley.

Fleischmann, Ulrich. 1978. 'Das Französisch-Kreolische in der Karibik'. Habilitations thesis, Free University Berlin.

Foley, William A. 1984. 'Nature vs. Nurture: The Genesis of Language. A Review Article'. *Comparative Studies in Society and History*, 26(2), 335–44.

Fourcade, Georges. 1930. *Z'istoires la caze*. Saint-Denis: Drouhet.

Frake, Charles O. 1971. 'Lexical Origins and Semantic Structure in Philippine Creole Spanish'. In Hymes (ed.), 223–42.

Freyberg, Paul G. 1975. 'Bai yumi mekim wanem bilong helpim Tok Pisin?' In McElhanon (ed.), 28–35.

Friederici, Georg. 1911. 'Pidgin-Englisch in Deutsch-Neuguinea'. *Koloniale Rundschau*, 3, 92–106.

Fromkin, V., Rodman, R., Collins, P. & Blair, D. 1983. *An Introduction to Language*. Sydney: Holt, Rinehart & Winston.

Gebhard, Jerry G. 1979. *Thai Adaption of English Language Features: A Study of Thai English*. Canberra: Pacific Linguistics, A–57, 201–16.

Genthe, Siegfried. 1908. *Samoa*. Berlin: Allgemeiner Verein für Deutsche Literatur.

Gilbert, Glenn. 1980. Pidgin and Creole Languages: Selected Essays by Hugo Schuchardt. London: Cambridge University Press.

—— 1983. 'Two Early Surveys of the World's Pidgins and Creoles: A Comparison between Schuchardt and Reinecke'. Paper presented at the York Creole Conference.

—— (ed.). Forthcoming. *Pidgin and Creole Languages: Essays in Memory of John E. Reinecke*. (Possibly) Hawaii University Press.

Gilman, Charles. 1978. 'A Comparison of Jamaican Creole and Cameroonian Pidgin English'. *English Studies*, 59(1), 57–65.

Givón, Talmy. 1979. 'Prolegomena to any Sane Creology'. In Hancock (ed.), 3–36.

Goodman, J. S. 1967. 'The Development of a Dialect of English–Japanese Pidgin'. *Anthropological Linguistics*, 9, 43–55.

Goodman, Morris F. 1964. *A Comparative Study of Creole French Dialects*. The Hague: Mouton.

—— 1971. 'The Strange Case of Mbugu'. In Hymes (ed.), 243–54.

Greenberg, Joseph H. (ed.). 1963. *Universals of Language*. Cambridge, Mass.: MIT Press.

Greenfield, William. 1830. *A Defence of the Surinam Negro–English version of the New Testament*, London.

Grimshaw, Allen D. 1971. 'Some Social Forces and some Social Functions of Pidgin and Creole Languages'. In Hymes (ed.), 427–46.

Grimshaw, Beatrice. 1912. *Guinea Gold.* London: Mills & Boon.

Gumperz, J. J. & Wilson, R. 1971. 'Convergence and Creolization: A Case from the Indo-Aryan-Dravidian Border'. In Hymes (ed.), 151–68.

Haas, Mary R. 1975. 'What is Mobilian?' In Crawford, J. M. (ed.), *Studies in South-Eastern Indian Languages*. Athens, Ga: University of Georgia Press, 257–63.

Hale, Horatio, E. 1890. *An International Idiom. A Manual of the Oregon Trade Language or 'Chinook Jargon'*. London: Whittaker.

Hall, Robert A. Jr. 1943. *Melanesian Pidgin English: Grammar, Texts, Vocabulary*. Baltimore, Md: Linguistic Society of America.

—— 1944. 'Chinese Pidgin English: Grammar and Texts'. *Journal of the American Oriental Society*, 64, 95–113.

—— 1948. 'The Linguistic Structure of Taki Taki'. *Language*, 24, 92–116.

—— 1953. *Haitian Creole: Grammar, Texts, Vocabulary*. American Folklore Society Memoir No. 43.

—— 1955a. 'Pidgin English in the British Solomon Islands'. *Australian Quarterly*, 27(4), 68–74.

—— 1955b. *Hands off Pidgin English*. Sydney: Pacific Publications.

—— 1956. 'Innovations in Melanesian Pidgin (Neo-Melanesian)'. *Oceania*, 26, 91–109.

—— 1958. 'Creolized Languages and Genetic Relationships'. *Word*, 14, 367–73.

—— 1961. 'How Pidgin English has Evolved'. *New Scientist*, 9, 413–15.

—— 1962. 'The Life Cycle of Pidgin Languages'. *Lingua*, 11, 151–6.

—— 1966. *Pidgin and Creole Languages*. Ithaca, NY: Cornell University Press.

—— 1972. 'Pidgins and Creoles as Standard Languages'. In Pride & Holmes (eds), 142–54.

—— 1975. *Stormy Petrel in Linguistics*. Ithaca, NY: Spoken Language Services.

Haller, Hermann W. 1981. 'Between Standard Italian and Creole'. *Word*, 32(3), 181–94.

Halliday, Michael A. K. 1974. *Explorations in the Functions of Language*. London: Edward Arnold.

—— 1976. 'Anti-Languages'. *American Anthropologist*, 78(3), 570–84.

Hancock, Ian F. 1969. 'A Provisional Comparison of the English-based Atlantic Creoles'. *African Languages Review*, 8, 7–72.

—— 1971. 'A Map and List of Pidgin and Creole Languages'. In Hymes (ed.), 509–624.

—— 1972. 'Some Dutch-derived Items, in Java Creole Portuguese'. *Orbis*, 12, 549–54.

—— 1974. 'Shelta: A Problem of Classification'. In Hancock & DeCamp (eds), 130–7.

—— 1975. 'Lexical Expansion within a Closed System'. Paper presented at the International Conference on Pidgins and Creoles, Honolulu.

—— 1976. 'Nautical Sources of Krio Vocabulary'. *International Journal of the Sociology of Language*, 7, 23–36.

—— 1977a. 'Appendix: Repertory of Pidgin and Creole Languages'. In Valdman (ed.), (1977b), 362–9.

—— 1977b. 'Recovering Pidgin Genesis: Approaches and Problems'. In Valdman (ed.) (1977b), 277–94.
—— (ed.). 1979. *Readings on Creole Studies*. Ghent: Story-scientia.
—— 1980. 'Lexical Expansion in Creole Languages'. In Valdman & Highfield (eds), 63–88.
—— 1983. 'A Preliminary Classification of Anglophone Atlantic Creoles'. Unpublished manuscript, University of Texas.
—— 1984. 'A Preliminary Classification of the Anglophone Atlantic Creoles'. Manuscript, University of Texas; to appear in Gilbert (ed.) (forthcoming).
Harding, E. M. 1983. 'The Effect of the Use of FT on Conversation'. Paper presented at the York Creole Conference.
Harris, John W. 1984. 'Language Contact, Pidgins and the Emergence of Kriol in the Northern Territory'. PhD thesis, University of Queensland.
Harris, Roy. 1977. *On the Possibility of Linguistic Change*. Oxford: Clarendon Press.
—— 1980. *The Language Makers*. London: Duckworth.
—— 1981. *The Language Myth*. London: Duckworth.
—— 1982. 'The Speech–Communication Model in 20th Century Linguistics and its Sources'. In Hattori & Inoue (eds), 864–9.
Hattori, Shirô & Kazuko, Inoue. 1982. *Proceedings of the XIIIth International Congress of Linguists*. Tokyo: CIPL.
Hawkes, Terence. 1977. *Structuralism and Semiotics*. London: Methuen.
Heine, Bernd. 1970. *Status and Use of African Lingua Francas*. Munich: Weltforum.
—— 1973. *Pidgin-Sprachen im Bantu-Bereich*. Kölner Beiträge zur Afrikanistik 3. Berlin: Reimer.
—— 1975. 'Some Generalizations of African-based Pidgins'. Paper presented at the International Conference on Pidgins and Creoles, Honolulu.
Hellinger, Marlis. 1972. 'Aspects of Belizean Creole'. *Folia Linguistica*, 6, 22–39.
—— 1979. 'Across Base Language Boundaries; The Creole of Belize'. In Hancock (ed.), 315–33.
Herman, L. & Herman, M. S. 1943. *Foreign Dialects: A Manual for Actors, Directors and Writers*. New York: Theatre Arts Books.
Hesseling, Dirk Christiaan. 1905. *Het Negerhollands der Deense Antillen*. Leiden: Sigthoff.
—— 1910. 'Overblijfsels van de Nederlandse taal op Ceylon'. *Tijdschrift voor Nederlandsche Taal-en Letterkunde*, 29, 303–12.
—— 1979. *On the Origin and Formation of Creoles: A Miscellany of Articles*. Translated by T. L. Markey & P. T. Roberge. Ann Arbor, Mich.: Karoma.
Hesse-Wartegg, Ernst von. 1898. *Schantung und Deutsch-China*. Leipzig: Weber.
—— 1902. *Samoa, Bismarckarchipel und Neuguinea*. Leipzig: Weber.
Hill, Kenneth C. (ed.). 1979. *The Genesis of Language*. Ann Arbor, Mich.: Karoma.
Hinnenkamp, Volker. 1982. *Foreigner Talk und Tarzanisch*. Hamburg: H. Buske.
—— 1983. 'Eye-witnessing Pidginization? Structural and Sociolinguistic Aspects of German and Turkish Foreigner-Talk'. Paper presented at the York Creole Conference.
Hockett, Charles F. 1950. 'Age-Grading and Linguistic Continuity'. *Language*, 26, 449–57.
—— 1958. *A Course in Modern Linguistics*. New York: Macmillan.

—— 1968. *The State of the Art*. The Hague: Mouton.
Hoenigswald, Henry M. 1971. 'Language History and Creole Studies'. In Hymes (ed.), 473–80.
Hollyman, K. J. 1976. 'Les pidgins européens de la région calédonienne'. *Te Reo*, 19, 25–65.
Holm, John. 1978. 'The Creole English of Nicaragua's Miskito Coast'. PhD thesis, University College London.
—— 1980. 'African Features in White Bahamian English'. *English Worldwide*, 1(1), 45–66.
Holthouse, H. 1969. *Cannibal Cargoes*. London and Adelaide: Angus & Robertson.
Hosali, Priya. 1983. 'Syntactic Peculiarities of Butler English'. Paper presented at the York Creole Conference.
Hudson, Richard. 1983. 'Linguistic Equality'. *Clie Working Paper*, 1, 1–6.
Hueskes, Joseph (ed.). 1932. *Pioniere der Südsee*. Hiltrup: Herz Jesu Mission.
Hull, Alexander. 1968. 'The Origins of New World French Phonology'. *Word*, 24, 255–69.
Huttar, George L. 1972. 'A Comparative Word List for Djuka'. In Grimes, J. E. (ed.), *Languages of the Guianas*. Norman, Oksa: SIL of the University of Oklahoma, 12–21.
—— 1975. 'Sources of Creole Semantic Structures'. *Language*, 51(3), 684–95.
Hymes, Dell (ed.). 1971. *Pidginization and Creolization of Languages*. London: Cambridge University Press.
—— 1980. Commentary. In Valdman & Highfield (eds), 389–424.
Jabłońska, Alina. 1969. 'The Sino-Russian Mixed Language in Manchuria' (translated by A. Lyovin). *Working Papers in Linguistics University of Hawaii*, 3, 135–64.
Jacobs, Melville. 1932. 'Notes on the Structure of Chinook Jargon'. *Language*, 8, 27–50.
Jacomb, Edward. 1914. *France and England in the New Hebrides*. Melbourne: George Robertson.
Jakobson, Roman. 1960. 'Linguistics and Poetics'. In Sebeok (ed.), 350–77.
Janson, Tore. 1983. 'A Language of Sophiatown, Alexandra and Soweto'. Paper presented at the York Creole Conference.
Janssen, Arnold P. 1932. 'Die Erziehungsanstalt für halbweisse Kinder'. In Hueskes (ed.), 150–4.
Jespersen, Otto. 1922. *Language, its Nature, Development and Origin*. London: Allen & Unwin.
—— 1948. *Growth and Structure of the English Language*. New York: Doubleday Anchor Books/Oxford: Basil Blackwell.
Johnson, Sister Mary Canice. 1974. 'Two Morpheme Structure Rules in an English Proto-Creole'. In DeCamp & Hancock (eds), 118–29.
Jones, E. 1971. 'Krio, an English-based Language of Sierra Leone'. In Spencer (ed.), 66–94.
Jones, Frederick, C. V. 1983. 'Aspects of the Morphology of English-Derived Words in Sierra Leone Krio'. Paper presented at the York Creole Conference.
Kahn, Morton C. 1931. *Djuka. The Bush Negroes of Dutch Guayana*. New York: Viking Press.
Kay, Paul & Sankoff, Gillian. 1974. 'A Language-universals Approach to Pidgins and Creoles'. In DeCamp & Hancock (eds), 61–72.

Keesing, Roger. n.d. 'Solomon Pidgin Pronouns: Predicate Markers and the Eastern Oceanic Substrate'. Unpublished manuscript, Department of Anthropology, RSPacS, Australian National University.

Kihm, Alain. 1983a. 'Is There Anything like Decreolization? Some Ongoing Changes in Bissau Creole'. Paper presented at the York Creole Conference.

—— 1983b. 'De l'intérêt d'étudier les créoles, ou qu'ont-ils d'espécial? *Espace créole*, 5, 75–100.

Klein, Wolfgang (ed.). 1975. 'Sprache Ausländischer Arbeiter'. *Lili*, 5, 18.

Koch, Harold. 1984. 'Central Australian Aboriginal Pidgin'. Paper presented at the 54th ANZAAS Congress, Canberra.

Koefoed, Geert. 1975. 'A Note on Pidgins, Creoles and Greenberg's Universals'. Paper presented at the International Conference on Pidgins and Creoles, Honolulu.

Laade, Wolfgang. 1968. 'Tales from the West Coast of Papua'. *Archiv für Völkerkunde*, 22, 93–112.

Labov, William. 1971a. 'On the Adequacy of Natural Languages: 1: The Development of Tense'. Unpublished manuscript, mimeo, University of Pennsylvania.

—— 1971b. 'The Notion of "System" in Creole Languages'. In Hymes (ed.), 447–72.

—— 1972. 'Some Principles of Linguistic Methodology'. *Language in Society*, 1, 97–120.

—— 1980. 'Is There a Creole Speech Community'. In Valdman & Highfield (eds), 369–88.

—— & Labov, T. 1978. 'Learning the Syntax of Questions'. In Campbell, R. N. & Smith, P. T. (eds), *Recent Advances in the Psychology of Language*. New York and London: Plenum Press.

Lakoff, G. & Johnson, M. 1980. *Metaphors We Live By*. London and Chicago: University of Chicago Press.

Landtman, Gunnar. 1917. *The Folk Tales of the Kiwai Papuans*. Acta Societatis Scientiarum Fennicæ, vol. XLVII, Helsinki.

—— 1918. 'The Pidgin English of British New Guinea'. *Neuphilologische Mitteilungen*, 19, 62–74.

Lass, Roger. 1979. *On Explaining Language Change*. Cambridge: Cambridge University Press.

Laycock, Donald C. 1970a. *Materials in New Guinea Pidgin*. Canberra: Pacific Linguistics, D–5.

—— 1970b. 'It was a peculiarly great year for Pidgin'. *Pacific Islands Monthly*, 41, 45–8.

Lawrence, Peter. 1964. *Road belong Cargo*. Melbourne: Melbourne University Press.

Leech, G. & Svartvik, J. 1975. *A Communicative Grammar of English*. London: Longman.

Lefèbvre, C., Magliore-Holly, H. & Pion, N. (eds). 1982. *Syntaxe de l'Haïtien*. Ann Arbor, Mich.: Karoma.

Le Jeune, Jean-Marie Raphael. 1886. *Practical Chinook Vocabulary*. Kamloops: St Louis' Mission (mimeo).

Leland, Charles G. 1876. *Pidgin-English Sing-song*. London: Trübner.

Lenz, Rodolfo. 1928. *El Papiamento, la lengua criolla de Curazao*. Santiago de Chile: Balcells.

Le Page, Robert B. 1960. *Jamaican Creole*. London: Macmillan.

—— (ed.). 1961. *Proceedings of the Conference on Creole Language Studies*. London: Macmillan.

—— 1966. 'Introduction'. In B. L. Bailey.

—— 1968. 'Problems to be Faced in the Use of English as the Medium of Education in Four West Indian Territories'. In J. A. Fishman et al. (eds), 431–42.
—— 1973. 'The Concept of Competence in a Creole/Contact Situation'. *York Papers in Linguistics*, vol. 3, 31–50.
—— 1980. 'Theoretical Aspects of Sociolinguistic Studies in Pidgin and Creole Languages'. In Valdman & Highfield (eds), 331–68.
—— 1983a. 'Introduction to York Creole Conference'. Paper presented at the York Creole Conference.
—— 1983b. Review of Bickerton: *Roots of Language*. Unpublished manuscript, University of York.
Liem, Nguyen Dang. 1979. 'Cases and Verbs in Pidgin French (Tay Boi) in Vietnam'. In *Papers in Pidgin and Creole Linguistics*, No. 3. Canberra: Pacific Linguistics, A–57, 217–46.
Lightfoot, D. 1979. *Principles of Diachronic Syntax*. Cambridge: Cambridge University Press.
Lincoln, P. C. 1975. 'Acknowledging Dual-Lingualism'. *Working Papers in Linguistics*, (University of Hawaii), 7(4), 39–45.
Lounsbury, Floyd D. 1968. 'One Hundred Years of Anthropological Linguistics'. In Brew, John O. (ed.), *One Hundred Years of Anthropology*. Cambridge, Mass.: Harvard University Press, 153–225.
Luke, Kang-Kwong. 1983. 'Language Mixing in Hong Kong'. Paper presented at the York Creole Conference.
Lynch, John (ed.). 1975b. *Pidgins and Tok Pisin*. Occasional Paper No. 1. University of Papua New Guinea, Department of Language.
—— 1979. 'Changes in Tok Pisin Morphology'. Paper presented at the 13th Congress of the Linguistic Society of Papua New Guinea: Port Moresby.
—— 1980. 'Mixed Languages'. In J. Lynch (ed.), *Readings in the Comparative Linguistics of Melanesia*, 283–96. Port Moresby: University of Papua New Guinea.
—— 1981. 'Austronesian "Loanwords" (?) in Trans-New Guinea Phylum Vocabulary'. In Daview, H. J. et al., *Papers in New Guinea Linguistics, No. 21*, 165–80. Canberra: Pacific Linguistics, A–61.
Lyons, John. 1981. *Language and Linguistics*. Cambridge: Cambridge University Press.
Mafeni, B. 1971. 'Nigerian English'. In Spencer (ed.), 95–112.
Magens, J. M. 1770. *Grammatica over det Creolske sprog*. Copenhagen: Gerhard Giese Salikath.
Malinowski, Bronislav. 1923. 'The Problem of Meaning in Primitive Languages'. In Ogden, C. K. & Richards, I. A. (eds), *The Meaning of Meaning*, 296–336. London: Kegan Paul.
Manessy, Gabriel. 1977. 'Processes of Pidginization in African Languages'. In Valdman (ed.) (1977b), 129–34.
Markey, Thomas L. 1980. 'Diffusion, Fusion and Creolization: A Field Guide to Developmental Linguistics'. Unpublished manuscript, University of Michigan and Technische Universität Berlin.
—— 1981. Review of P. Muysken, *Generative Studies on Creole Languages. English World-Wide*, 2(2), 269–74.
—— 1982. 'Afrikaans: Creole or Non-Creole'. *Zeitschrift für Dialektologie und Linguistik*, IL, 2, 169–207.

—— 1983. 'Static vs. Dynamic in Germanic Linguistics'. *Monatshefte*, 75(2), 110–14.

—— 1985. 'On Suppletion'. Paper presented at VIIth ISHC Conference, Pavia.

——, Roberge, Paul T., Muysken, P., Meijer, Guus. (eds). 1979. *On the Origin and Formation of Creoles: A Miscellany of Articles by Dirk Christiaan Hesseling*. Ann Arbor, Mich.: Karoma.

Martyn-Jones, Marilyn & Romaine, Suzanne. 1984. 'Semilingualism: A Half-baked Theory of Communicative Competence'. Paper presented at the fourth Nordic Symposium on Bilingualism, Uppsala.

Mayerthaler, Willi. 1978. 'Morphologische Natürlichkeit'. Habilitations Thesis, Technische Universität Berlin.

Mead, Margaret. 1931. 'Talk Boy'. *Asia*, 31 (141–51), 191.

—— 1956. *New Lives for Old*. New York: W. Morrow.

Meillet, Antoine. 1921. *Linguistique historique et linguistique générale*. Paris: Honoré Champion.

Meisel, Jürgen M. 1975. 'Ausländerdeutsch und Deutsch ausländischer Arbeiter'. In Klein (ed.), 9–53.

—— 1976. 'Linguistic Simplification. A Study of Immigrant Workers' Speech and Foreigner Talk'. In Corder & Roulet (eds), 83–113.

—— (ed.). 1977. *Pidgins – Creoles – Languages in Contact*. Tübingen: Narr.

—— 1983. 'Transfer as a Second-Language Strategy'. *Language and Communication* 3(1), 11–46.

Mihalic, Francis. 1957. *Grammar and Dictionary of Neo-Melanesian*. Westmead, New South Wales: Mission Press.

—— 1969. 'Neo-Melanesian – A Compromise'. In F. Mihalic, *The Word in the World*. Epping, New South Wales: Divine Word Publications.

—— 1971. *The Jacaranda Dictionary and Grammar of Melanesian Pidgin*. Brisbane: Jacaranda Press.

Milroy, Lesley. 1980. *Language and Social Networks*. Oxford: Basil Blackwell.

Mintz, Sidney W. 1971. 'The Socio-historical Background to Pidginization and Creolization'. In Hymes (ed.), 481–98.

Molony, Carol H. 1973. 'Lexical Change in Philippine Creole Spanish'. Unpublished manuscript, Standford University.

——, Zobl, H. & Stölting, W. (eds). 1977. *German in Contact with other Languages*. Kronberg: Scriptor.

Moravcsik, Edith A. 1978. 'Universals of Language Contact'. In Greenberg, J. (ed.), *Universals of Human Language Vol. 1: Methods and Theory*, 93–122. Stanford, Conn.: Stanford University Press.

Morris, Desmond, Collett, Peter, Marsh, Peter, O'Shaughnessy, Marie. 1979. *Gestures, Their Origins and Distribution*. London: Book Club Associates.

Mosel, Ulrike. 1980. *Tolai and Tok Pisin*. Canberra: Pacific Linguistics, B–73.

Mühlhäusler, Peter. 1974. *Pidginization and Simplification of Language*. Canberra: Pacific Linguistics, B–26.

—— 1977a. 'Bermerkungen zum "Pidgin Deutsch" von Neuguinea'. In Molony, Zobl & Stölting (eds), 58–70.

—— 1977b. 'Creolization of New Guinea Pidgin'. In Wurm (ed.), 567–76.

—— 1978a. 'Papuan Pidgin English Rediscovered'. In Wurm & Carrington (eds), 1377–446.

—— 1978b. 'Samoan Plantation Pidgin English and the Origin of New Guinea Pidgin'.

In *Papers in Pidgin and Creole Linguistics, No. 1*. Canberra: Pacific Linguistics, A–54, 67–120.

—— 1978c. 'Synonymy and Communication across Lectal Boundaries in Tok Pisin'. In *Papers in Pidgin and Creole Linguistics, No. 2*. Canberra: Pacific Linguistics, A–57, 1–20.

—— 1978d. 'The Functional Possibilities of Lexical Bases in New Guinea Pidgin'. In *Papers in Pidgin and Creole Linguistics, No. 1*. Canberra: Pacific Linguistics, A–54, 121–74.

—— 1979. *Growth and Structure of the Lexicon of New Guinea Pidgin*. Canberra: Pacific Linguistics, C–52.

—— 1980a. 'Warum sind Pidginsprachen keine gemischten Sprachen'. In P. S. Ureland (ed.), *Sprachvariation und Sprachwandel*. Tübingen: Niemeyer, 139–60.

—— 1980b. 'Phases in the Development of Tok Pisin'. In Hüllen, W. (ed.), *Understanding Bilingualism*, 119–30. Frankfurt: Lang.

—— 1980c. 'Structural Expansion and the Process of Creolization'. In Valdman & Highfield (eds), 19–56.

—— 1981a. 'Foreigner Talk: Tok Masta in New Guinea'. *International Journal of the Sociology of Language*, 28, 93–113.

—— 1981b. 'Melanesian Pidgin English (Kanaka English) in Australia'. *Kabar Seberang*, 819, 93–105.

—— 1982a. 'Kritische Bemerkungen zu Sprachmischungsuniversalien'. In Ureland, P. S. (ed.), *Die Leistung der Strataforschung und der Kreolistik*, 407–32. Tübingen Niemeyer.

—— 1982b. 'Language and Communication Efficiency: The Case of Tok Pisin'. *Language and Communication*, 2(2), 105–22.

—— 1983. 'Stinkiepoos, Cuddles and Related Matters'. *Australian Journal of Linguistics*, 3(1), 75–92.

—— 1984a. 'Discontinuity in the Development of Pidgins and Creoles'. In Enninger, W. (ed.), *Studies in Language Ecology*, 118–34. Wiesbaden: Steiner.

—— 1984b. 'Tracing the Roots of Pidgin German'. *Language and Communication*, 4(1), 27–58.

—— 1984c. 'Learning to Speak about Speaking in a Pidgin Language'. In *Papers in Pidgins and Creole Linguistics, No. 3*. Canberra: Pacific Linguistics, A–65, 93–103.

—— 1985. 'Patterns of Contact, Mixture, Creation and Nativization: Their Contribution to a General Theory of Language'. In Bailey & Harris (eds), 51–88.

Muysken, Pieter, 1975. 'Pidginization in the Quechua of the Lowlands of Eastern Ecuador'. Paper presented at the conference on Pidgins and Creoles, Honolulu.

—— (ed.). 1981. *Generative Studies on Creole Languages*. Dordrecht: Foris.

McDonald, R. (ed.). 1977. 'Georg Friederici's Pidgin Englisch in Deutsch-Neuguinea'. Occasional Paper No. 14. University of Papua New Guinea, Department of Language.

McElhanon, K. A. (ed.). 1975. *Tok Pisin i go we? Kivung*. Special Publication No. 1. Port Moresby: Linguistic Society of Papua New Guinea.

Nagara, Susumu. 1972. *Japanese Pidgin English in Hawaii: A Bilingual Description*. Honolulu: University Press of Hawaii.

Naro, Anthony J. 1978. 'A Study on the Origins of Pidginization'. *Language*, 54(2), 314–47.

Neffgen, H. 1915. 'Pidgin-English'. *Samoan Times*, 23 January and 27 March.

Neumann, Günther. 1965. 'Russennorwegisch und Pidginenglisch'. *Nachrichten der Giessener Hochschulgesellschaft*, 34, 219–32.

—— 1966. 'Zur Chinesisch-Russischen Behelfssprache von Kjachta'. *Sprache*, 12, 237–51.

Neustupný, Jiri V. 1983. 'Communication with the Japanese'. *The Wheel Extended*, xiii(1), 28–30.

Newton, Henry. 1914. *In Far New Guinea*. London: Seeley, Service.

Nichols, P. 1976. 'Linguistic Change in Gullah'. PhD thesis, Stanford University.

Noss, Philip A. 1979. 'Fula: A Language of Change'. In Hancock (ed.), 175–90.

O'Barr, William M. & O'Barr, Jean F. (eds). 1976. *Language and Politics*. The Hague: Mouton.

Ochs, Elinor. 1979. 'Planned and Unplanned Discourse'. In Givón, Talmy (ed.), *Syntax and Semantics*, vol. 12, 51–80. New York: Academic Press.

Paul, Hermann. 1970. *Prinzipien der Sprachgeschichte*. Tübingen: Niemeyer.

Pawley, Andrew. 1975. 'On Epenthetic Vowels in New Guinea Pidgin'. In McElhanon (ed.), 215–28.

Peet, William Jr. 1979. 'The Nominative Shift in Hawaiian Creole Pronominalization'. In *Papers in Pidgin and Creole Linguistics, No. 2*. Canberra: Pacific Linguistics, A–57, 151–61.

Platt, John T. 1975. 'The Singapore English Speech Continuum and its Basilect "Singlish" as a "creoloid"'. *Anthropological Linguistics*, 17(7), 363–74.

Politzer, R. L. 1949. 'On the Emergence of Romance from Latin'. *Word*, 5, 126–30.

Pollard, Velma. 1983. 'Rastafarian Language in St Lucia and Barbados'. Paper presented at the York Creole Conference.

Posner, Rebecca. 1983. 'The Origins and Affinities of French Creoles: New Perspectives'. *Language and Communication*, 3(2), 191–202.

Pradelles de Latour, Marie-Lorraine. 1983. 'Urban Pidgin in Douala'. Paper presented at the York Creole Conference.

Pride, J. B. & Holmes J. (ed.). 1972. *Sociolinguistics*. Harmondsworth: Penguin.

Raidt, Edith H. 1983. *Einführung in die Geschichte und Struktur des Afrikaans*. Darmstadt: Wissenschaftliche Buchgesellschaft.

Ramson, William S. (ed.). 1970. *English Transported*. Canberra: Australian National University Press.

Ray, Sidney H. 1907. 'The Jargon English of the Torres Straits'. In *Reports of the Cambridge Anthropological Expedition to Torres Straits*, 251–4. Cambridge: Cambridge University Press.

—— 1926. *A Comparative Study of Melanesian Island Languages*. Cambridge: Cambridge University Press.

Reddy, Michael J. 1979. 'The Conduit Metaphor – A Case of Frame Conflict in our Language about Language'. In Ortony, A. (ed.), *Metaphor and Thought*, 284–324. Cambridge: Cambridge University Press.

Reed, S. W. 1943. *The Making of Modern New Guinea*. Philadelphia, Penn.: American Philosophical Society Memoir No. 18.

Reinecke, John E. 1937. 'Marginal Languages'. Unpublished PhD thesis, Yale University.

—— 1964. 'Trade Jargons and Creole Dialects as Marginal Languages'. In Hymes, D. (ed.), *Language in Culture and Society*, 534–42. New York: Harper & Row.

—— 1971. 'Tây Bồi: Notes on the Pidgin French Spoken in Vietnam'. In Hymes (ed.), 47–56.

—— 1980. 'William Greenfield, A Neglected Pioneer Creolist'. Paper presented at the Conference of the Society for Caribbean Linguistics, Aruba.

—— 1981. *Selective Chronology of Creole Studies*, Special supplementary issue to the *Carrier Pidgin, vol. 9*.

—— DeCamp, David, Hancock, Ian F., Wood, Richard E. 1975. *A Bibliography of Pidgin and Creole Languages*. Oceanic Linguistics Special Publication No. 14. Honolulu: University Press of Hawaii.

Reisman, Karl. 1974. 'Contrapuntal Conversations in an Antiguan Village'. In Bauman & Sherzer (eds), 110–24.

Ribbe, Carl. 1903. *Zwei Jahre unter den Kannibalen der Salomo Inseln*. Dresden: Elbgau.

Richardson, I. 1961. 'Some Observations on the Status of Town Bemba in Northern Rhodesia'. *African Language Studies*, 2, 25–36.

Rickford, John R. 1977. 'The Question of Prior Creolization in Black English'. In Valdman (ed.) (1977b), 190–221.

—— 1983a. 'What Happens in Decreolization'. In Andersen, R. W. (ed.), *Pidginization and Creolization as Language Acquisition*. Rowley, Mass.: Newbury House, 1983, 298–318.

—— 1983b. 'Standard and Non-Standard Language Attitudes in a Creole Continuum'. *Society for Caribbean Linguistics Occasional Paper 16*, 3–30.

—— 1984. 'Me Tarzan, you Jane! Cognition and Expression in the Creole Speaker'. Unpublished manuscript, Stanford University.

—— & Traugott, Elisabeth. Forthcoming. 'Symbol of Powerlessness and Degeneracy, or Symbol of Solidarity and Truth? Paradoxical Attitudes toward Pidgins and Creoles'. To appear in Greenbaum, S. *The English Language Today*.

Rigsby, Bruce. 1984. 'English Pidgin/Creole Varieties on Cape York Peninsula'. Paper presented at the 54th ANZAAS Conference, Canberra.

—— & Sutton, Peter. 1982. 'Speech Communities in Aboriginal Australia'. *Anthropological Forum*, V(1), 8–23.

Riley, Carroll L. 1952. 'Trade Spanish of the Piñaguero Panare'. *Studies in Linguistics*, 10(1), 6–11.

Roberts, Peter A. 1977. 'Duont: A Case for Spontaneous Development'. *Journal of Creole Studies*, 1(1), 101–8.

Robertson, Frank. 1971. 'Comic Opera Talk Talk; English as she is broken is the New Guinea tongue that strangers love'. *Asia Magazine*, 22 August 1971, 13–16, (Tokyo).

Robinson, W. P. 1974. *Language and Social Behaviour*, Harmondsworth: Penguin.

Romaine, Suzanne. 1982a. 'What is a Speech Community?' In Romaine (ed.) (1982b), 13–24.

—— (ed.). 1982b. *Sociolinguistic Variation in Speech Communities*. London: Edward Arnold.

—— 1984. Review of P. Muysken (ed.), *Generative Studies on Creole Languages*. *Australian Journal of Linguistics*, 4(1), 116–22.

Ross, A. S. C. 1964. *The Pitcairnese Language*. London: Deutsch.

Royal Commission into Labour. 1885. 'Recruiting Labourers in New Guinea and Adjacent Islands. *Votes and Proceedings of the Legislative Assembly*, Brisbane, 2, 813–987.

Russel, Thomas. 1868. *The Etymology of Jamaica Grammar, by a young gentleman.* Kingston: De Cordova, McDougall.

Salisbury, R. F. 1967. 'Pidgin's Respectable Past'. *New Guinea*, 2(2), 44–8.

—— 1972. 'Notes on Bilingualism and Linguistic Change in New Guinea'. In J. B. Pride and J. Holmes (eds), 52–64.

Samarin, William J. 1953. *Learning Sango. A Pedagogical Grammar.* Bozoum: Mission Evangelique de l'Oubangui-Chari.

—— 1961. 'The Vocabulary of Sango'. *Word*, 17, 17–22.

—— 1966. 'Self-annulling Prestige Factors among Speakers of a Creole Language'. In Bright (ed.), 188–213.

—— 1969. 'The Art of Gbeya Insults'. *International Journal of African Languages*, 35, 323–9.

—— 1971. *Salient and Substantive Pidginization.* In Hymes (ed.), 117–40.

—— 1975. 'Historical, Ephemeral and Inevitable Verbal Categories'. Paper presented at the International Conference on Pidgins and Creoles, Honolulu.

—— 1980. 'Standardization and Instrumentalization of Creole Languages'. In Valdman & Highfield (eds), 213–36.

—— 1982. 'Colonization and Pidginization on the Ubangi river'. Unpublished manuscript, Toronto.

Sandefur, John R. 1981. 'Kriol – An Aboriginal Language'. *Hemisphere*, 25(4), 252–6.

—— 1984. 'A Language Coming of Age: Kriol of North Australia'. MA thesis, University of Western Australia.

Sankoff, Gillian. 1975a. 'Wanpela lain manmeri ibin kisim Tok Pisin i kamap olsem tok ples bilong ol'. In McElhanon (ed.), 102–7.

—— 1975b. 'Sampela nupela lo i kamap long Tok Pisin'. In McElhanon (ed.), 235–40.

—— 1976. 'Political Power and Linguistic Inequality in Papua New Guinea'. In O'Barr & O'Barr (eds), 283–310.

—— 1977. 'Variability and Explanation in Language and Culture'. In Saville-Troike (ed.), 59–74.

—— 1979. 'The Genesis of a Language'. In Hill (ed.), 23–47.

—— 1980. 'Variation, Pidgins and Creoles'. In Valdman & Highfield (eds), 139–65.

—— & Brown, Penelope. 1976. 'On the Origins of Syntax in Discourse: A Case Study of Tok Pisin Relatives'. *Language*, 52(3), 631–66.

—— & Laberge, Suzanne. 1973. 'On the Acquisition of Native Speakers by a Language'. *Kivung*, 6(1), 32–47.

Saville-Troike, Muriel (ed.). 1977. *Linguistics and Anthropology.* Washington, DC: Georgetown University Press.

Schegloff, E. A. 1978. 'On Some Questions and Ambiguities in Conversation'. In Dressler, U. (ed.), *Current Trends in Textlinguistics*, 81–102. New York and London: Academic Press.

Schellong, Otto. 1934. *Alte Dokumente aus der Südsee.* Königsberg.

Scherer, Klaus R. & Giles, Howard (eds). 1980. *Social Markers in Speech.* Cambridge: Cambridge University Press.

Schnee, Heinrich, von. 1904. *Bilder aus der Südsee.* Berlin: Reimer.

Schneider, Gilbert D. 1974. 'West African Pidgin English'. PhD thesis, Hartford Seminary Foundation.

Schuchardt, Hugo. 1882. 'Sur le créole de la Réunion'. *Romania*, 11, 589–93.

—— 1889a. 'Beiträge zur Kenntnis des englischen Kreolisch: II. Melaneso-Englisches'. *Englische Studien*, 13, 158–62.

—— 1889b. 'Beiträge zur Kenntnis des Kreolischen Romanisch V. Allgemeines über das Indoportugiesische'. *Zeitschrift für Romanische Philologie*, 13, 476–516.

—— 1891. 'Beiträge zur Kenntnis des englischen Kreolisch: III. Das Indo-Englische'. *Englische Studien*, 15, 286–305.

—— 1979. *The Ethnography of Variation, Selected Writings on Pidgins and Creoles*. Translated by T. L. Markey. Ann Arbor, Mich.: Karoma.

—— n.d. 'Kreolische Studien X: Ueber das Negerenglische von Westafrika'. Unpublished manuscript, Schuchardt collection, Graz.

Schultze, Ernst. 1933. 'Sklaven und Dienersprachen'. *Sociologus*, 9, 378–418.

Schumann, John H. 1978. *The Pidginization Process*. Rowley: Newbury House.

Schwartz, Theodore. 1957. 'The Paliau Movement in the Admiralty Islands – 1946 to 1954'. PhD thesis, University of Pennsylvania.

Schwörer, E. 1916. *Kolonial-Deutsch. Vorschläge einer künftigen deutschen Kolonialsprache in systematisch-grammatikalischer Darstellung und Begründung*. Munich: Huber.

Scotton, C. M. 1969. 'A Look at the Swahili of Two Groups of Up-country Speakers'. *Swahili*, 39(1–2), 101–10.

Sebba, Mark. 1981. 'Derivational Regularities in a Creole Lexicon: the Case of Sranan'. *Linguistics*, 19, 101–17.

Sebeok, T. A. (ed.). 1960. *Style in Language*. Cambridge, Mass.: MIT Press.

Seiler, Walter. 1982. 'The Spread of Malay to Kaiser Wilhelmsland'. In Carle et al. (eds), 67–86.

Shelton-Smith. 1929. '"Pidgin" English in New Guinea'. *Rabaul Times*, 24 May 1929.

Shilling, Alison. 1980. 'Bahamian English – A Non-Continuum?' In Day (ed.), 133–46.

Shnukal, Anna. 1984. 'Variation in Torres Strait Creole'. Paper presented at the 54th ANZAAS Conference, Canberra.

Shuy, Roger W. and Fasold, Ralph W. 1973. *Language Attitudes: Current Trends and Prospects*. Washington, DC: Georgetown University Press.

Siegel, Jeff. 1975. 'Fiji Hindustani'. Unpublished manuscript, University of Hawaii.

—— 1982. 'Plantation Languages in Fiji'. Unpublished manuscript, Australian National University.

1983a. 'Koines and Koineization'. Unpublished manuscript, Australian National University.

—— 1983b. 'Plantation Pidgin Fijian'. Paper presented at the 15th Pacific Science Congress, Dunedin.

—— 1984. 'Pidgin English in Fiji'. Paper presented at the 54th ANZAAS Congress, Canberra.

—— 1985. 'Media Tok Pisin'. In *Papers in Pidgin and Creole Linguistics, No. 3*. Canberra: Pacific Linguistics, A–65, 81–92.

Silverstein, Michael. 1972a. 'Chinook Jargon: Language Contact and the Problem of Multi-level Generative Systems', I and II. *Language*, 48(2), 378–406 and 48(3), 596–625.

—— 1972b. 'Goodbye Columbus: Language and Speech Community in Indian-European Contact Situations'. Unpublished manuscript, University of Chicago.

—— 1977. 'Cultural Prerequisites to Grammatical Analysis'. In Saville-Troike (ed.), 139–52.

—— n.d. 'Who shall Regiment Language? Intuition, Authority and Politics in Linguistic Communication'. Unpublished manuscript, University of Chicago.

Smith, David M. 1972. 'Some Implications for the Social Status of Pidgin Languages'. In Smith, D. M. and Shuy, R. W. *Sociolinguistics in Cross-Cultural Analysis*. Washington: Georgetown University Press, 47–56.

Smith, Ian, R. 1983. 'The Development of Morphosyntax in Sri Lanka Portuguese'. Paper presented at the York Creole Conference.

Smith, Norval. 1977a. 'Vowel Epenthesis in the Surinam Creoles'. *Amsterdam Creole Studies*, I, 1–31.

—— 1977b. 'The Development of the Liquids in the Surinam Creoles'. *Amsterdam Creole Studies*, I, 32–54.

Southworth, Franklin C. 1971. 'Detecting Prior Creolization: An Analysis of the Historical Origins of Marathi'. In Hymes (ed.), 255–74.

Speiser, Felix. 1913. *Südsee, Urwald, Kannibalen*. Leipzig: Voigtländer.

Spencer, J. (ed.). 1971. *The English Language in West Africa*. London: Longman.

Sreedhar, M. V. 1977. 'Standardization of Naga Pidgin'. *Journal of Creole Studies*, 1(1), 157–70.

—— 1983. 'Coining of Words in Pidgins/Creoles: A Case Study of Naga Pidgin'. Paper presented at the York Creole Conference.

Stefánsson, A. 1909. 'The Eskimo Trade Jargon of Herschel Island'. *American Anthropologist*, II, 217–32.

Steffensen, Margaret S. 1977. 'Double Talk: When it means something and when it doesn't'. *Chicago Linguistic Society, Papers from the Regional Meetings*, 13, 603–11.

—— 1979. 'Reduplication in Bamyili Creole'. In *Papers in Pidgin and Creole Linguistics, No. 2*. Canberra: Pacific Linguistics, A–57, 119–34.

Steinberg, Danny D. & Jakobovits, Leon A. (eds). 1971. *Semantics: An Interdisciplinary Reader in Philosophy, Linguistics and Psychology*. Cambridge: Cambridge University Press.

Stewart, William A. 1962. 'The Functional Distribution of Creole and French in Haiti'. *Georgetown Monograph Series on Languages and Linguistics*, 15, 149–59.

Sylvain, Suzanne. 1936. *Le Créole Haïtien*. Wetteren: Imprimèrie de Meester.

Taber, Charles R. 1979. 'French Loan Words in Sango: The Motivation of Lexical Borrowing'. In Hancock (ed.), 191–200.

Tabouret-Keller, Andrée. 1980. 'Psychological Terms used in Creole Studies'. In Valdman & Highfield (eds), 313–30.

Tauli, Valter. 1968. *Introduction to a Theory of Language Planning*. Uppsala: Almquist & Wiksells.

Taylor, Andrew J. 1978. 'Evidence of a Pidgin Motu in the Earliest Written Motu Materials'. In Wurm & Carrington (eds), 1325–50.

Taylor, Douglas. 1963. 'The Origin of West Indian Creole Languages: Evidence from Grammatical Categories'. *American Anthropologist*, 65, 800–14.

Taylor, Insup. 1976. *Introduction to Psycholinguistics*. New York: Holt, Rinehart & Winston.

Taylor, Talbot & Mühlhäusler, Peter. 1982. 'Review of K. R. Scherer and H. Giles *Social Markers in Speech*'. *Journal of Literary Semantics*, XI(2), 125–35.

Temple, Sir William. 1690. *An Essay upon the Ancient and Modern Learning*.

Tetaga, Jeremiah E. 1971. 'Prenasalization as an Aspect of New Guinea Tok Pisin'. Unpublished manuscript, Linguistic Institute, University of Michigan.

Thomas, John J. 1869. *The Theory and Practice of Creole Grammar*. Port-of-Spain: Chronicle Publishing Office.

Thomason, Sarah Grey. 1981. 'Chinook Jargon in Areal and Historical Context'. *University of Montana Occasional Papers in Linguistics*, 2, 295–396.

Thompson, Robert W. 1961. 'A Note on some Possible Affinities between the Creole Dialects of the Old World and those of the New'. In Le Page (ed.), 107–13.

—— 1967. 'On the Portuguese Dialect of Hong Kong'. In *Symposium on Historical, Archaeological and Linguistic Studies on Southern China*. Hong Kong: Hong Kong University Press, 238–40.

Todd, Loreto. 1974. *Pidgins and Creoles*. London: Routledge & Kegan Paul.

—— 1975. 'Pidgins and Creoles: the Case for the Creoloid'. Paper presented at the International Conference on Pidgins and Creoles, Honolulu.

—— 1979. 'Cameroonian: a consideration of "what's in a name?"' In Hancock (ed.), 281–94.

—— 1982. 'The English Language in West Africa'. In Bailey & Görlach (eds), 281–305.

—— 1984. *Modern Englishes*. Oxford: Basil Blackwell.

—— Forthcoming. 'The CM2 Process: A Selection of Riddles in Cameroon Pidgin English'. In Gilbert (ed.).

Traugott, Elisabeth. 1976. 'Natural Semantax: Its Role in the Study of Second Language Acquisition'. In Corder & Roulet (eds), 132–62.

—— & Romaine, Suzanne. 1982. 'Style in Sociohistorical Linguistics'. Unpublished manuscript, Universities of Stanford and Birmingham, 32 pp.

Trudgill, Peter. 1977. 'Creolization in Reverse: Reduction and Simplification in the Albanian Dialects of Greece'. *Transactions of the Philological Society, 1976–7*, 32–50.

—— 1983. *On Dialect*. Oxford: Basil Blackwell.

Turner, G. W. 1966. *The English Language in Australia and New Zealand*. London: Longman.

Ullmann, Stephen. 1957. *Principles of Semantics*. Glasgow: Jackson.

Unesco. 1963. *The Use of Vernacular Languages in Education*. Monographs on Fundamental Education 8. Paris: Unesco.

Urry, James & Walsh, Michael. 1981. 'The lost "Macassarese Language" of Northern Australia'. *Aboriginal History*, 5(2), 91–108.

Valdman, Albert. 1977a. 'Creolization: Elaboration in the Development of Creole French Dialects'. In Valdman (ed.), 155–89.

—— (ed.). 1977b. *Pidgin and Creole Linguistics*. London and Bloomington, Ind.: Indiana University Press.

Valkhoff, Marius F. 1966. *Studies in Portuguese and Creole*. Johannesburg: Witwatersrand University Press.

—— 1972. *New Light on Afrikaans and Malayo-Portuguese*. Louvain: Peeters.

Van Name, Addison. 1869. 'Contributions to Creole Grammar'. *Transactions of the American Philological Association*, 1, 123–67.

Vico, G. B. 1725. *The New Science*.

Voegelin, Carl & Voegelin, Florence. 1964. 'Languages of the World: Ibero-Caucasian and Pidgin-Creole fascicle one'. *Anthropological Linguistics*, 6, 1–71.

Volker, Craig Alan. 1982. 'An Introduction to Rabaul Creole German (Unserdeutsch)'. MA thesis, University of Queensland.

Voorhœve, Jan. 1961. 'Linguistic Experiments in Syntactic Analysis'. In Le Page (ed.), 37–60.

—— 1962. 'Creole Languages and Communication'. In *Committee for Technical Cooperation in Africa: Symposium on Multilingualism*. London: CCTA Publishing Bureau, 233–42.

—— 1971. 'Church Creole and Pagan Cult Languages'. In Hymes (ed.), 323–6.

—— 1973. 'Historical and Linguistic Evidence in favour of the Relexification Theory in the Formation of Creoles'. *Language in Society*, 2, 133–45.

—— 1981. 'Multifunctionality as a Derivational Problem'. In Muysken (ed.), 25–34.

—— & Kramp, André. 1982. 'Syntactic Developments in Sranan'. Paper presented at the Fourth Biannual Conference of the Society for Caribbean Linguistics, Paramaribo.

Wales, Kathleen. 1980. 'Exophora Re-examined: The Uses of the Personal Pronoun WE in Present-day English'. *UEA Papers in Linguistics* (University of East Anglia), 12, 21–44.

Walsh, D. S. 1984. 'Is "English-based" an adequately Accurate Label for Bislama?' Paper presented at the 54th ANZAAS Congress, Canberra.

Washabaugh, William. 1975. 'Challenges of Pidgins and Creoles to Current Linguistic Theory: For Prepositions to become Complementizers'. Paper presented at the International Conference on Pidgins and Creoles, Honolulu.

—— & Greenfield, S. M. 1983. 'The Development of the Atlantic Creole Languages'. In Woolford & Washabaugh (eds), 106–19.

Werkgroep Taal Buitenlandse. Werknemers. 1978. *Nederlands tegen Buitenlanders*. Amsterdam: Publications of the Institute for General Linguistics, 18.

Whinnom, Keith. 1971. 'Linguistic Hybridization and the "Special Case" of Pidgins and Creoles'. In Hymes (ed.), 91–115.

Wode, Henning. 1977. 'Developmental Principles in Naturalistic L2 Acquisition'. In Drachman, G. (ed.), *Akten der 3. Salzburger Jahrestagung für Linguistik*, Salzburg: Neugebauer, 207–20.

Woolford, Ellen. 1979. 'The Developing Complementizer System of Tok Pisin'. In Hill (ed.), 108–24.

—— & Washabaugh, William (eds). 1983. *The Social Context of Creolization*. Ann Arbor, Mich.: Karoma.

Wullschlaegel. 1858. *Deutsch-Negerenglisches Wörterbuch*. Löbau: T. U. Duroldt. Reprinted Amsterdam: S. Emmering, 1965.

Wurm, Stephen A. 1964. 'Motu and Police Motu: A Study in Typological Contrasts'. *Papers in New Guinea Linguistics, No. 2*. Canberra: Pacific Linguistics, A–4, 19–41.

—— 1969. 'English, Pidgin and what else?' *New Guinea*, 4(2), 30–42.

—— 1970. *New Guinea Highlands Pidgin: Course Materials*. Canberra: Pacific Linguistics, D–3.

—— 1971. 'Pidgins, Creoles and Lingue Franche'. In *Current Trends in Linguistics*, vol. 8, 999–1021. The Hague: Mouton.

—— 1977a. 'Pidgins, Creoles, Lingue Franche and National Development'. In Valdman (ed.), 333–57.

—— 1977b. 'The Nature of Pidgin'. In Wurm (ed.) (1977c), 511–30.

—— (ed.). 1977c. *Language, Culture, Society and the Modern World.* New Guinea Area Languages and Language Study, Vol. 3. Canberra: Pacific Linguistics, C–40.

—— (ed.). 1979. *New Guinea and Neighboring Areas: A Sociolinguistic Laboratory*. The Hague: Mouton.

—— 1980. 'Standardization and Instrumentalization in Tok Pisin'. In Valdman & Highfield (eds), 237–45.

—— 1983. 'Grammatical Decay in Papuan Languages'. Paper presented at the 15th Pacific Science Congress, Dunedin. To appear in Proceedings. Canberra: Pacific Linguistics.

—— et al. 1981. 'Pidgin Languages, Trade Languages and Lingue Franche in Oceania and Australia'. In Wurm and Hattôri *Language Atlas, Pacific Area I*, map 24. Stuttgart: Geocenter.

—— & Carrington, L. (eds). 1978. *Second International Conference on Austronesian Linguistics: Proceedings*. Canberra: Pacific Linguistics, C–61.

—— & Harris, John B. 1963. *Police Motu*. Canberra: Pacific Linguistics, 31.

——, Laycock, D. C. & Mühlhäusler, P. 1984. 'Notes on Attitudes to Pronunciation in the New Guinea Area'. *International Journal of the Sociology of Language*, 50, 123–46.

—— & Mühlhäusler, P. 1979. 'Attitudes towards New Guinea Pidgin and English'. In Wurm (ed.), 243–62.

—— & ——1983. 'Registers in New Guinea Pidgin'. *International Journal of the Sociology of Language*, 35, 69–86.

Zettersten, A. 1969. *The English of Tristan da Cunha*. Lund Studies in English, 37.

Zöller, Hugo. 1891. *Deutsch-Neuguinea und meine Ersteigung des Finisterre Gebirges*. Stuttgart, Berlin and Leipzig: Union.

Zyhlarz, Ernst. 1932–3. 'Ursprung und Sprachcharacter des Altägyptischen'. *Zeitschrift für Eingeborenensprachen*, 23, 25–45, 81–110, 161–94, 241–54.

Index

Aitchison 141, 221, 237, 269
Aub-Buscher 228–9

Bailey 45, 108, 134, 241, 272
Baker 60, 83, 99, 212–13, 228
Bickerton 10, 37, 42, 45, 47–9, 62, 64, 88, 93, 97, 114, 122–3, 205, 222, 238, 240, 257, 261, 304
bioprogram 10, 79, 88, 97, 115, 221, 222, 247, 259
Bloomfield 38, 90, 100, 193
Bollée 91, 96, 166, 219

cargo cult 66–7, 203
Cassidy 233, 268
catastrophe 76, 249, 258
causatives 184, 217
Chomsky 116, 276
Churchill 25, 97, 145
circumlocution 146–7, 171
Clark 17, 18, 36, 93, 143, 161
Clyne 69, 101, 103, 160, 264
common core grammar 118
conduit metaphor 278
Corne 60, 83, 212–13, 239
creolization 205–30
creoloid 10–11
critical threshold 164, 264–5

DeCamp 43, 45, 220, 232, 237, 240, 273
dependency hypothesis 276, 295
desert-island approach 92
diffusion 57, 76, 99, 225
discontinuity 18, 55, 76, 94, 107, 134, 220, 237, 252, 255–8, 265, 285
Dutton 13, 51, 77, 78, 109, 110, 134, 138, 145, 162, 188, 189, 269

embedding 162, 187
equality 23–4, 39, 48, 61, 91, 259–61
expansion phase 176–205

family tree 32–7, 252–5
Ferguson 101, 137
Ferraz 234
Figueroa 48–9
Foley 225–6
foreigner talk 38, 40, 57, 82, 99, 152
Franke 233–4
functions of language 77–9, 81–8

Givón 6, 160, 230, 246
Goodman 53, 144–5, 152, 172

Haas 77
Hale 52, 53
Hall 15, 28, 29, 35, 38, 89, 118, 153, 239, 241, 252–4
Halliday 81, 86, 87
Hancock 16, 17, 36, 98, 111, 195, 219, 236
Harris, R. 56, 255, 259, 278
Heine 31–2, 114–15, 148–50, 158

Hesseling 33
Hinnenkamp 75, 101, 105–6, 144
Hoenigswald 256
Holm 123, 206, 229–30
Huttar 112, 230–1
Hymes 48, 147
hypercorrection 239, 248, 258

implicational scaling 44–5, 108, 239, 274
impoverishment 4, 135, 154, 266
inflection 152–4, 181–2, 213–16, 240–1

jargon stage 135–47
Jones, E. 207
Jones, F. 243

Keesing 37, 293
Kihm 210, 251, 295
Koch 221, 246
Koine 11, 12, 33

Labov 69, 71, 96, 137, 151, 209, 217, 258, 273
language death 89, 236, 269
language mixing 5, 7, 32, 62, 89, 90, 113, 117, 120–9, 231, 277
Laycock 107, 116, 238
learnability 261–4, 267
Le Page 43, 93, 206, 273
lexical encounters 1, 2, 144, 247
lexicon 165–75, 191–9, 228–36, 243–9
literacy 90, 91, 203–4
Lynch 268

Mafeni 174, 176, 179, 194
Markey 256, 294
Mayerthaler 71, 210
Meisel 56, 115, 125, 129, 267
metalinguistics 41, 47, 65, 69, 70, 85, 278–9, 281
Mosel 122–4, 149, 154, 193, 196, 237, 261
multifunctionality 146, 153, 171–3, 185, 218
Muysken 189

Naro 106, 114
naturalness 23, 30, 46, 47, 49, 60–3, 71, 94, 102, 117, 128, 141, 151–2, 233, 259, 279–80
nautical language 96, 97–100
Neustupný 53, 296

Pawley 180
Peet 244–5
phonology 139–42, 148–52, 177–81, 206–13, 238–40, 262–3
plurals 115–16, 182–3, 214–15, 228, 241, 294
Posner 130
post-creole continuum 11, 33, 237–49
pronouns 57, 60, 103–4, 130–1, 158–9, 233

question words 163, 224

Ray 34, 37
reanalysis 161, 182, 187, 190, 227
reduplication 57, 120, 123, 196, 218
Reinecke 30, 37, 39, 72–3, 98, 152, 175, 196, 276
regression 53, 56, 69, 70, 83, 106, 262
relativization 189–90, 221, 245
relexification 14, 35, 52, 56, 74, 79, 107–13
Rickford 208, 237, 245, 268, 271
Rigsby 273
Romaine 90, 273
Ross 206–7

Samarin 30, 38, 69, 85, 89, 152, 248
Sandefur 72, 74, 79, 85, 237, 240
Sankoff 59, 76, 83, 95, 118, 151, 164, 181, 187
Schuchardt 33, 79, 100, 114, 119, 128, 140–1, 158, 253
second-language acquisition 24, 40, 41
Shnukal 235
Siegel 11, 12, 16, 73, 145, 157, 166, 204
sign language 52–4
Silverstein 146, 174, 267
simplification 4, 101, 104, 135, 141, 154, 208, 266–8

Smith 208–9, 211–12
speech community 273–4
stabilization 147–70
Steffensen 219
Stewart 88, 90, 240
substratum 33, 39–40, 56, 119–29, 194–6, 207–9
superstratum 129–31, 206, 225
SVO order 155–6, 225
systematicity 258–9

Taber 191–2
Tabouret-Keller 278
Taylor 35, 131
Thomason 140, 154–6, 165
Thompson 107, 112, 219
Todd 14, 36, 54, 96, 176–7, 200–1, 247, 257
tone 149–50
transformational-generative grammar 39–43, 259, 262, 267
Traugott 90, 161, 247, 266
Trudgill 69, 89

uniformitarianism 55, 89, 134, 249, 252, 256
universals 40–3, 56, 83, 89, 94, 113–19, 285

Valdman 205, 227
verb serialization 160, 246
Volker 221–3
Voorhoeve 35, 111, 112, 172, 218, 226
vowel epenthesis 140–1, 207

Whinnom 58, 78, 89, 138, 147, 260
Wode 261
Woolford 188
Wurm 16, 38, 83, 89, 121, 172, 188, 272, 282